5/06

VIZ GRAPHIC NOVEL

D0201331

THE ALL-NEW
TENCHI MUYŌ!

DARK WASHU

STORY AND ART BY
HITOSHI OKUDA

The All-New Tenchi Muyô!
Vol. 3: Dark Washu
Action Edition

STORY AND ART BY HITOSHI OKUDA

English Adaptation/Fred Burke
Translation/Lillian Olsen
Touch-up & Lettering/Dan Nakrosis
Cover Design/Hidemi Sahara
Graphic Design/Carolina Ugalde
Editor/Eric Searleman

Managing Editor/Annette Roman
Editor-in-Chief/William Flanagan
Sr. Dir. of Licensing & Acquisitions/Rika Inouye
VP of Sales & Marketing/Liza Coppola
Sr. VP of Editorial/Hyoe Narita
Publisher/Seiji Horibuchi

Printed in Canada

Published by VIZ, LLC
P.O. Box 77010
San Francisco, CA 94107

Action Edition
10 9 8 7 6 5 4 3 2 1
First printing, October 2003

For advertising rates or media kit,
e-mail advertising@viz.com

www.animerica-mag.com
www.viz.com   store.viz.com

CONTENTS

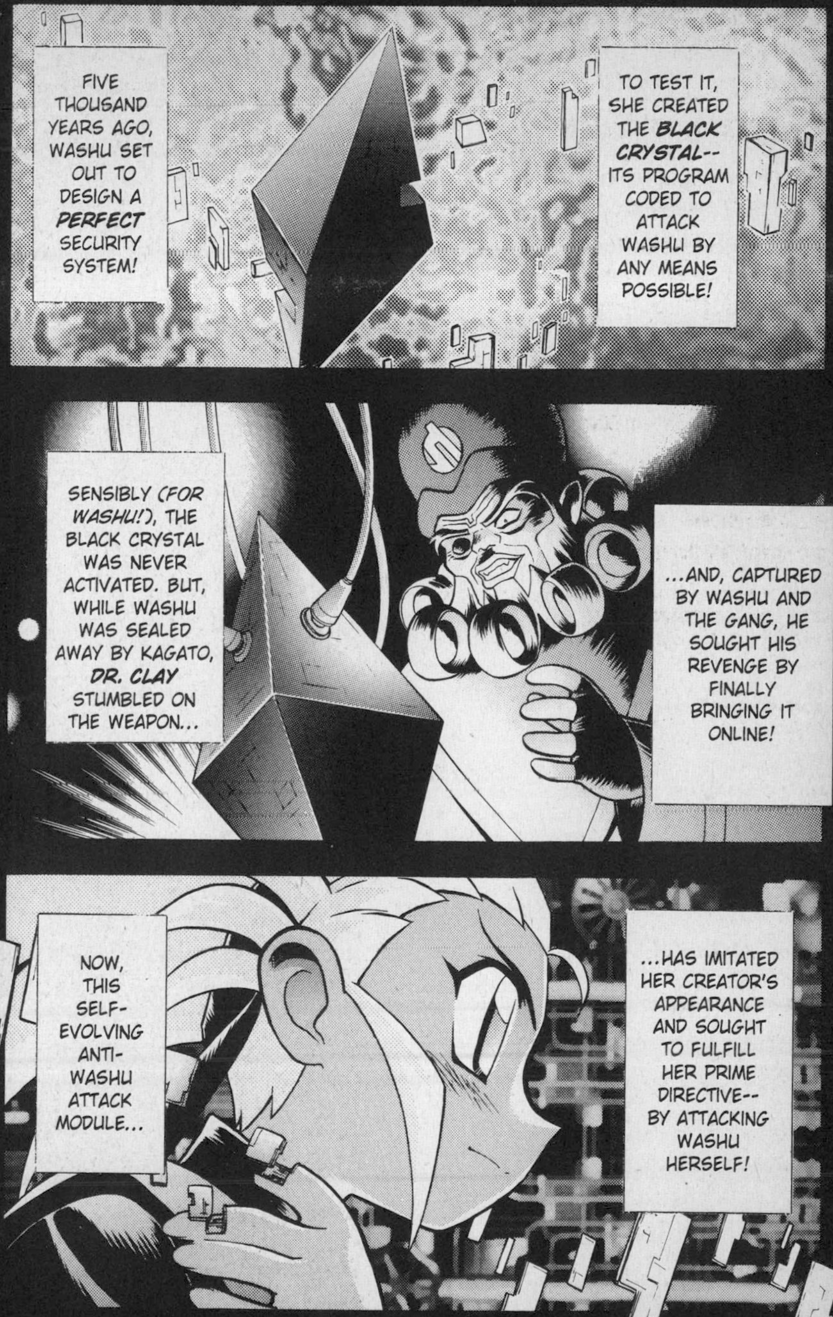
FIVE THOUSAND YEARS AGO, WASHU SET OUT TO DESIGN A **PERFECT** SECURITY SYSTEM!
TO TEST IT, SHE CREATED THE ***BLACK CRYSTAL***-- ITS PROGRAM CODED TO ATTACK WASHU BY ANY MEANS POSSIBLE!
SENSIBLY (*FOR WASHU!*), THE BLACK CRYSTAL WAS NEVER ACTIVATED. BUT, WHILE WASHU WAS SEALED AWAY BY KAGATO, ***DR. CLAY*** STUMBLED ON THE WEAPON...
...AND, CAPTURED BY WASHU AND THE GANG, HE SOUGHT HIS REVENGE BY FINALLY BRINGING IT ONLINE!
NOW, THIS SELF-EVOLVING ANTI-WASHU ATTACK MODULE...
...HAS IMITATED HER CREATOR'S APPEARANCE AND SOUGHT TO FULFILL HER PRIME DIRECTIVE-- BY ATTACKING WASHU HERSELF!

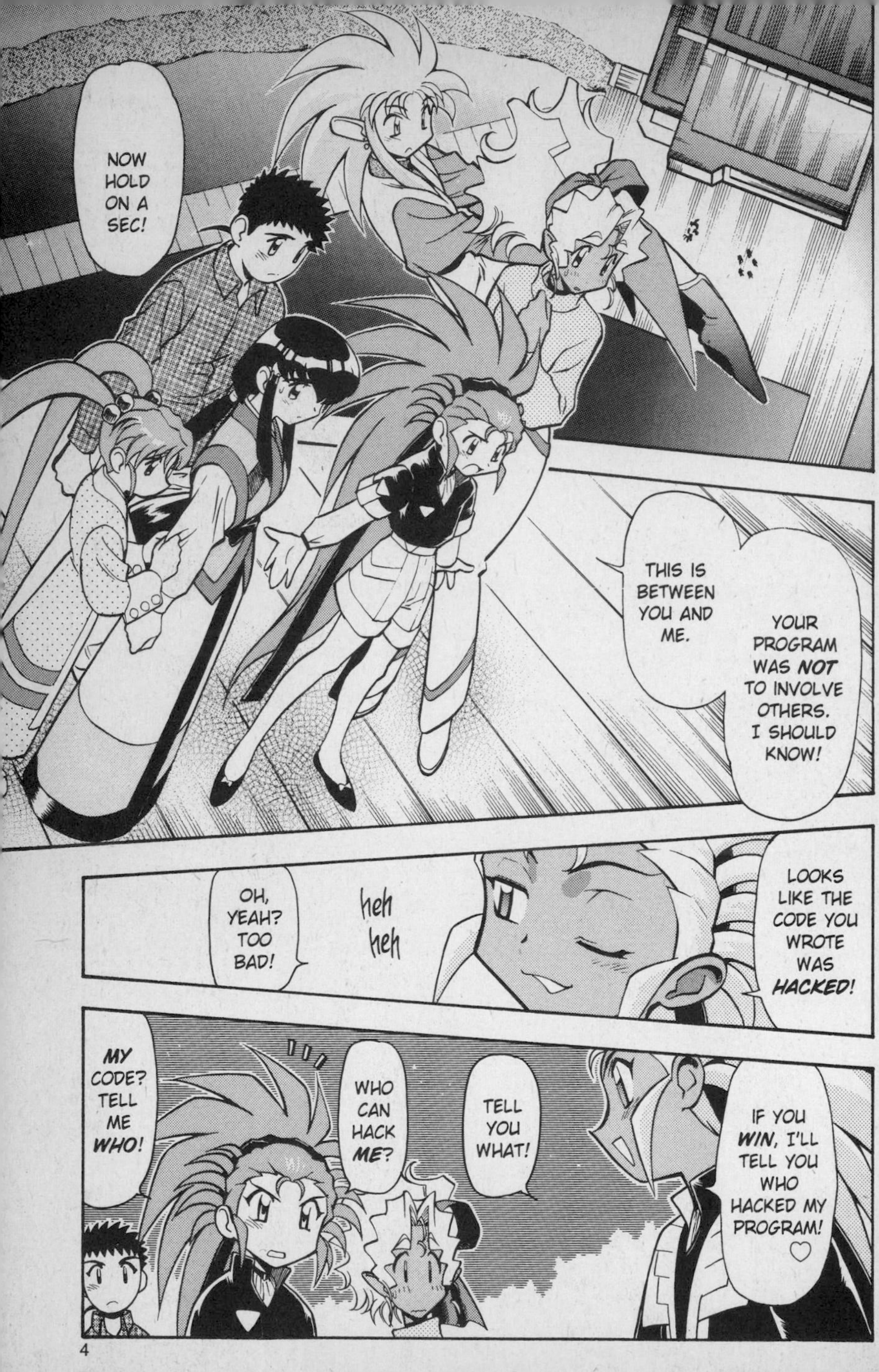
NOW HOLD ON A SEC!
THIS IS BETWEEN YOU AND ME.
YOUR PROGRAM WAS **NOT** TO INVOLVE OTHERS. I SHOULD KNOW!
OH, YEAH? TOO BAD!
heh heh
LOOKS LIKE THE CODE YOU WROTE WAS **HACKED**!
MY CODE? TELL ME **WHO**!
WHO CAN HACK **ME**?
TELL YOU WHAT!
IF YOU **WIN**, I'LL TELL YOU WHO HACKED MY PROGRAM! ♡

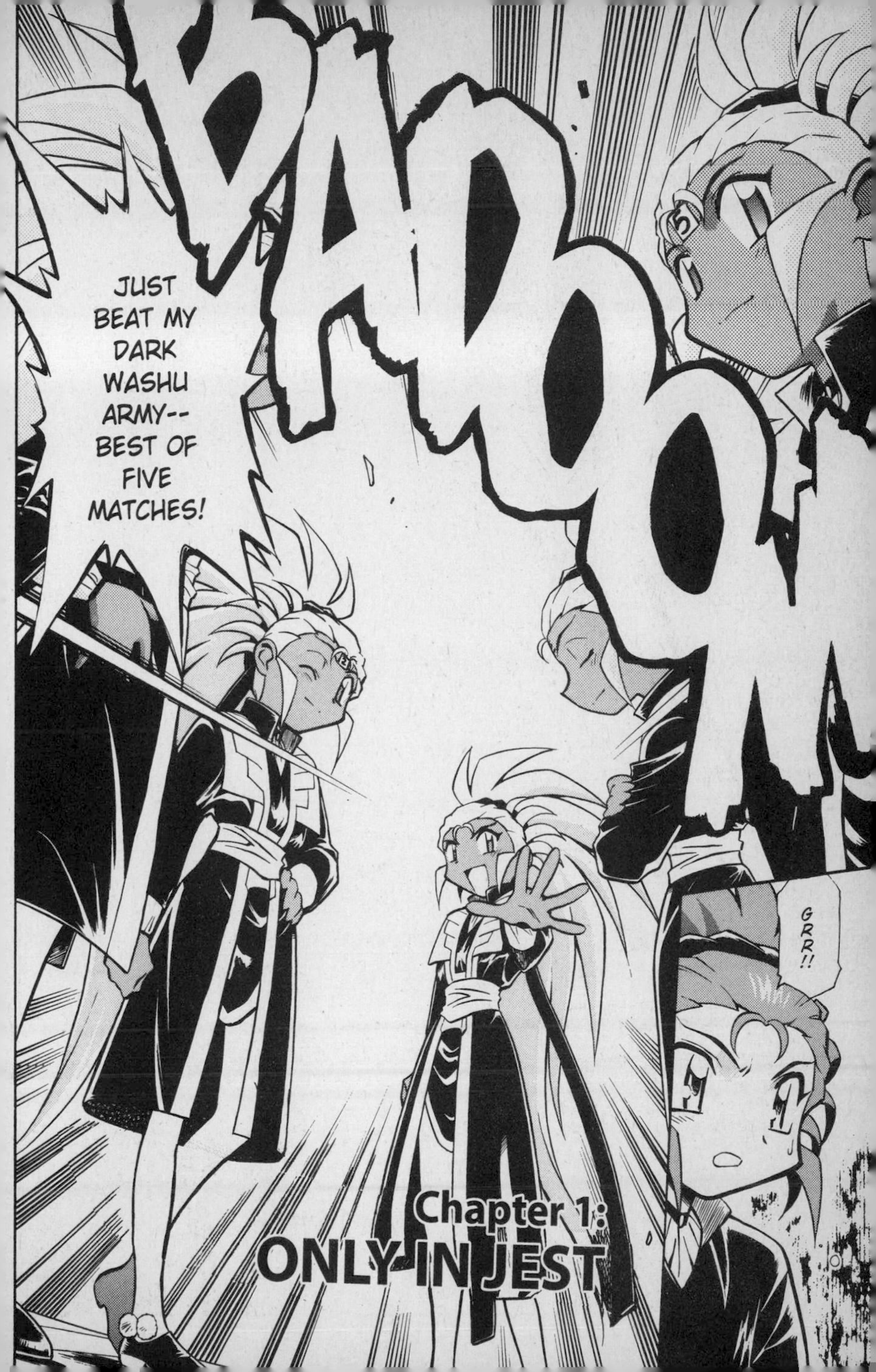
BADOOM
JUST BEAT MY DARK WASHU ARMY-- BEST OF FIVE MATCHES!
GRR!!
Chapter 1:
ONLY IN JEST

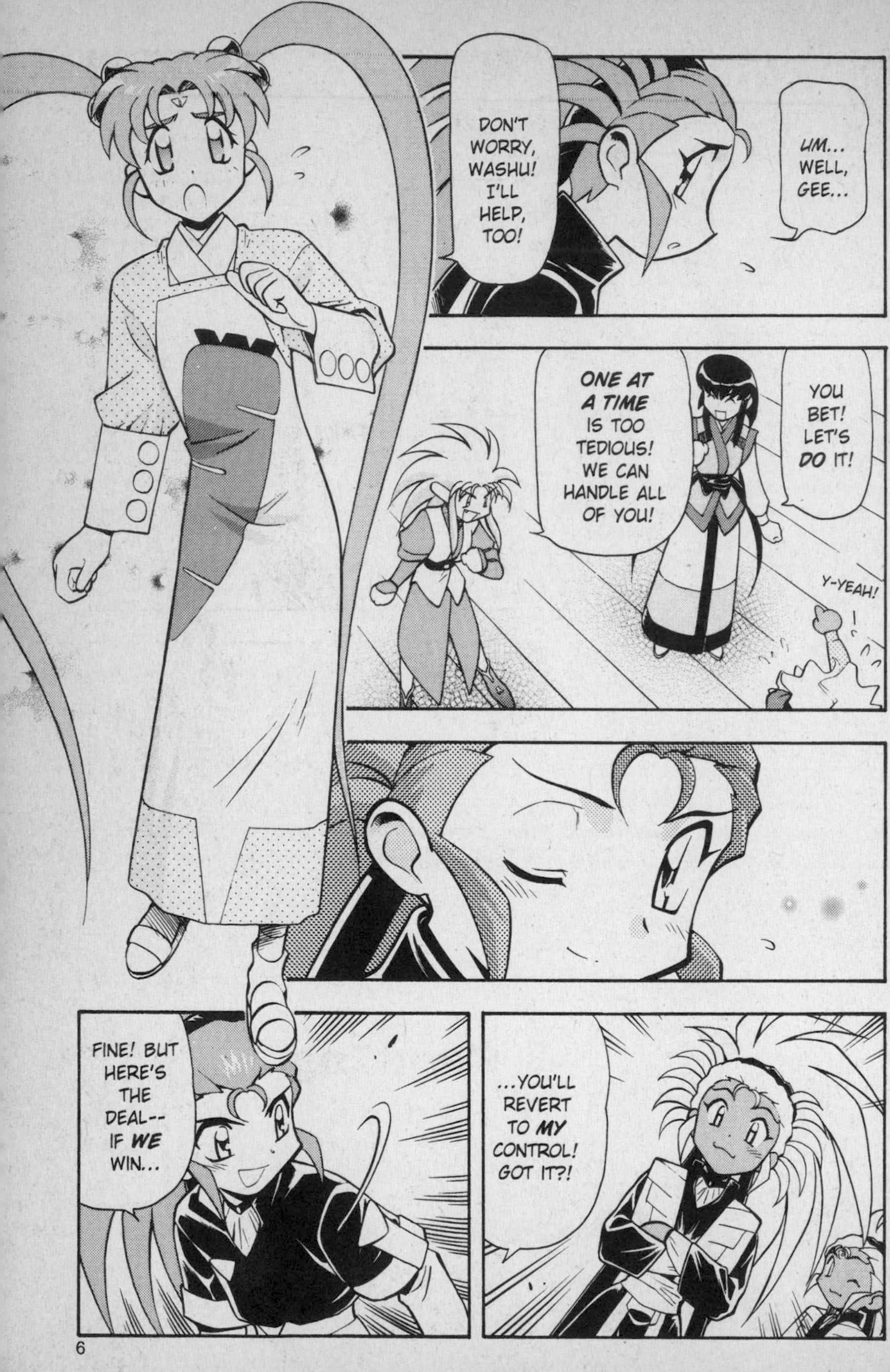
DON'T WORRY, WASHU! I'LL HELP, TOO!
UM... WELL, GEE...
ONE AT A TIME IS TOO TEDIOUS! WE CAN HANDLE ALL OF YOU!
YOU BET! LET'S DO IT!
Y-YEAH!
FINE! BUT HERE'S THE DEAL-- IF WE WIN...
...YOU'LL REVERT TO MY CONTROL! GOT IT?!

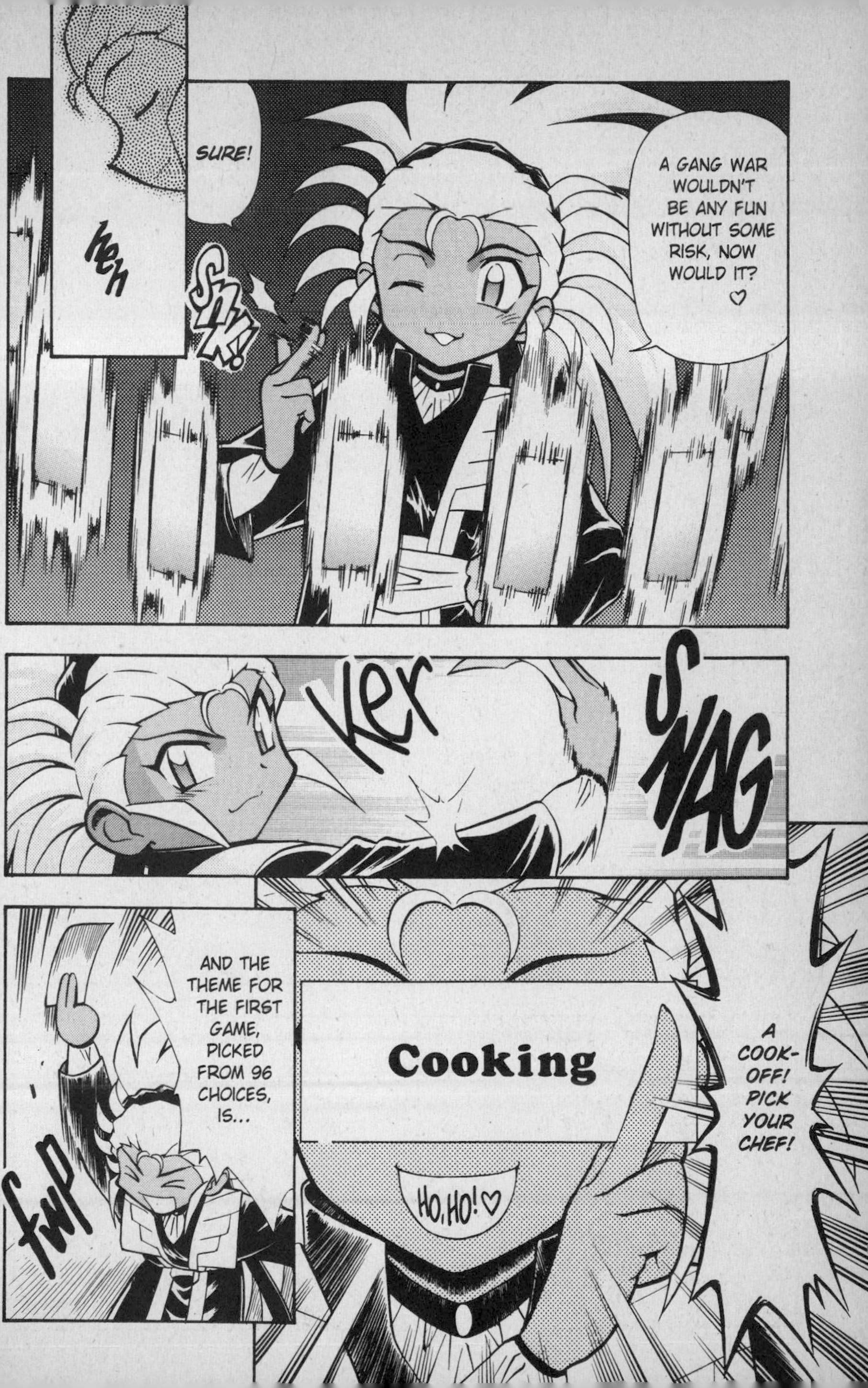
SURE!
heh
SNIK!
A GANG WAR WOULDN'T BE ANY FUN WITHOUT SOME RISK, NOW WOULD IT? ♡
KER
SNAG
AND THE THEME FOR THE FIRST GAME, PICKED FROM 96 CHOICES, IS...
fwip
Cooking
HO, HO! ♡
A COOK-OFF! PICK YOUR CHEF!

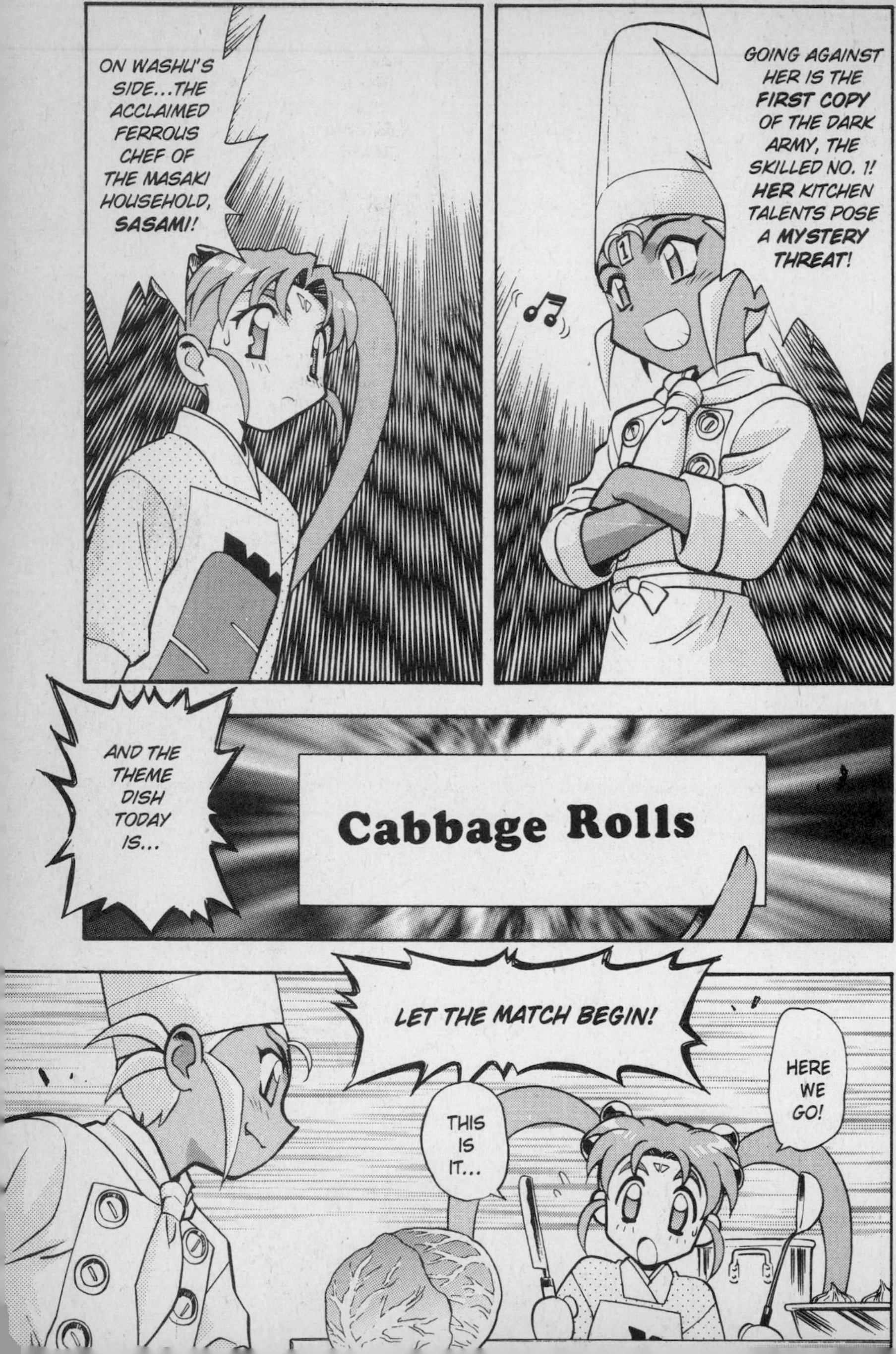
ON WASHU'S SIDE...THE ACCLAIMED FERROUS CHEF OF THE MASAKI HOUSEHOLD, SASAMI!
GOING AGAINST HER IS THE FIRST COPY OF THE DARK ARMY, THE SKILLED NO. 1! HER KITCHEN TALENTS POSE A MYSTERY THREAT!
AND THE THEME DISH TODAY IS...
Cabbage Rolls
LET THE MATCH BEGIN!
THIS IS IT...
HERE WE GO!

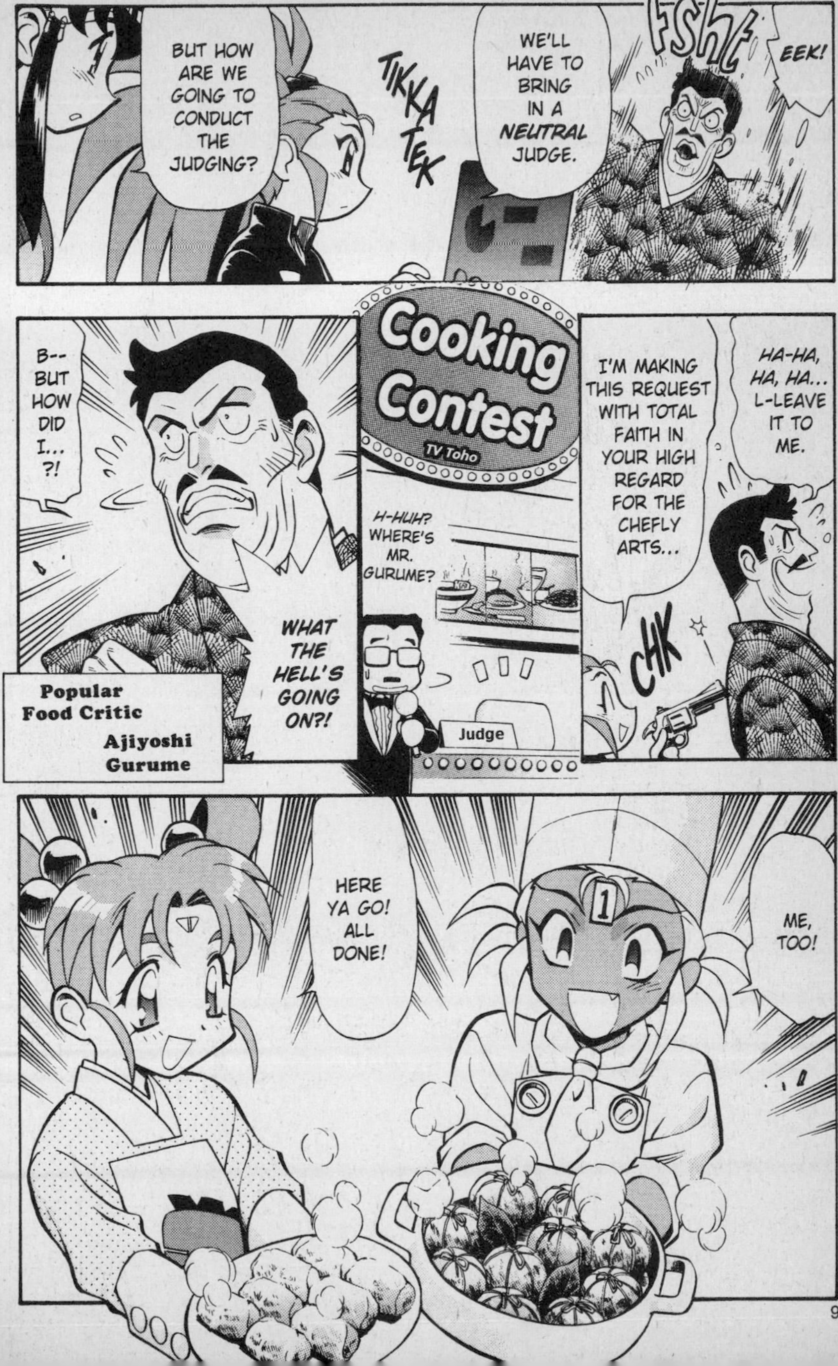
BUT HOW ARE WE GOING TO CONDUCT THE JUDGING?
TIKKA TEK
WE'LL HAVE TO BRING IN A NEUTRAL JUDGE.
fsht
EEK!
B-- BUT HOW DID I... ?!
WHAT THE HELL'S GOING ON?!
Popular Food Critic Ajiyoshi Gurume
Cooking Contest
TV Toho
H-HUH? WHERE'S MR. GURUME?
Judge
I'M MAKING THIS REQUEST WITH TOTAL FAITH IN YOUR HIGH REGARD FOR THE CHEFLY ARTS...
HA-HA, HA, HA... L-LEAVE IT TO ME.
CHK
HERE YA GO! ALL DONE!
ME, TOO!

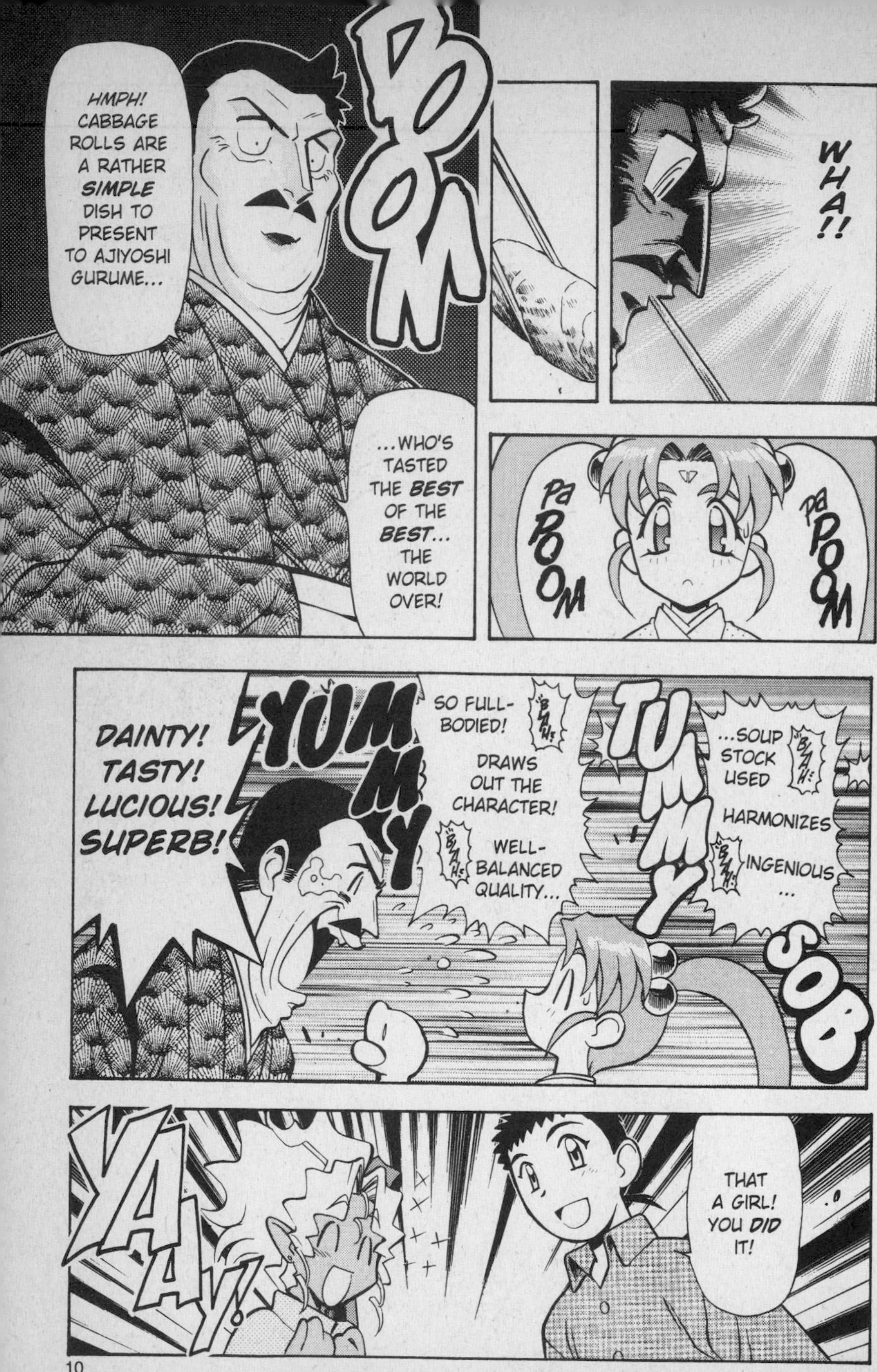
HMPH! CABBAGE ROLLS ARE A RATHER SIMPLE DISH TO PRESENT TO AJIYOSHI GURUME...
BOOM
...WHO'S TASTED THE BEST OF THE BEST... THE WORLD OVER!
WHA!!
PaPOOM
PaPOOM
DAINTY! TASTY! LUCIOUS! SUPERB!
YUMMY
SO FULL-BODIED!
BLAH
DRAWS OUT THE CHARACTER!
BLAH
WELL-BALANCED QUALITY...
TUMMY
...SOUP STOCK USED
BLAH
HARMONIZES
BLAH
INGENIOUS...
SOB
YAAY
THAT A GIRL! YOU DID IT!

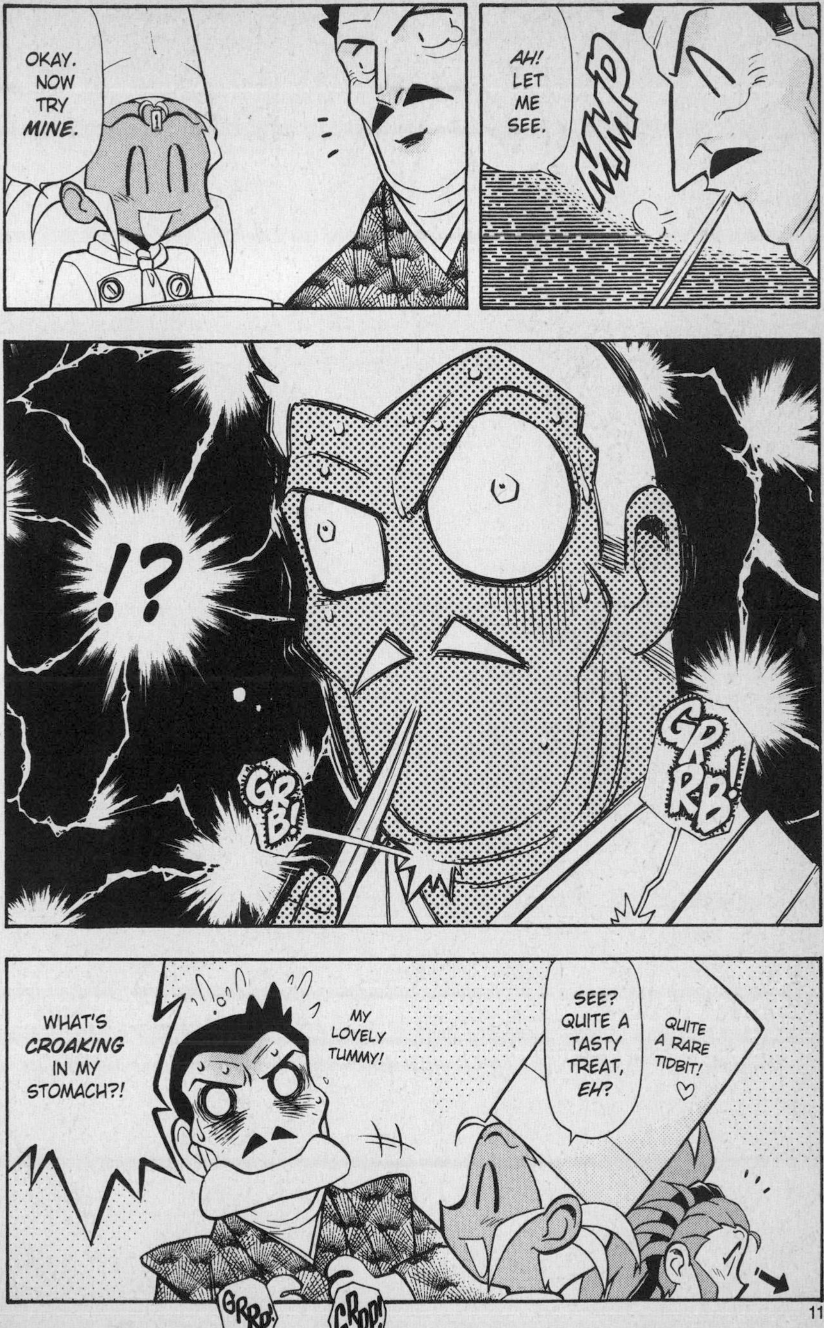
OKAY. NOW TRY MINE.
AH! LET ME SEE.
NMP
!?
GRB!
GRRB!
WHAT'S CROAKING IN MY STOMACH?!
MY LOVELY TUMMY!
SEE? QUITE A TASTY TREAT, EH?
QUITE A RARE TIDBIT! ♡
GRRP!
GRRP!

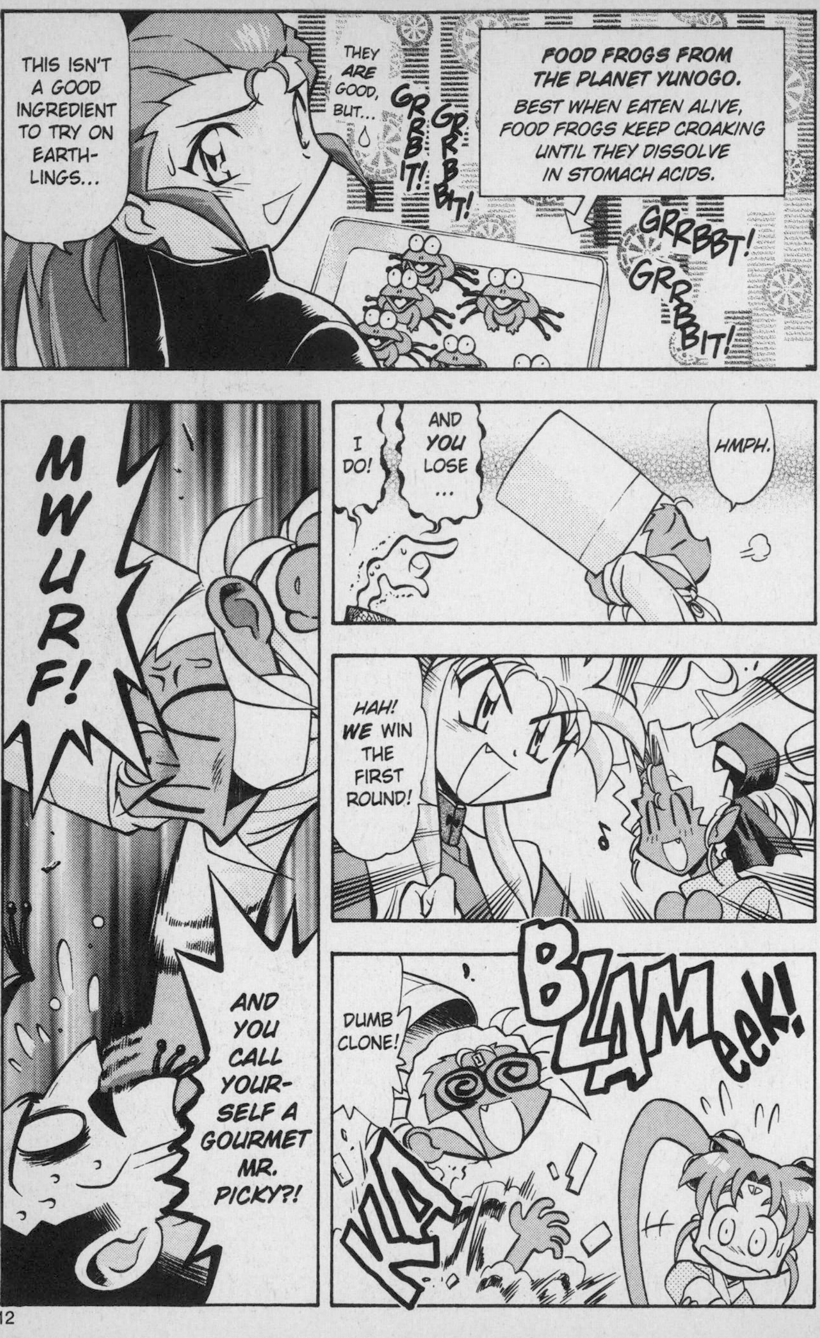
THIS ISN'T A GOOD INGREDIENT TO TRY ON EARTH-LINGS...
THEY ARE GOOD, BUT...
GRRBBIT!
GRRBBBIT!
FOOD FROGS FROM THE PLANET YUNOGO.
BEST WHEN EATEN ALIVE, FOOD FROGS KEEP CROAKING UNTIL THEY DISSOLVE IN STOMACH ACIDS.
GRRRBBT!
GRRBBBIT!
MWURF!
AND YOU CALL YOURSELF A GOURMET MR. PICKY?!
I DO!
AND YOU LOSE ...
HMPH.
HAH! WE WIN THE FIRST ROUND!
DUMB CLONE!
BLAM
eek!

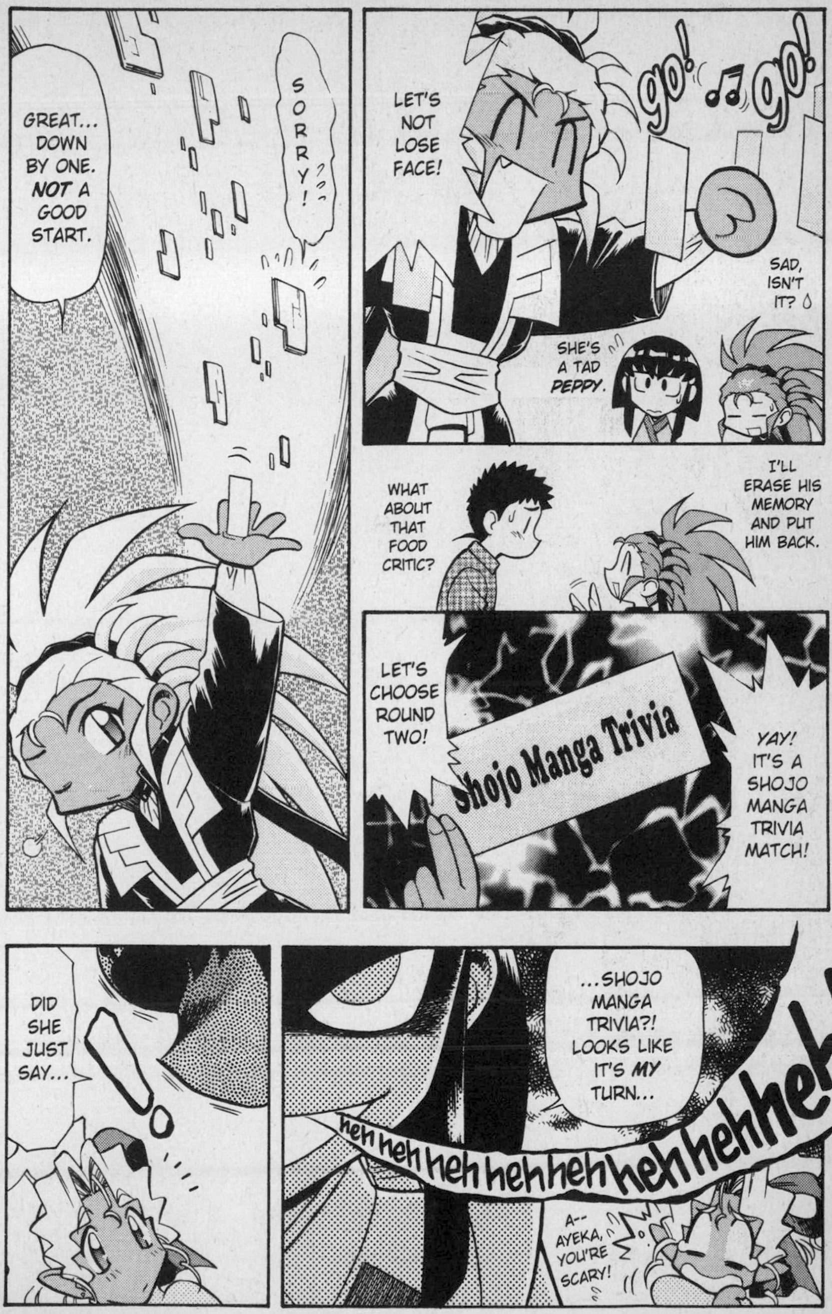
GREAT... DOWN BY ONE. *NOT* A GOOD START.
SORRY!
LET'S NOT LOSE FACE!
go! ♫ go!
SHE'S A TAD *PEPPY*.
SAD, ISN'T IT?
WHAT ABOUT THAT FOOD CRITIC?
I'LL ERASE HIS MEMORY AND PUT HIM BACK.
LET'S CHOOSE ROUND TWO!
Shojo Manga Trivia
YAY! IT'S A SHOJO MANGA TRIVIA MATCH!
DID SHE JUST SAY...
!
...SHOJO MANGA TRIVIA?! LOOKS LIKE IT'S *MY* TURN...
heh heh heh heh heh heh heh heh heh!
A-- AYEKA, YOU'RE SCARY!

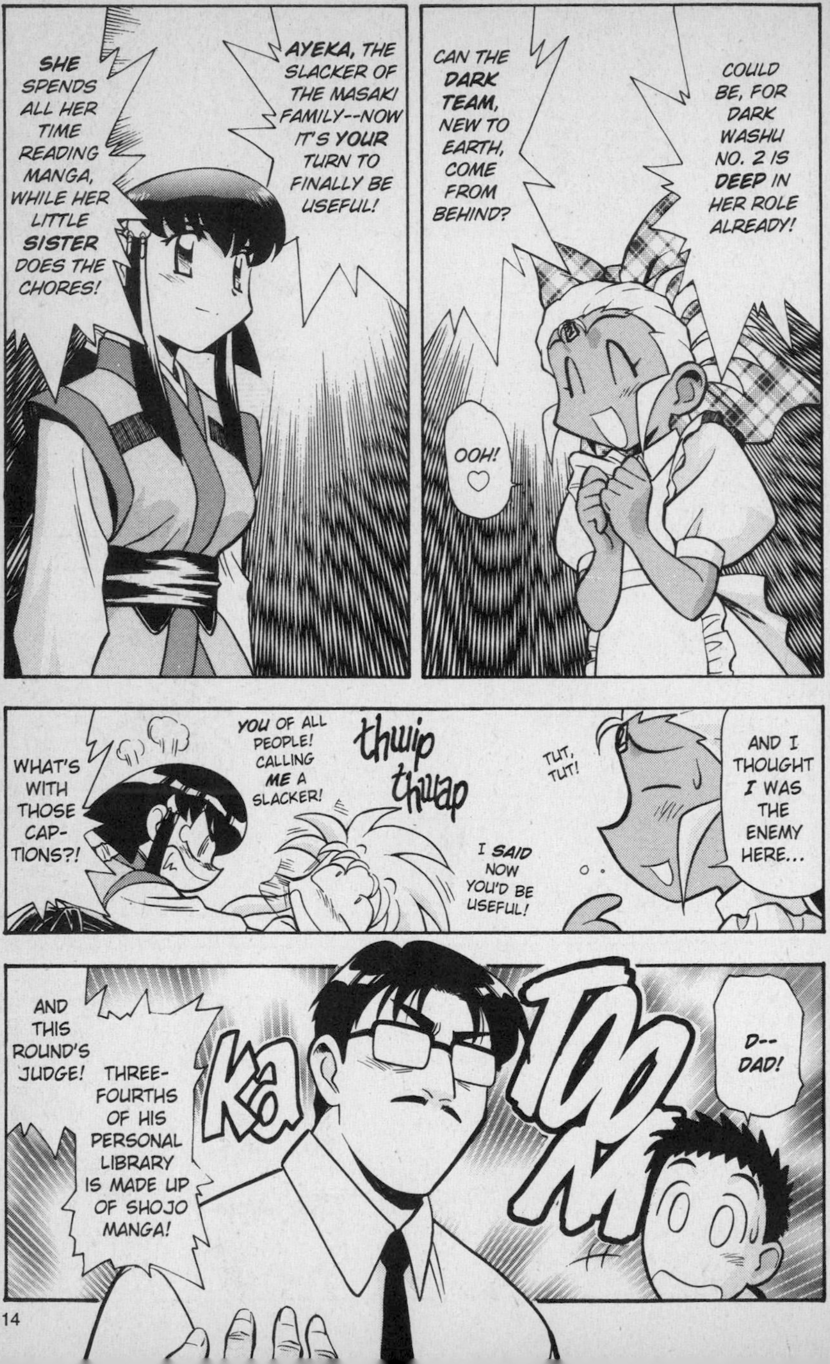
SHE SPENDS ALL HER TIME READING MANGA, WHILE HER LITTLE SISTER DOES THE CHORES!
AYEKA, THE SLACKER OF THE MASAKI FAMILY--NOW IT'S YOUR TURN TO FINALLY BE USEFUL!
CAN THE DARK TEAM, NEW TO EARTH, COME FROM BEHIND?
COULD BE, FOR DARK WASHU NO. 2 IS DEEP IN HER ROLE ALREADY!
OOH! ♡
WHAT'S WITH THOSE CAP-TIONS?!
YOU OF ALL PEOPLE! CALLING ME A SLACKER!
thwip thwap
TUT, TUT!
I SAID NOW YOU'D BE USEFUL!
AND I THOUGHT I WAS THE ENEMY HERE...
AND THIS ROUND'S JUDGE!
THREE-FOURTHS OF HIS PERSONAL LIBRARY IS MADE UP OF SHOJO MANGA!
KA TOOM
D--DAD!

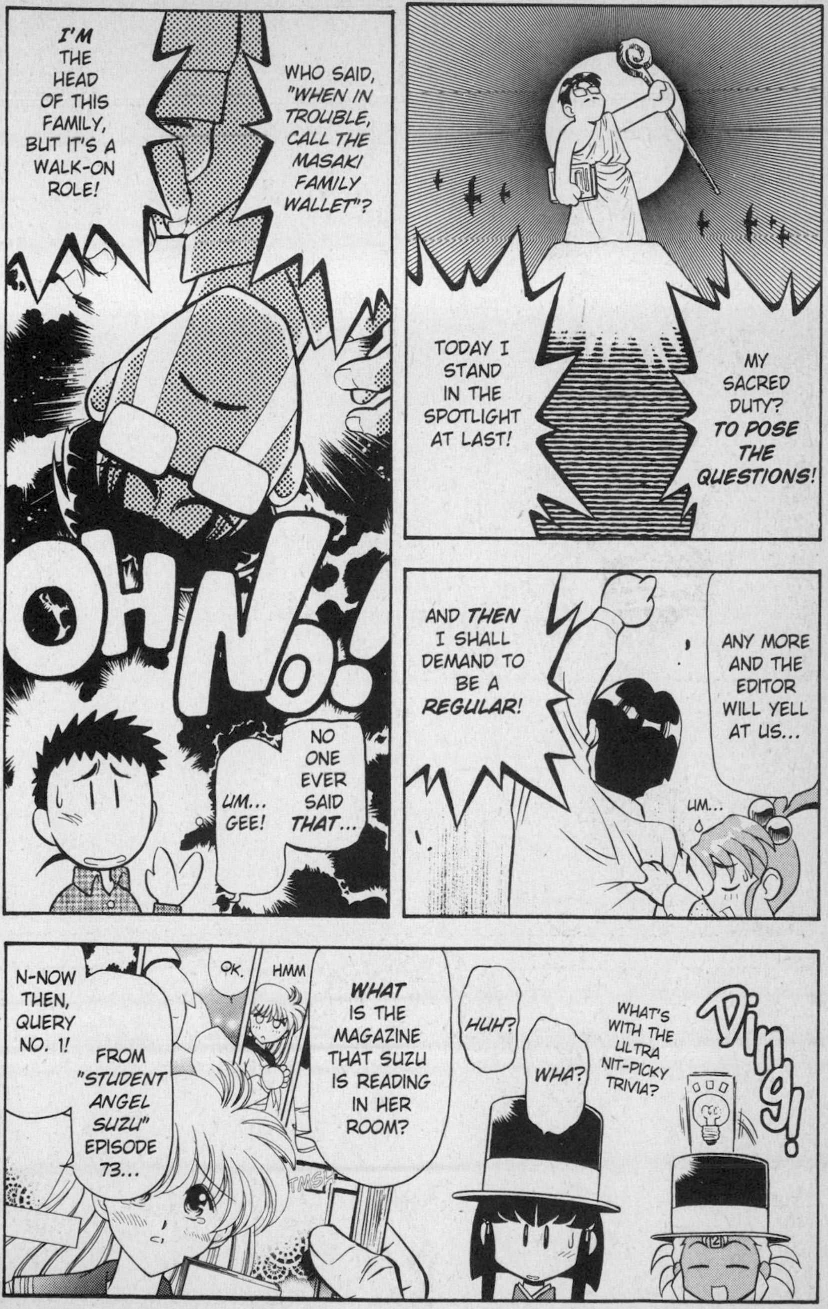
I'M THE HEAD OF THIS FAMILY, BUT IT'S A WALK-ON ROLE!
WHO SAID, "WHEN IN TROUBLE, CALL THE MASAKI FAMILY WALLET"?
OH NO!!
UM... GEE!
NO ONE EVER SAID THAT...
TODAY I STAND IN THE SPOTLIGHT AT LAST!
MY SACRED DUTY? TO POSE THE QUESTIONS!
AND THEN I SHALL DEMAND TO BE A REGULAR!
ANY MORE AND THE EDITOR WILL YELL AT US...
UM...
N-NOW THEN, QUERY NO. 1!
FROM "STUDENT ANGEL SUZU" EPISODE 73...
OK.
HMM
WHAT IS THE MAGAZINE THAT SUZU IS READING IN HER ROOM?
TMSH
HUH?
WHA?
WHAT'S WITH THE ULTRA NIT-PICKY TRIVIA?
Ding!

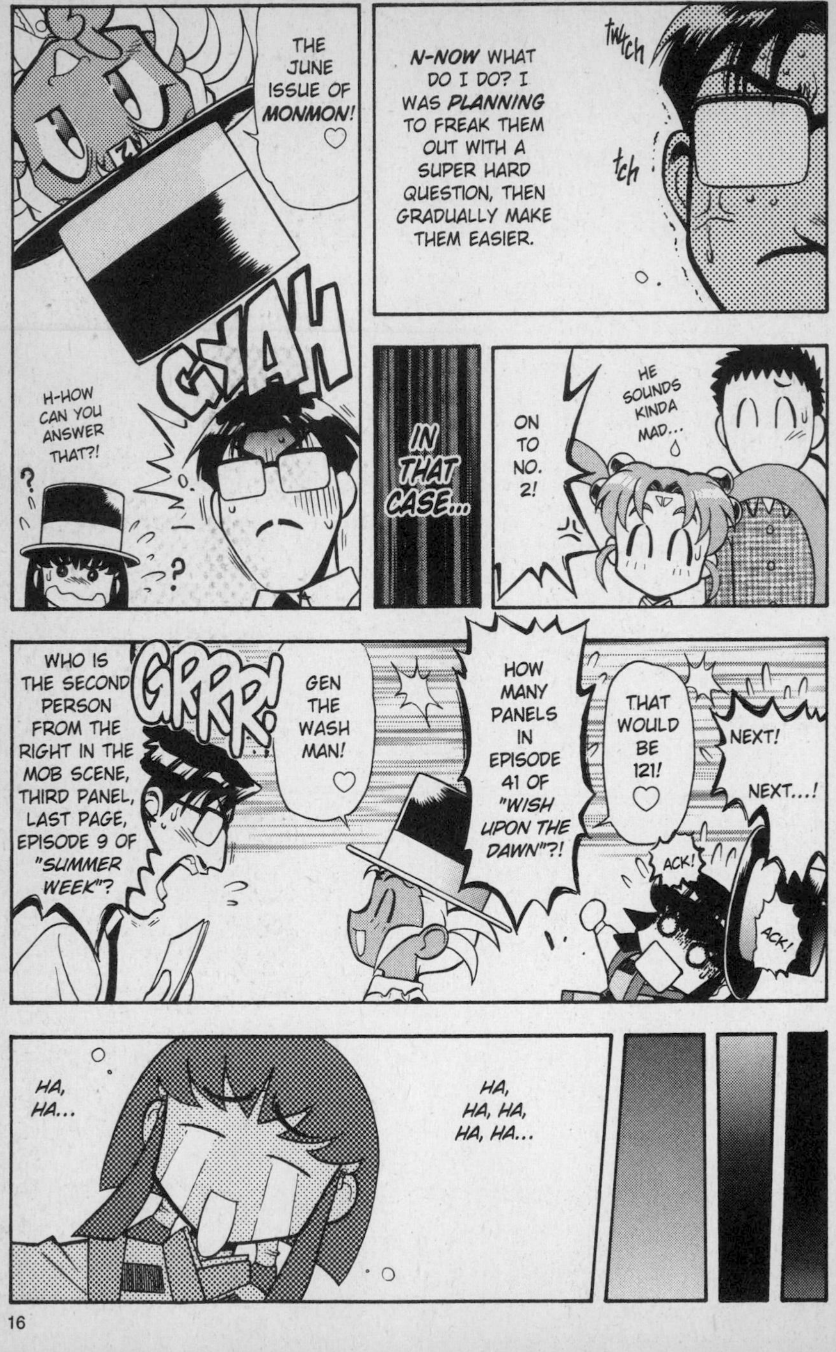
THE JUNE ISSUE OF MONMON! ♡
GYAH
H-HOW CAN YOU ANSWER THAT?!
?
?
N-NOW WHAT DO I DO? I WAS PLANNING TO FREAK THEM OUT WITH A SUPER HARD QUESTION, THEN GRADUALLY MAKE THEM EASIER.
twitch
tch
IN THAT CASE...
ON TO NO. 2!
HE SOUNDS KINDA MAD...
WHO IS THE SECOND PERSON FROM THE RIGHT IN THE MOB SCENE, THIRD PANEL, LAST PAGE, EPISODE 9 OF "SUMMER WEEK"?
GRRR!
GEN THE WASH MAN! ♡
HOW MANY PANELS IN EPISODE 41 OF "WISH UPON THE DAWN"?!
THAT WOULD BE 121! ♡
NEXT!
NEXT...!
ACK!
ACK!
HA, HA...
HA, HA, HA, HA, HA...

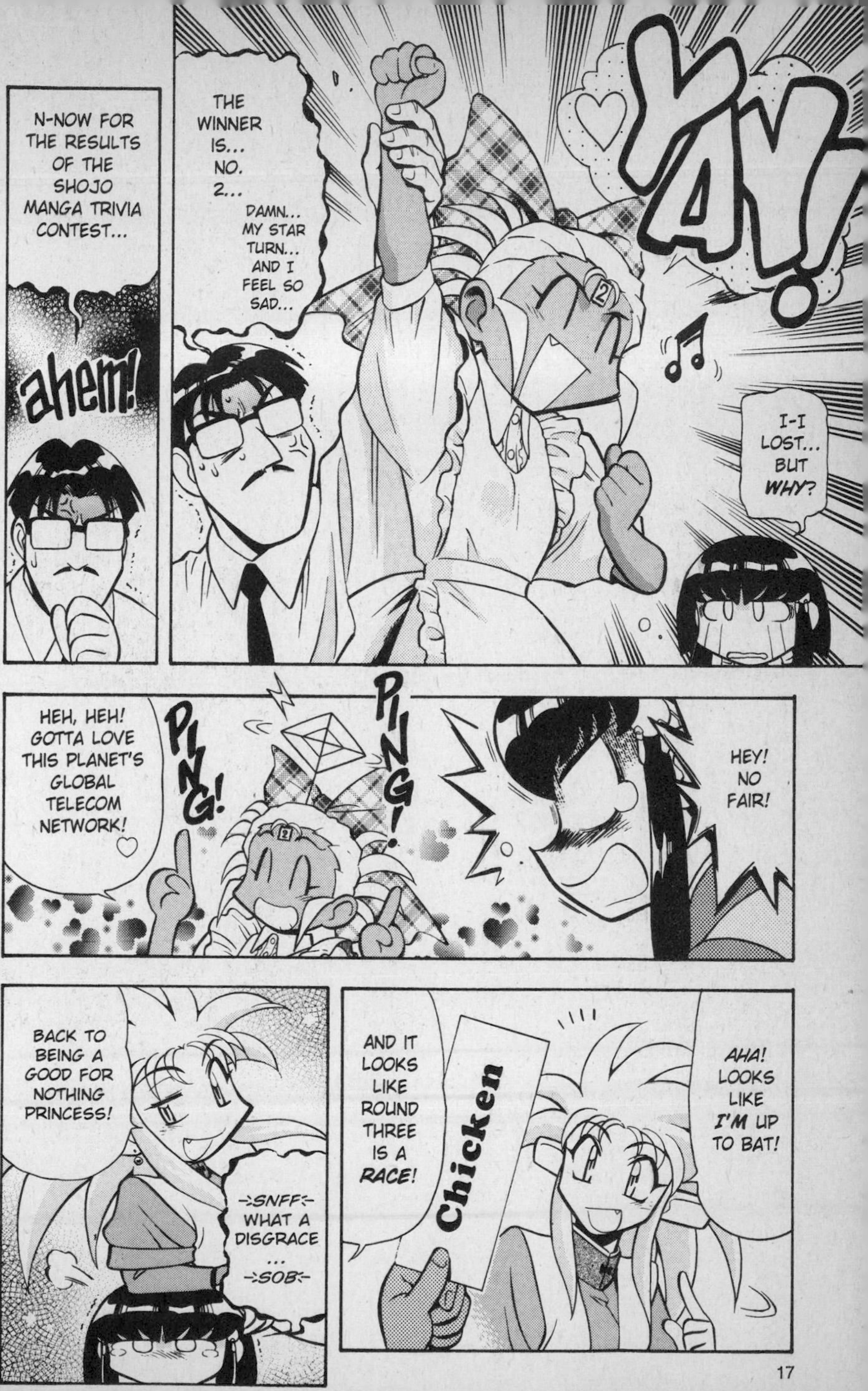
N-NOW FOR THE RESULTS OF THE SHOJO MANGA TRIVIA CONTEST...
ahem!
THE WINNER IS... NO. 2...
DAMN... MY STAR TURN... AND I FEEL SO SAD...
YAY!
I-I LOST... BUT *WHY?*
HEH, HEH! GOTTA LOVE THIS PLANET'S GLOBAL TELECOM NETWORK!
PING!
PING!
HEY! NO FAIR!
BACK TO BEING A GOOD FOR NOTHING PRINCESS!
SNFF WHAT A DISGRACE ... *SOB*
AND IT LOOKS LIKE ROUND THREE IS A *RACE!*
Chicken
AHA! LOOKS LIKE *I'M* UP TO BAT!

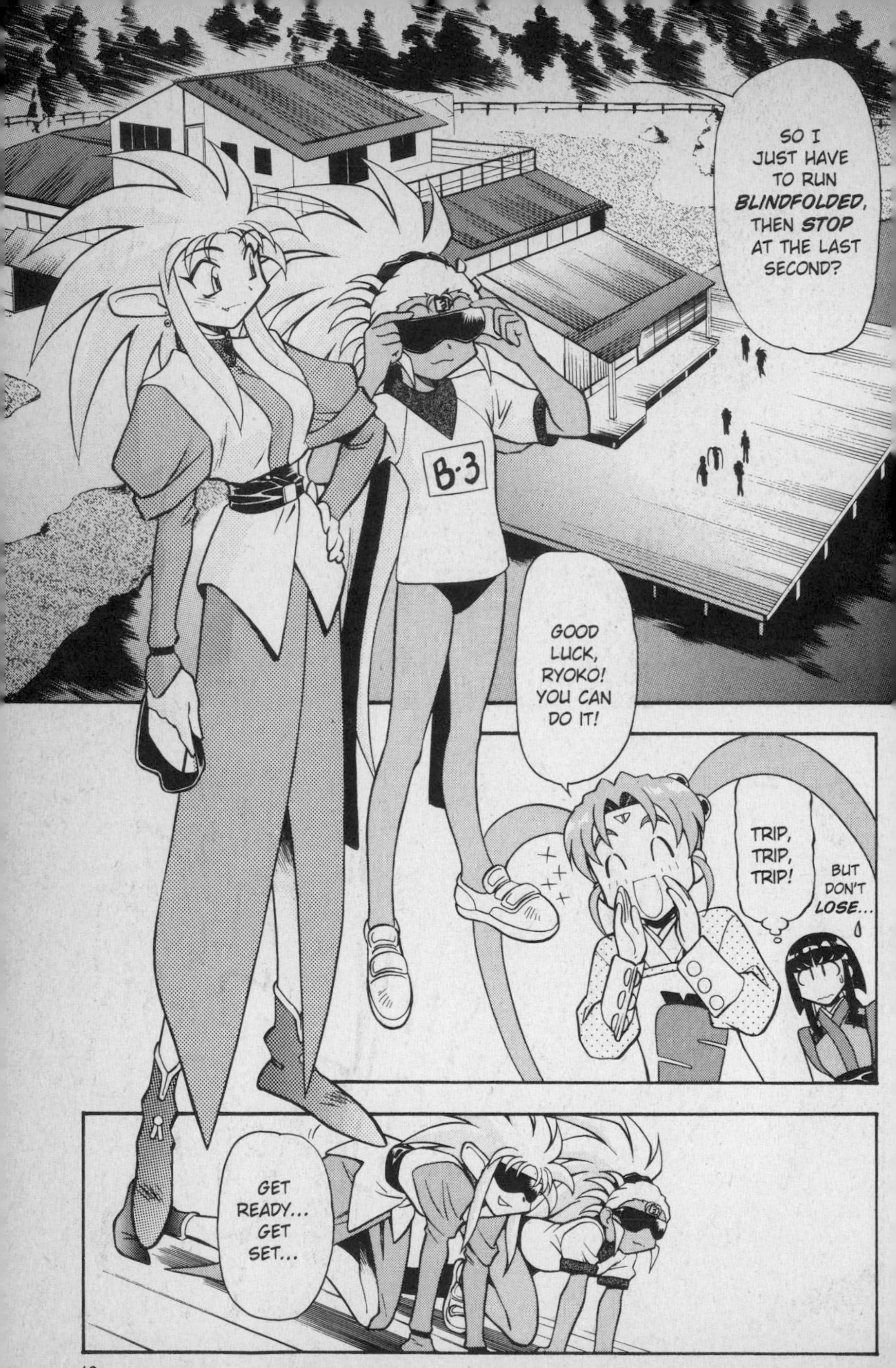
SO I JUST HAVE TO RUN **BLINDFOLDED**, THEN **STOP** AT THE LAST SECOND?
B-3
GOOD LUCK, RYOKO! YOU CAN DO IT!
TRIP, TRIP, TRIP!
BUT DON'T **LOSE**...
GET READY... GET SET...

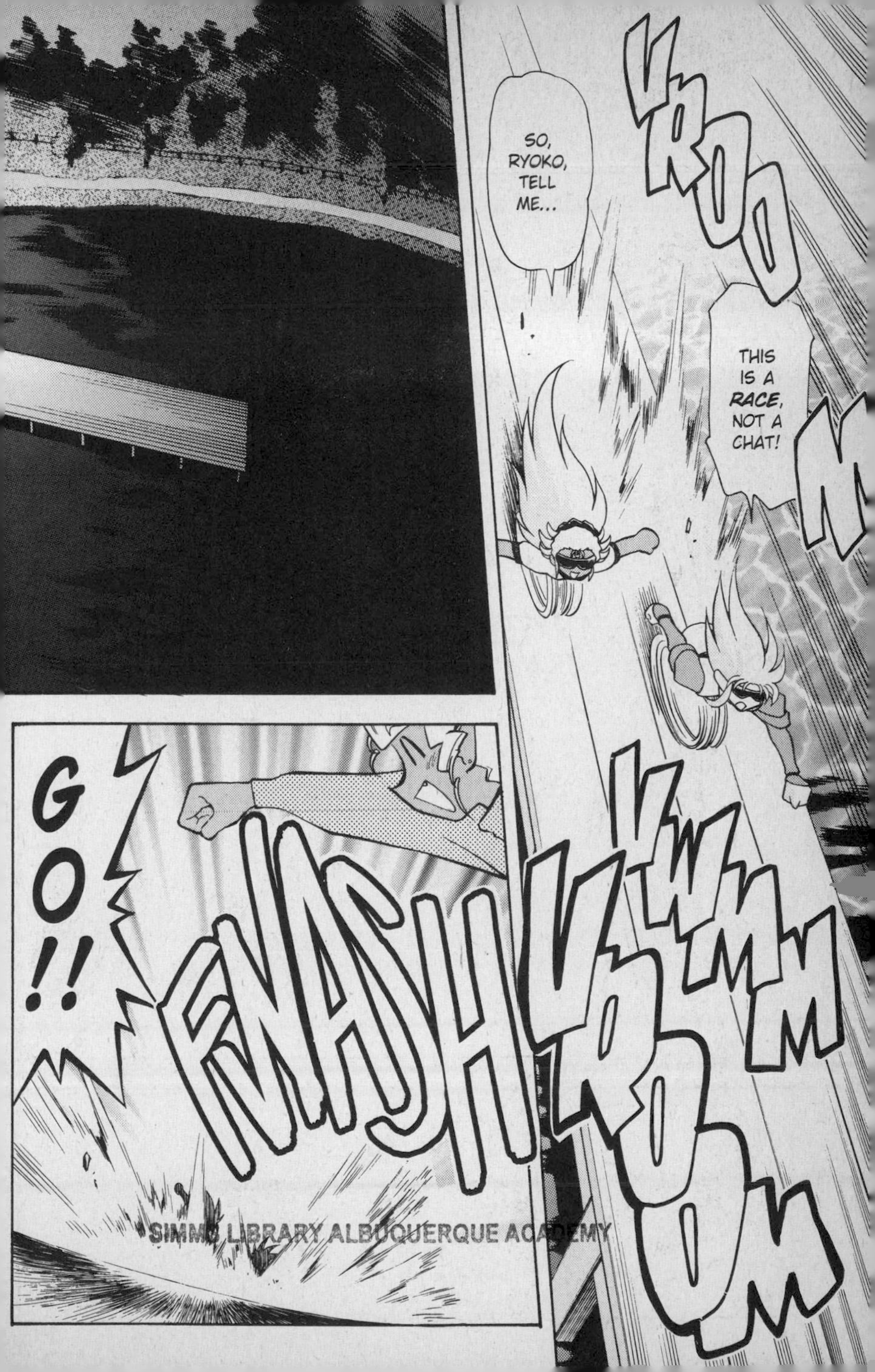
GO!!
FWASH
VROOOM
SO, RYOKO, TELL ME...
THIS IS A RACE, NOT A CHAT!

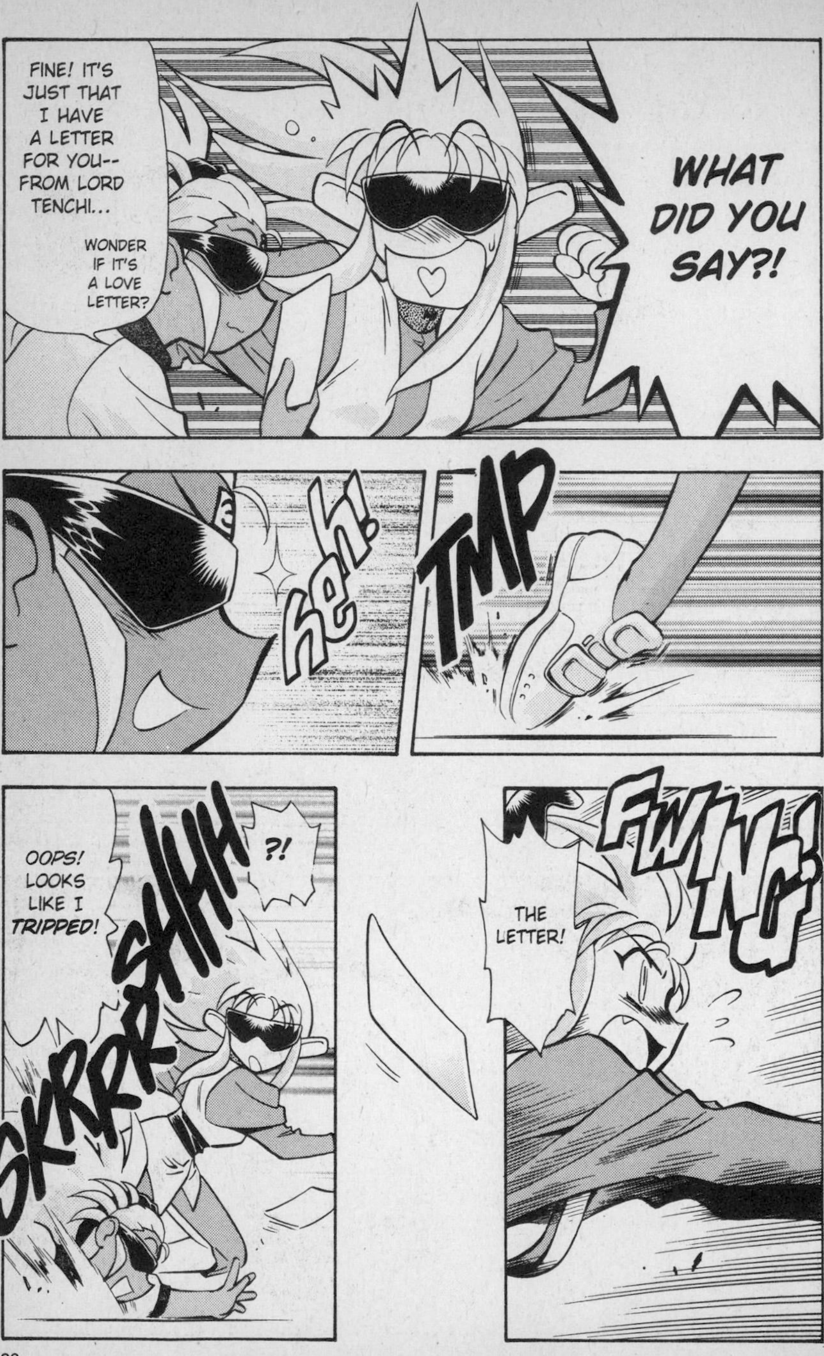

FINE! IT'S JUST THAT I HAVE A LETTER FOR YOU-- FROM LORD TENCHI...
WONDER IF IT'S A LOVE LETTER?
WHAT DID YOU SAY?!
heh!
TMP
OOPS! LOOKS LIKE I *TRIPPED!*
SKRRRSHHH
?!
THE LETTER!
FWING!

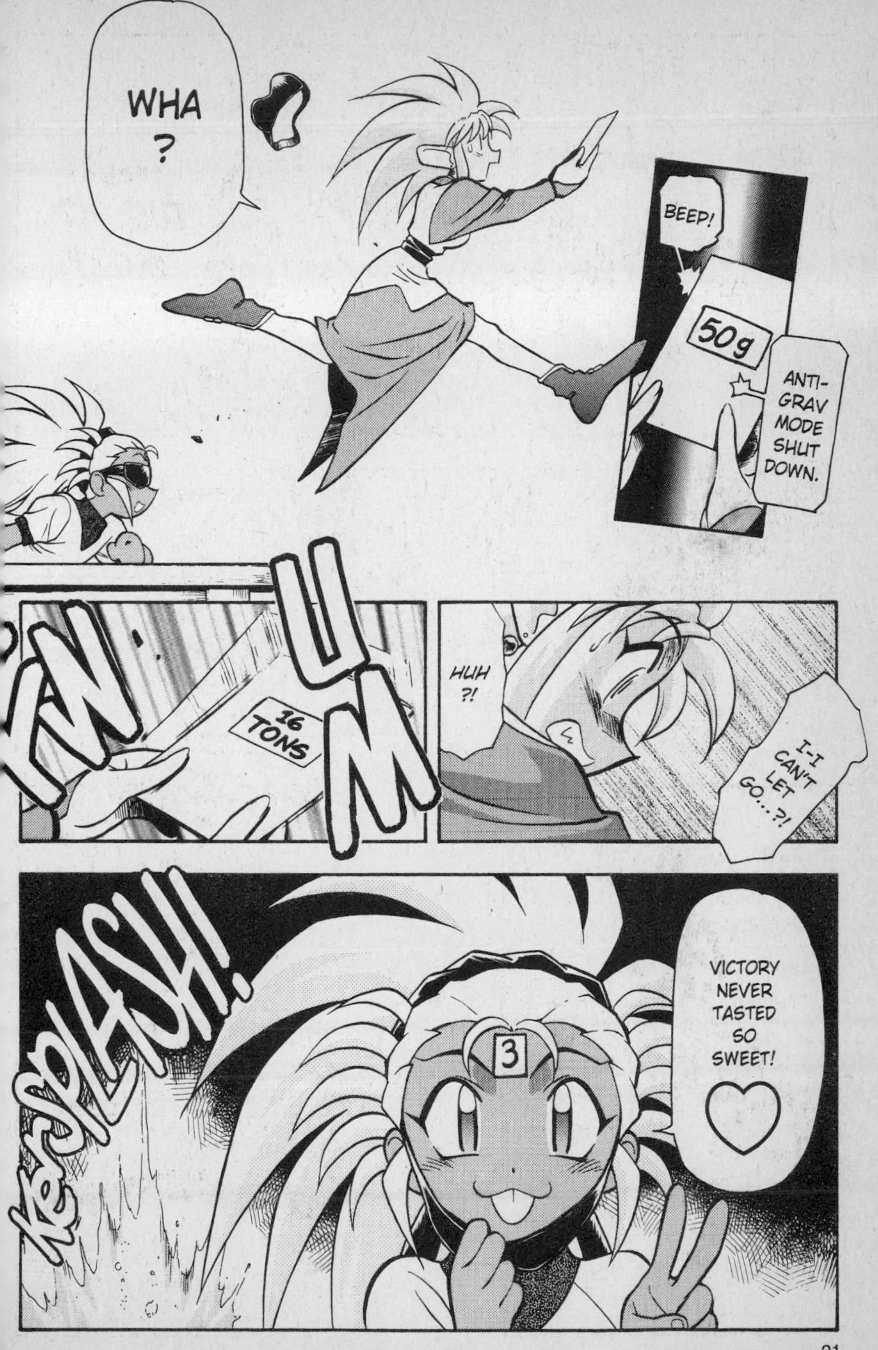
WHA ?
BEEP!
50g
ANTI-GRAV MODE SHUT DOWN.
16 TONS
HUH ?!
I-I CAN'T LET GO...?!
kerSPLASH!!
VICTORY NEVER TASTED SO SWEET!

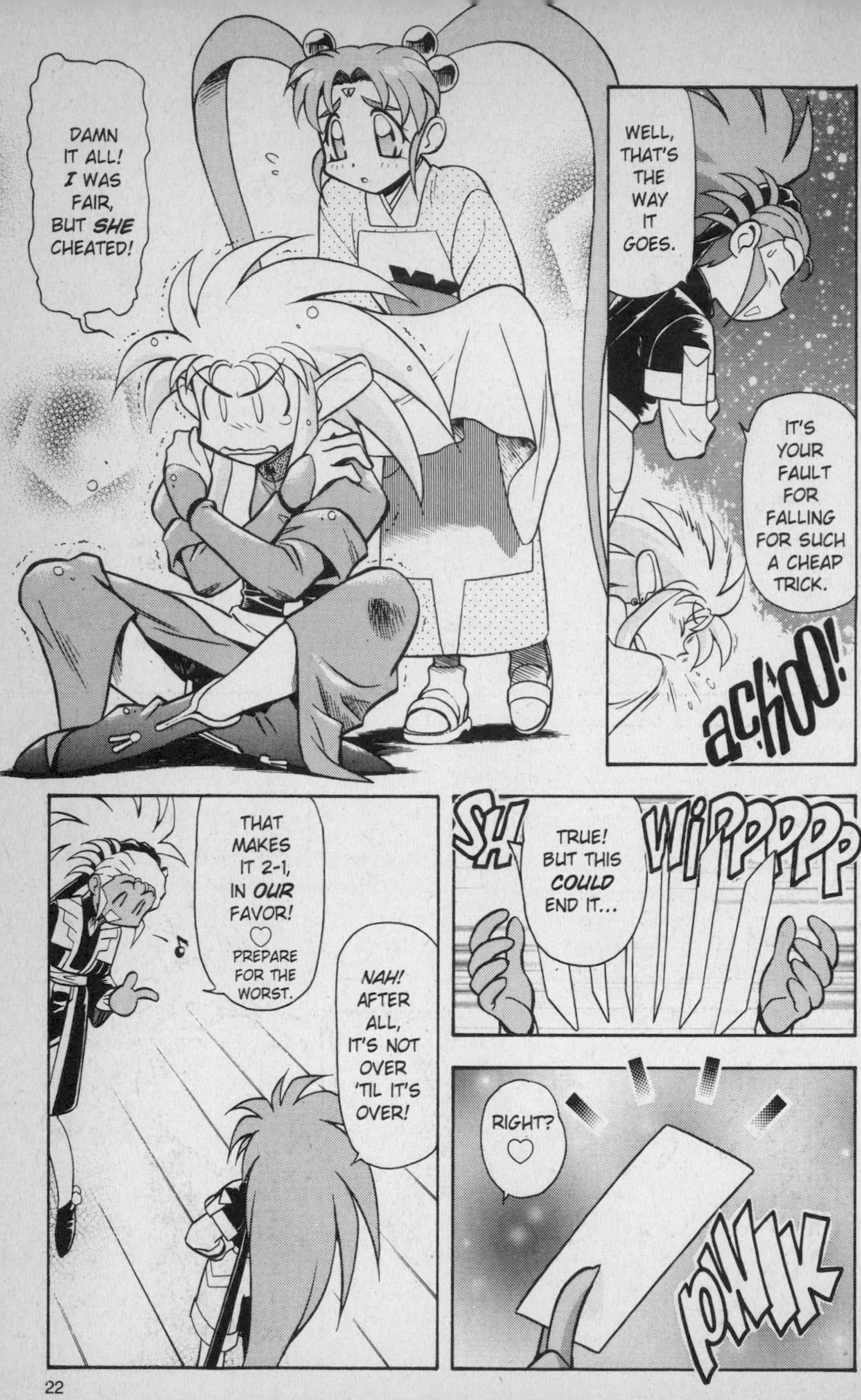
DAMN IT ALL! I WAS FAIR, BUT SHE CHEATED!
WELL, THAT'S THE WAY IT GOES.
IT'S YOUR FAULT FOR FALLING FOR SUCH A CHEAP TRICK.
ACHOO!
THAT MAKES IT 2-1, IN OUR FAVOR! ♡ PREPARE FOR THE WORST.
NAH! AFTER ALL, IT'S NOT OVER 'TIL IT'S OVER!
SH
TRUE! BUT THIS COULD END IT...
WIPPPPP
RIGHT? ♡
PINK

Drawing Lots

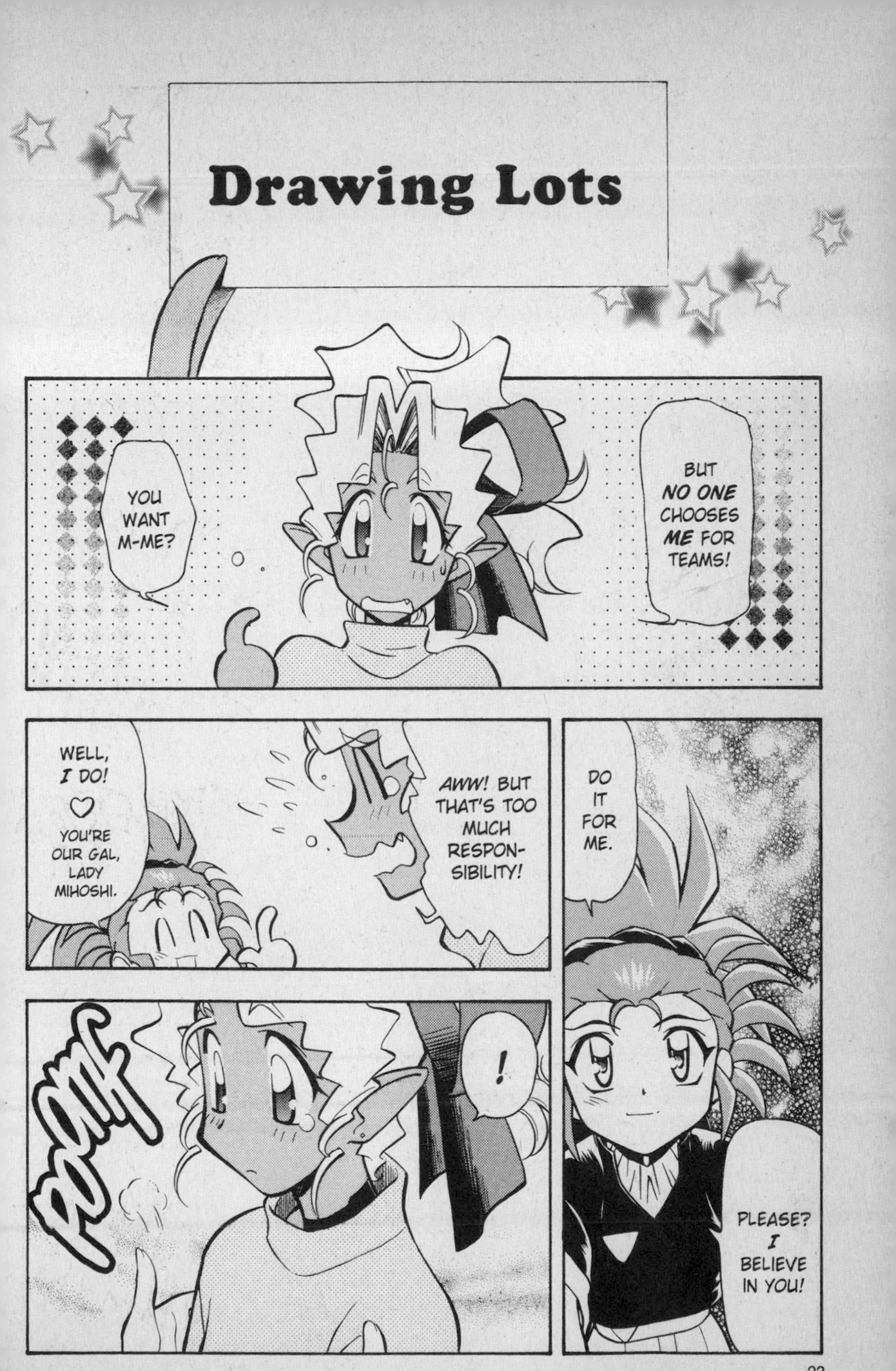
YOU WANT M-ME?
BUT NO ONE CHOOSES ME FOR TEAMS!
WELL, I DO! ♡ YOU'RE OUR GAL, LADY MIHOSHI.
AWW! BUT THAT'S TOO MUCH RESPONSIBILITY!
POOF
!
DO IT FOR ME.
PLEASE? I BELIEVE IN YOU!

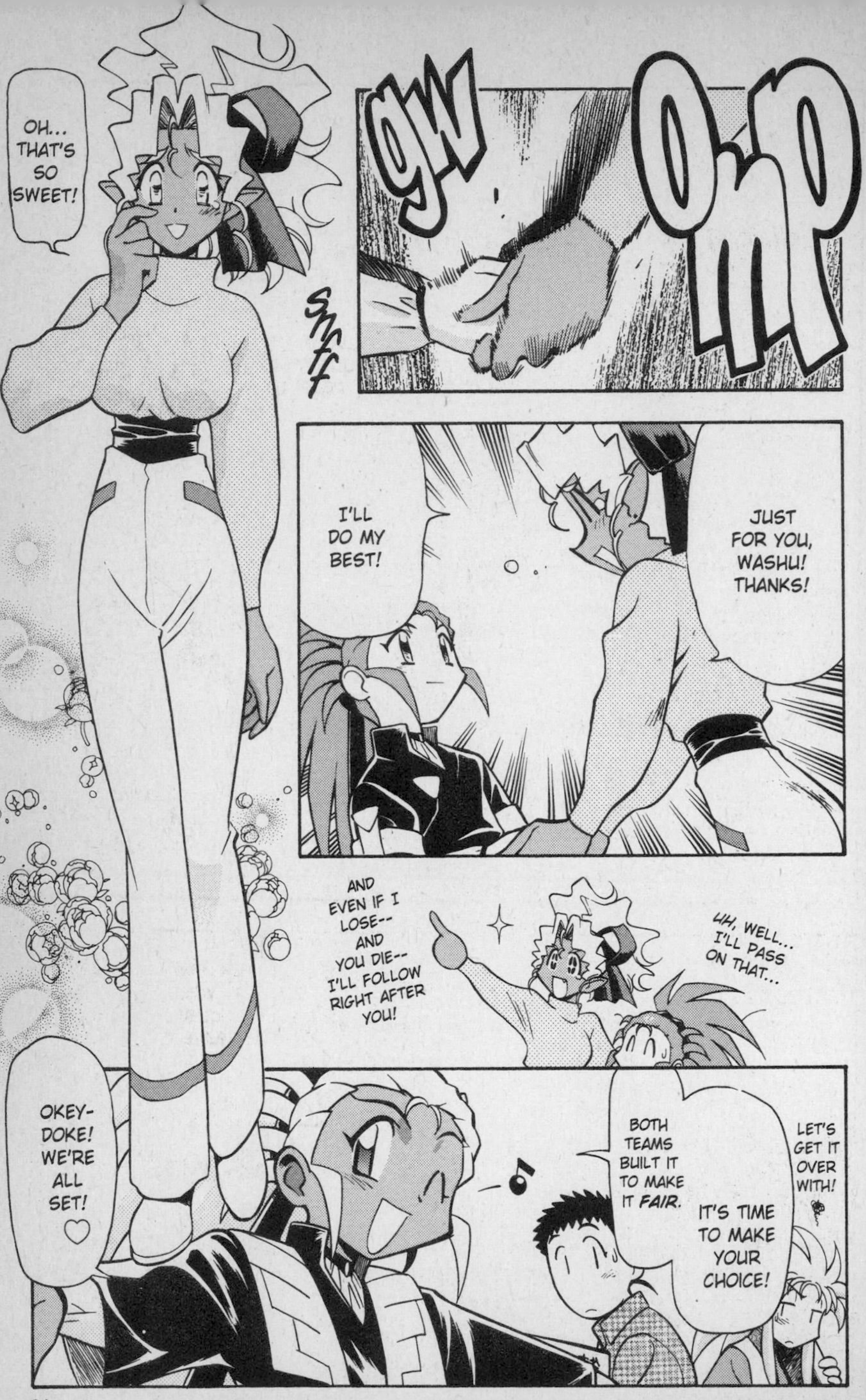

OH... THAT'S SO SWEET!
SNIFF
GW
OMP
I'LL DO MY BEST!
JUST FOR YOU, WASHU! THANKS!
AND EVEN IF I LOSE-- AND YOU DIE-- I'LL FOLLOW RIGHT AFTER YOU!
UH, WELL... I'LL PASS ON THAT...
OKEY-DOKE! WE'RE ALL SET!
BOTH TEAMS BUILT IT TO MAKE IT **FAIR**.
IT'S TIME TO MAKE YOUR CHOICE!
LET'S GET IT OVER WITH!

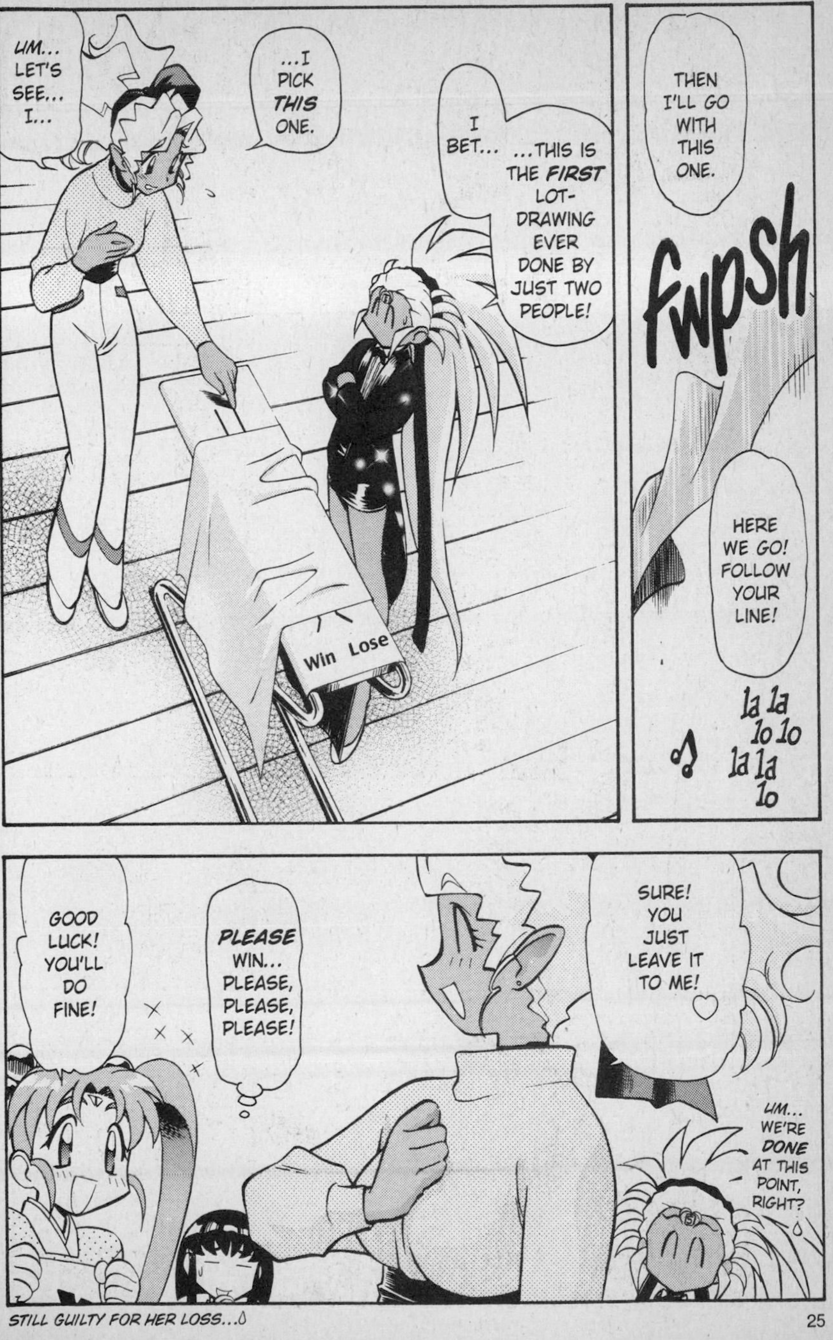
UM... LET'S SEE... I...
...I PICK *THIS* ONE.
I BET...
...THIS IS THE *FIRST* LOT-DRAWING EVER DONE BY JUST TWO PEOPLE!
Win Lose
THEN I'LL GO WITH THIS ONE.
fwpsh
HERE WE GO! FOLLOW YOUR LINE!
la la lo lo la la lo
GOOD LUCK! YOU'LL DO FINE!
PLEASE WIN... PLEASE, PLEASE, PLEASE!
SURE! YOU JUST LEAVE IT TO ME!
UM... WE'RE *DONE* AT THIS POINT, RIGHT?

STILL GUILTY FOR HER LOSS...

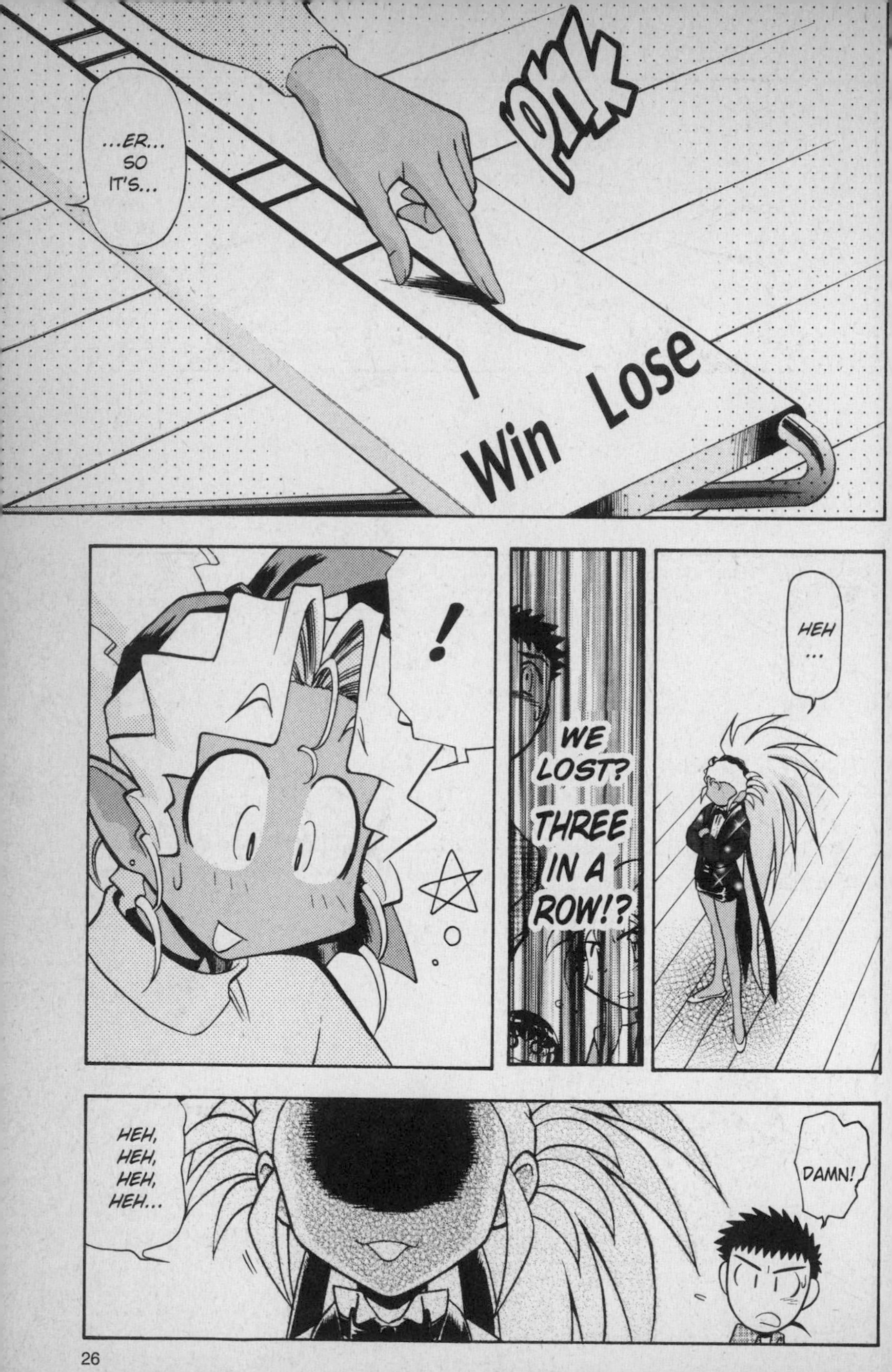
...ER... SO IT'S...
PIK
Win
Lose
!
WE LOST? THREE IN A ROW!?
HEH ...
HEH, HEH, HEH, HEH...
DAMN!

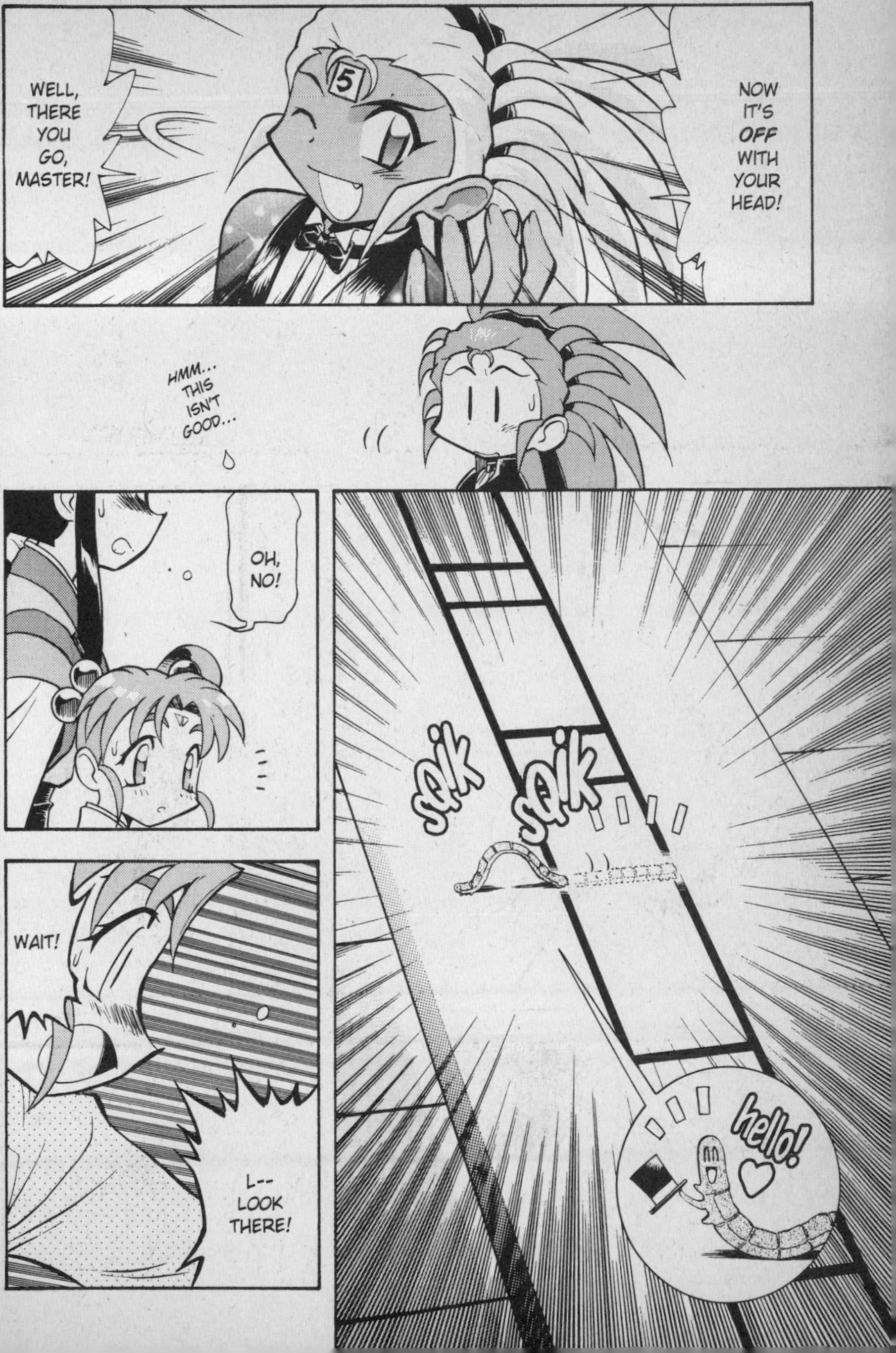
WELL, THERE YOU GO, MASTER!
NOW IT'S OFF WITH YOUR HEAD!
HMM... THIS ISN'T GOOD...
OH, NO!
WAIT!
L-- LOOK THERE!
sqik
sqik
hello!

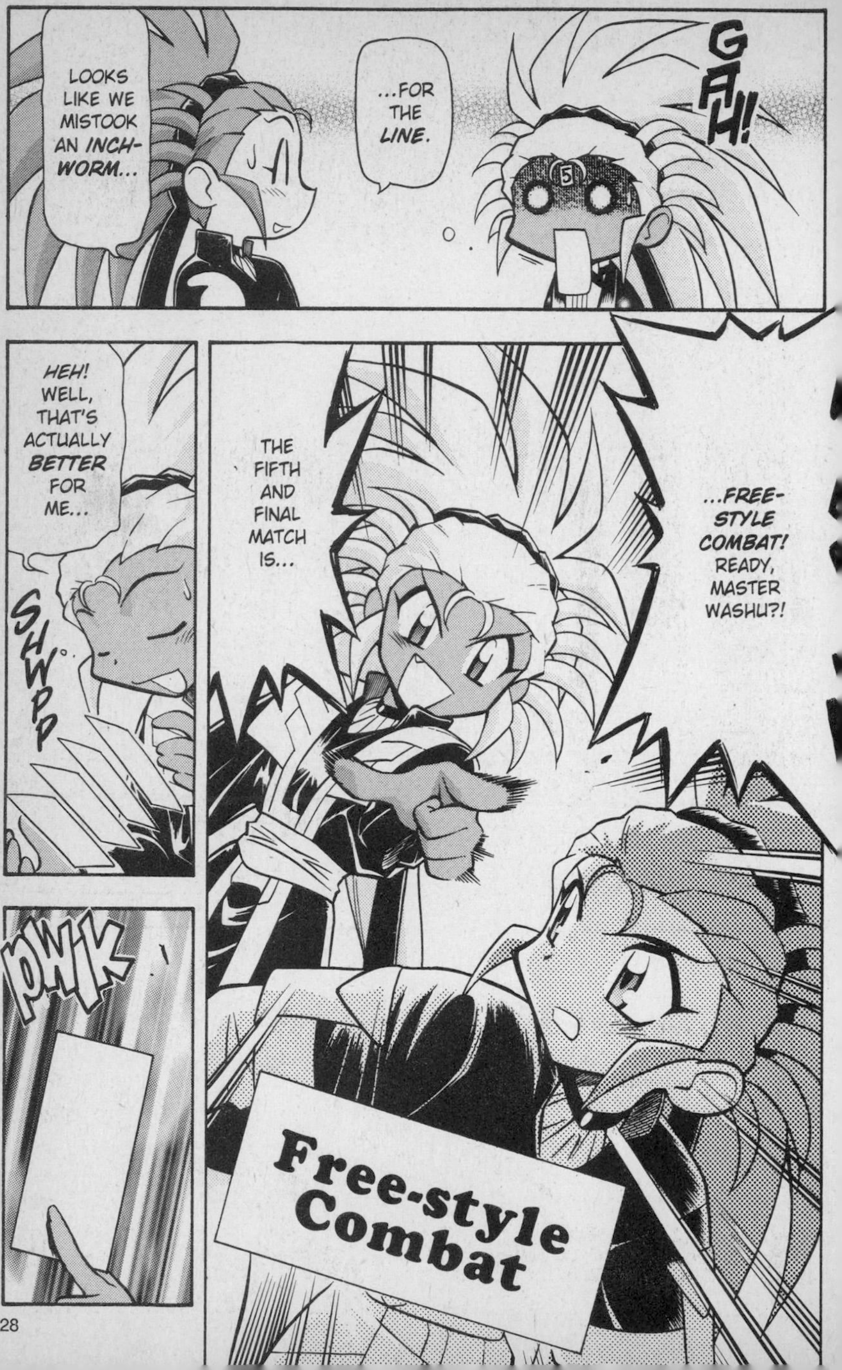
LOOKS LIKE WE MISTOOK AN *INCH-WORM*...
...FOR THE *LINE*.
GAH!
HEH! WELL, THAT'S ACTUALLY *BETTER* FOR ME...
SHWPP
PWIK
THE FIFTH AND FINAL MATCH IS...
...*FREE-STYLE COMBAT!* READY, MASTER WASHU?!
Free-style Combat

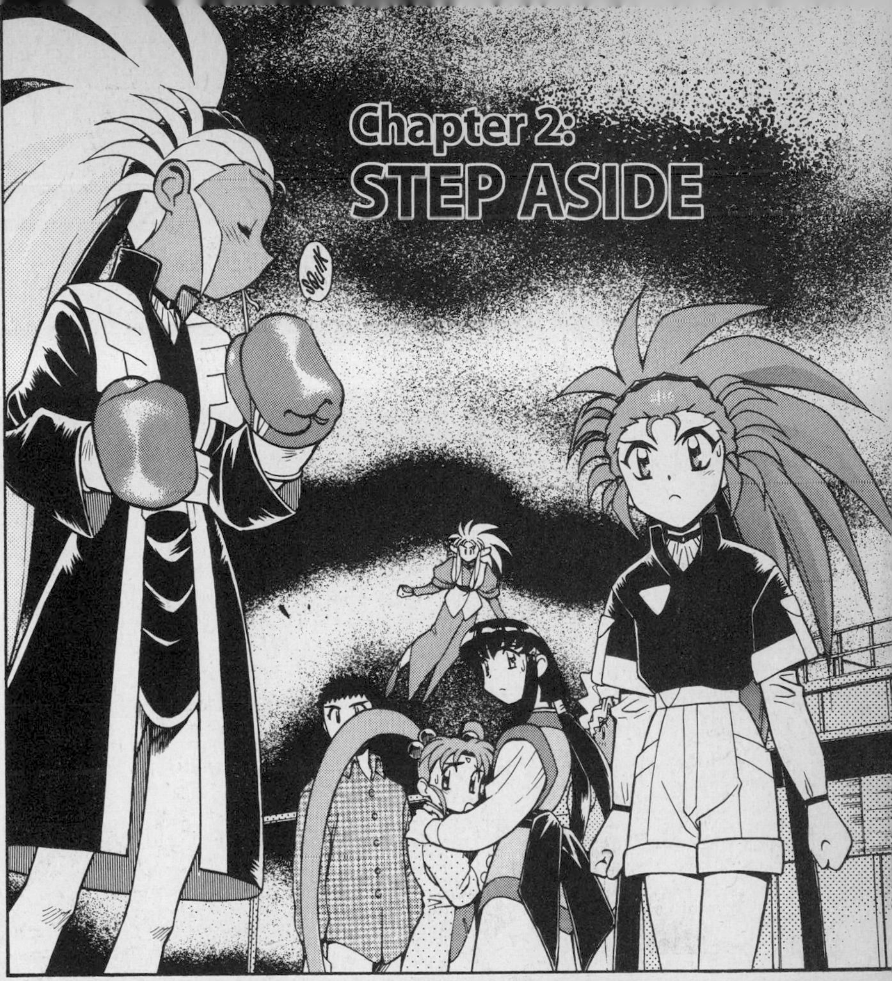
Chapter 2:
STEP ASIDE
SQUIK

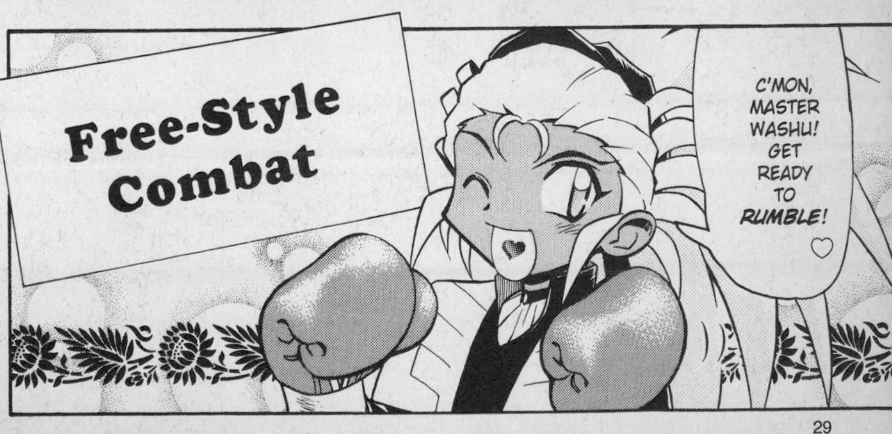
Free-Style Combat
C'MON, MASTER WASHU! GET READY TO *RUMBLE!* ♡

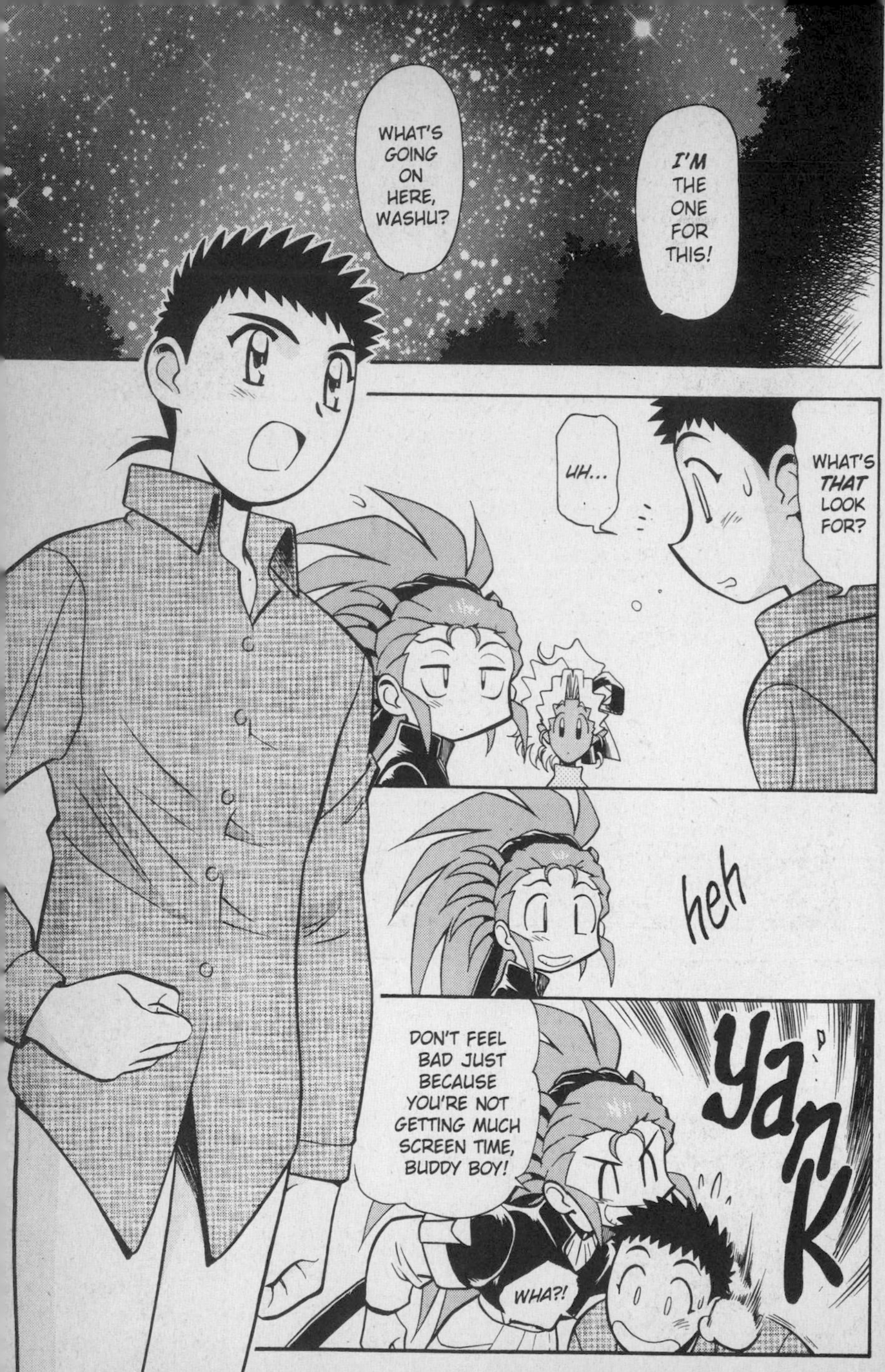
WHAT'S GOING ON HERE, WASHU?
I'M THE ONE FOR THIS!
UH...
WHAT'S THAT LOOK FOR?
heh
DON'T FEEL BAD JUST BECAUSE YOU'RE NOT GETTING MUCH SCREEN TIME, BUDDY BOY!
YANK
WHA?!

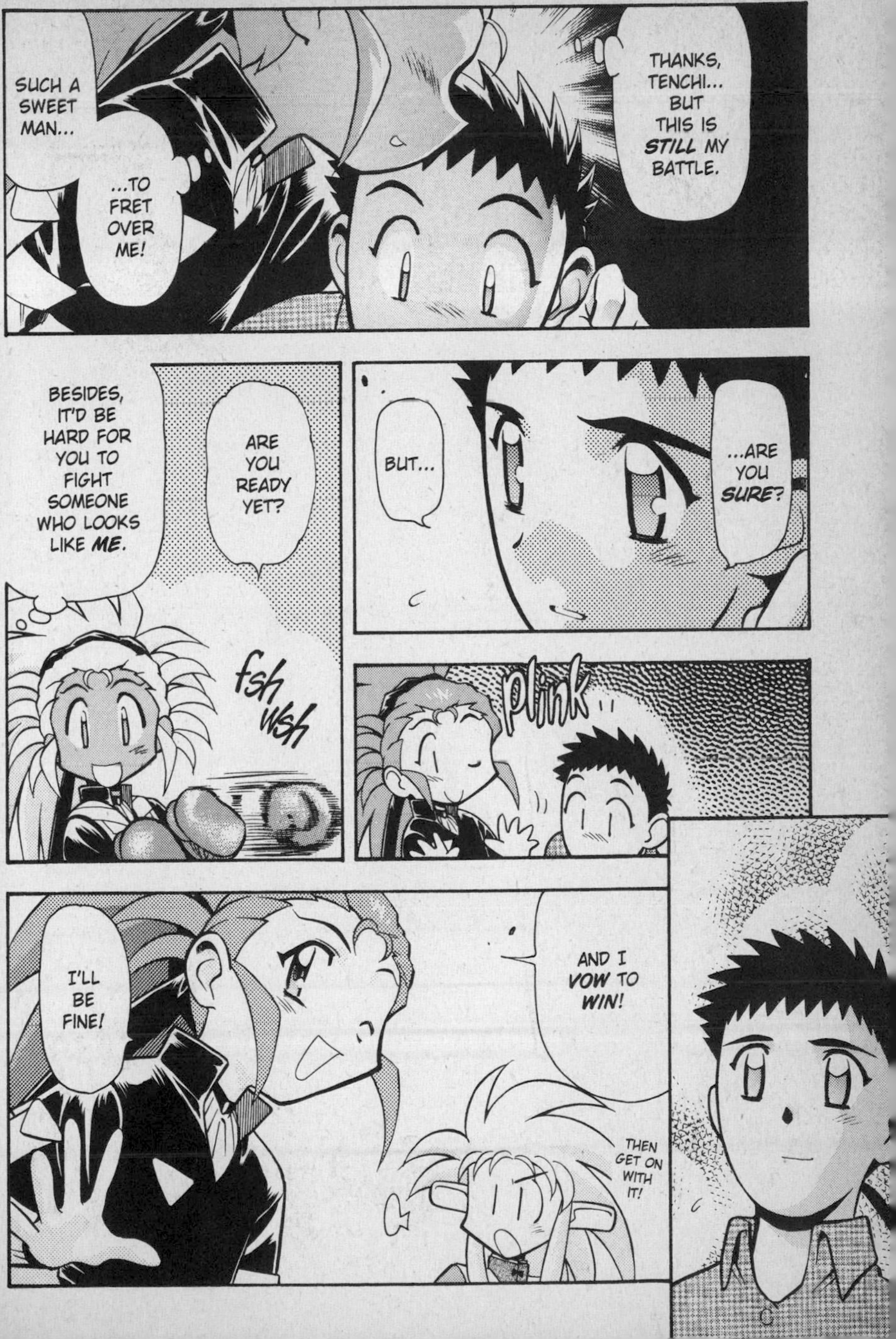
SUCH A SWEET MAN...
...TO FRET OVER ME!
THANKS, TENCHI... BUT THIS IS STILL MY BATTLE.
BESIDES, IT'D BE HARD FOR YOU TO FIGHT SOMEONE WHO LOOKS LIKE ME.
ARE YOU READY YET?
fsh wsh
BUT...
...ARE YOU SURE?
plink
I'LL BE FINE!
AND I VOW TO WIN!
THEN GET ON WITH IT!

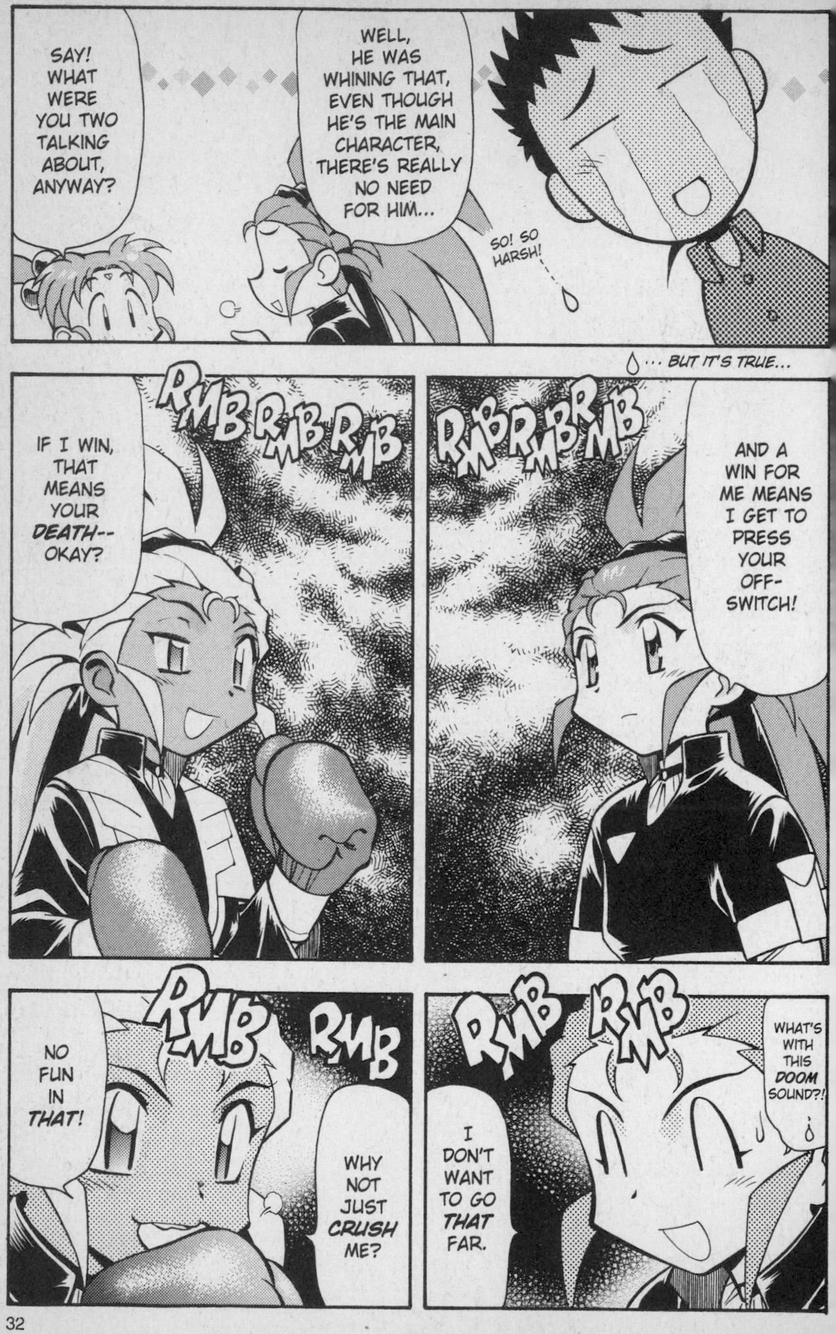
SAY! WHAT WERE YOU TWO TALKING ABOUT, ANYWAY?
WELL, HE WAS WHINING THAT, EVEN THOUGH HE'S THE MAIN CHARACTER, THERE'S REALLY NO NEED FOR HIM...
SO! SO HARSH!
... BUT IT'S TRUE...
RMB RMB RMB
IF I WIN, THAT MEANS YOUR *DEATH*-- OKAY?
RMB RMB RMB RMB
AND A WIN FOR ME MEANS I GET TO PRESS YOUR OFF-SWITCH!
RMB RMB
NO FUN IN *THAT*!
WHY NOT JUST *CRUSH* ME?
RMB RMB
I DON'T WANT TO GO *THAT* FAR.
WHAT'S WITH THIS *DOOM* SOUND?!

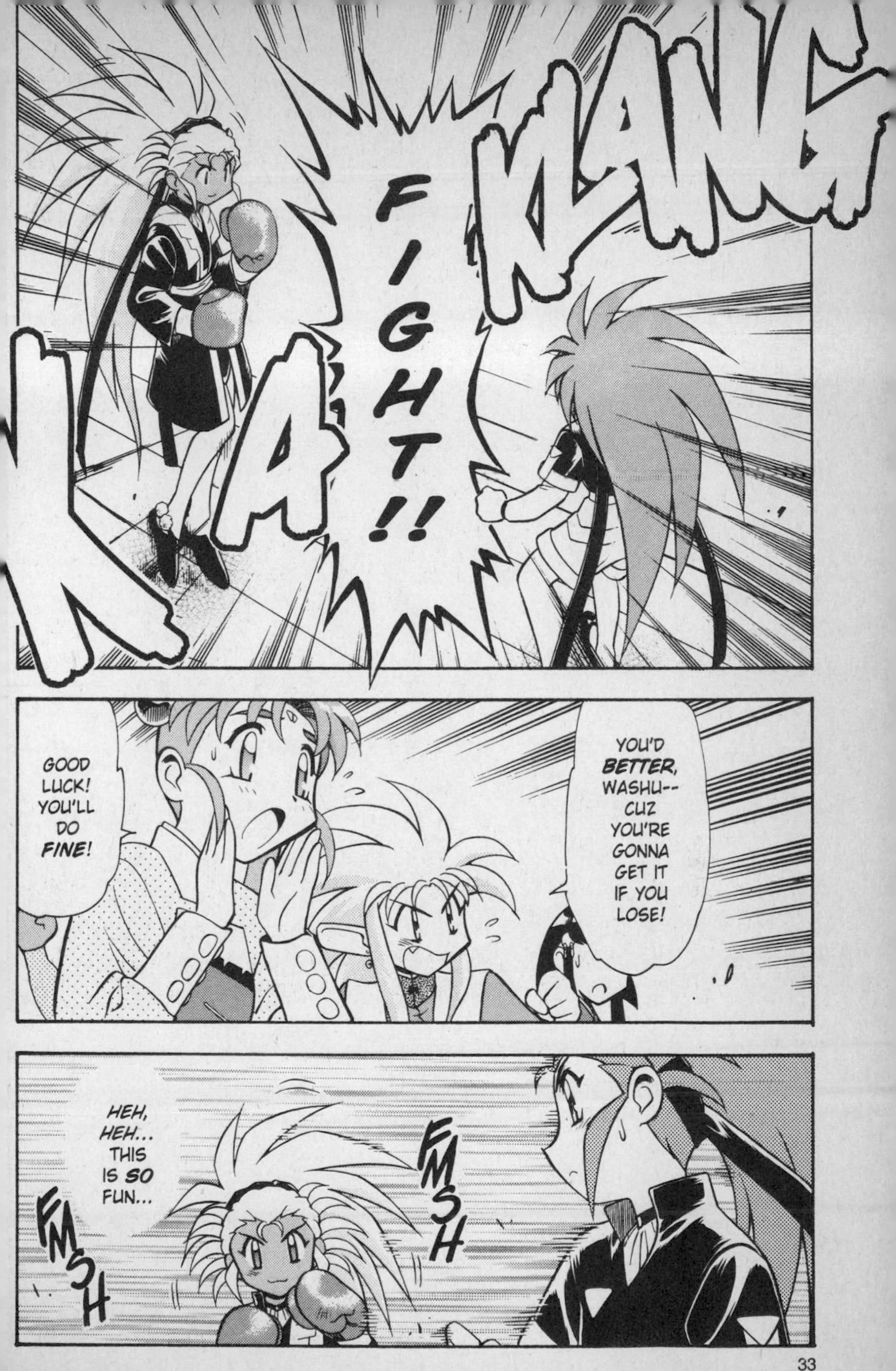
KLANG
KLANG
FIGHT!!
GOOD LUCK! YOU'LL DO FINE!
YOU'D BETTER, WASHU-- CUZ YOU'RE GONNA GET IT IF YOU LOSE!
HEH, HEH... THIS IS SO FUN...
FMSH
FMSH

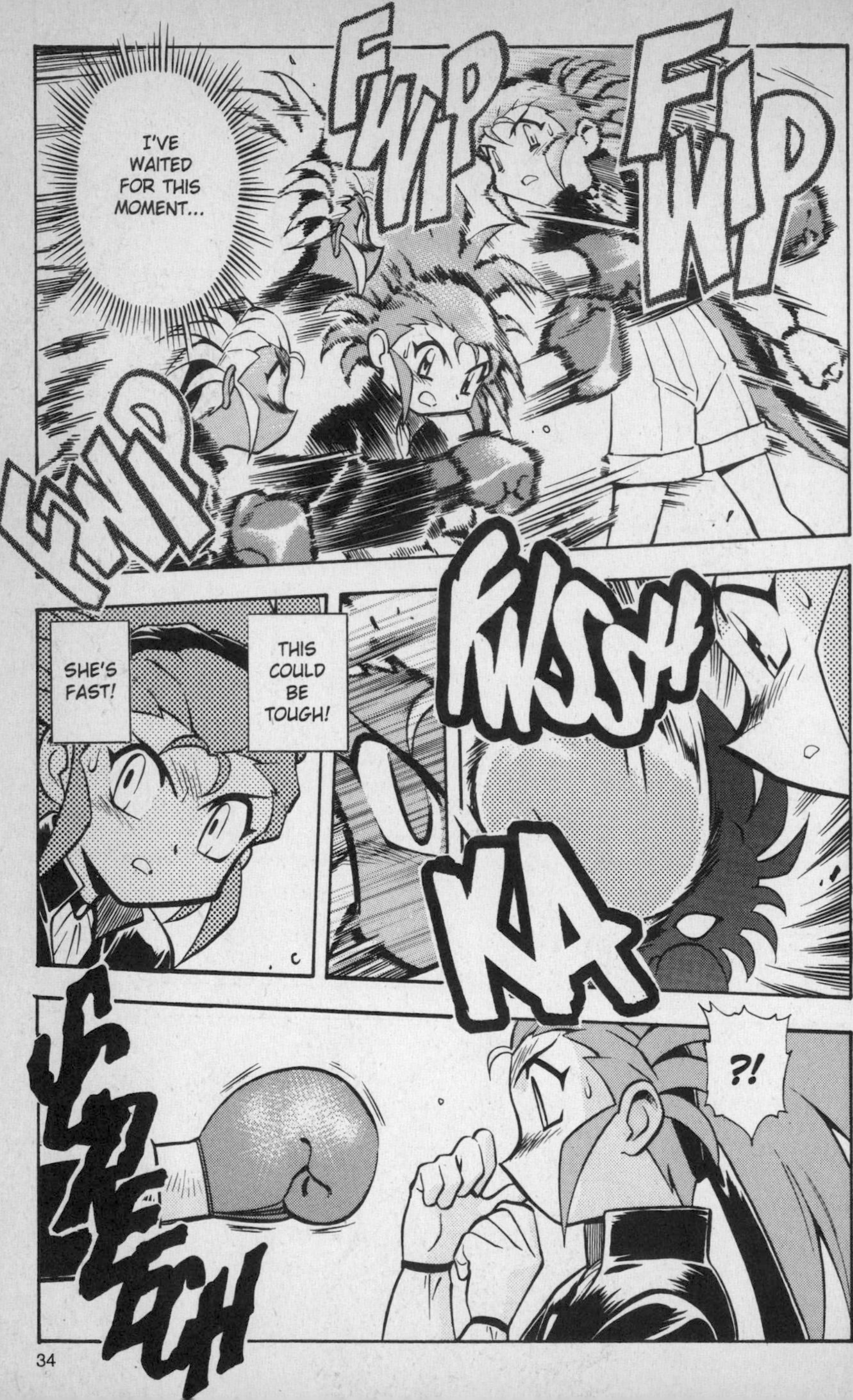
FWIP
I'VE WAITED FOR THIS MOMENT...
FWIP
FWIP
SHE'S FAST!
THIS COULD BE TOUGH!
FWSSH
KA
?!

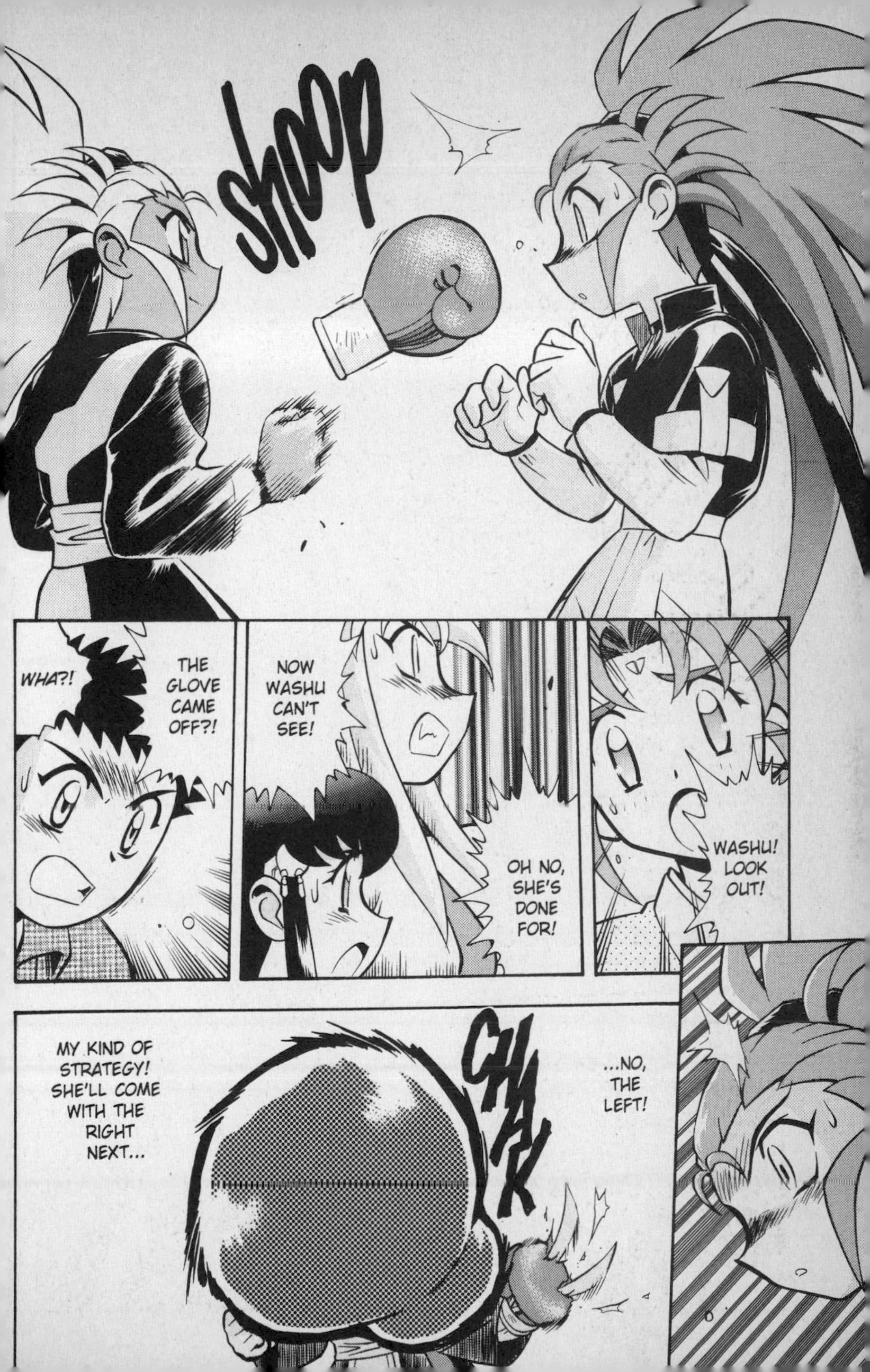
SHOOP
WHA?!
THE GLOVE CAME OFF?!
NOW WASHU CAN'T SEE!
OH NO, SHE'S DONE FOR!
WASHU! LOOK OUT!
MY KIND OF STRATEGY! SHE'LL COME WITH THE RIGHT NEXT...
CHAK
...NO, THE LEFT!

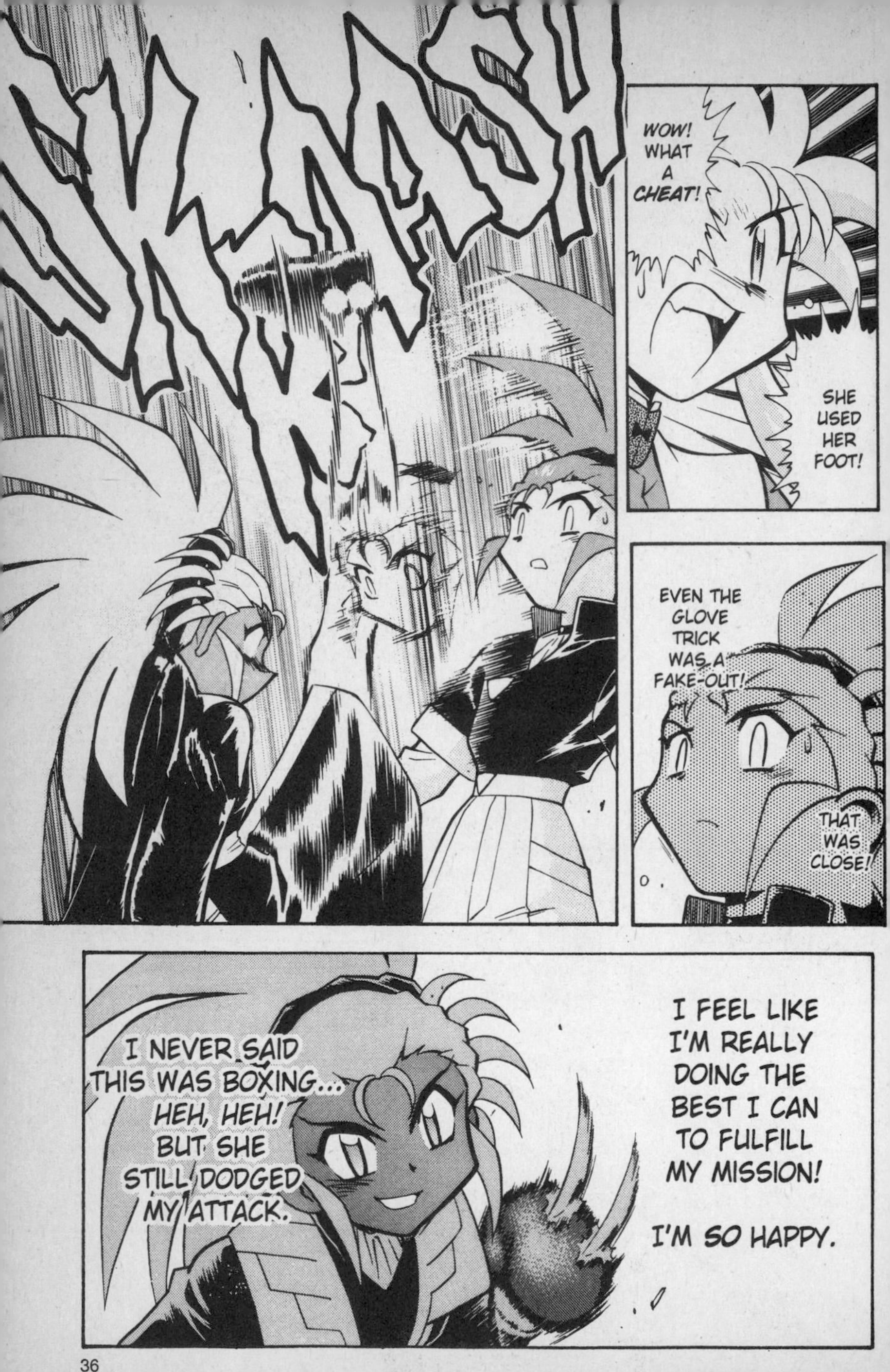
WOW! WHAT A CHEAT!
SHE USED HER FOOT!
EVEN THE GLOVE TRICK WAS A FAKE-OUT!
THAT WAS CLOSE!
I NEVER SAID THIS WAS BOXING... HEH, HEH! BUT SHE STILL DODGED MY ATTACK.
I FEEL LIKE I'M REALLY DOING THE BEST I CAN TO FULFILL MY MISSION!
I'M SO HAPPY.

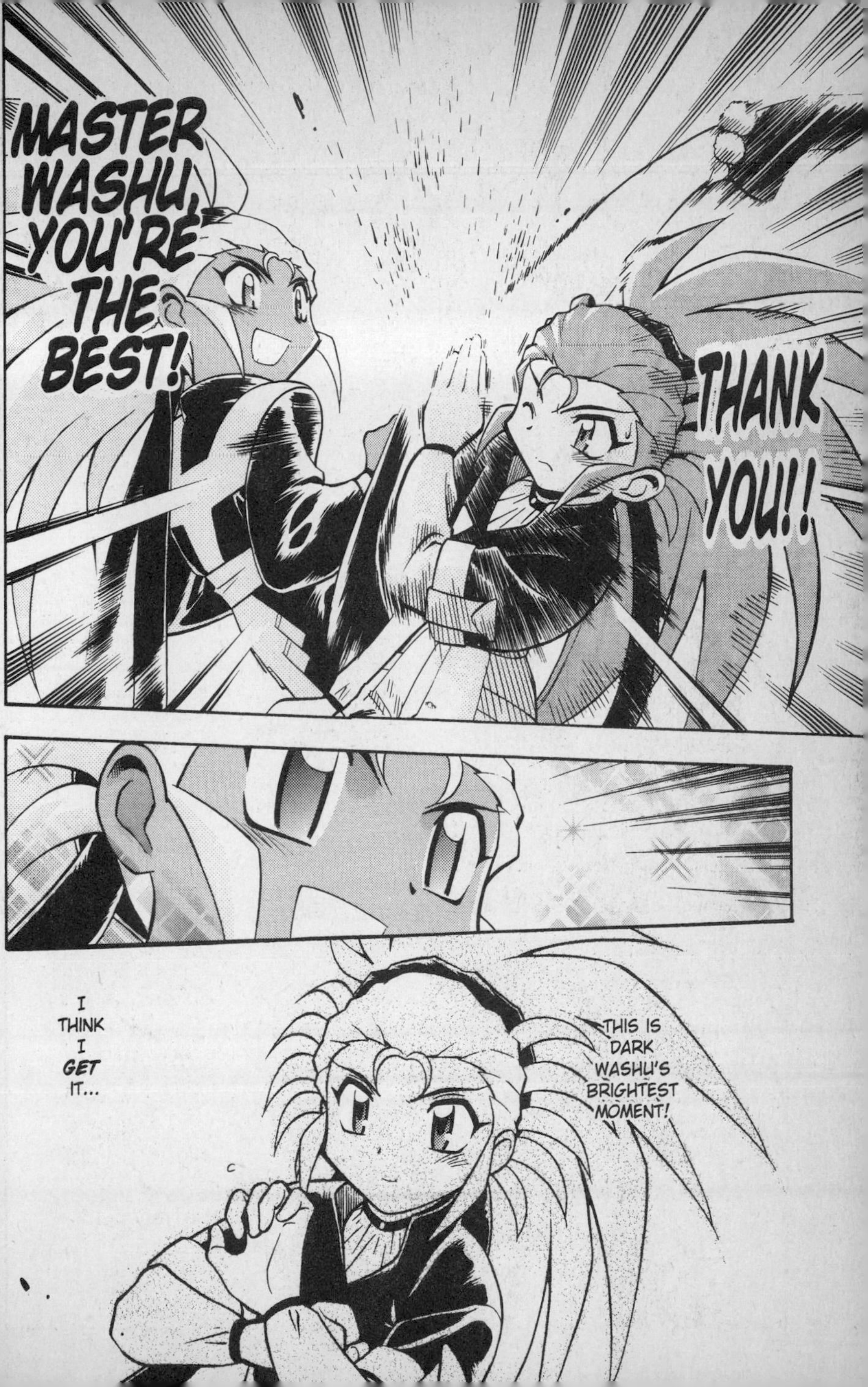
MASTER WASHU, YOU'RE THE BEST!
THANK YOU!!
I THINK I GET IT...
THIS IS DARK WASHU'S BRIGHTEST MOMENT!

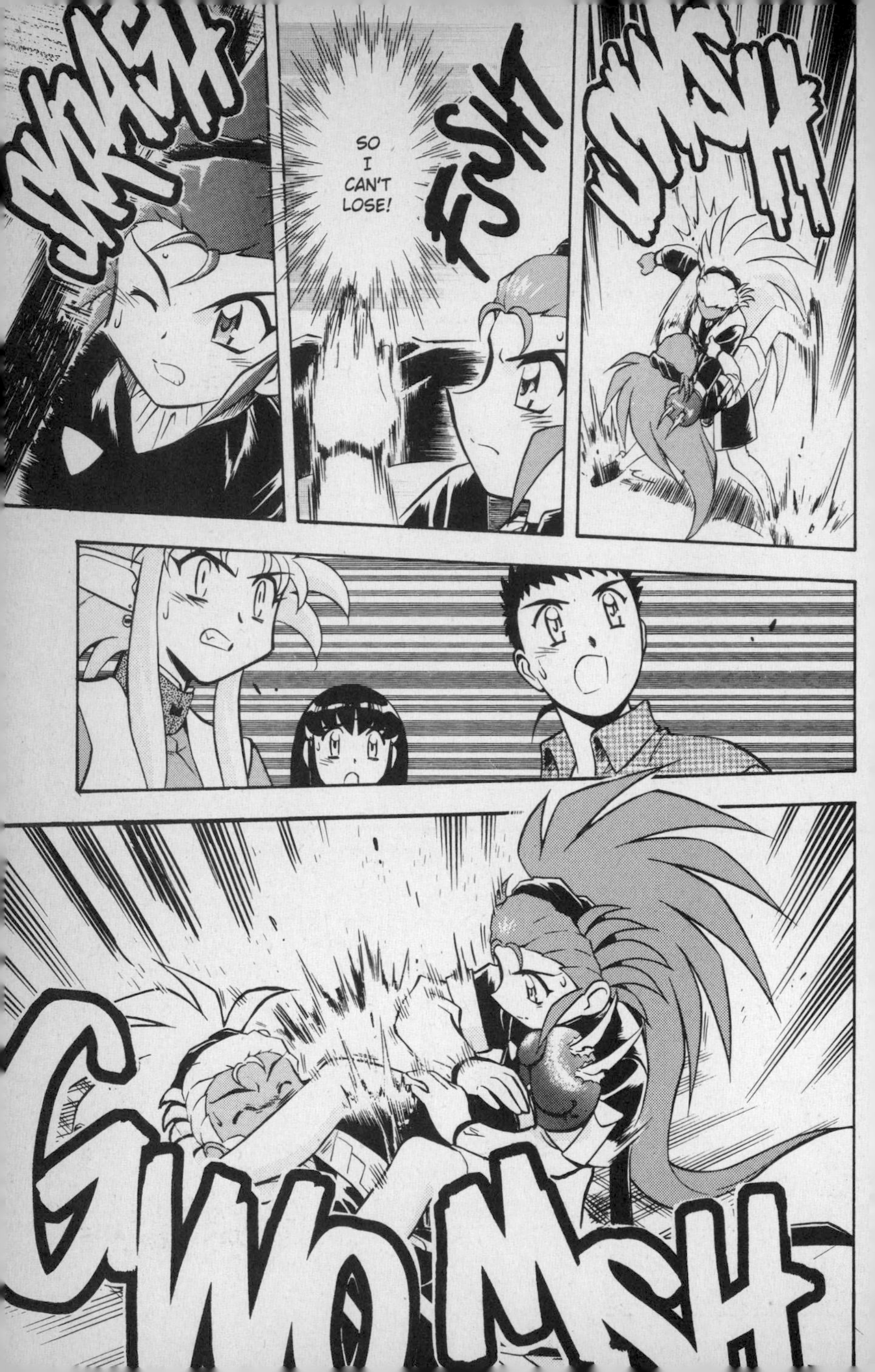
SO I CAN'T LOSE!

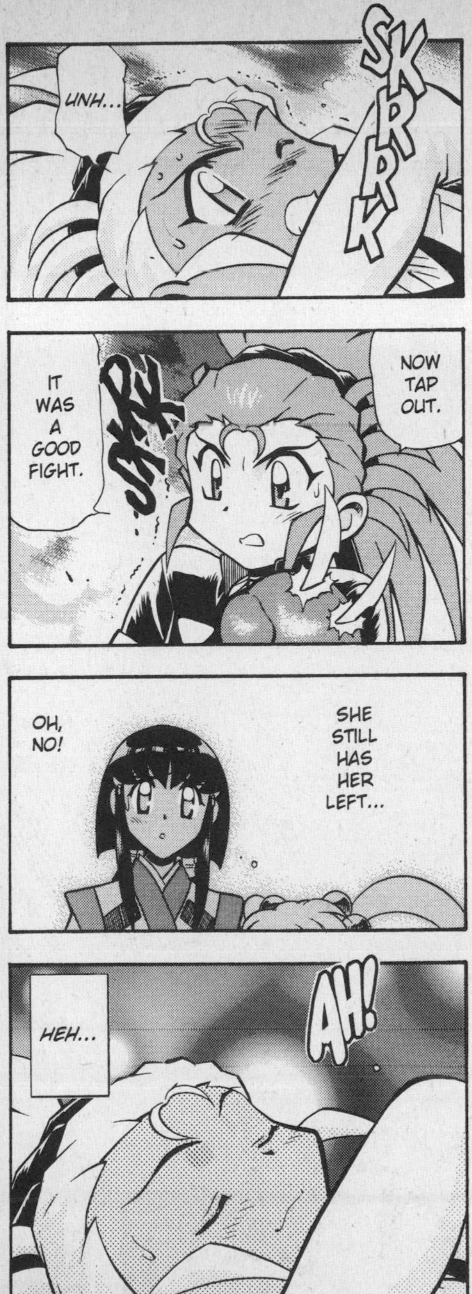
UNH...
SKRRK
IT WAS A GOOD FIGHT.
NOW TAP OUT.
OH, NO!
SHE STILL HAS HER LEFT...
HEH...
AH!

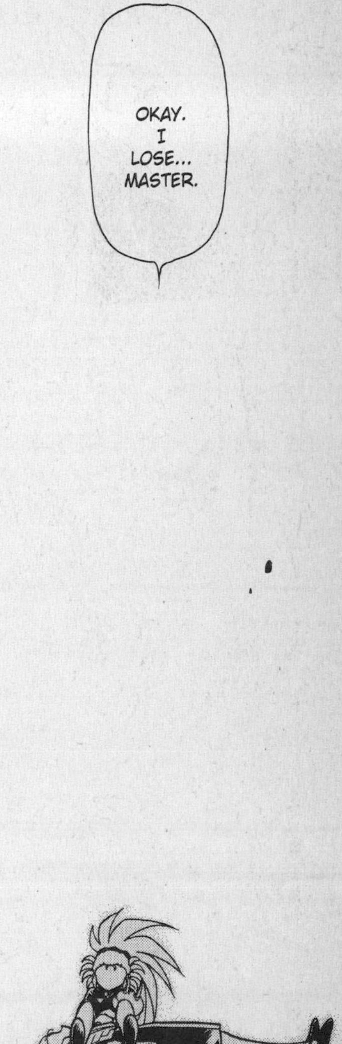
OKAY. I LOSE... MASTER.

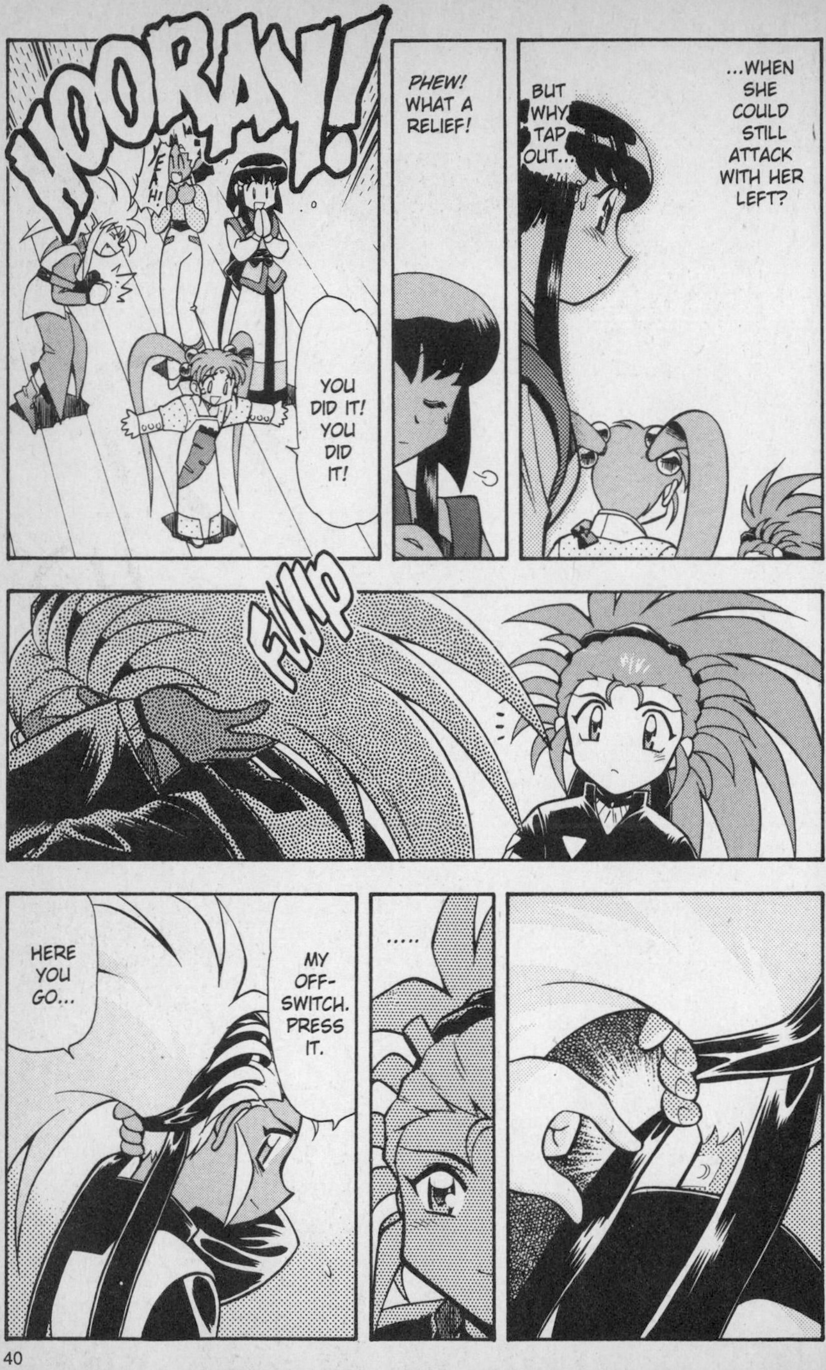
HOORAY!
YEAH!
YOU DID IT! YOU DID IT!
PHEW! WHAT A RELIEF!
BUT WHY TAP OUT...
...WHEN SHE COULD STILL ATTACK WITH HER LEFT?
FWIP
HERE YOU GO...
MY OFF-SWITCH. PRESS IT.
.....

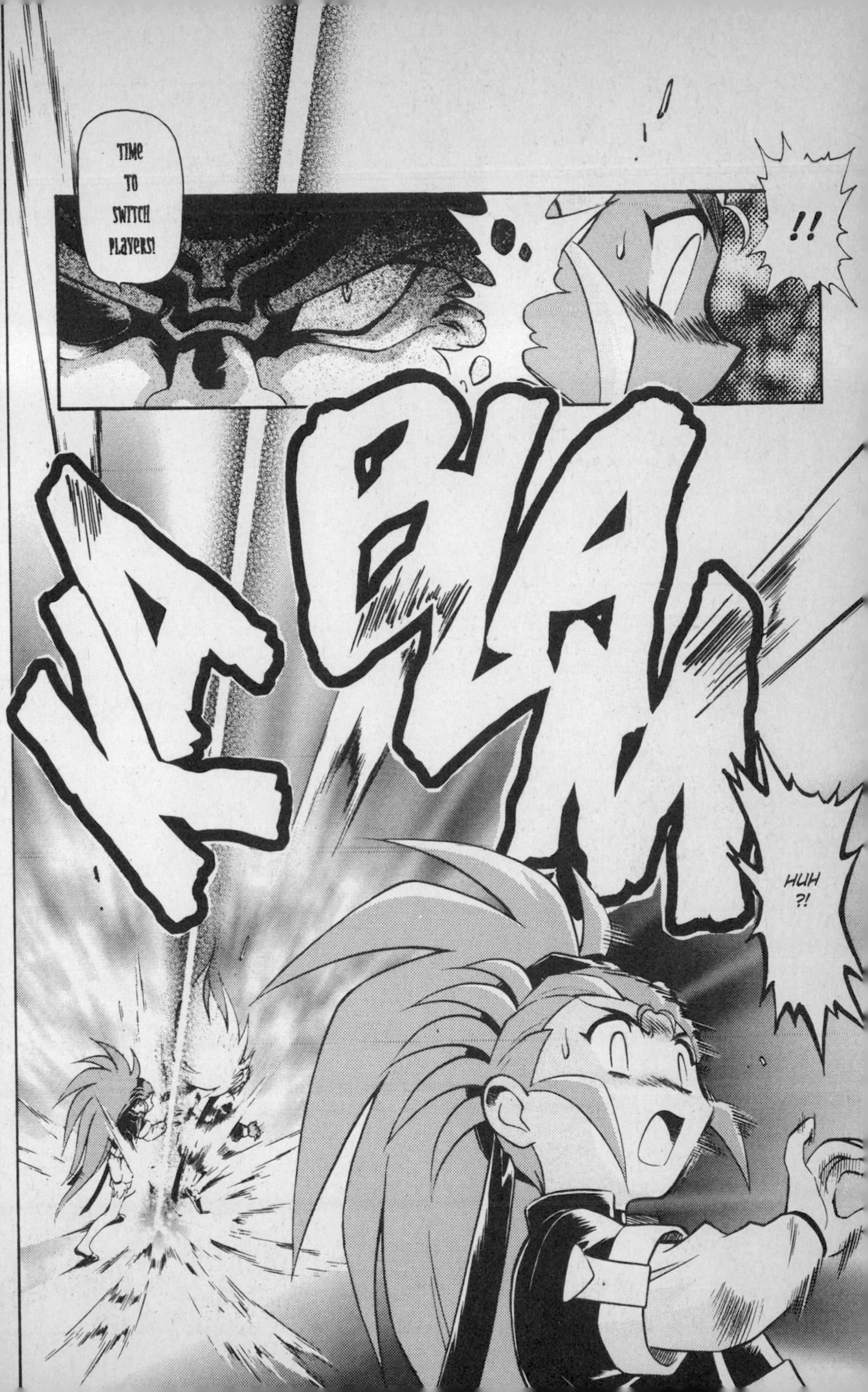
TIME TO SWITCH PLAYERS!
!!
HUH ?!

*POWER TO MAX LEVEL FOR NEXT SHOT!

WILL FIRE IN THREE, TWO, O--

!!

WHAM WHAM

ZWN ZWN

KERZ WASHT

JING!

THAT'S FOR USING SUCH A *FOUL* TRICK.

GOT YA!

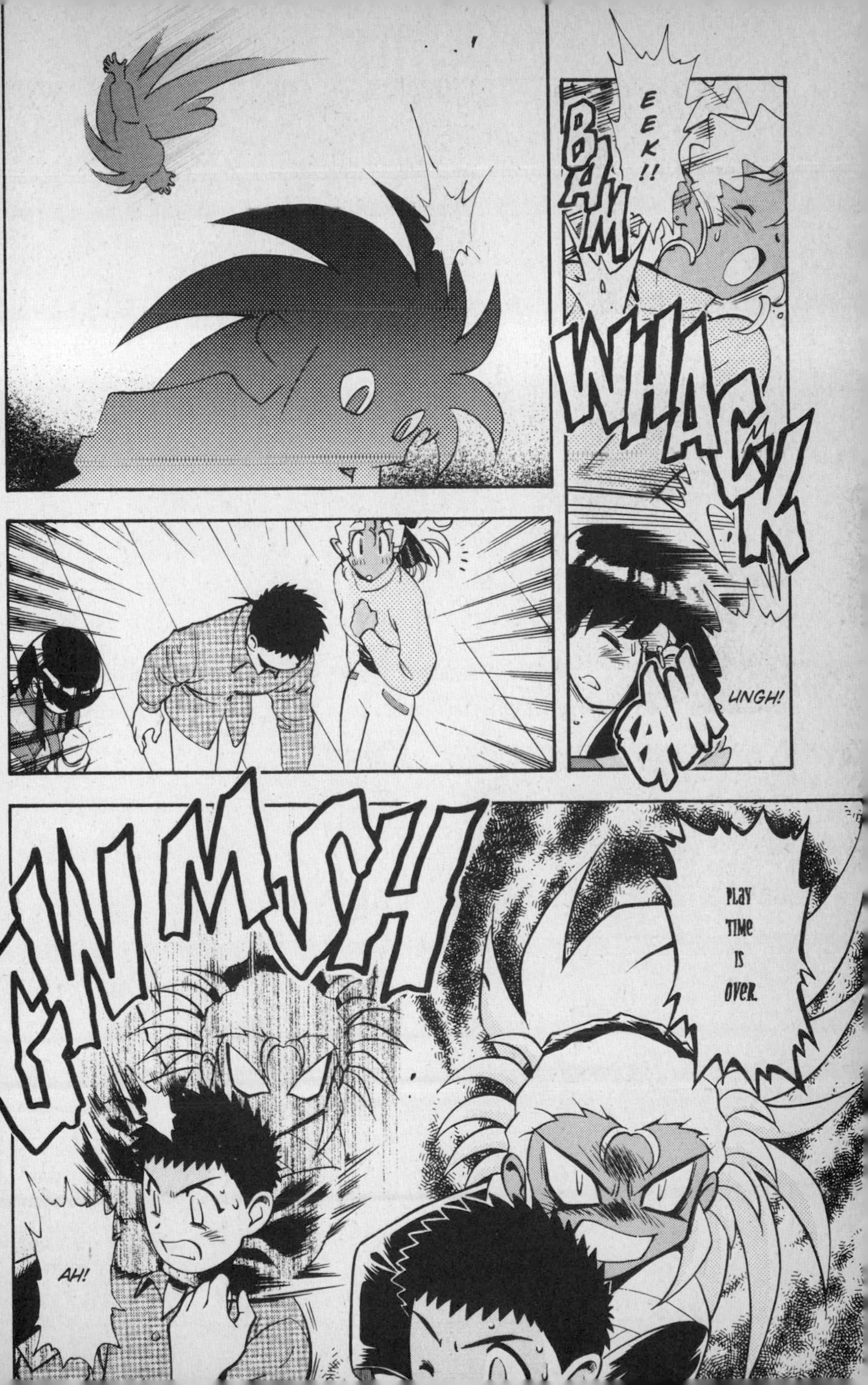
BAM
EEK!!
WHACK
BAM
UNGH!
PLAY TIME IS OVER.
AH!

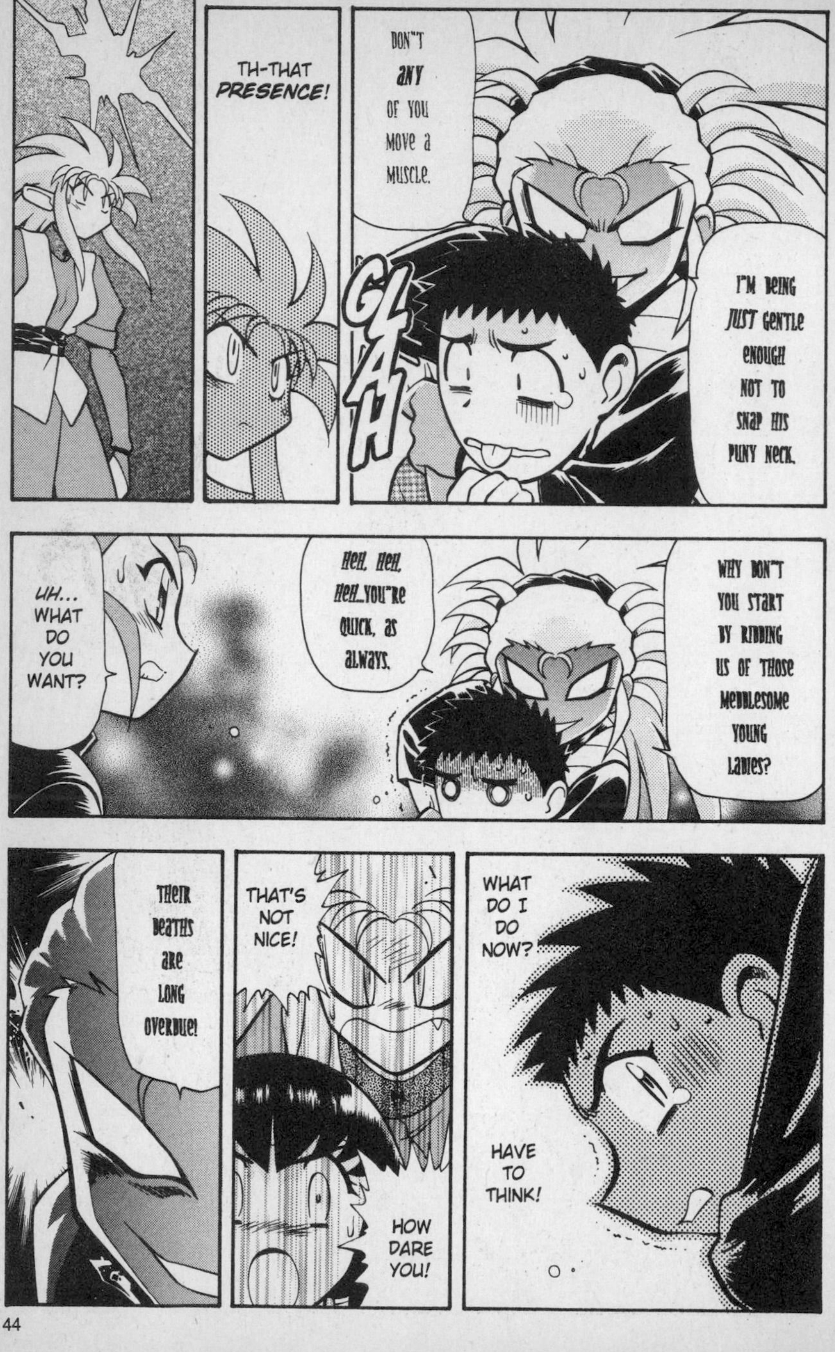
TH-THAT PRESENCE!
DON'T ANY OF YOU MOVE A MUSCLE.
GLAH
I'M BEING JUST GENTLE ENOUGH NOT TO SNAP HIS PUNY NECK.
UH... WHAT DO YOU WANT?
HEH, HEH, HEH...YOU'RE QUICK, AS ALWAYS.
WHY DON'T YOU START BY RIDDING US OF THOSE MEDDLESOME YOUNG LADIES?
THEIR DEATHS ARE LONG OVERDUE!
THAT'S NOT NICE!
HOW DARE YOU!
WHAT DO I DO NOW?
HAVE TO THINK!

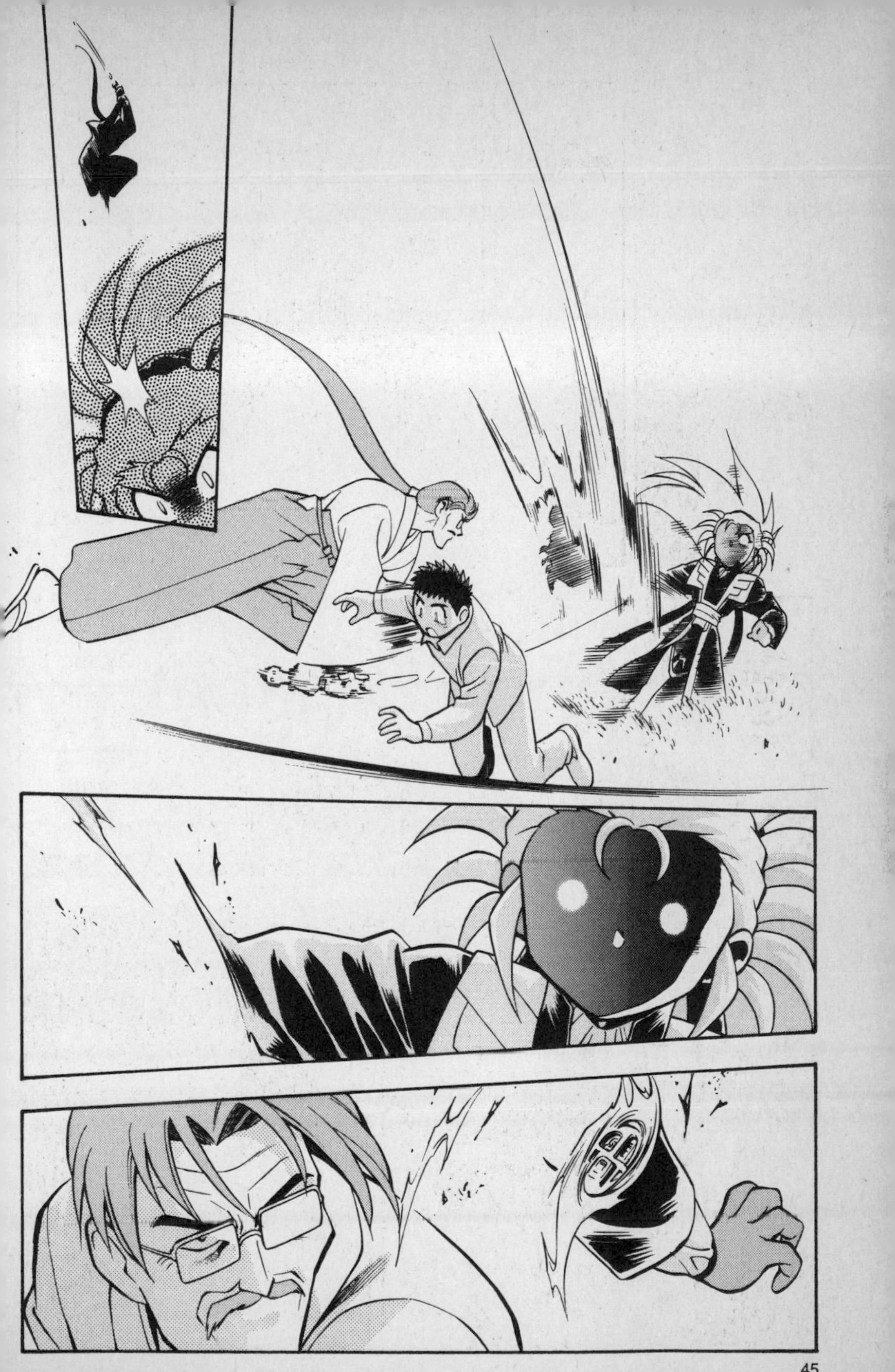

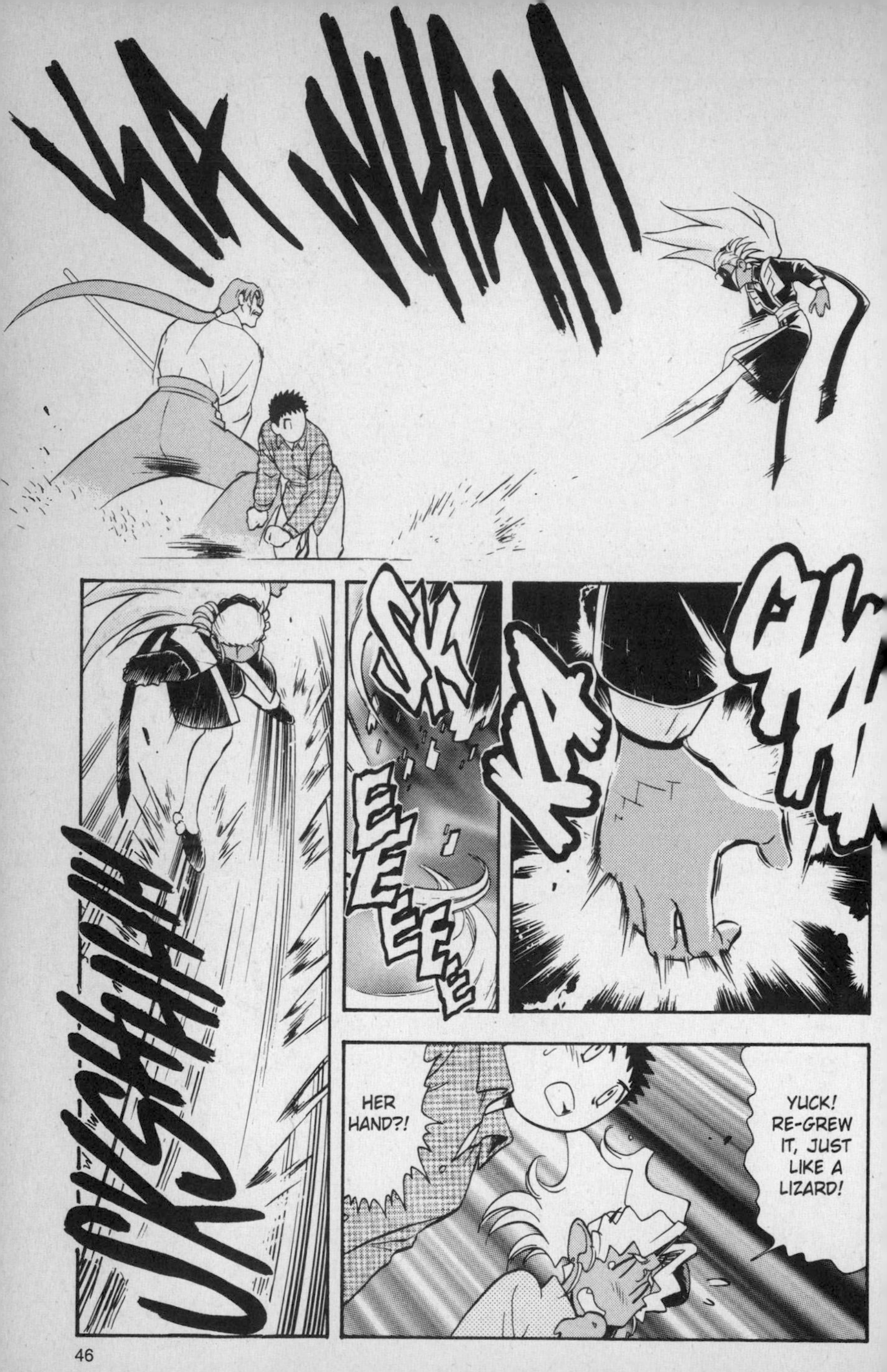
HER HAND?!
YUCK! RE-GREW IT, JUST LIKE A LIZARD!

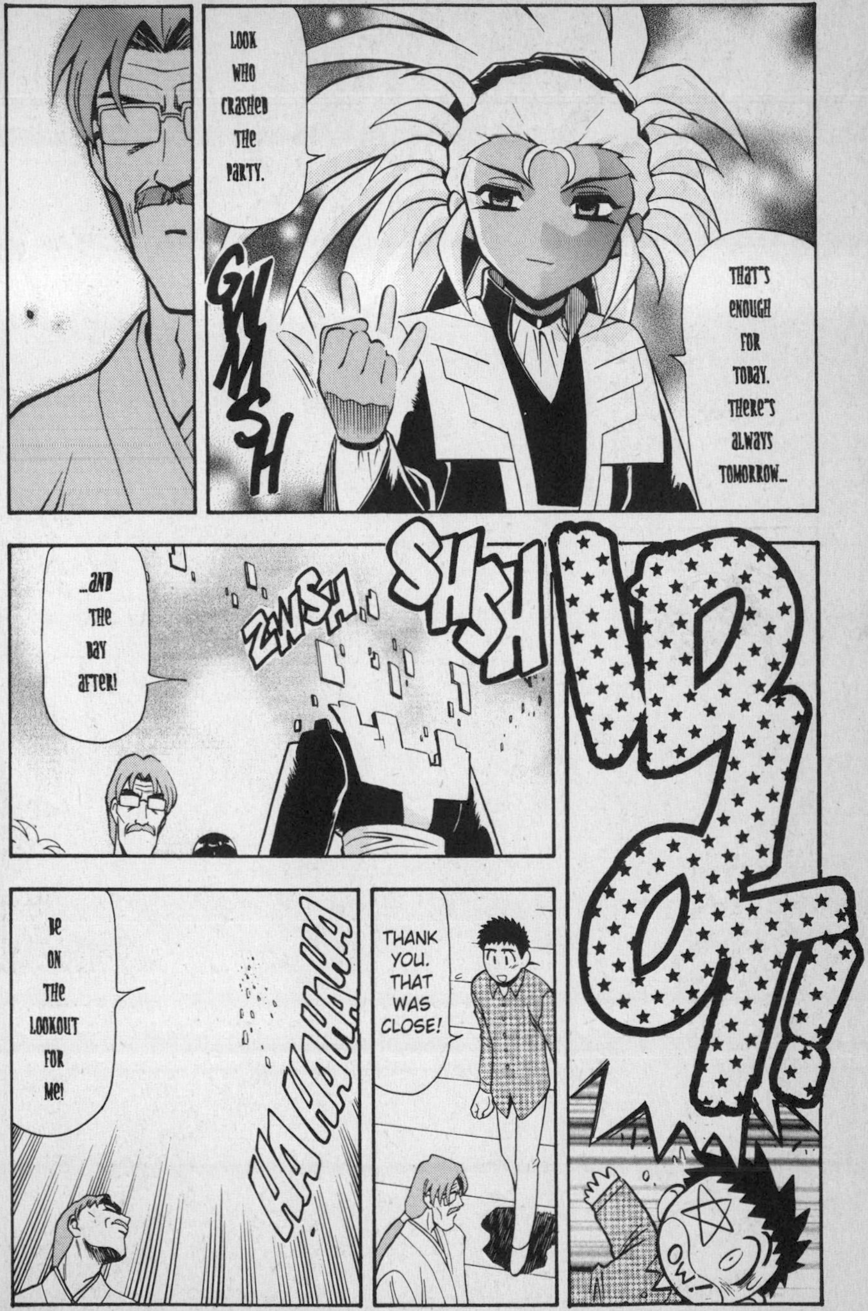
LOOK WHO CRASHED THE PARTY.
GWMSH
THAT'S ENOUGH FOR TODAY. THERE'S ALWAYS TOMORROW...
...AND THE DAY AFTER!
ZWSH
SHSH
BE ON THE LOOKOUT FOR ME!
HA HAHAHAHA
THANK YOU. THAT WAS CLOSE!
OW!

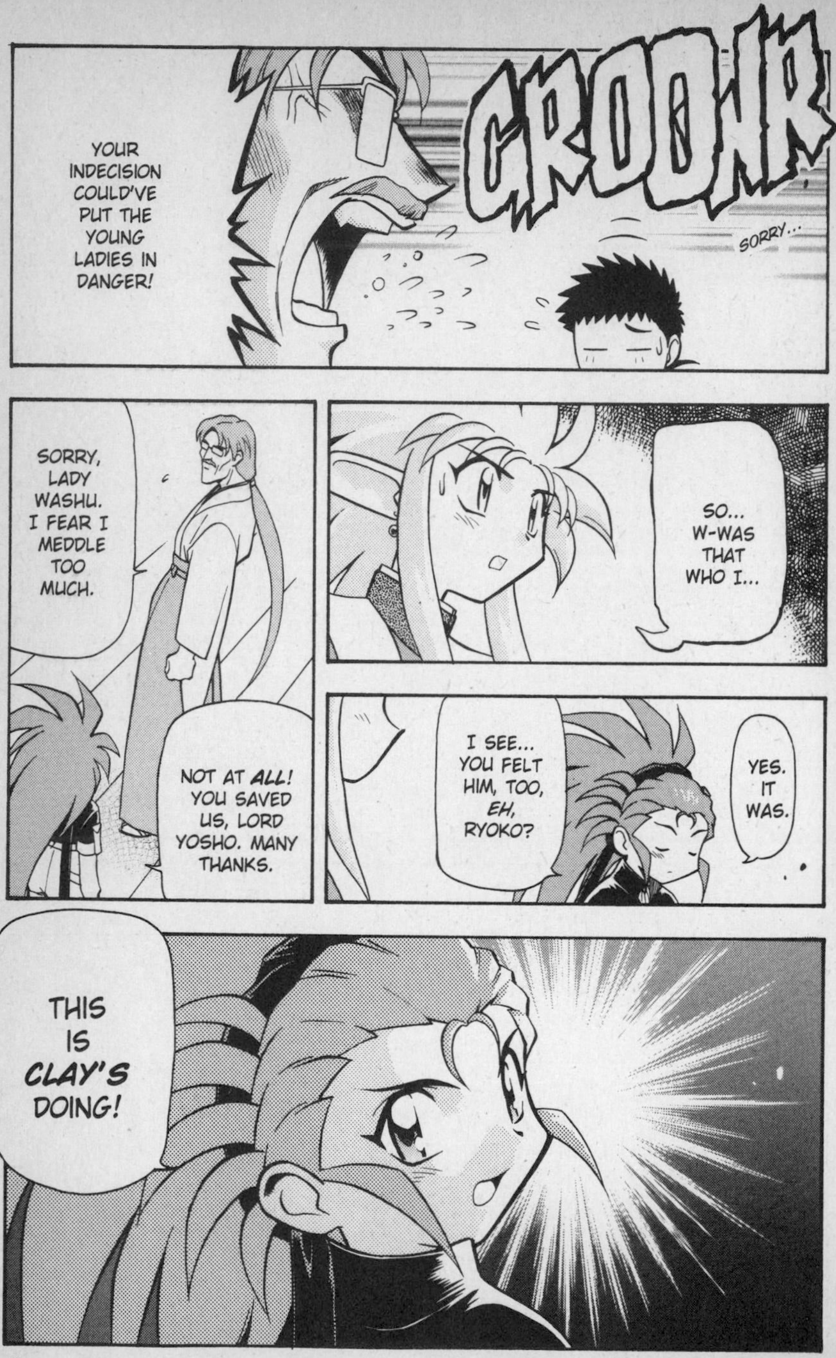
YOUR INDECISION COULD'VE PUT THE YOUNG LADIES IN DANGER!
CROONK!
SORRY...
SORRY, LADY WASHU. I FEAR I MEDDLE TOO MUCH.
NOT AT ALL! YOU SAVED US, LORD YOSHO. MANY THANKS.
SO... W-WAS THAT WHO I...
I SEE... YOU FELT HIM, TOO, EH, RYOKO?
YES. IT WAS.
THIS IS CLAY'S DOING!

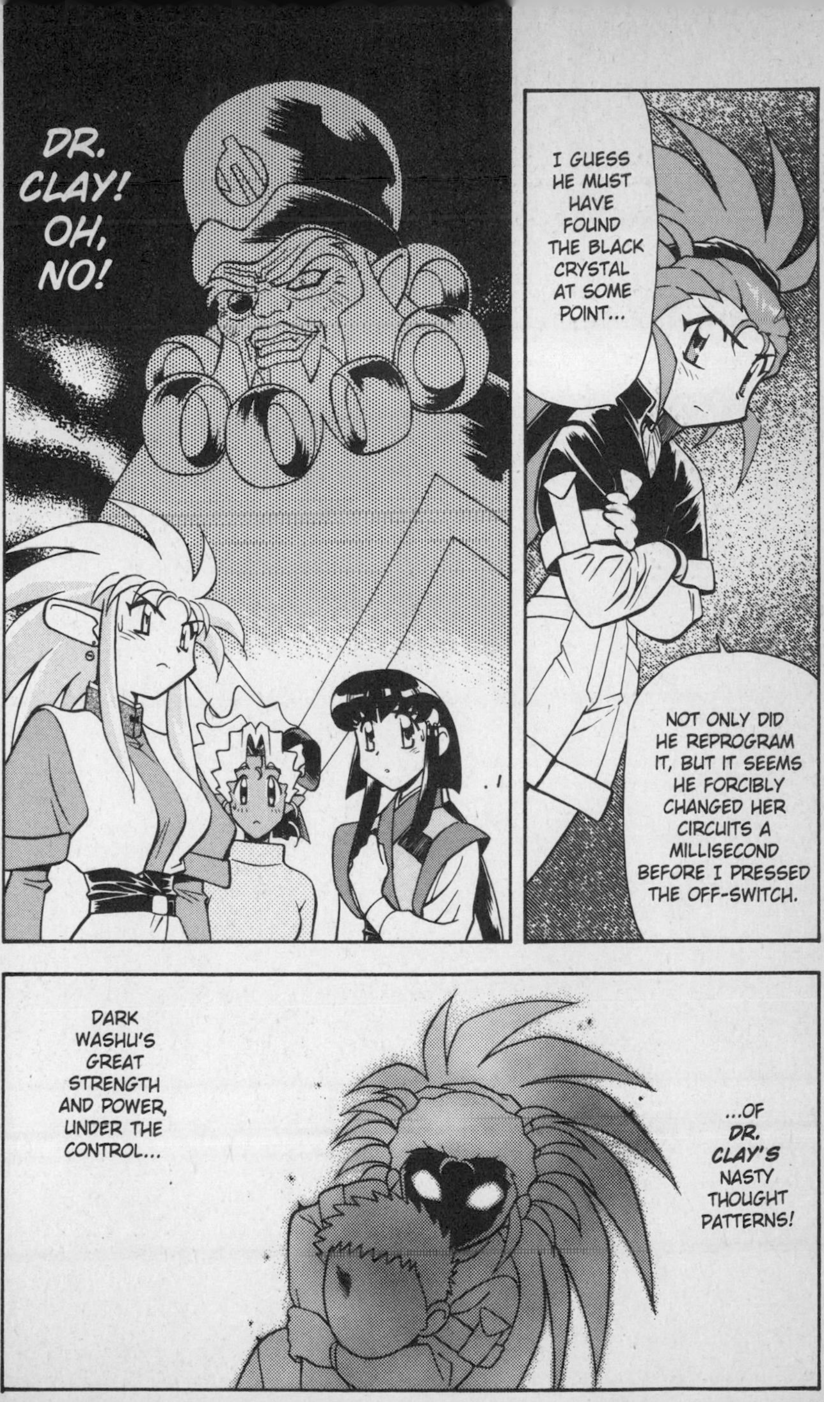
DR. CLAY! OH, NO!
I GUESS HE MUST HAVE FOUND THE BLACK CRYSTAL AT SOME POINT...
NOT ONLY DID HE REPROGRAM IT, BUT IT SEEMS HE FORCIBLY CHANGED HER CIRCUITS A MILLISECOND BEFORE I PRESSED THE OFF-SWITCH.
DARK WASHU'S GREAT STRENGTH AND POWER, UNDER THE CONTROL...
...OF DR. CLAY'S NASTY THOUGHT PATTERNS!

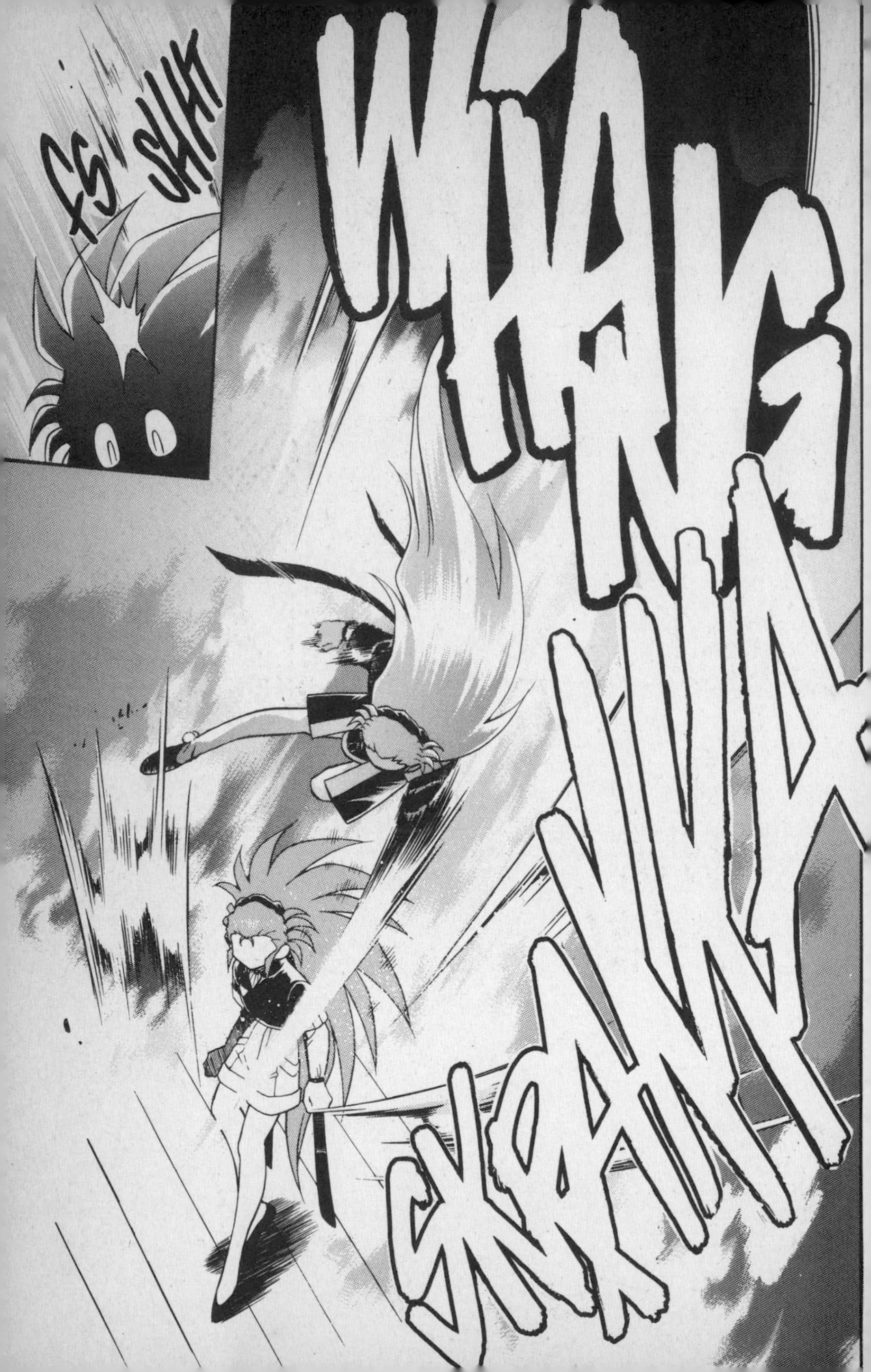
FS SHHT
WHANG
SKRANNG

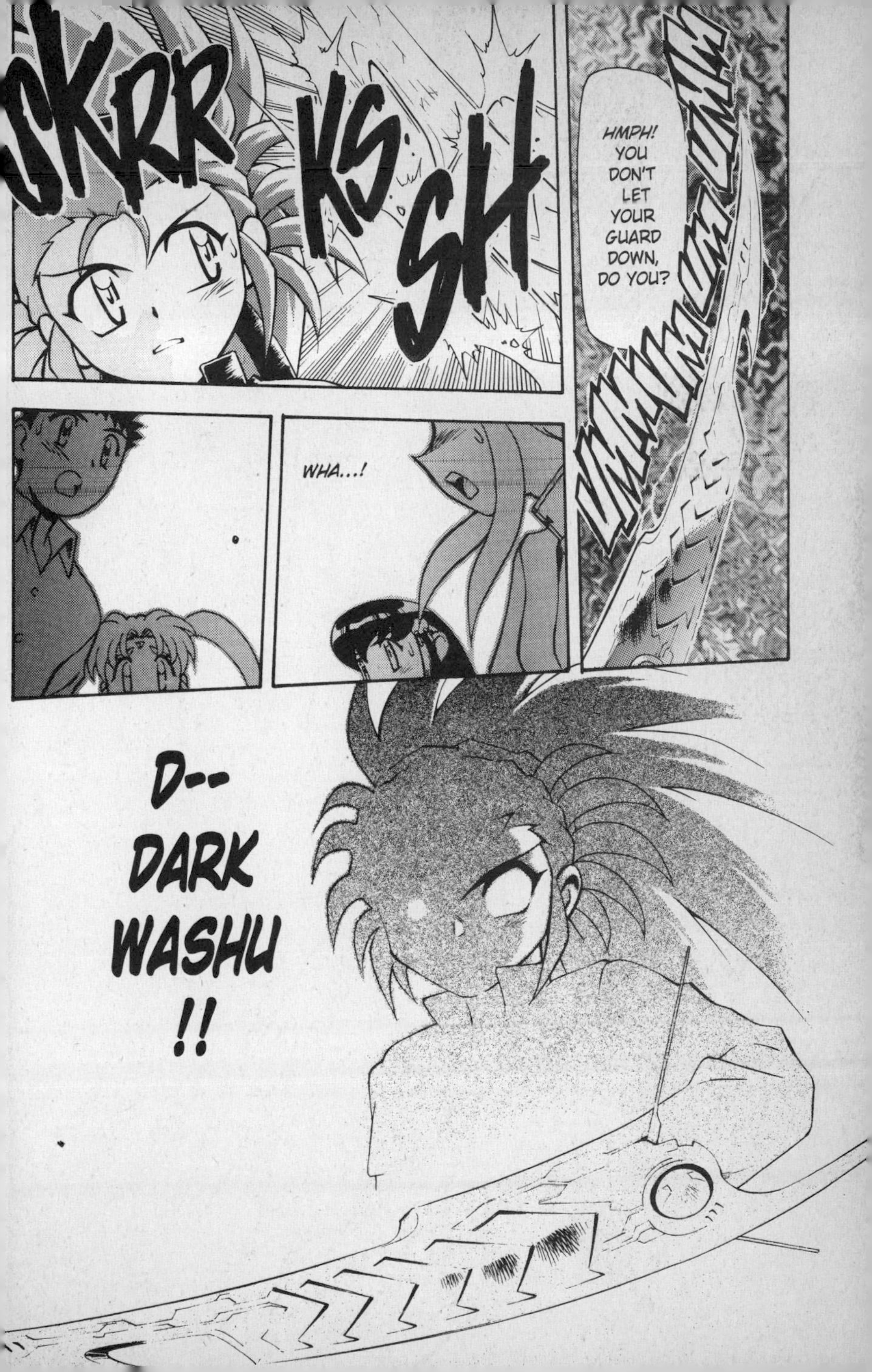
SKRR
KSSH
WHA...!
HMPH! YOU DON'T LET YOUR GUARD DOWN, DO YOU?
D-- DARK WASHU !!

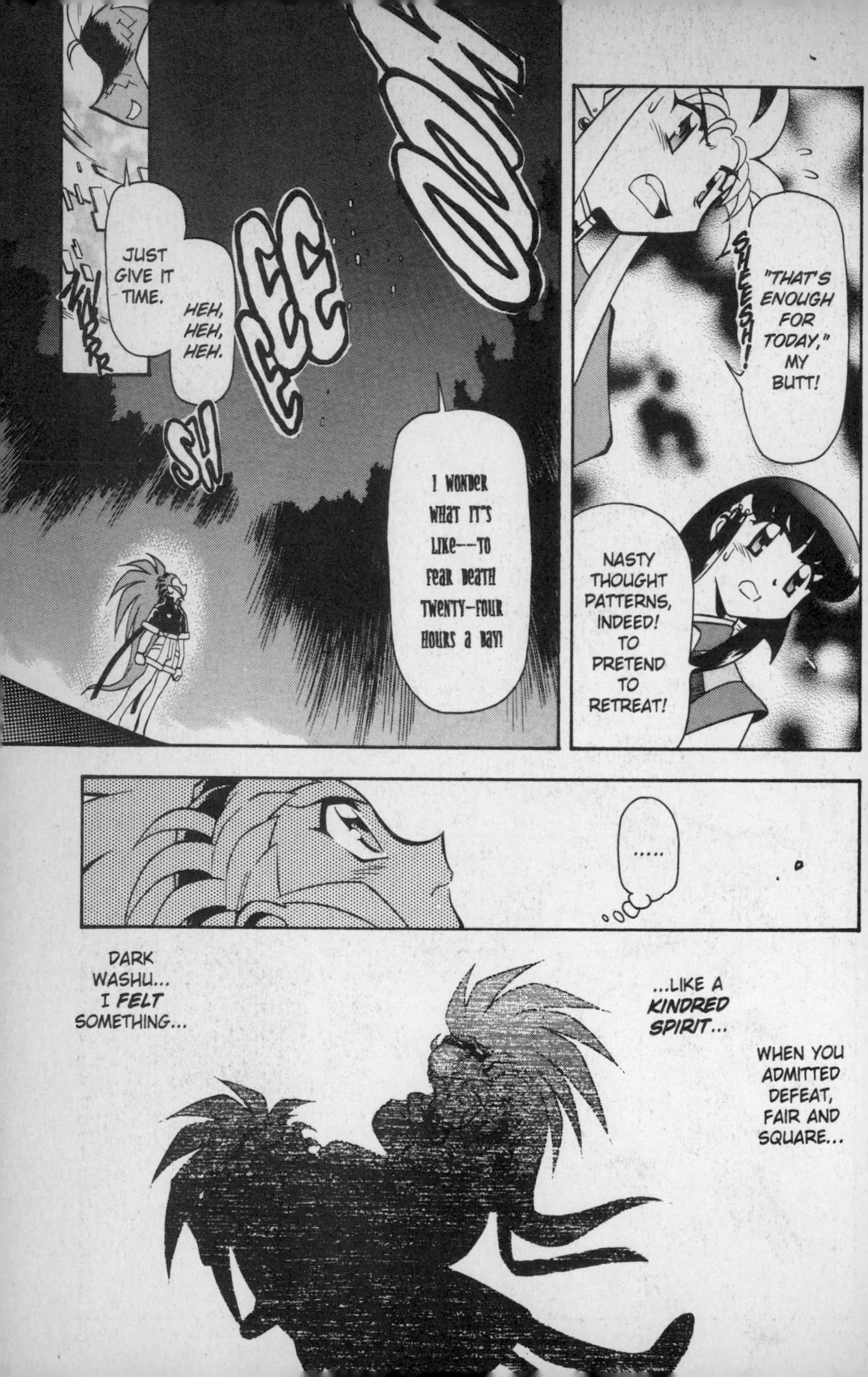
JUST GIVE IT TIME.
HEH, HEH, HEH.
I WONDER WHAT IT'S LIKE--TO FEAR DEATH TWENTY-FOUR HOURS A DAY!
SHEESH!
"THAT'S ENOUGH FOR TODAY," MY BUTT!
NASTY THOUGHT PATTERNS, INDEED! TO PRETEND TO RETREAT!
.....
DARK WASHU... I FELT SOMETHING...
...LIKE A KINDRED SPIRIT...
WHEN YOU ADMITTED DEFEAT, FAIR AND SQUARE...

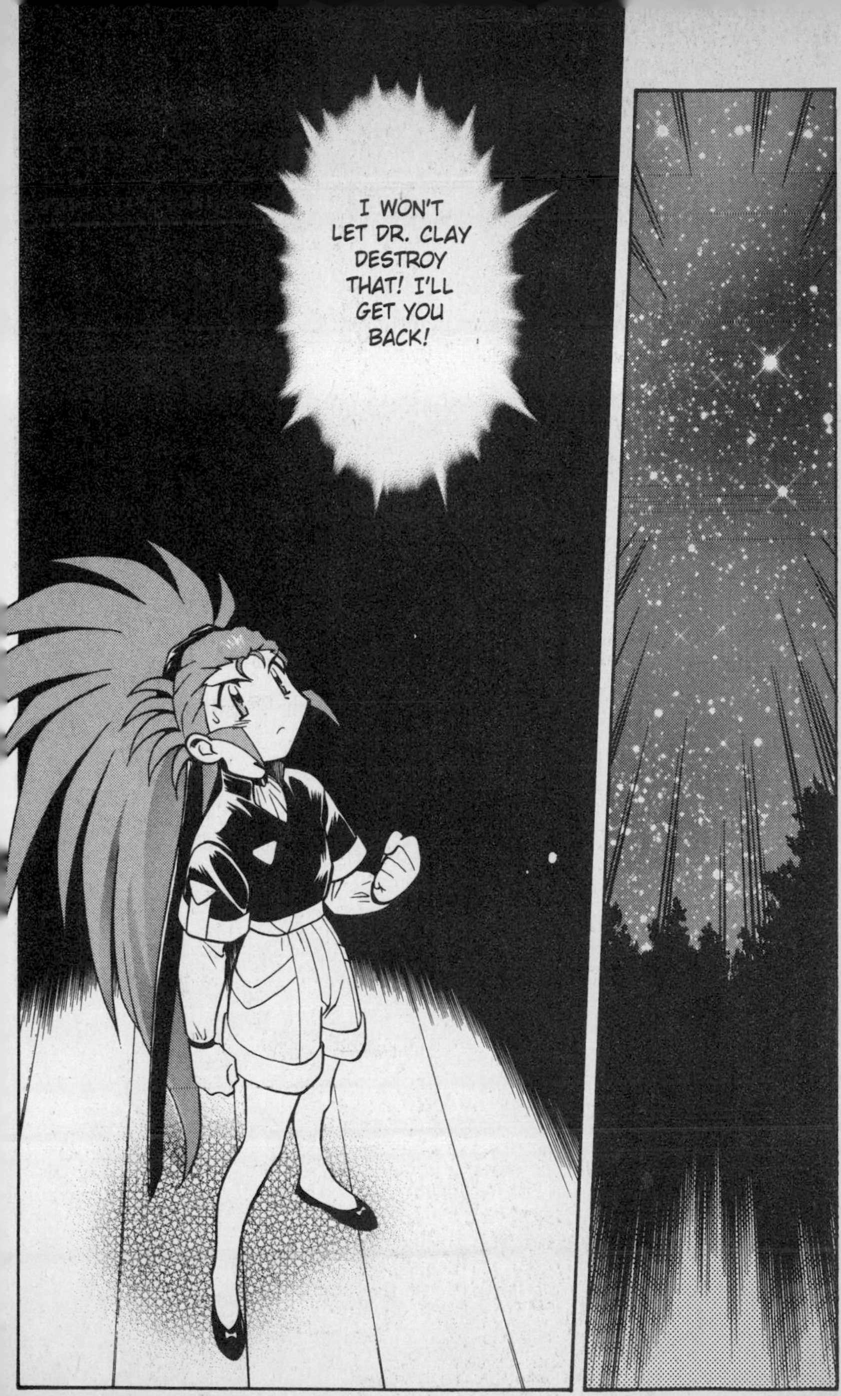
I WON'T LET DR. CLAY DESTROY THAT! I'LL GET YOU BACK!

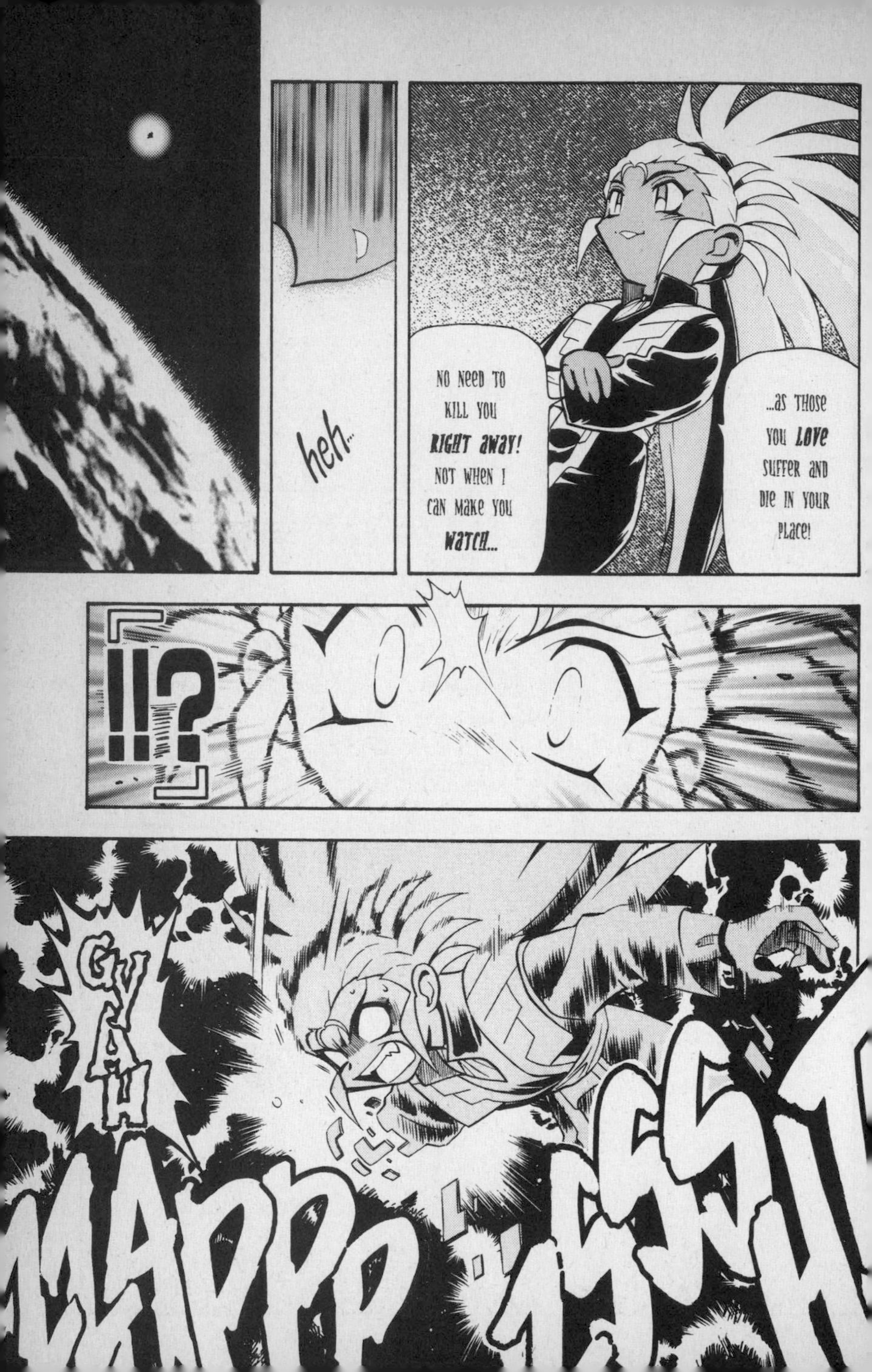
heh...
NO NEED TO KILL YOU **RIGHT AWAY!** NOT WHEN I CAN MAKE YOU **WATCH...**
...AS THOSE YOU **LOVE** SUFFER AND DIE IN YOUR PLACE!
!!?
GYAAH

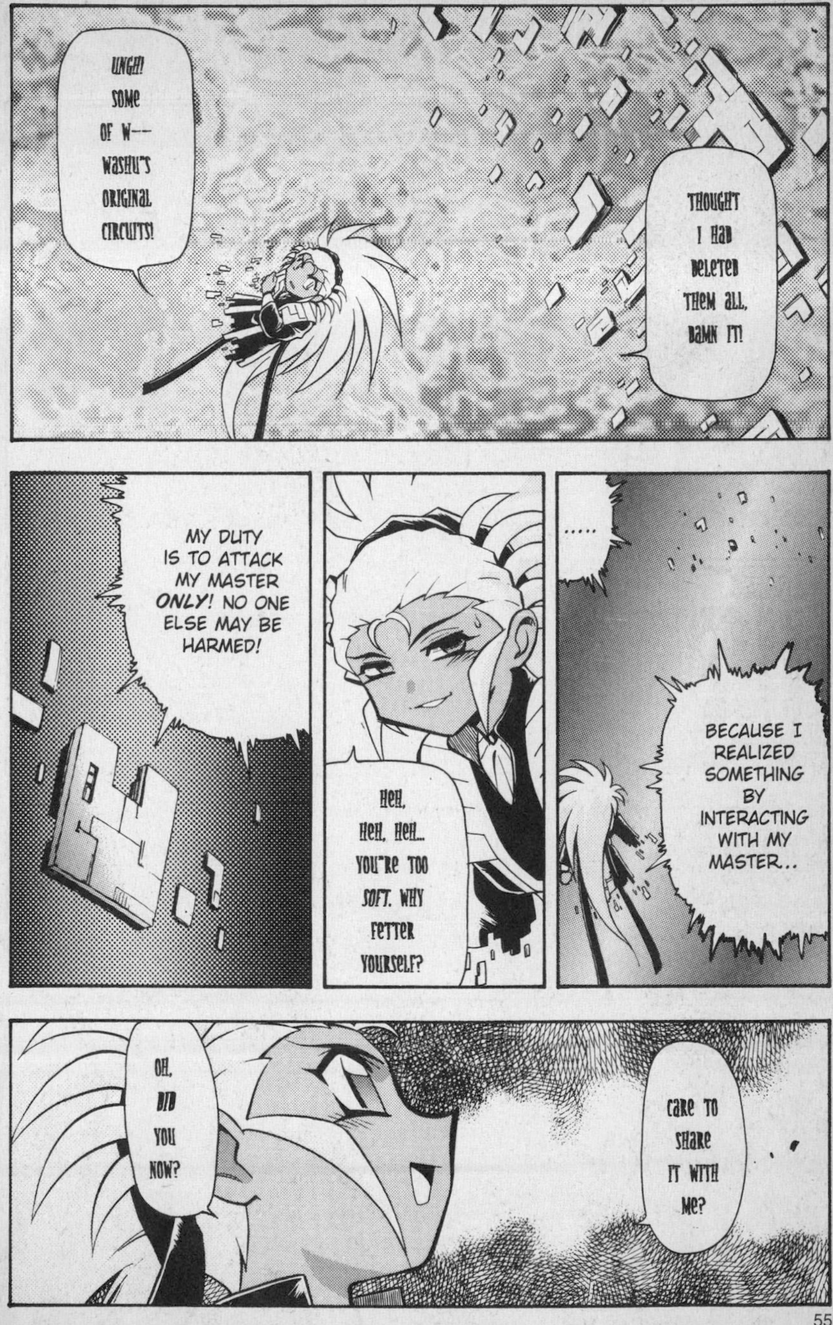
UNGH! SOME OF W-- WASHU'S ORIGINAL CIRCUITS!
THOUGHT I HAD DELETED THEM ALL, DAMN IT!
MY DUTY IS TO ATTACK MY MASTER ONLY! NO ONE ELSE MAY BE HARMED!
HEH, HEH, HEH... YOU'RE TOO SOFT. WHY FETTER YOURSELF?
.....
BECAUSE I REALIZED SOMETHING BY INTERACTING WITH MY MASTER..
OH, DID YOU NOW?
CARE TO SHARE IT WITH ME?

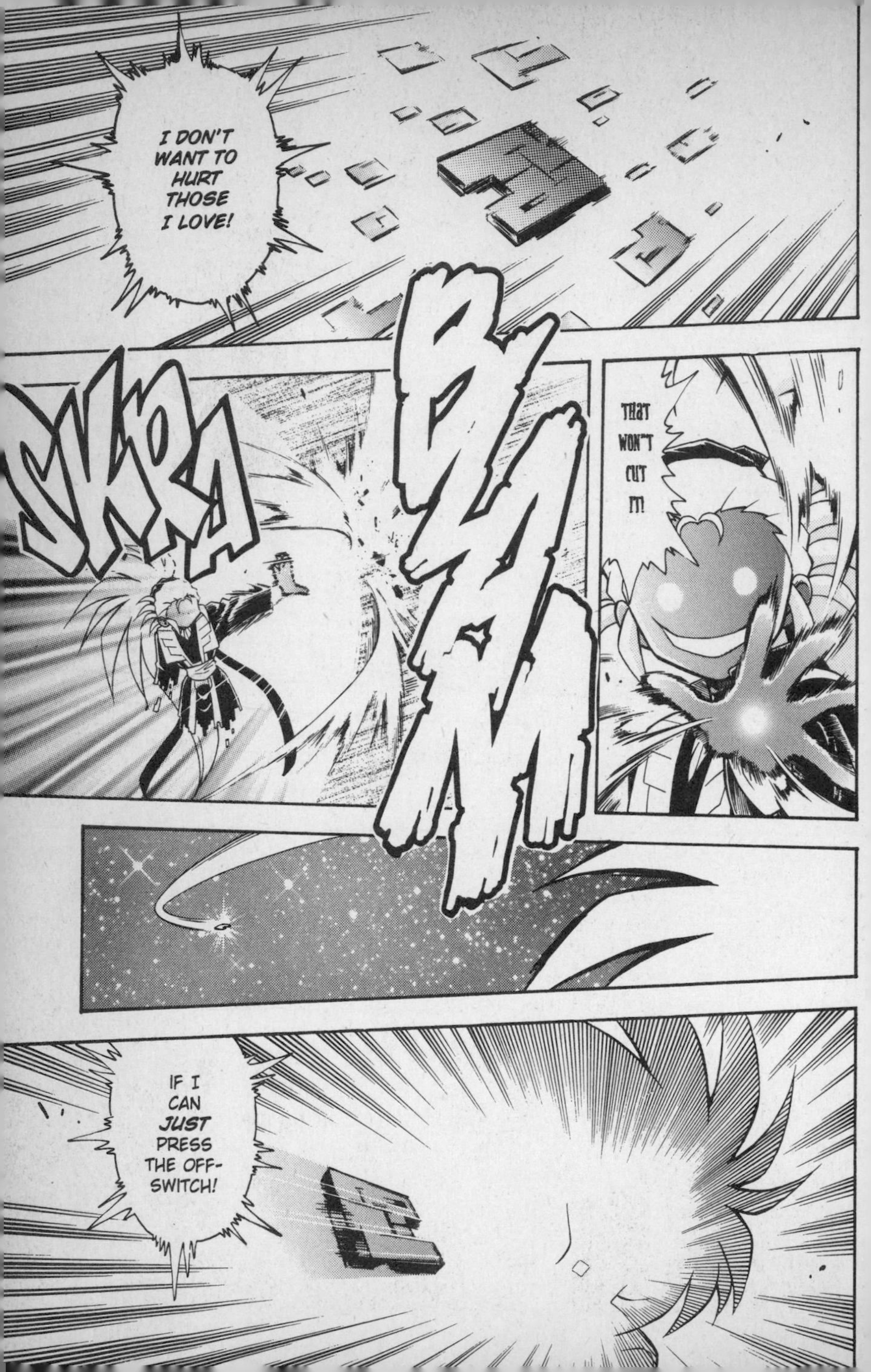
I DON'T WANT TO HURT THOSE I LOVE!
THAT WON'T CUT IT!
IF I CAN *JUST* PRESS THE OFF-SWITCH!

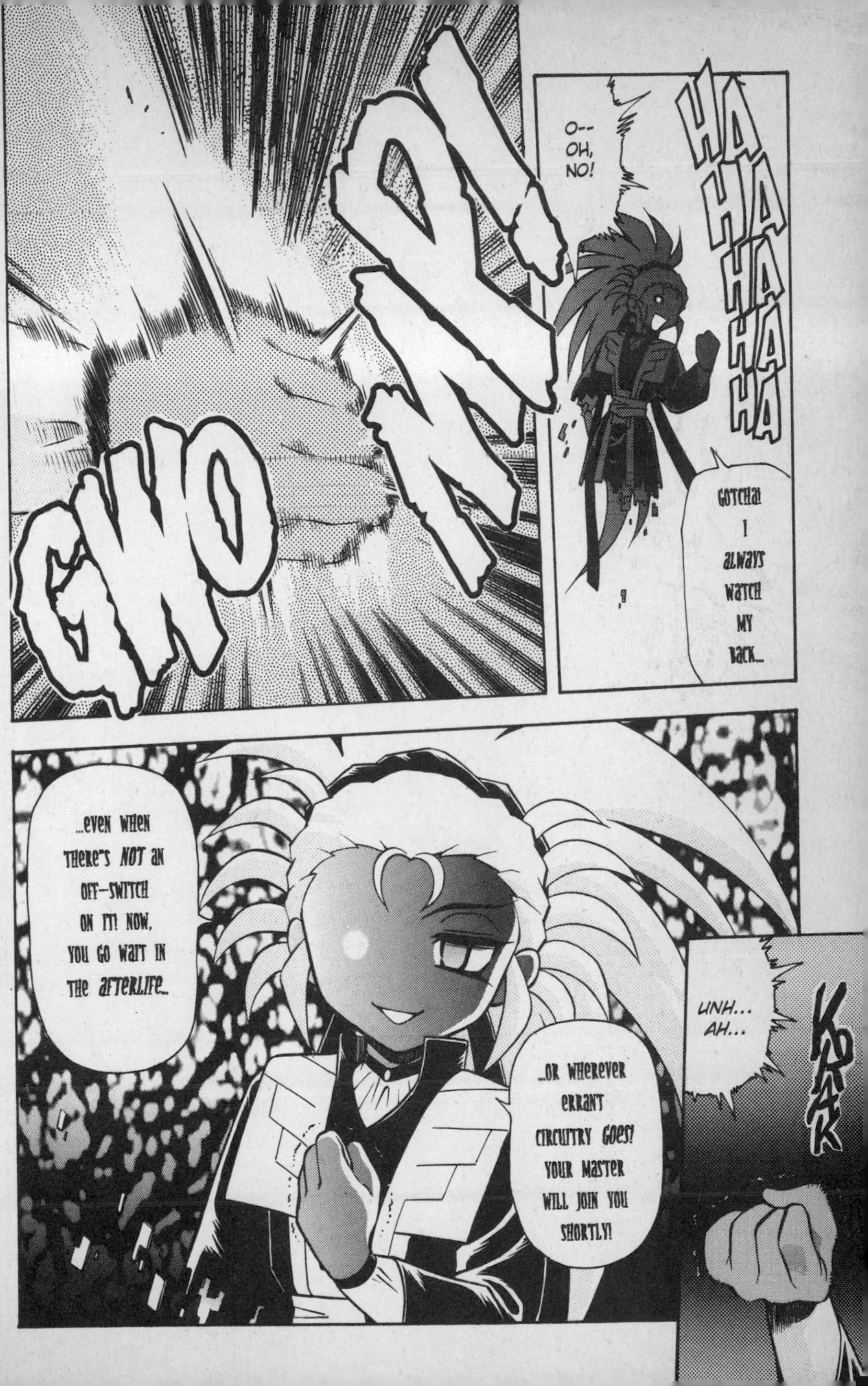
GNOKK!
O-- OH, NO!
HA HA HA HA HA HA
GOTCHA! I ALWAYS WATCH MY BACK...
...EVEN WHEN THERE'S *NOT* AN OFF-SWITCH ON IT! NOW, YOU GO WAIT IN THE *AFTERLIFE*...
...OR WHEREVER ERRANT CIRCUITRY *GOES*! YOUR MASTER WILL JOIN YOU SHORTLY!
UNH... AH...
KRAK

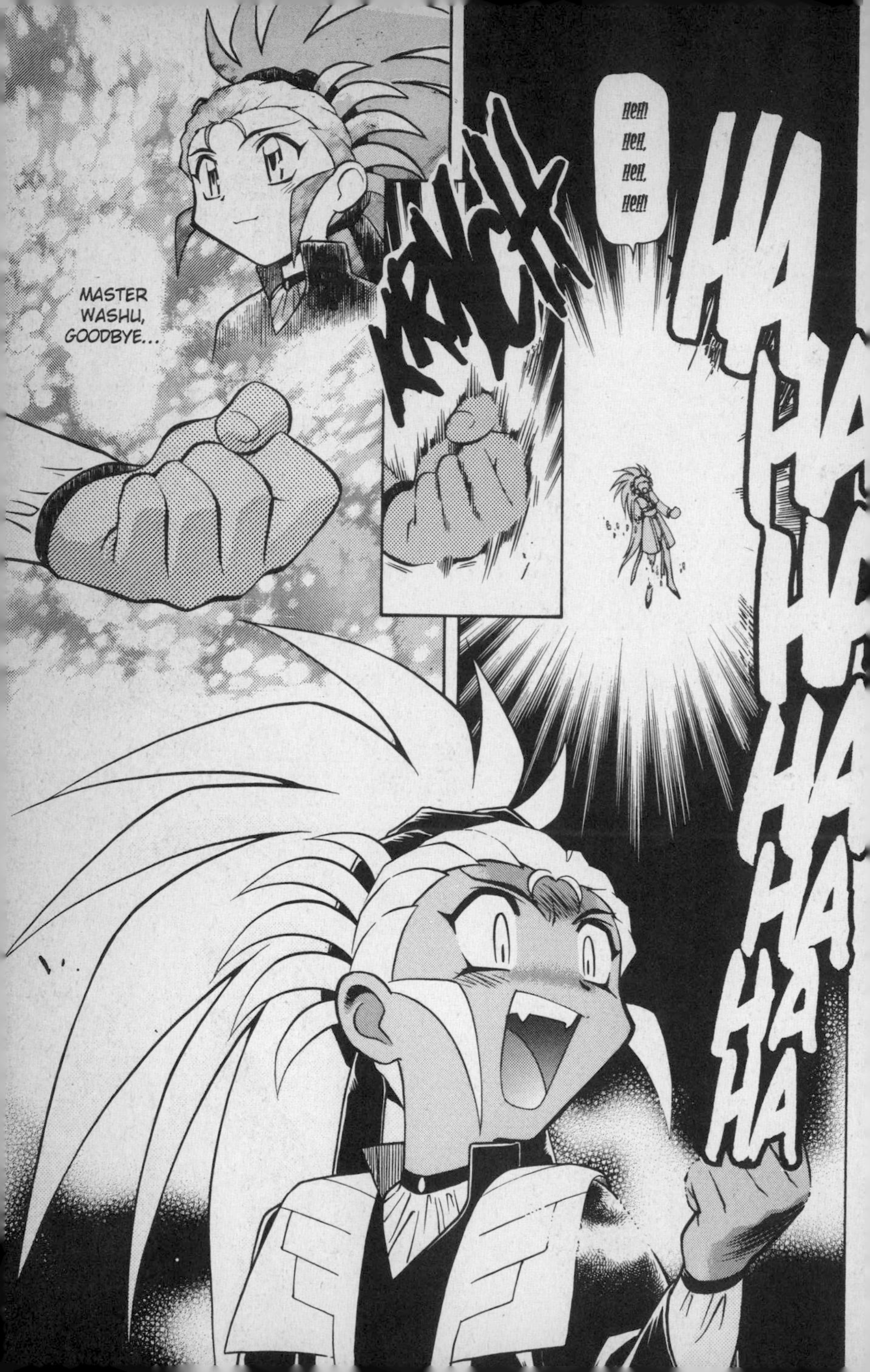
MASTER WASHU, GOODBYE...
KRACK!!
HEH! HEH, HEH, HEH!
HAHAHAHAHAHAHA

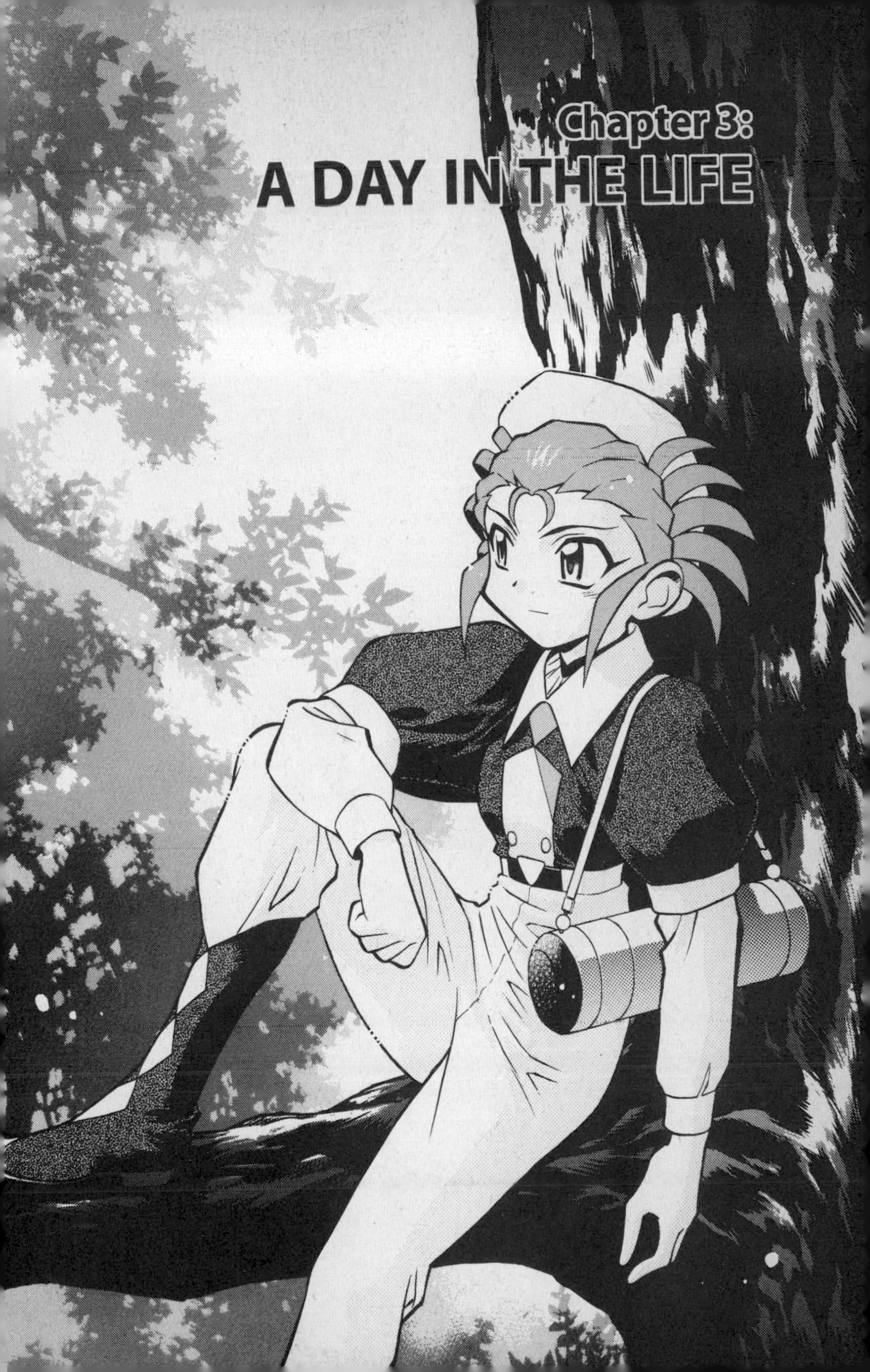
Chapter 3:
A DAY IN THE LIFE

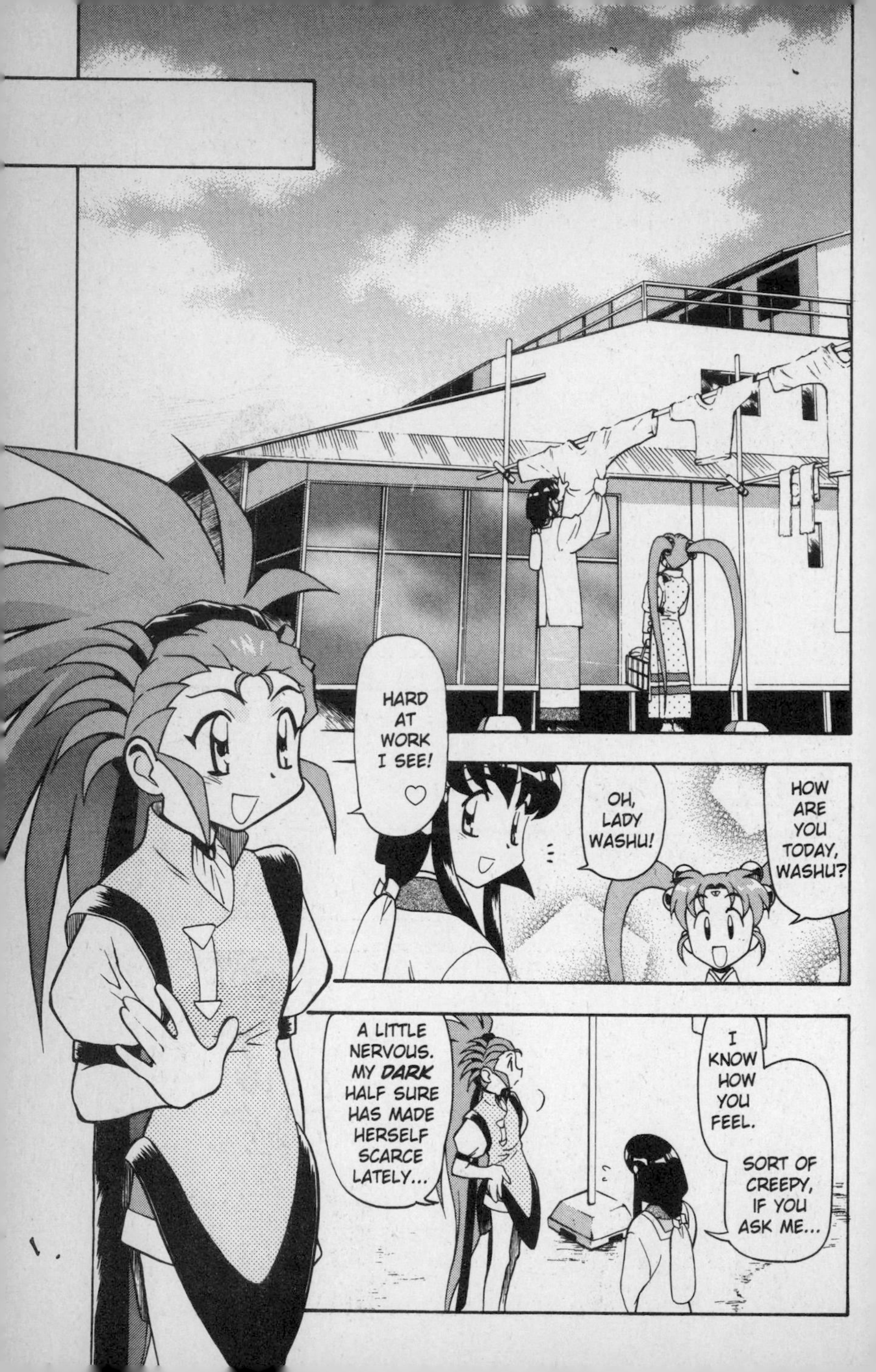
HARD AT WORK I SEE! ♡
OH, LADY WASHU!
HOW ARE YOU TODAY, WASHU?
A LITTLE NERVOUS. MY *DARK* HALF SURE HAS MADE HERSELF SCARCE LATELY...
I KNOW HOW YOU FEEL.
SORT OF CREEPY, IF YOU ASK ME...

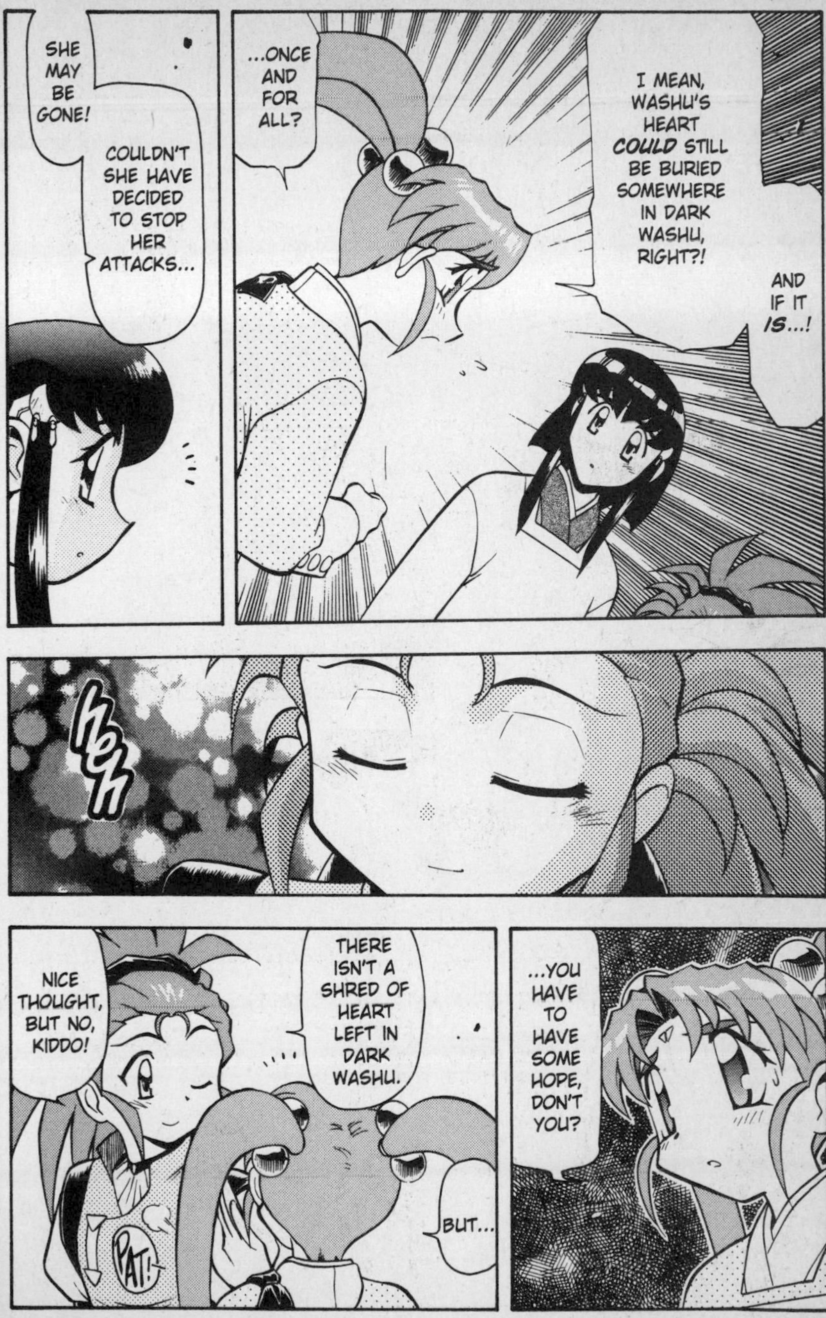

SHE MAY BE GONE!
COULDN'T SHE HAVE DECIDED TO STOP HER ATTACKS...
...ONCE AND FOR ALL?
I MEAN, WASHU'S HEART COULD STILL BE BURIED SOMEWHERE IN DARK WASHU, RIGHT?!
AND IF IT IS...!
heh
NICE THOUGHT, BUT NO, KIDDO!
THERE ISN'T A SHRED OF HEART LEFT IN DARK WASHU.
PAT!
BUT...
...YOU HAVE TO HAVE SOME HOPE, DON'T YOU?

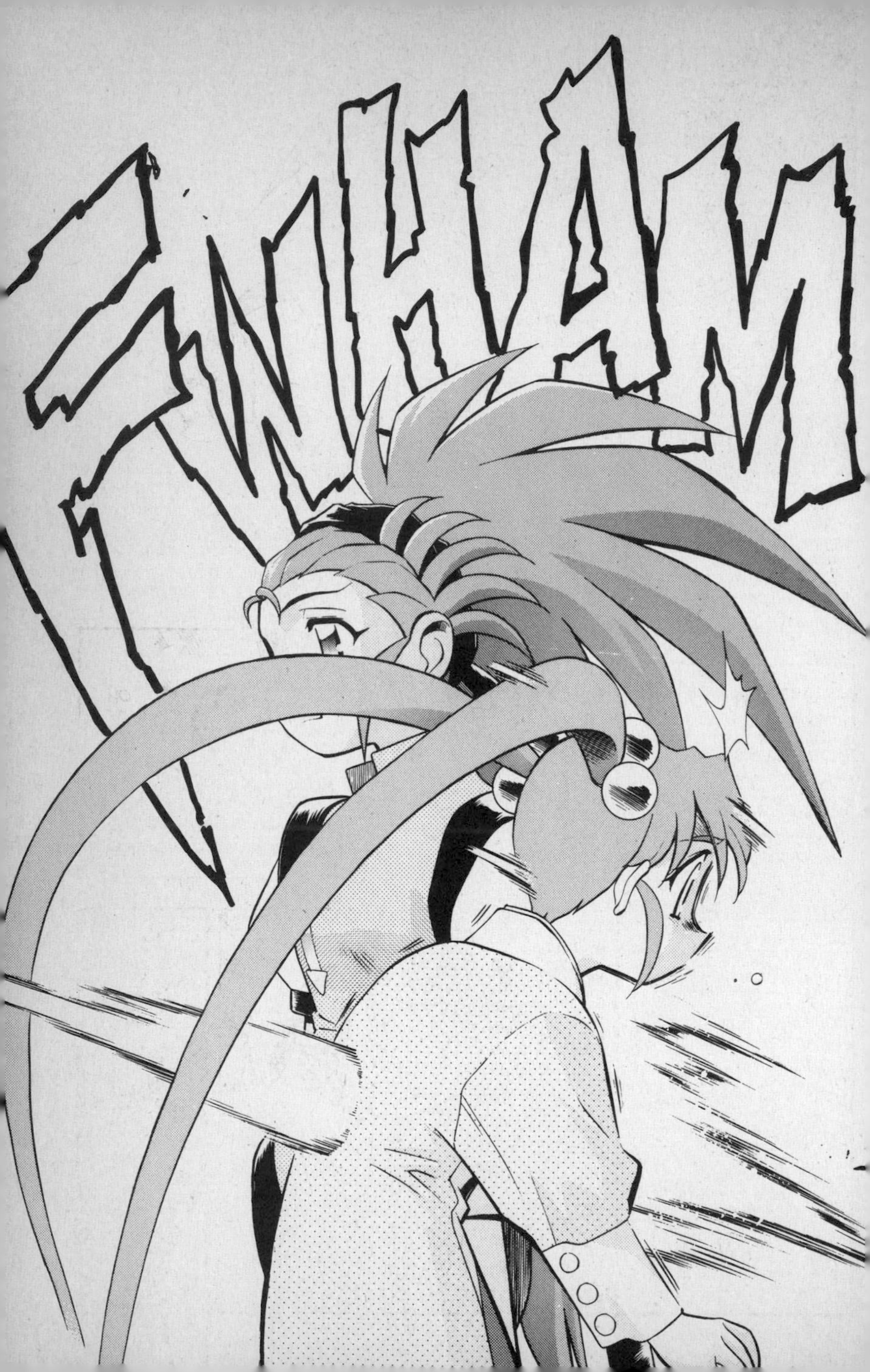
WHAM

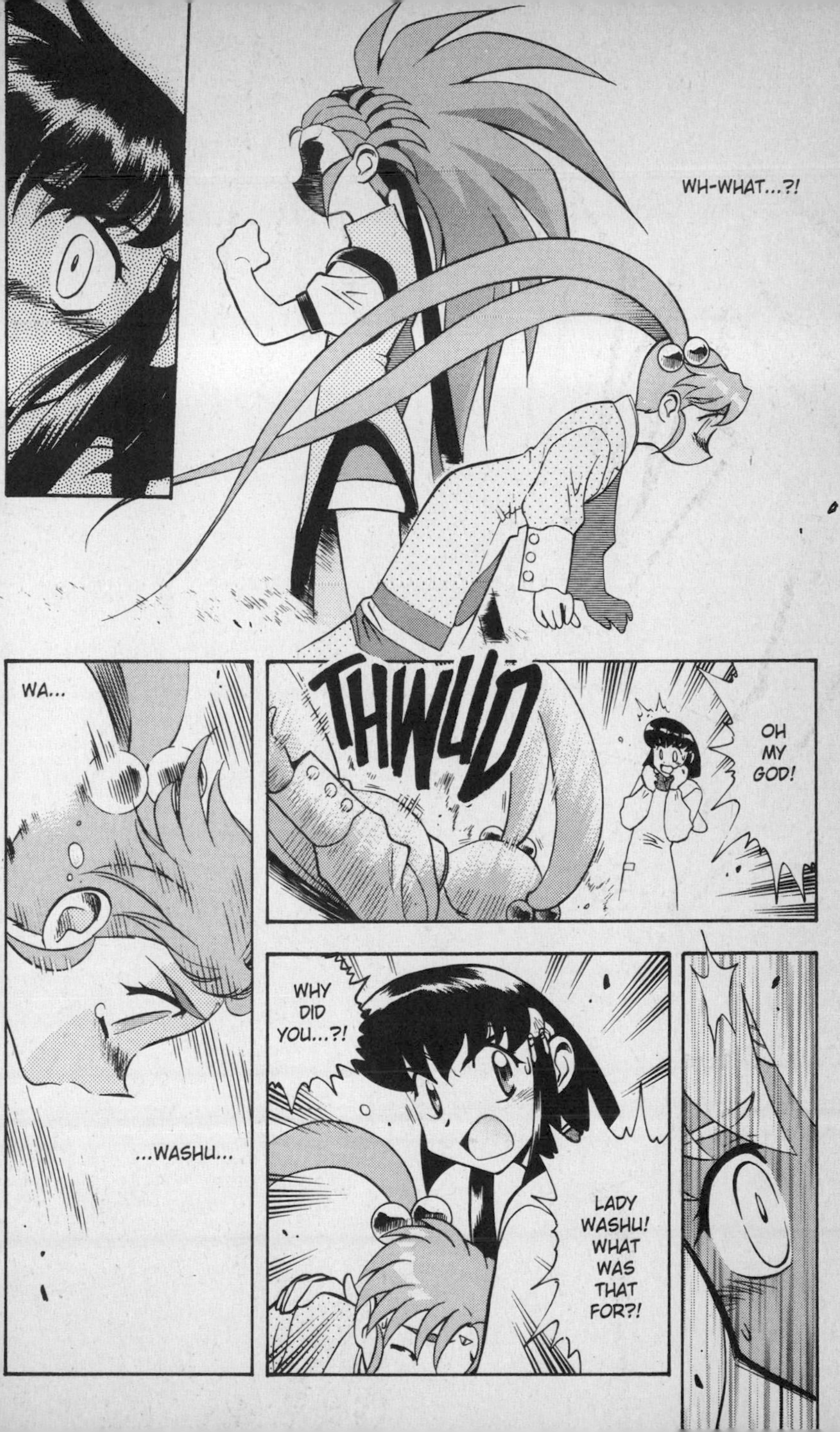
WH-WHAT...?!
WA...
...WASHU...
THWUD
OH MY GOD!
WHY DID YOU...?!
LADY WASHU! WHAT WAS THAT FOR?!

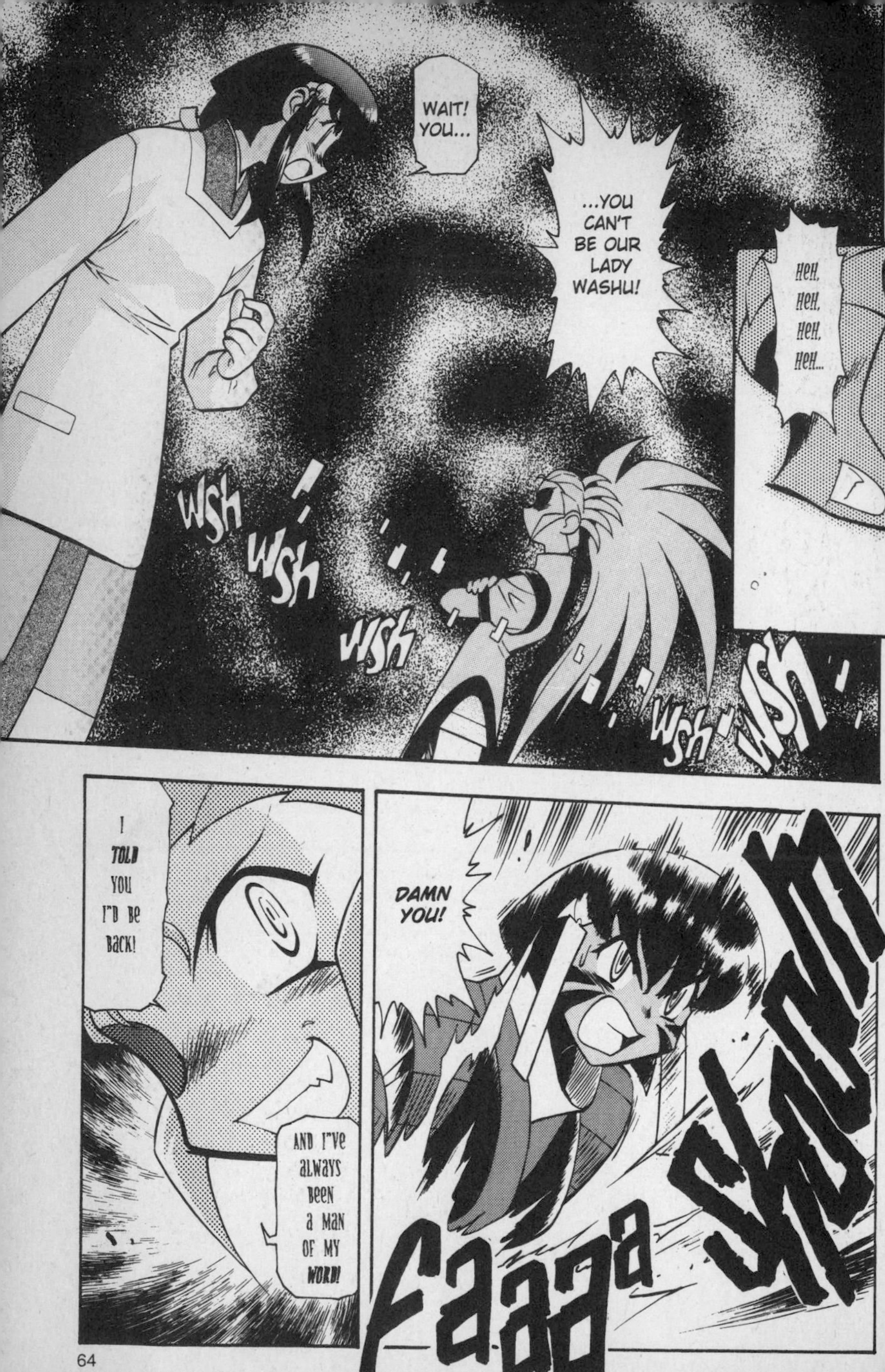
HEH, HEH, HEH, HEH...
...YOU CAN'T BE OUR LADY WASHU!
WAIT! YOU...
WSH WSH WSH
WSH WSH
DAMN YOU!
FAAAA-SHOOM
I TOLD YOU I'D BE BACK!
AND I'VE ALWAYS BEEN A MAN OF MY WORD!

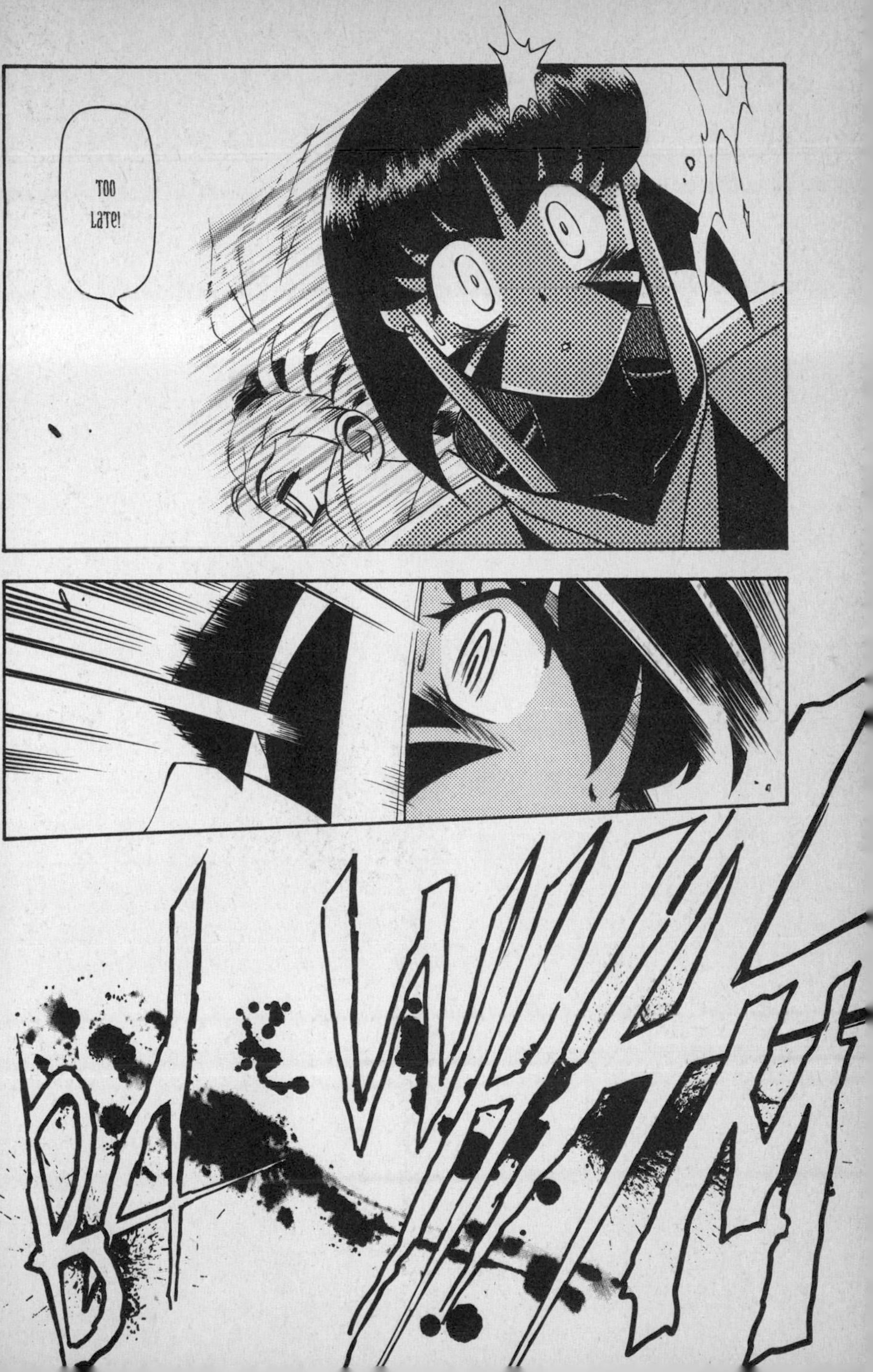
TOO LATE!
BAWAM

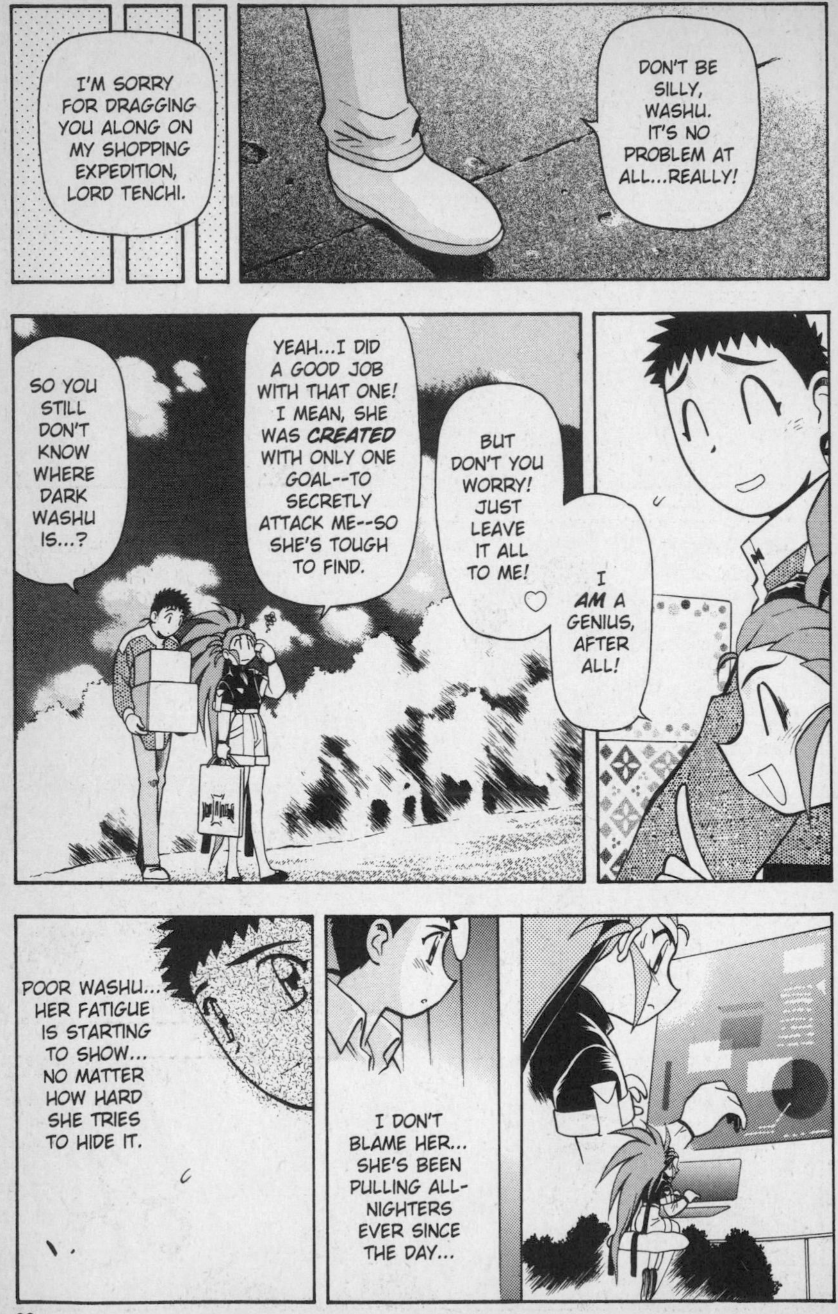
I'M SORRY FOR DRAGGING YOU ALONG ON MY SHOPPING EXPEDITION, LORD TENCHI.
DON'T BE SILLY, WASHU. IT'S NO PROBLEM AT ALL...REALLY!
SO YOU STILL DON'T KNOW WHERE DARK WASHU IS...?
YEAH...I DID A GOOD JOB WITH THAT ONE! I MEAN, SHE WAS *CREATED* WITH ONLY ONE GOAL--TO SECRETLY ATTACK ME--SO SHE'S TOUGH TO FIND.
BUT DON'T YOU WORRY! JUST LEAVE IT ALL TO ME! ♡
I *AM* A GENIUS, AFTER ALL!
POOR WASHU... HER FATIGUE IS STARTING TO SHOW... NO MATTER HOW HARD SHE TRIES TO HIDE IT.
I DON'T BLAME HER... SHE'S BEEN PULLING ALL-NIGHTERS EVER SINCE THE DAY...

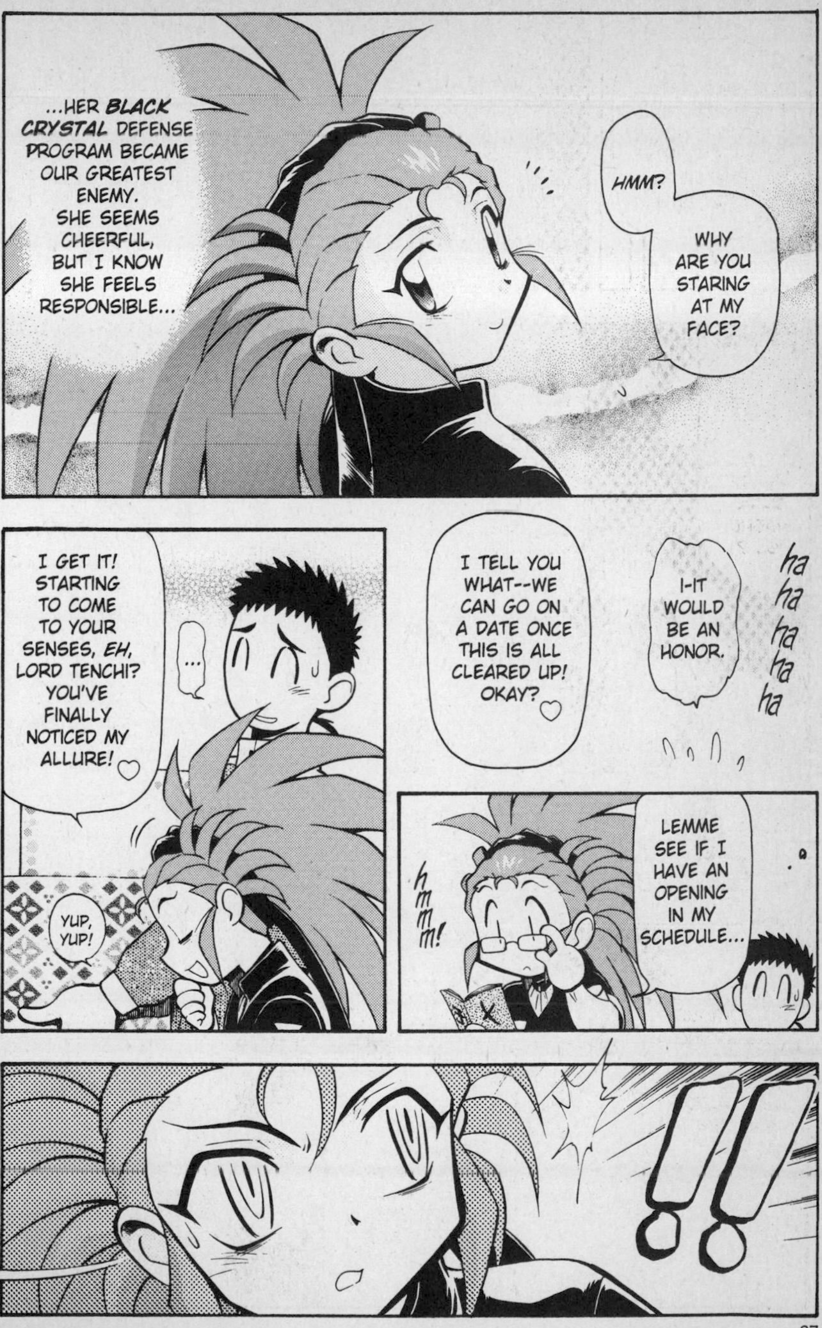
...HER BLACK CRYSTAL DEFENSE PROGRAM BECAME OUR GREATEST ENEMY. SHE SEEMS CHEERFUL, BUT I KNOW SHE FEELS RESPONSIBLE...
HMM?
WHY ARE YOU STARING AT MY FACE?
I GET IT! STARTING TO COME TO YOUR SENSES, EH, LORD TENCHI? YOU'VE FINALLY NOTICED MY ALLURE! ♡
...
YUP, YUP!
I TELL YOU WHAT--WE CAN GO ON A DATE ONCE THIS IS ALL CLEARED UP! OKAY? ♡
I-IT WOULD BE AN HONOR.
ha ha ha ha ha
hmmm!
LEMME SEE IF I HAVE AN OPENING IN MY SCHEDULE...
!!

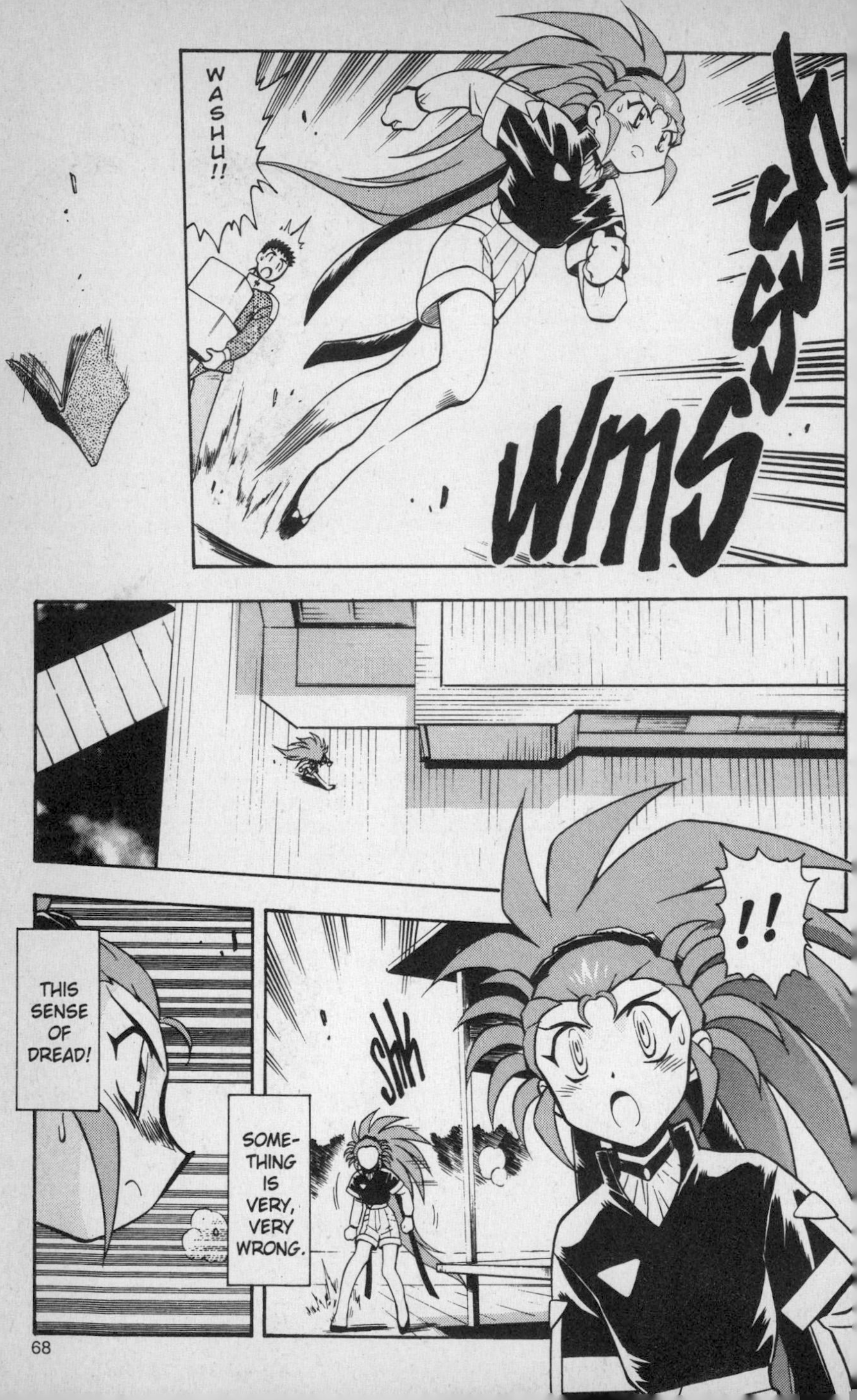
WASHU!!
WMSSH
THIS SENSE OF DREAD!
!!
SHKK
SOME-THING IS VERY, VERY WRONG.

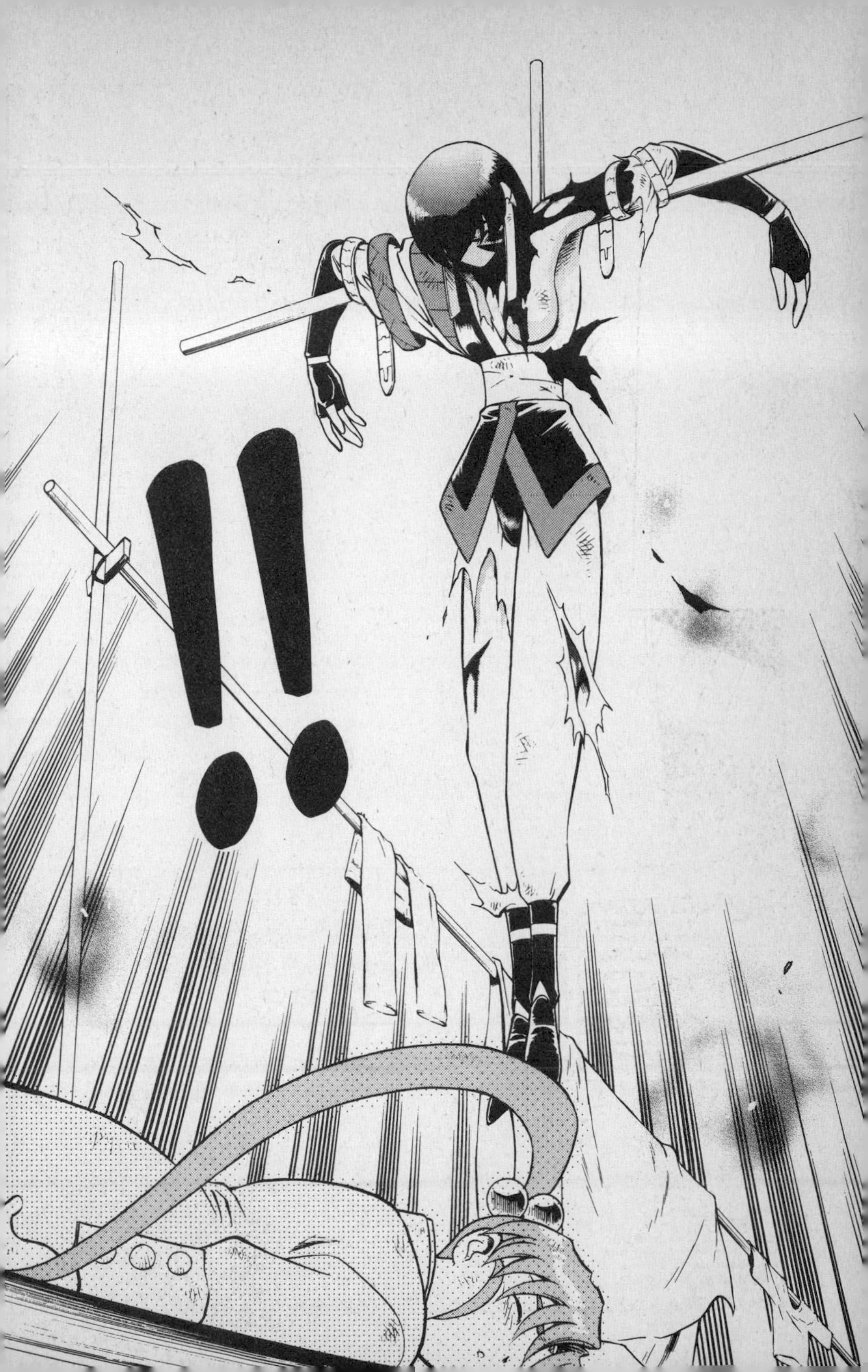
!!

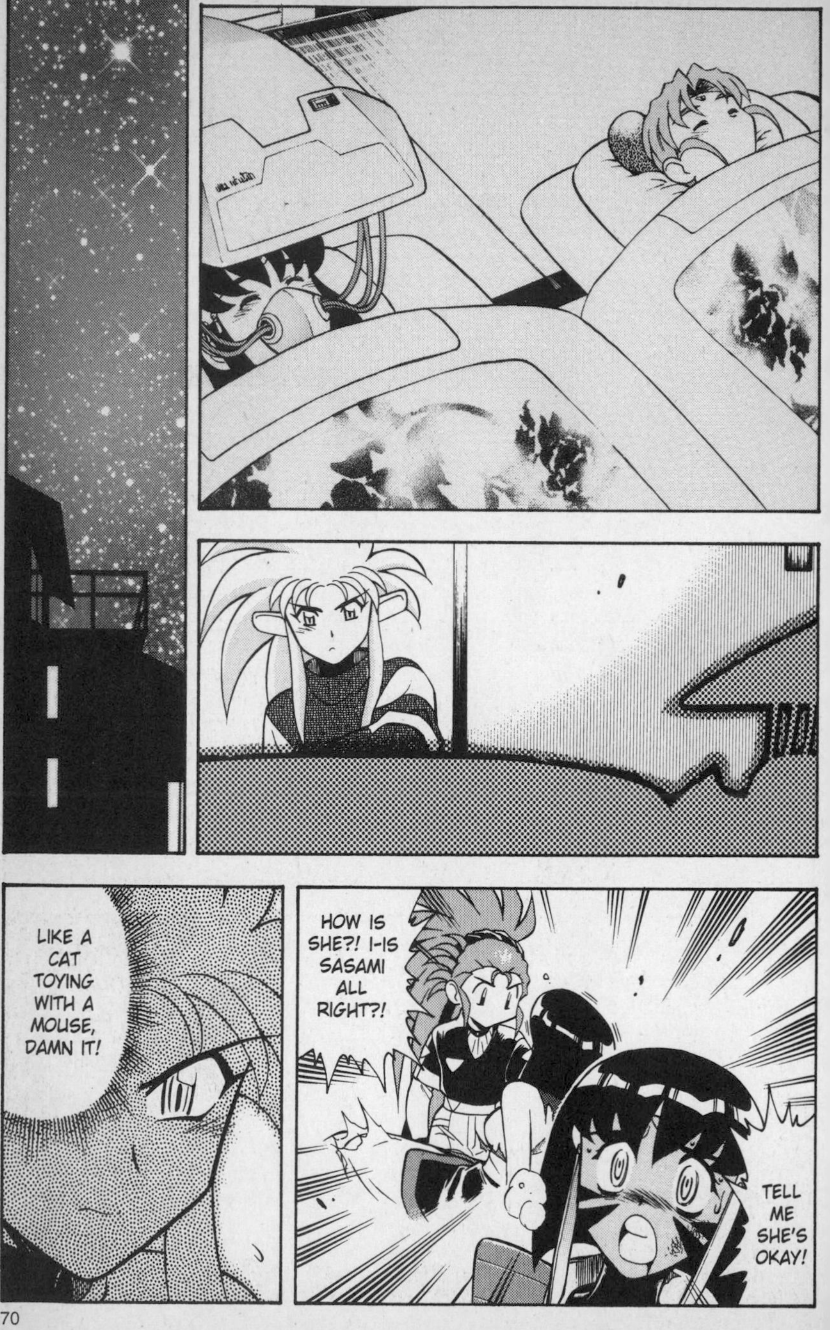
LIKE A CAT TOYING WITH A MOUSE, DAMN IT!
HOW IS SHE?! I-IS SASAMI ALL RIGHT?!
TELL ME SHE'S OKAY!

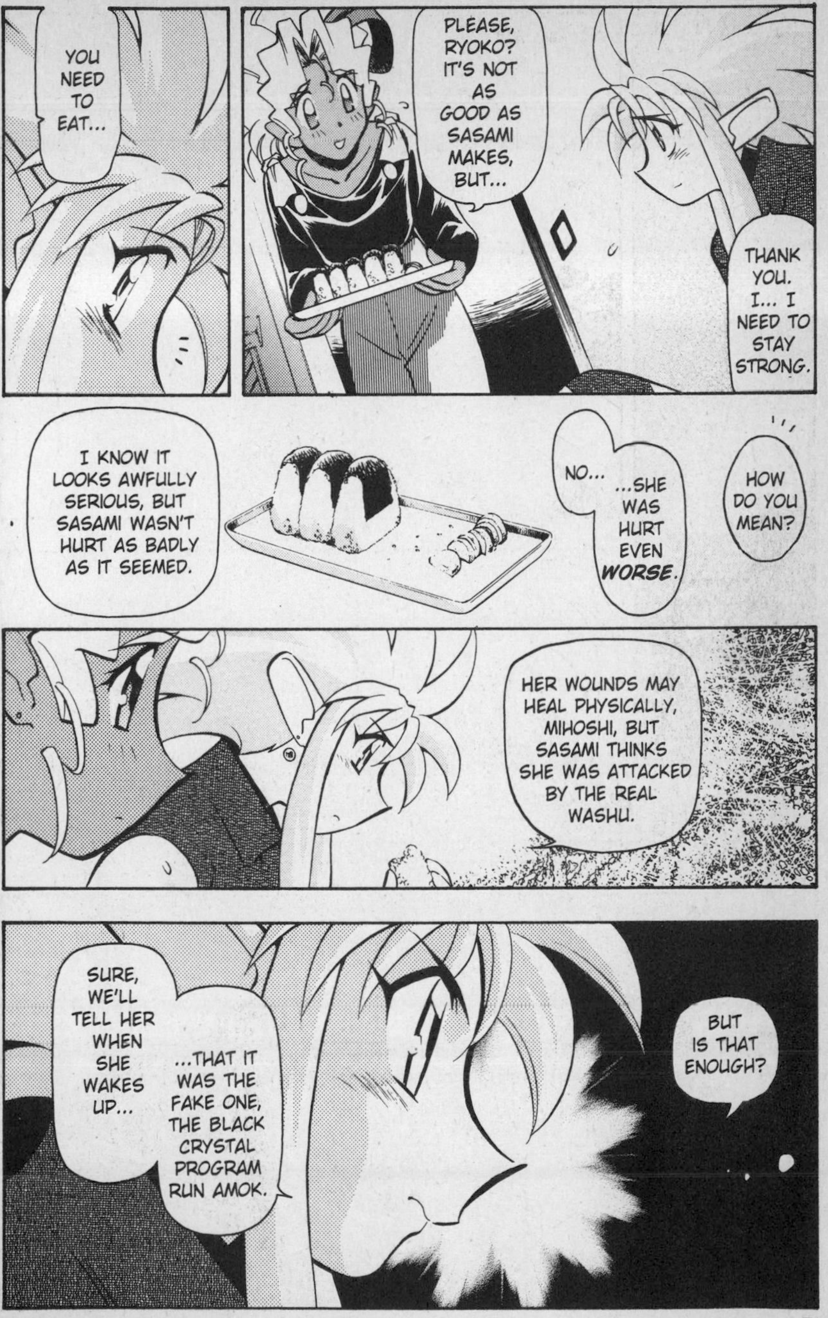
YOU NEED TO EAT...
PLEASE, RYOKO? IT'S NOT AS GOOD AS SASAMI MAKES, BUT...
THANK YOU. I... I NEED TO STAY STRONG.
I KNOW IT LOOKS AWFULLY SERIOUS, BUT SASAMI WASN'T HURT AS BADLY AS IT SEEMED.
NO...
...SHE WAS HURT EVEN ***WORSE***.
HOW DO YOU MEAN?
HER WOUNDS MAY HEAL PHYSICALLY, MIHOSHI, BUT SASAMI THINKS SHE WAS ATTACKED BY THE REAL WASHU.
SURE, WE'LL TELL HER WHEN SHE WAKES UP...
...THAT IT WAS THE FAKE ONE, THE BLACK CRYSTAL PROGRAM RUN AMOK.
BUT IS THAT ENOUGH?

THAT MOMENT-- IT'S *FOREVER* ETCHED IN HER MEMORY!

A SCAR THAT CAN'T BE ERASED!

RYOKO...

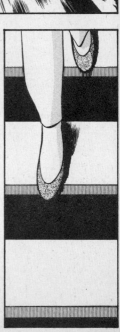

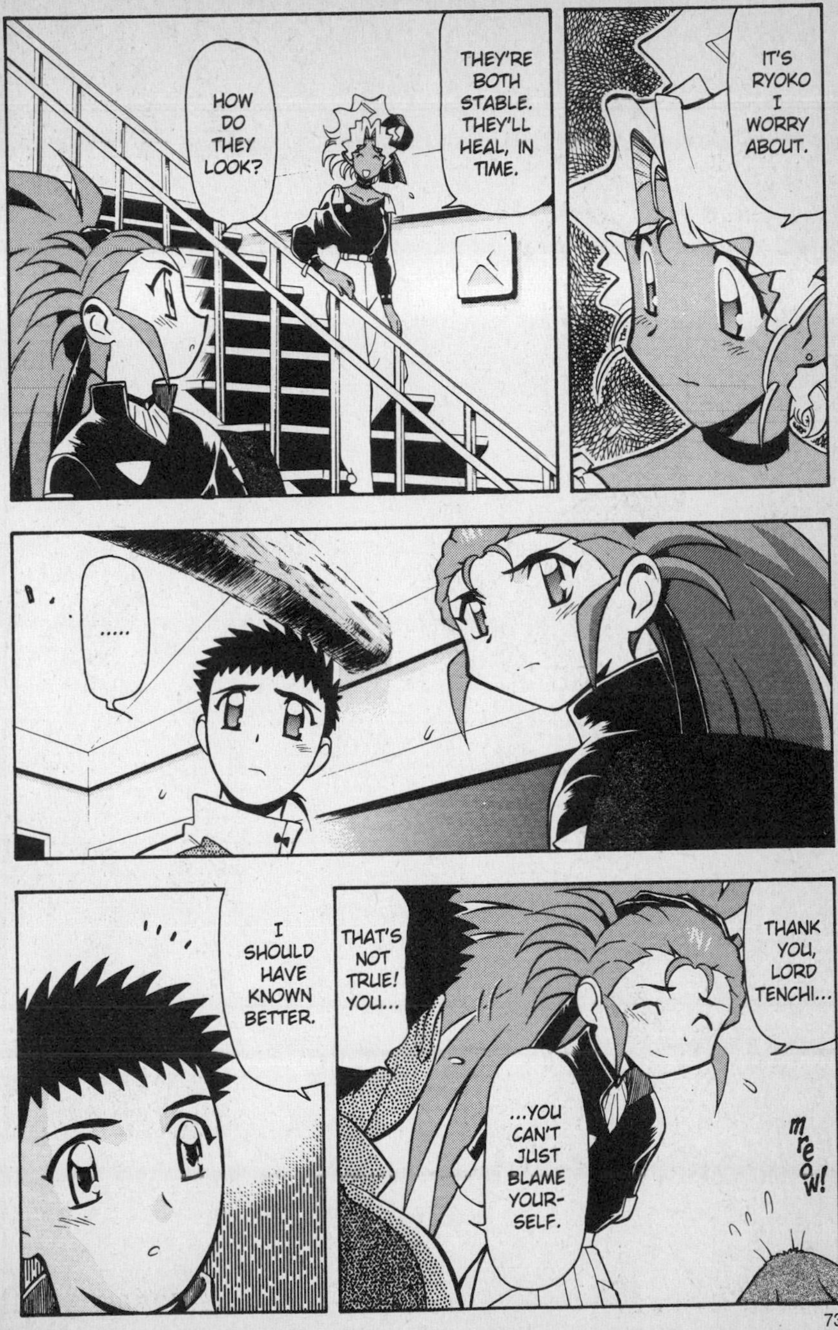
HOW DO THEY LOOK?
THEY'RE BOTH STABLE. THEY'LL HEAL, IN TIME.
IT'S RYOKO I WORRY ABOUT.
.....
I SHOULD HAVE KNOWN BETTER.
THAT'S NOT TRUE! YOU...
...YOU CAN'T JUST BLAME YOURSELF.
THANK YOU, LORD TENCHI...
mreow!

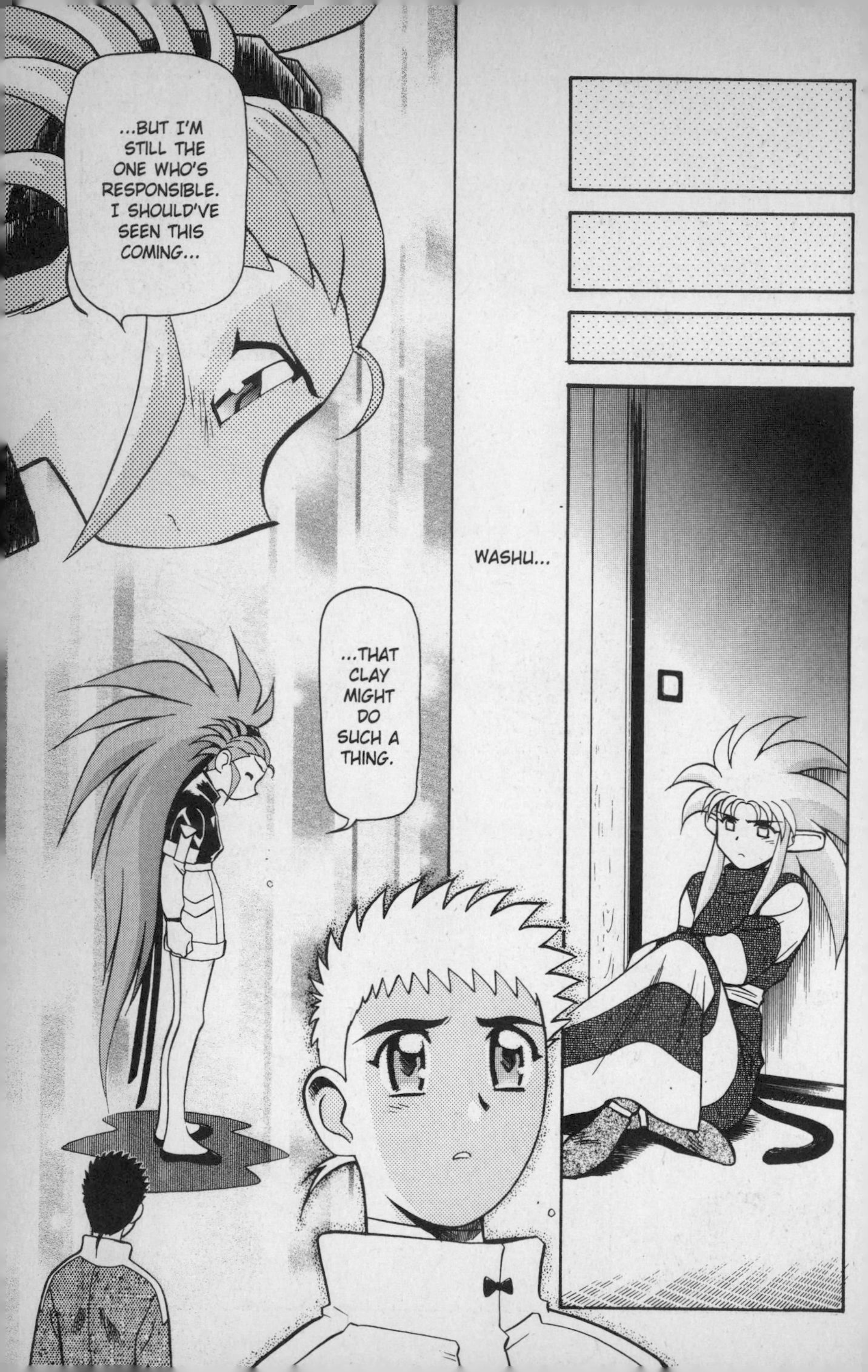
...BUT I'M STILL THE ONE WHO'S RESPONSIBLE. I SHOULD'VE SEEN THIS COMING...
...THAT CLAY MIGHT DO SUCH A THING.
WASHU...

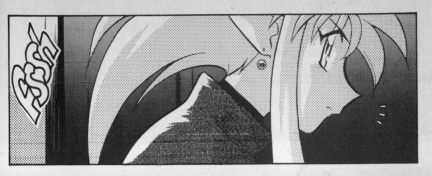

IT'S NOT GOOD FOR YOU TO STRESS YOURSELF OUT THIS WAY.

LORD TENCHI'S WORRIED ABOUT YOU, TOO...

krrrrm

SO TELL ME.

ARE YOU *SURE* YOU'RE NOT DARK WASHU?

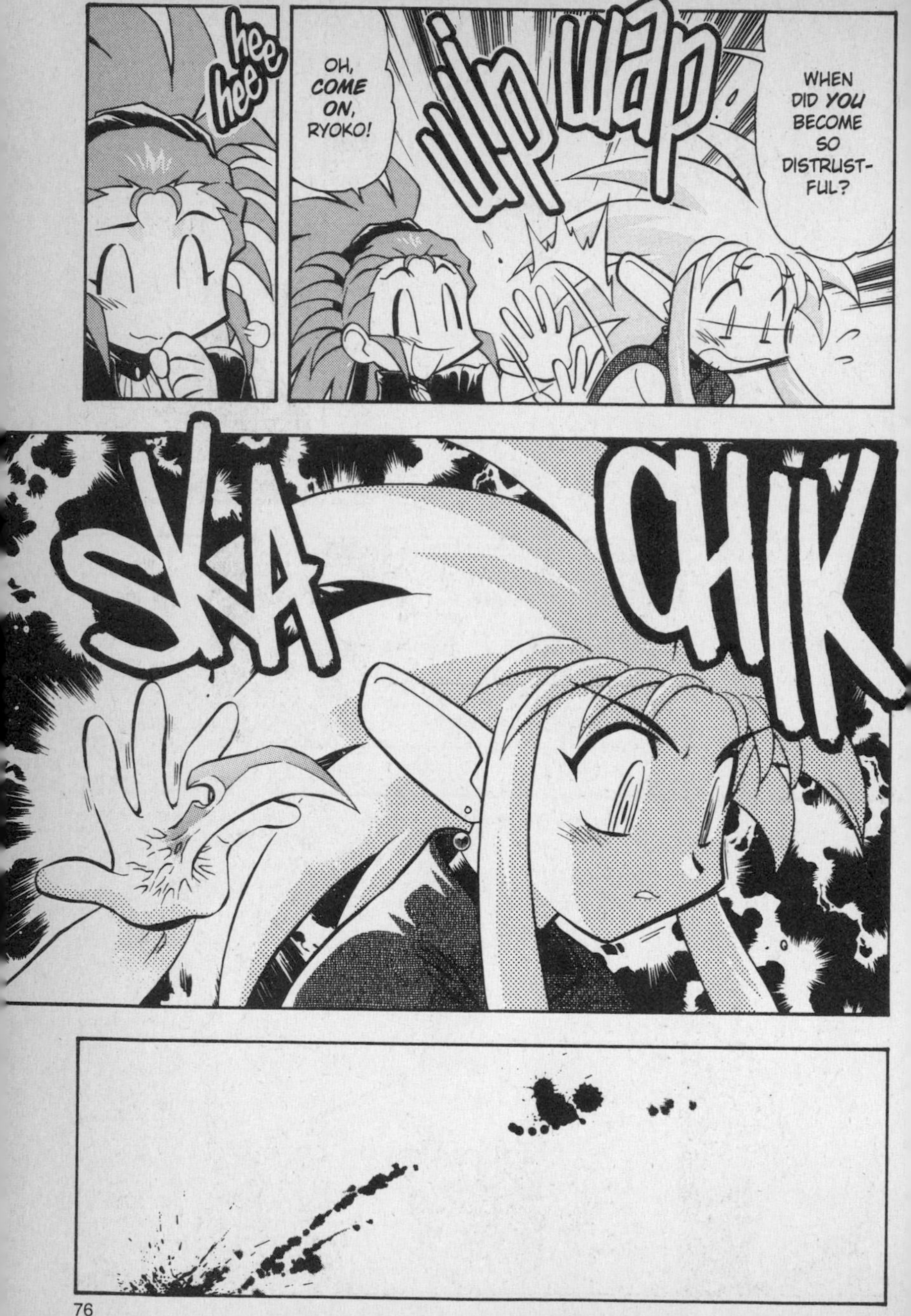
hee hee
OH, COME ON, RYOKO!
wip wap
WHEN DID YOU BECOME SO DISTRUST-FUL?
SKA CHIK

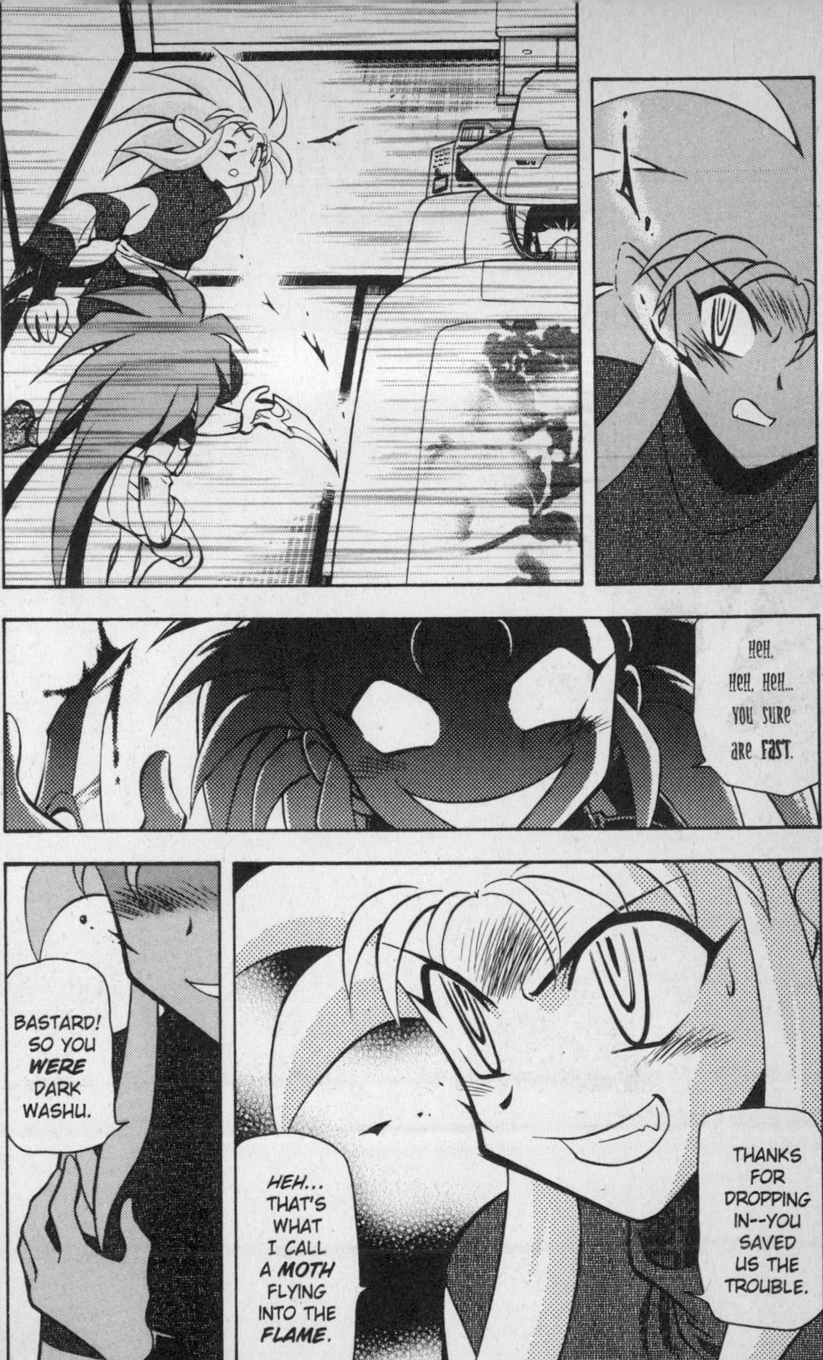
HEH, HEH, HEH... YOU SURE ARE FAST.
BASTARD! SO YOU WERE DARK WASHU.
HEH... THAT'S WHAT I CALL A MOTH FLYING INTO THE FLAME.
THANKS FOR DROPPING IN--YOU SAVED US THE TROUBLE.

I'LL SHOW *YOU*, YOU--

Fwmsh!?

fs SSSHHTSH

GYAAAH!

AH! THERE WE GO--IT FINALLY STARTED WORKING. DON'T BOTHER TRYING TO REGENERATE THAT...HEH!

UNH... BUT THIS... THIS IS JUST A FLESH WOUND...

HARDLY! I INJECTED YOU WITH A VIRUS THAT TARGETS YOUR REGENERATIVE ENZYMES. HEH. HEH. HEH...

SAY HELLO TO WASHU FOR ME-- WHEN YOU SEE HER! HEH...

WSH

WSH

WSH

WSH

WSH

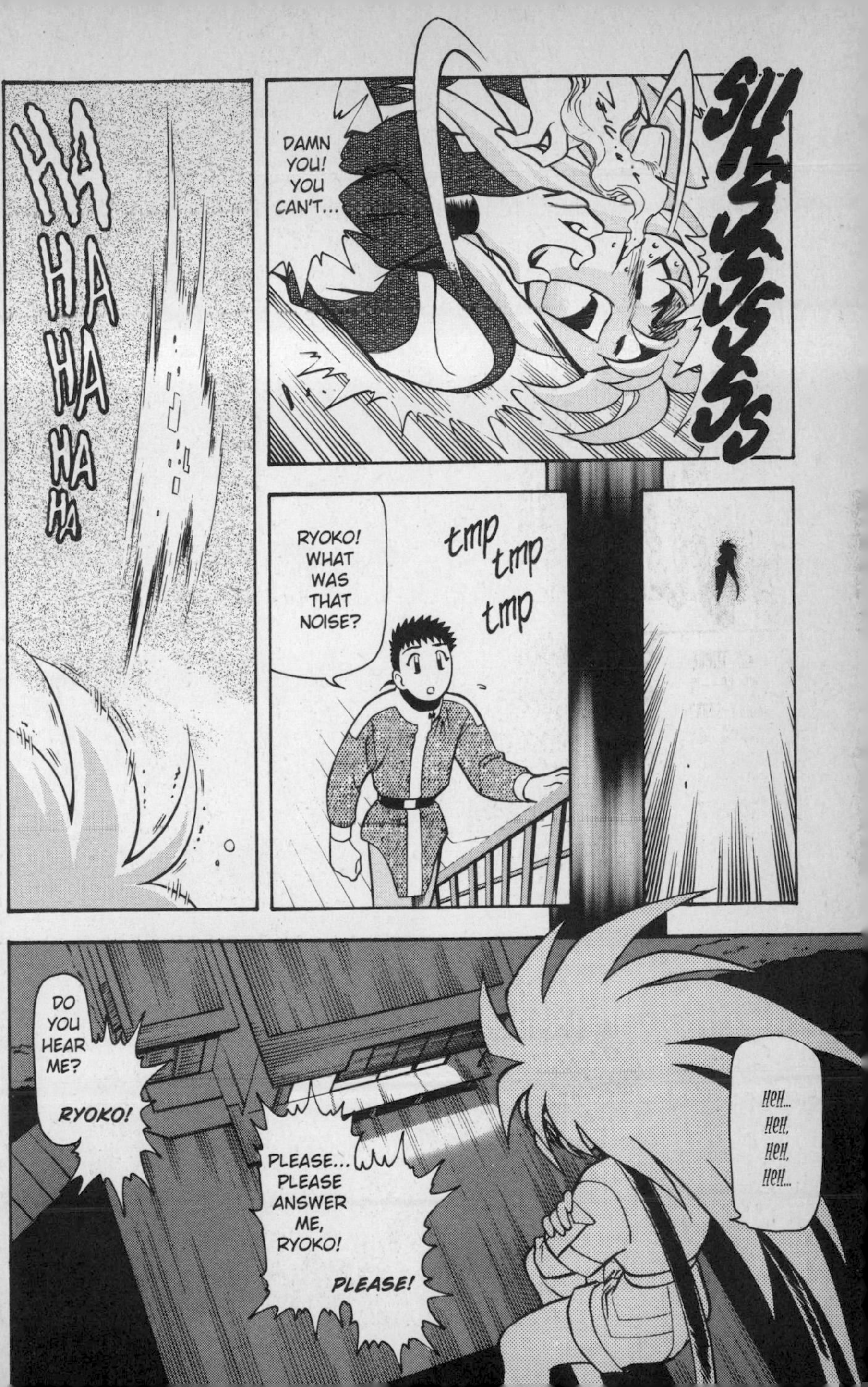

HA HA HA HA HA
DAMN YOU! YOU CAN'T...
SHSSSSSS
RYOKO! WHAT WAS THAT NOISE?
tmp tmp tmp
DO YOU HEAR ME?
RYOKO!
PLEASE... PLEASE ANSWER ME, RYOKO!
PLEASE!
HEH... HEH, HEH, HEH...

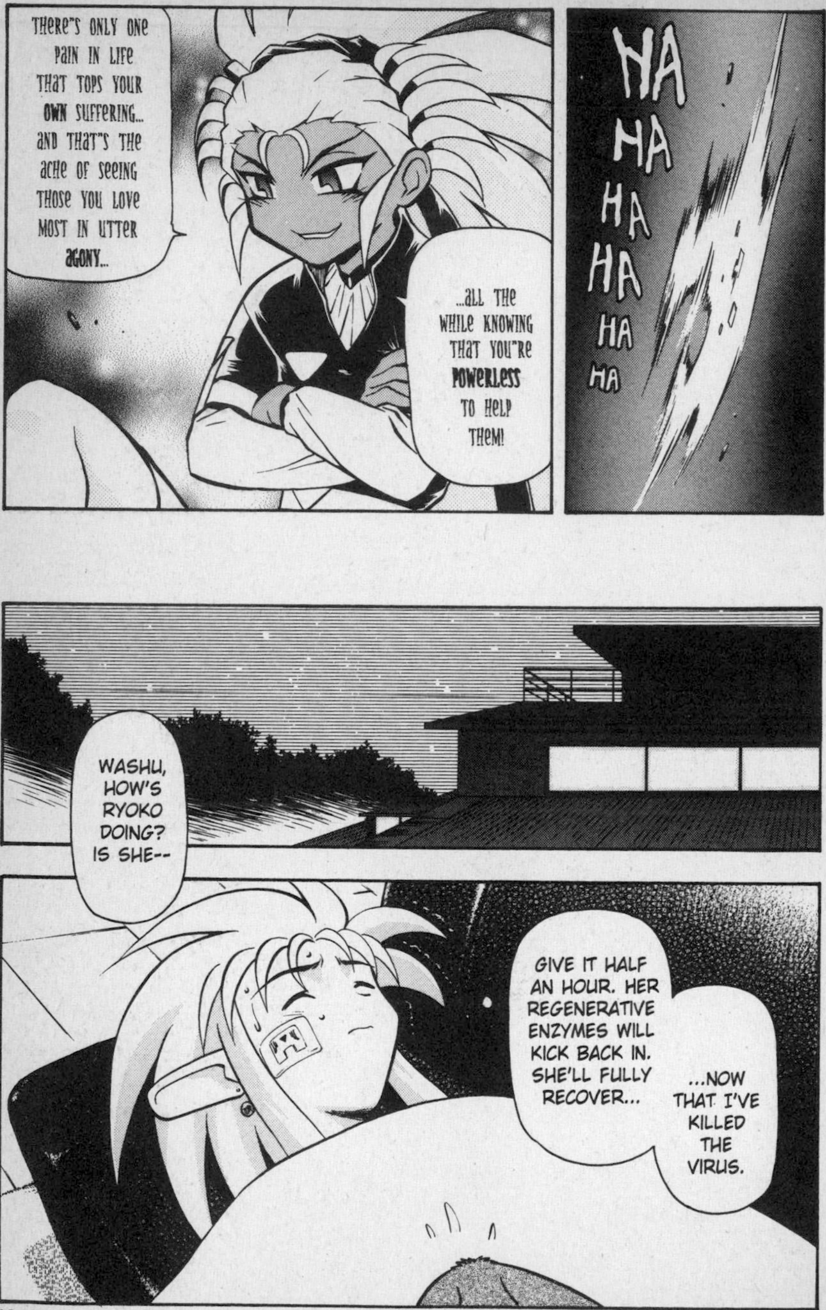

THERE'S ONLY ONE PAIN IN LIFE THAT TOPS YOUR OWN SUFFERING... AND THAT'S THE ACHE OF SEEING THOSE YOU LOVE MOST IN UTTER AGONY...
...ALL THE WHILE KNOWING THAT YOU'RE POWERLESS TO HELP THEM!
HA HA HA HA HA HA HA
WASHU, HOW'S RYOKO DOING? IS SHE--
GIVE IT HALF AN HOUR. HER REGENERATIVE ENZYMES WILL KICK BACK IN. SHE'LL FULLY RECOVER...
...NOW THAT I'VE KILLED THE VIRUS.

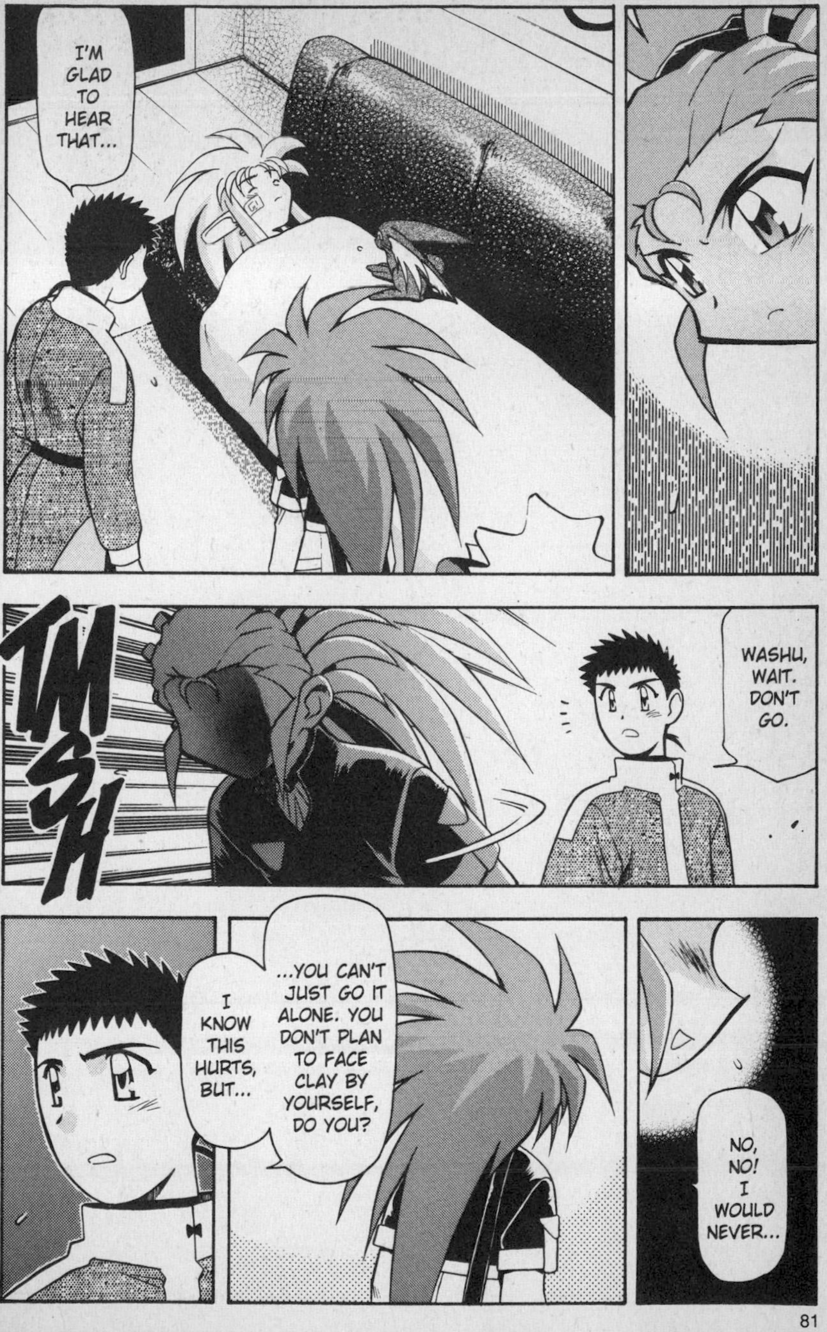
I'M GLAD TO HEAR THAT...
TMSH
WASHU, WAIT. DON'T GO.
I KNOW THIS HURTS, BUT...
...YOU CAN'T JUST GO IT ALONE. YOU DON'T PLAN TO FACE CLAY BY YOURSELF, DO YOU?
NO, NO! I WOULD NEVER...

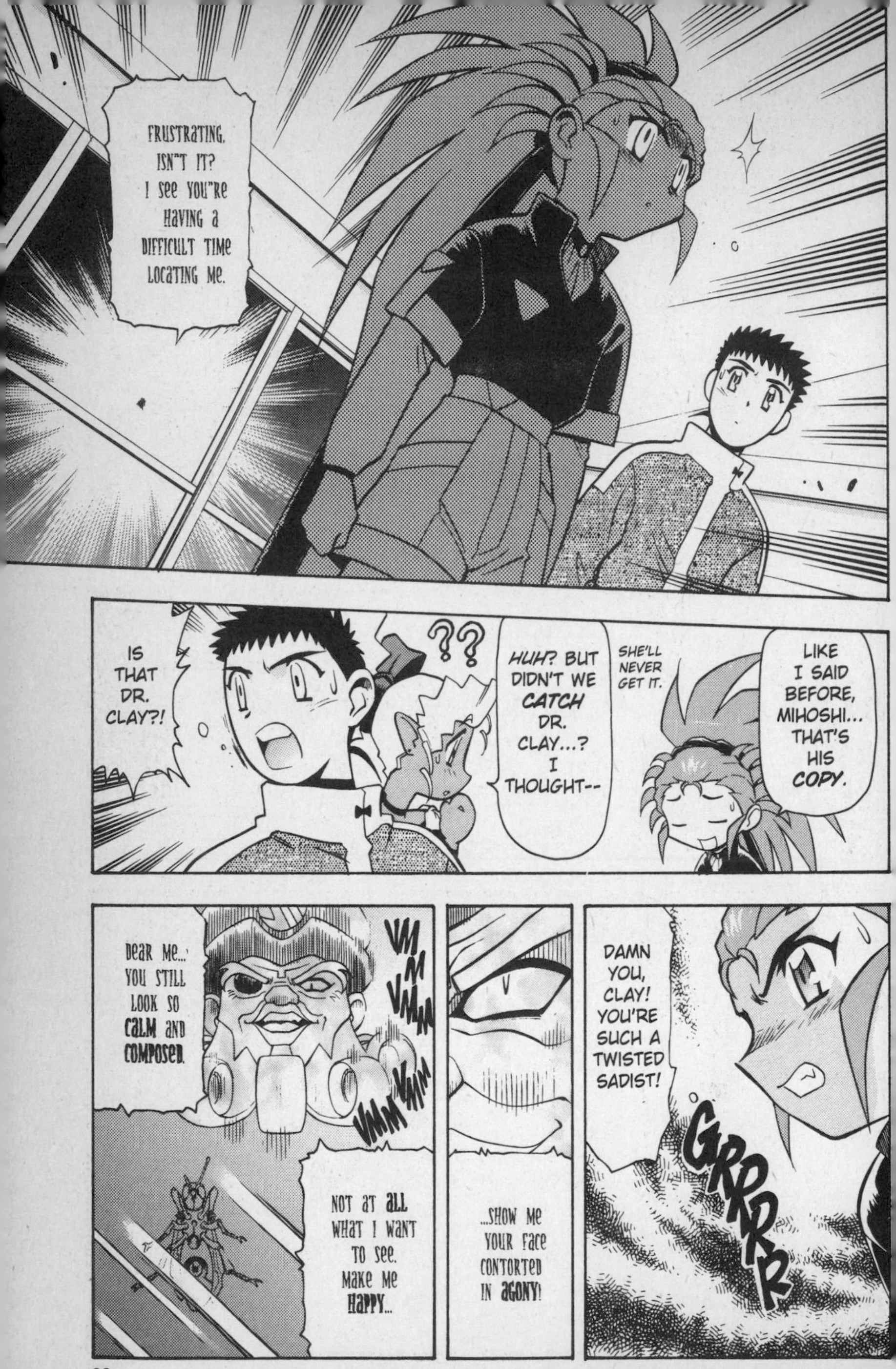

FRUSTRATING, ISN'T IT? I SEE YOU'RE HAVING A DIFFICULT TIME LOCATING ME.
IS THAT DR. CLAY?!
??
HUH? BUT DIDN'T WE CATCH DR. CLAY...? I THOUGHT--
SHE'LL NEVER GET IT.
LIKE I SAID BEFORE, MIHOSHI... THAT'S HIS COPY.
DEAR ME... YOU STILL LOOK SO CALM AND COMPOSED.
VMM VMM VMM
VMM VMM
NOT AT ALL WHAT I WANT TO SEE. MAKE ME HAPPY...
...SHOW ME YOUR FACE CONTORTED IN AGONY!
DAMN YOU, CLAY! YOU'RE SUCH A TWISTED SADIST!
GRRRR

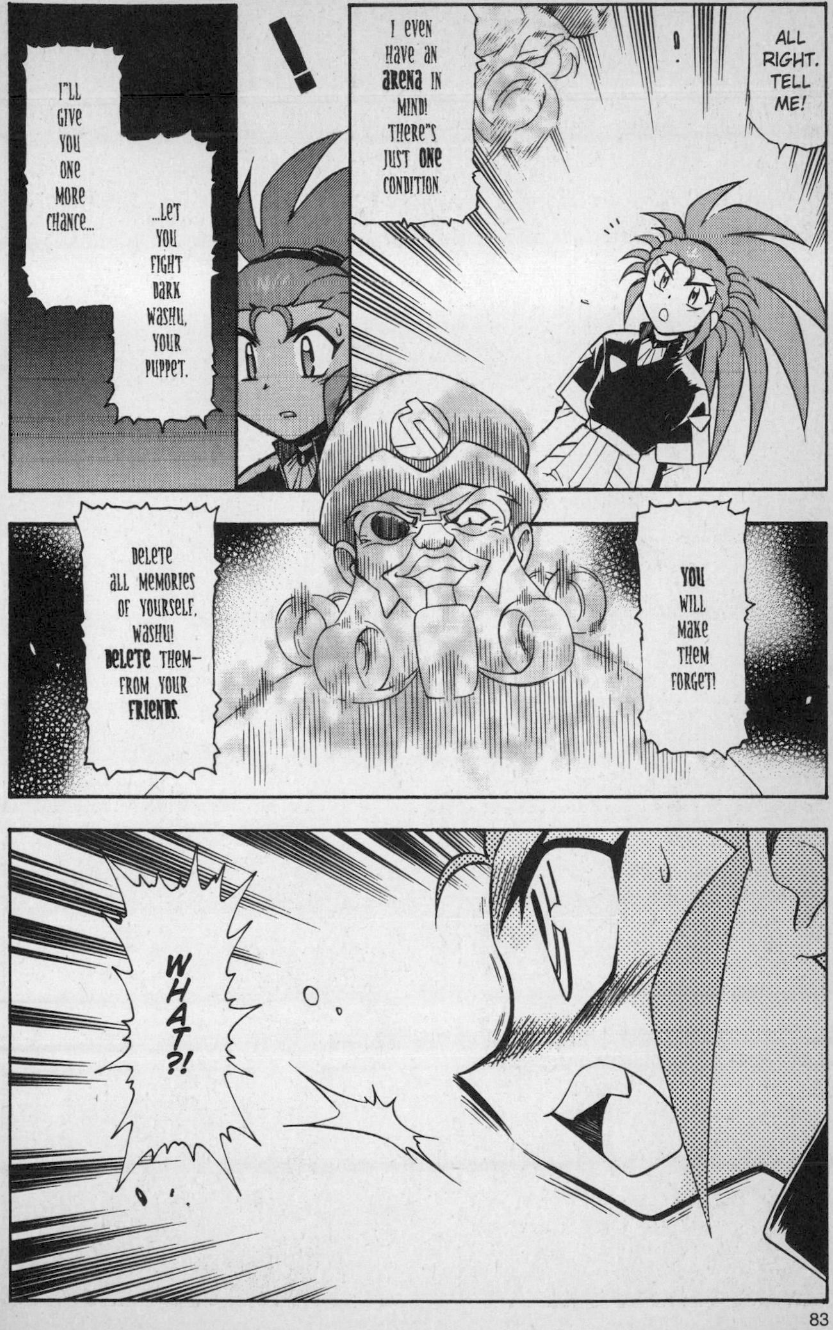

I'LL GIVE YOU ONE MORE CHANCE...
...LET YOU FIGHT DARK WASHU, YOUR PUPPET.
!
I EVEN HAVE AN ARENA IN MIND! THERE'S JUST ONE CONDITION.
!
ALL RIGHT. TELL ME!
DELETE ALL MEMORIES OF YOURSELF, WASHU! DELETE THEM--FROM YOUR FRIENDS.
YOU WILL MAKE THEM FORGET!
WHAT?!

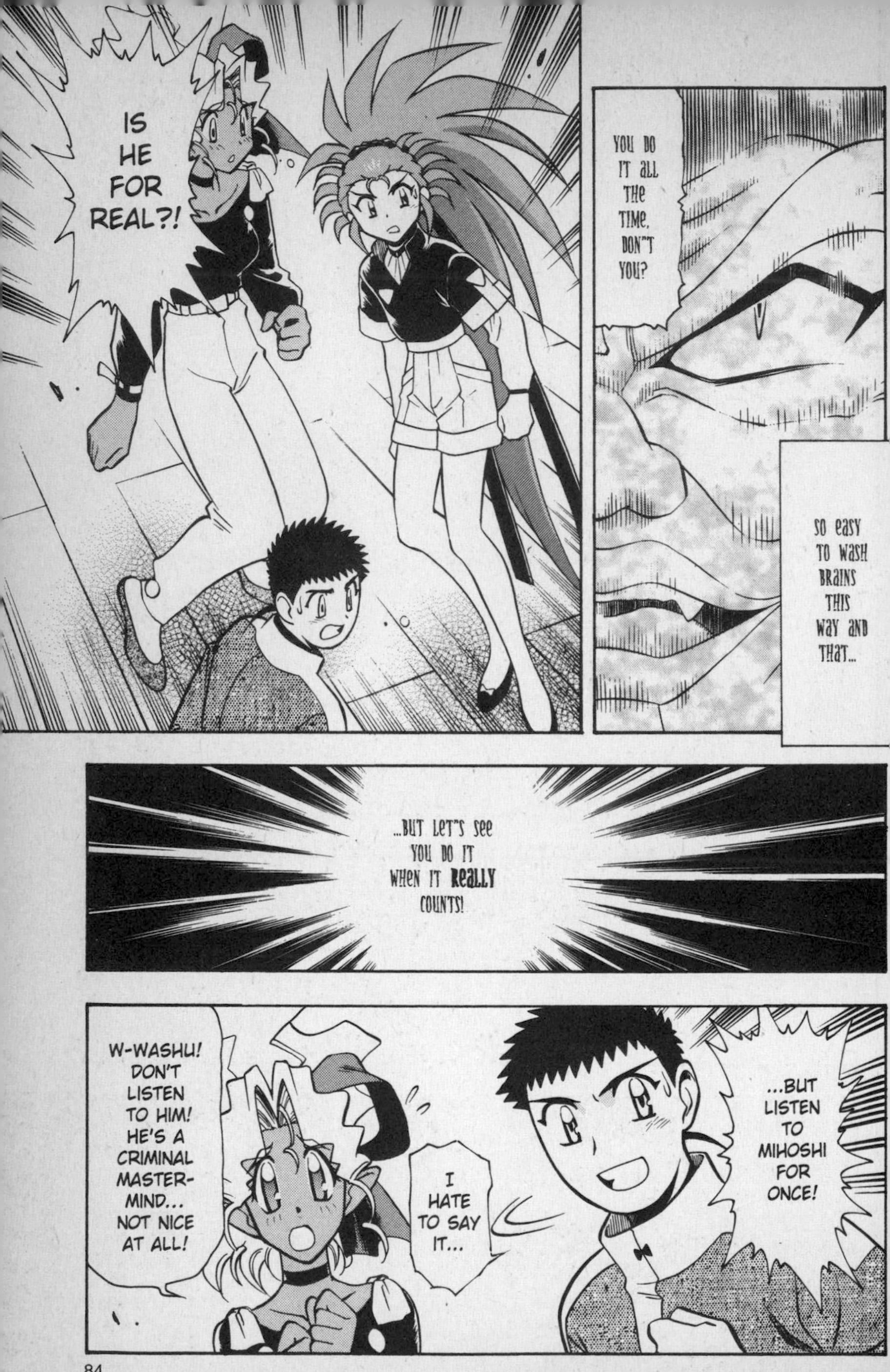
IS HE FOR REAL?!
YOU DO IT ALL THE TIME, DON'T YOU?
SO EASY TO WASH BRAINS THIS WAY AND THAT...
...BUT LET'S SEE YOU DO IT WHEN IT REALLY COUNTS!
W-WASHU! DON'T LISTEN TO HIM! HE'S A CRIMINAL MASTER-MIND... NOT NICE AT ALL!
I HATE TO SAY IT...
...BUT LISTEN TO MIHOSHI FOR ONCE!

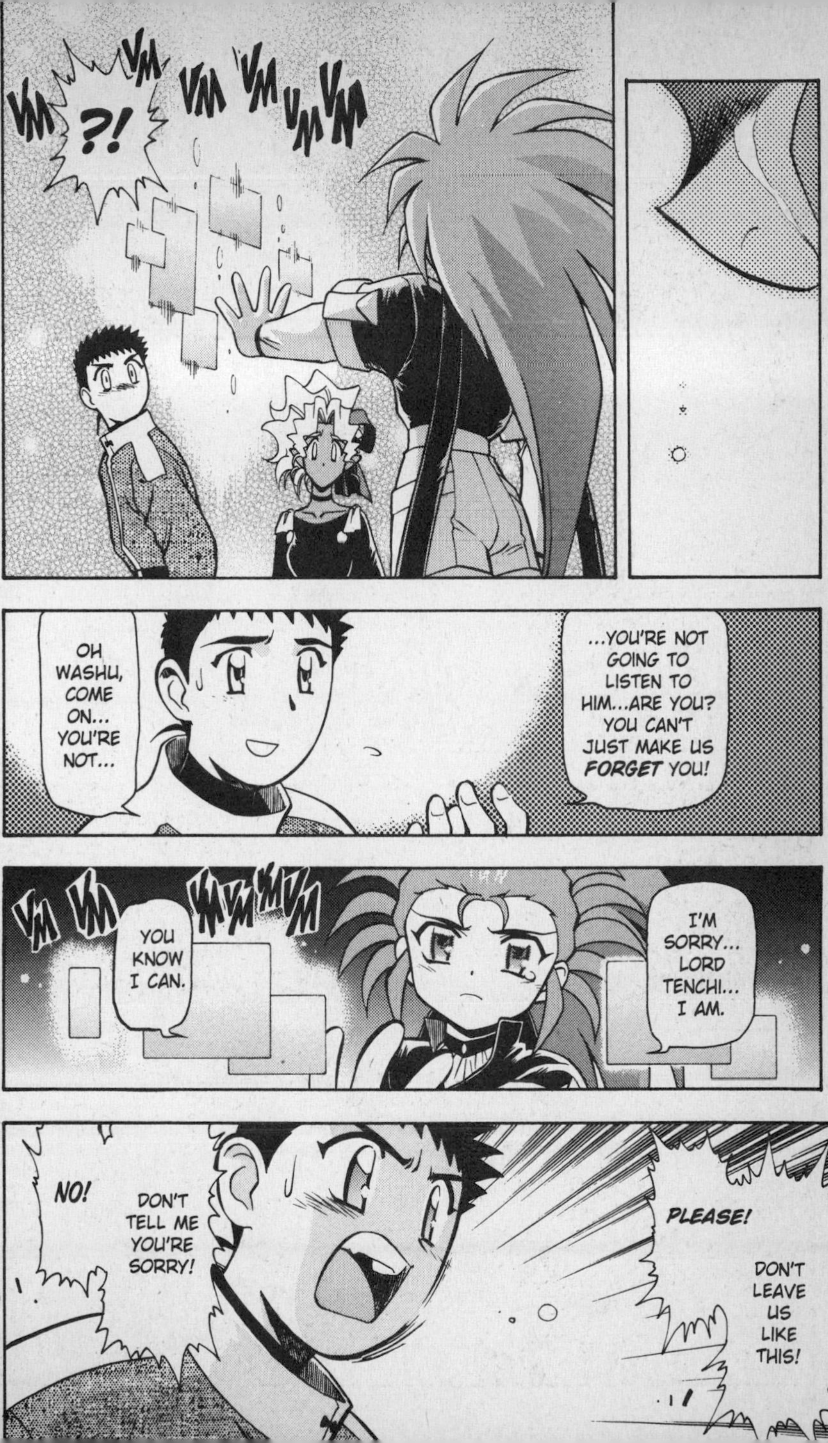
VM
?!
VM
VM
VM
VM
VM
OH WASHU, COME ON... YOU'RE NOT...
...YOU'RE NOT GOING TO LISTEN TO HIM...ARE YOU? YOU CAN'T JUST MAKE US FORGET YOU!
VM VM VMVMVMVM
YOU KNOW I CAN.
I'M SORRY... LORD TENCHI... I AM.
NO!
DON'T TELL ME YOU'RE SORRY!
PLEASE!
DON'T LEAVE US LIKE THIS!

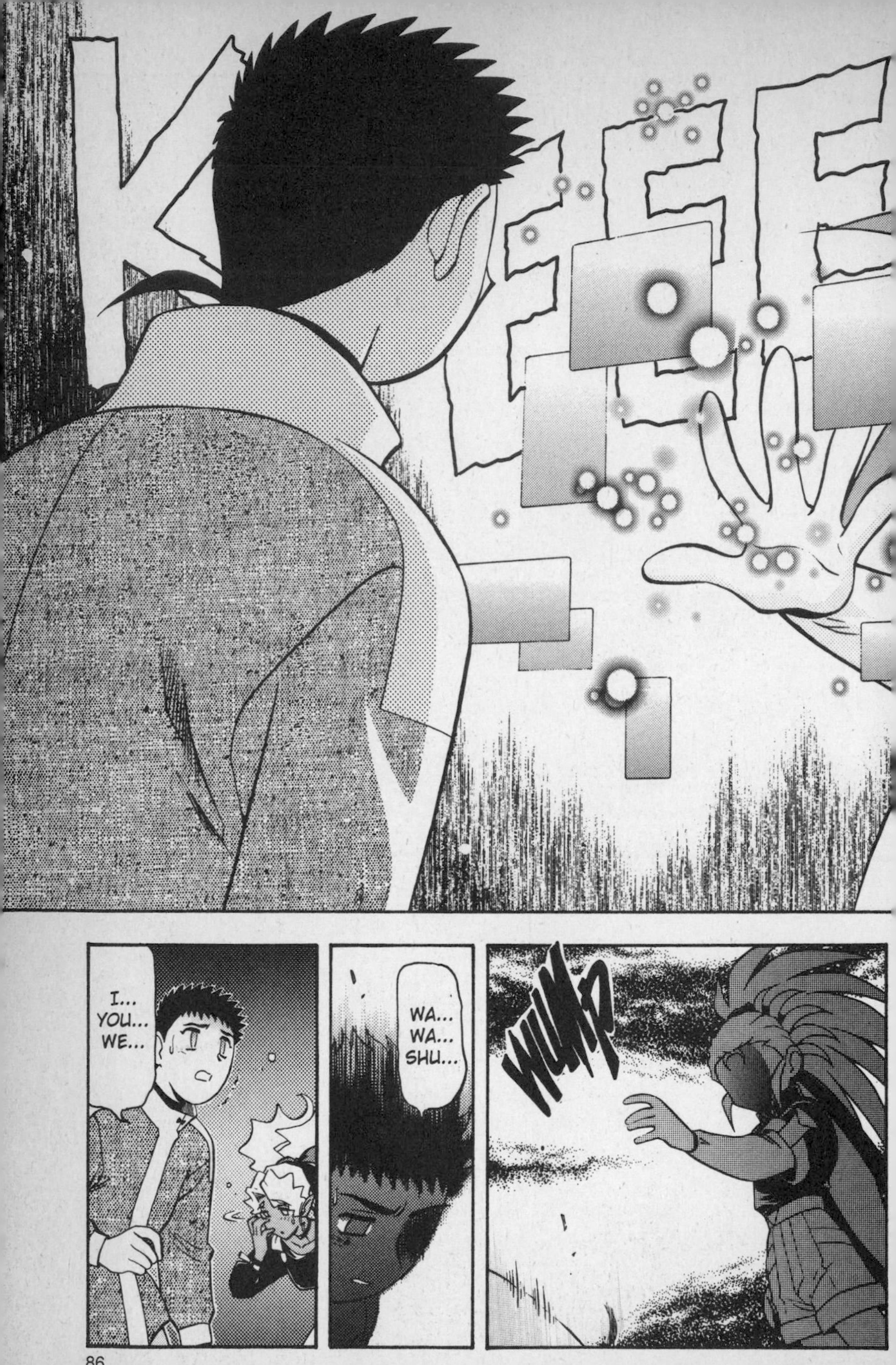
I... YOU... WE...
WA... WA... SHU...
WUMP

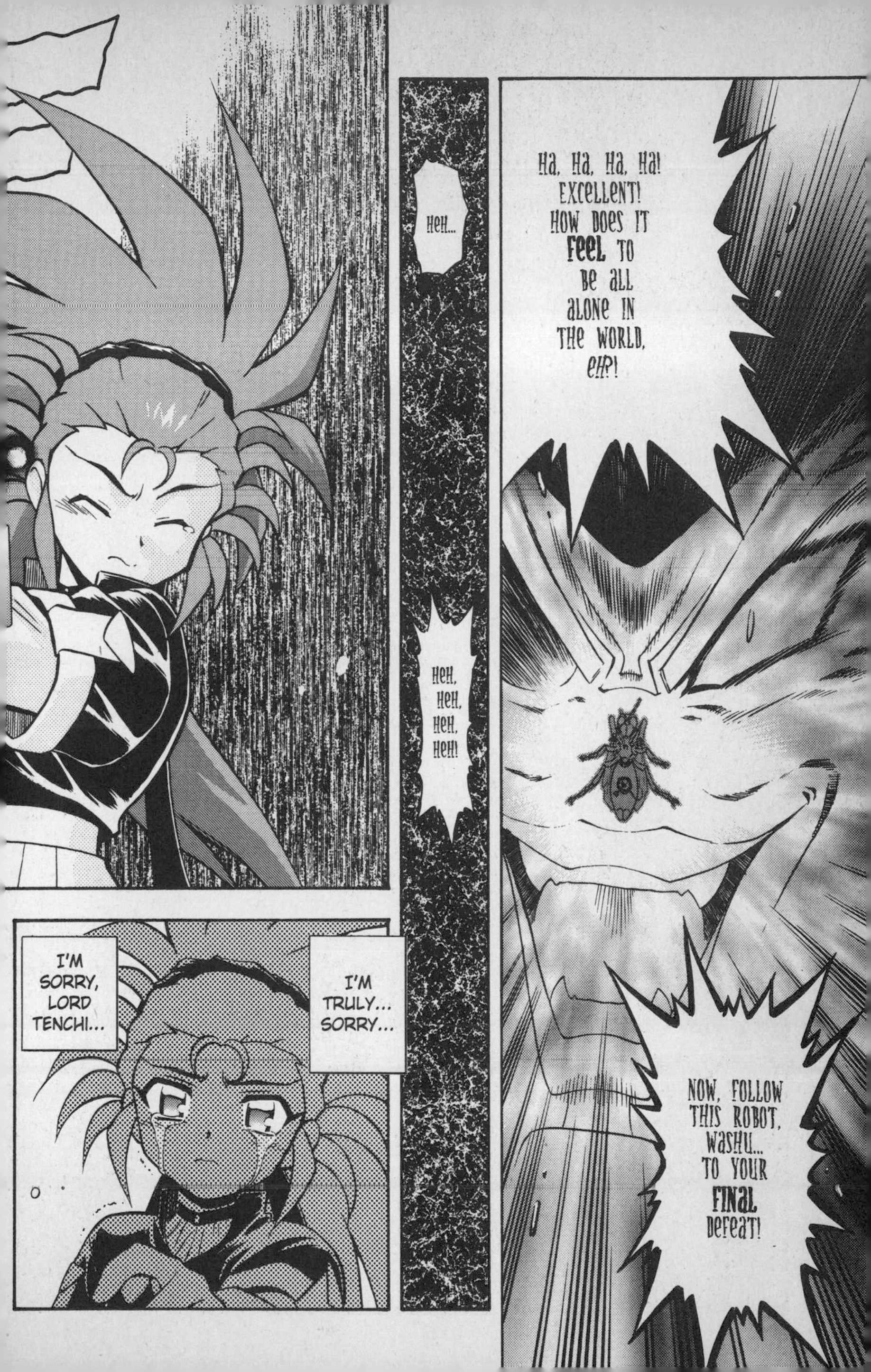

I'M SORRY, LORD TENCHI...
I'M TRULY... SORRY...
HEH...
HEH, HEH, HEH, HEH!
HA, HA, HA, HA! EXCELLENT! HOW DOES IT FEEL TO BE ALL ALONE IN THE WORLD, EH?!
NOW, FOLLOW THIS ROBOT, WASHU... TO YOUR FINAL DEFEAT!

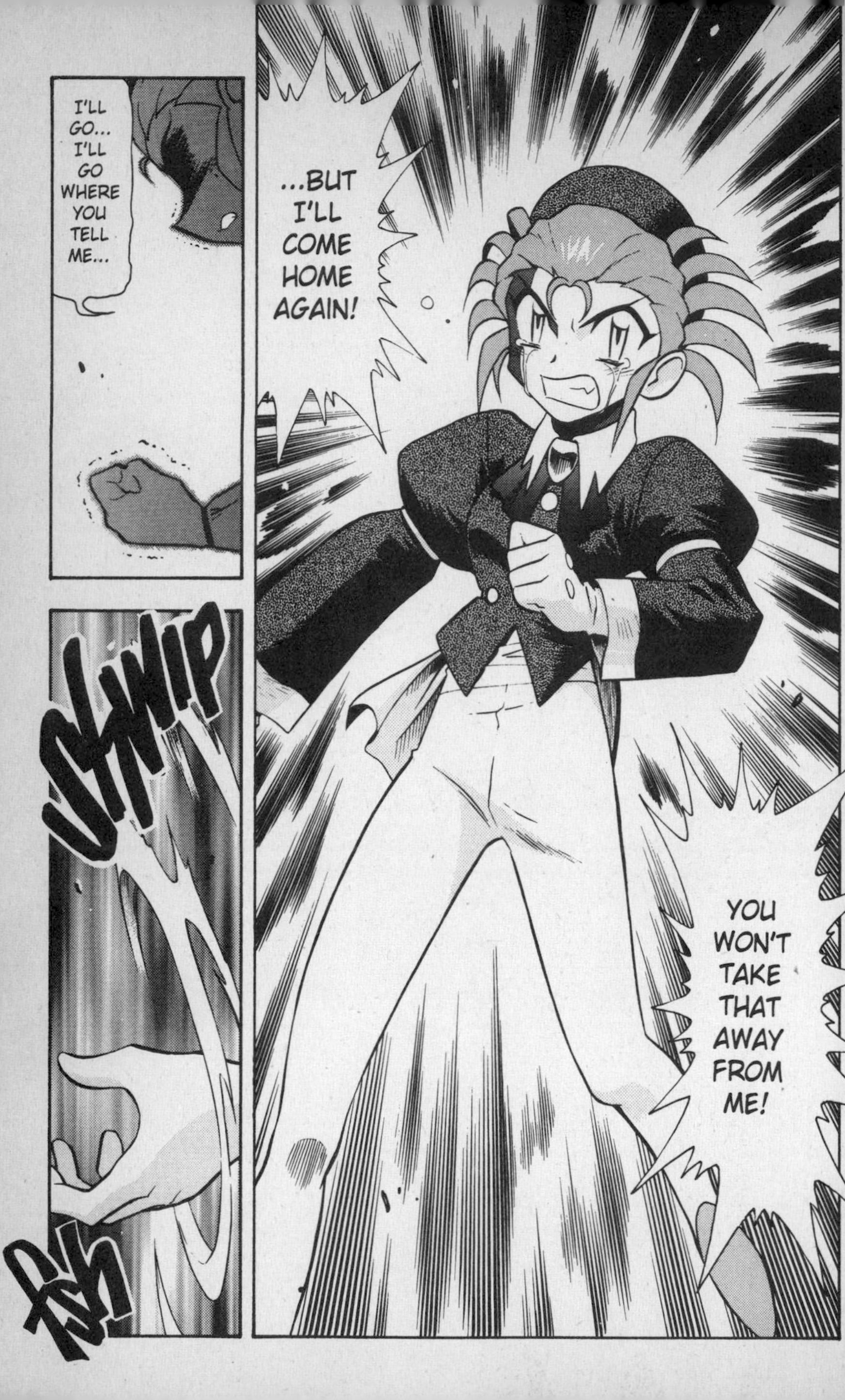
I'LL GO... I'LL GO WHERE YOU TELL ME...
SWHIP
FSH
...BUT I'LL COME HOME AGAIN!
YOU WON'T TAKE THAT AWAY FROM ME!

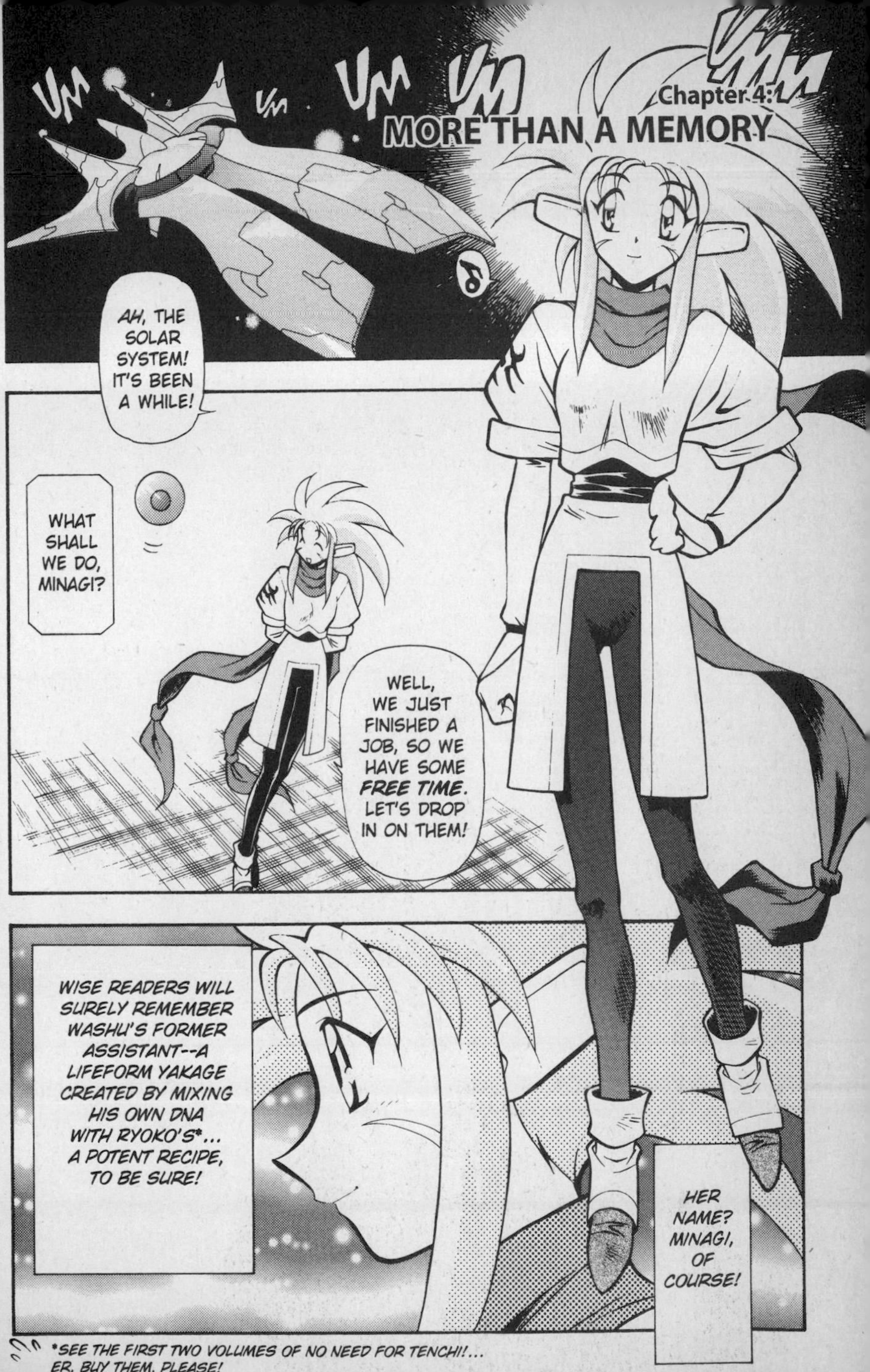
UM
UM
UM
UM
UMM
Chapter 4:
MORE THAN A MEMORY
AH, THE SOLAR SYSTEM! IT'S BEEN A WHILE!
WHAT SHALL WE DO, MINAGI?
WELL, WE JUST FINISHED A JOB, SO WE HAVE SOME FREE TIME. LET'S DROP IN ON THEM!
WISE READERS WILL SURELY REMEMBER WASHU'S FORMER ASSISTANT--A LIFEFORM YAKAGE CREATED BY MIXING HIS OWN DNA WITH RYOKO'S*... A POTENT RECIPE, TO BE SURE!
HER NAME? MINAGI, OF COURSE!

*SEE THE FIRST TWO VOLUMES OF NO NEED FOR TENCHI!... ER, BUY THEM, PLEASE!

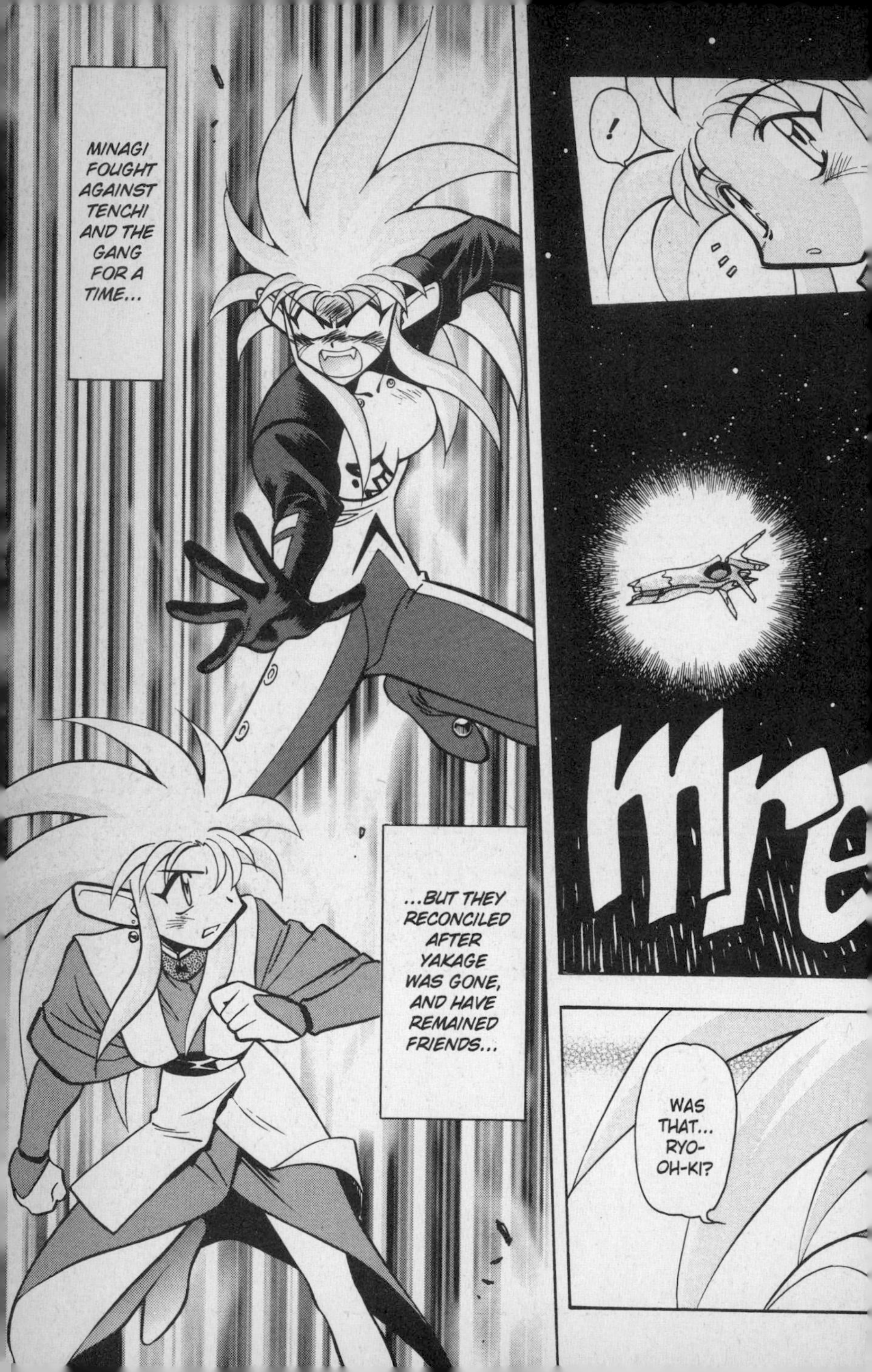
MINAGI FOUGHT AGAINST TENCHI AND THE GANG FOR A TIME...
...BUT THEY RECONCILED AFTER YAKAGE WAS GONE, AND HAVE REMAINED FRIENDS...
!
WAS THAT... RYO-OH-KI?

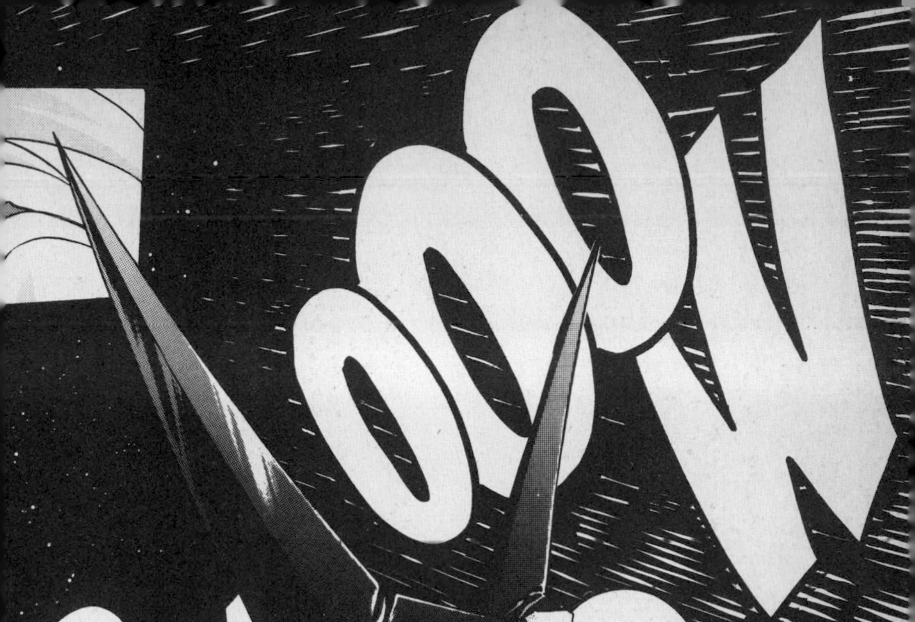
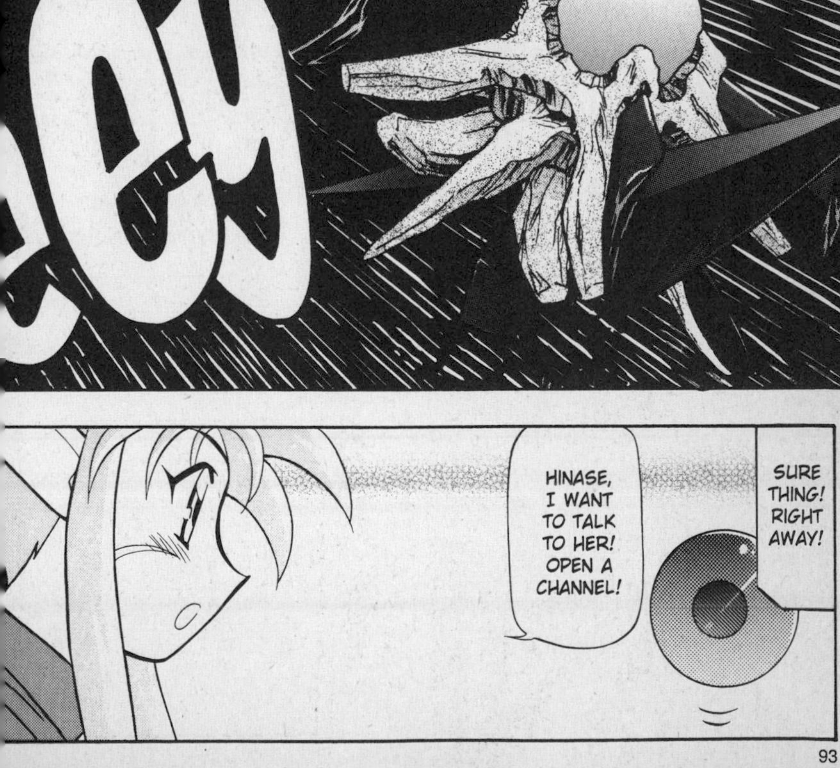
HINASE, I WANT TO TALK TO HER! OPEN A CHANNEL!
SURE THING! RIGHT AWAY!

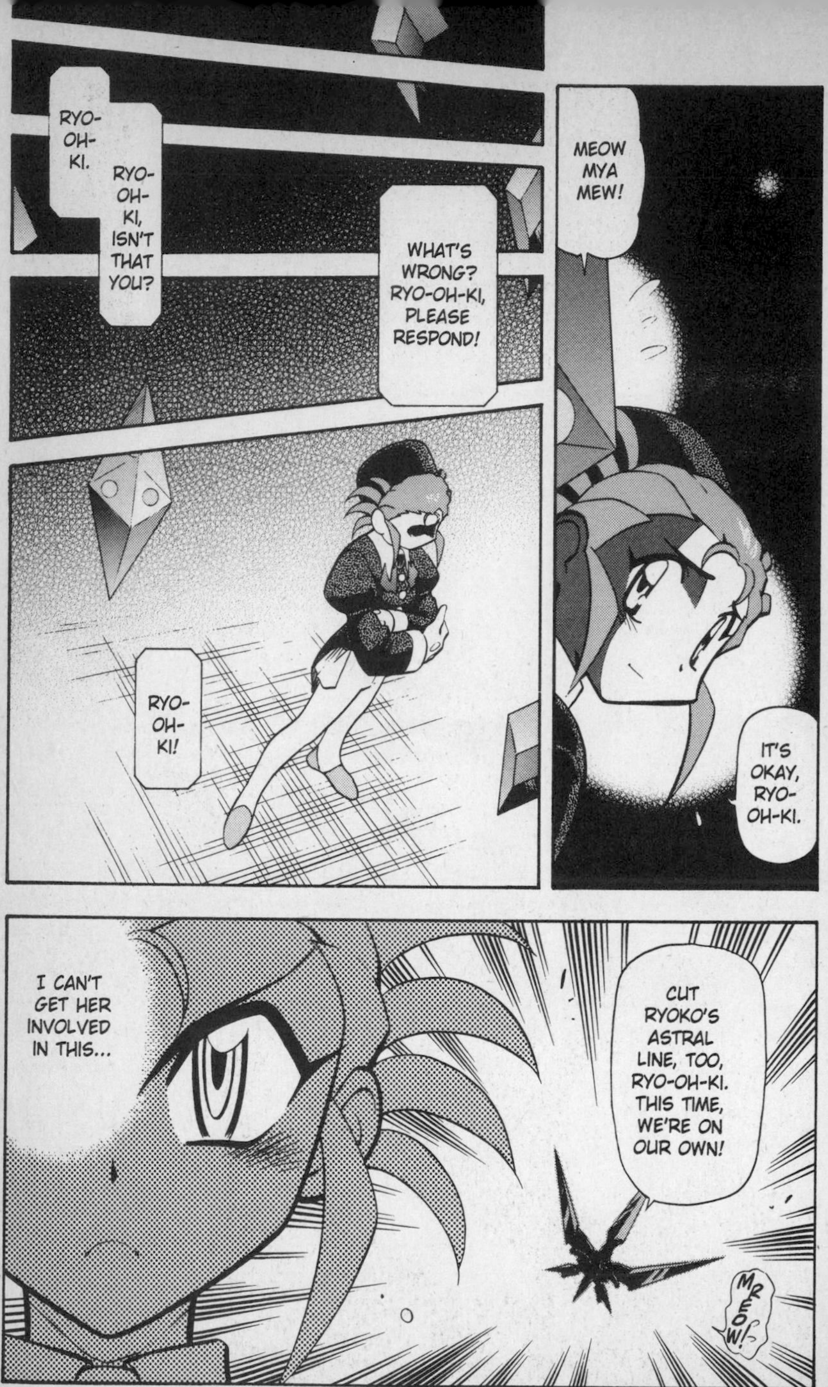
RYO-OH-KI.
RYO-OH-KI, ISN'T THAT YOU?
WHAT'S WRONG? RYO-OH-KI, PLEASE RESPOND!
RYO-OH-KI!
MEOW MYA MEW!
IT'S OKAY, RYO-OH-KI.
I CAN'T GET HER INVOLVED IN THIS...
CUT RYOKO'S ASTRAL LINE, TOO, RYO-OH-KI. THIS TIME, WE'RE ON OUR OWN!
MREOW!

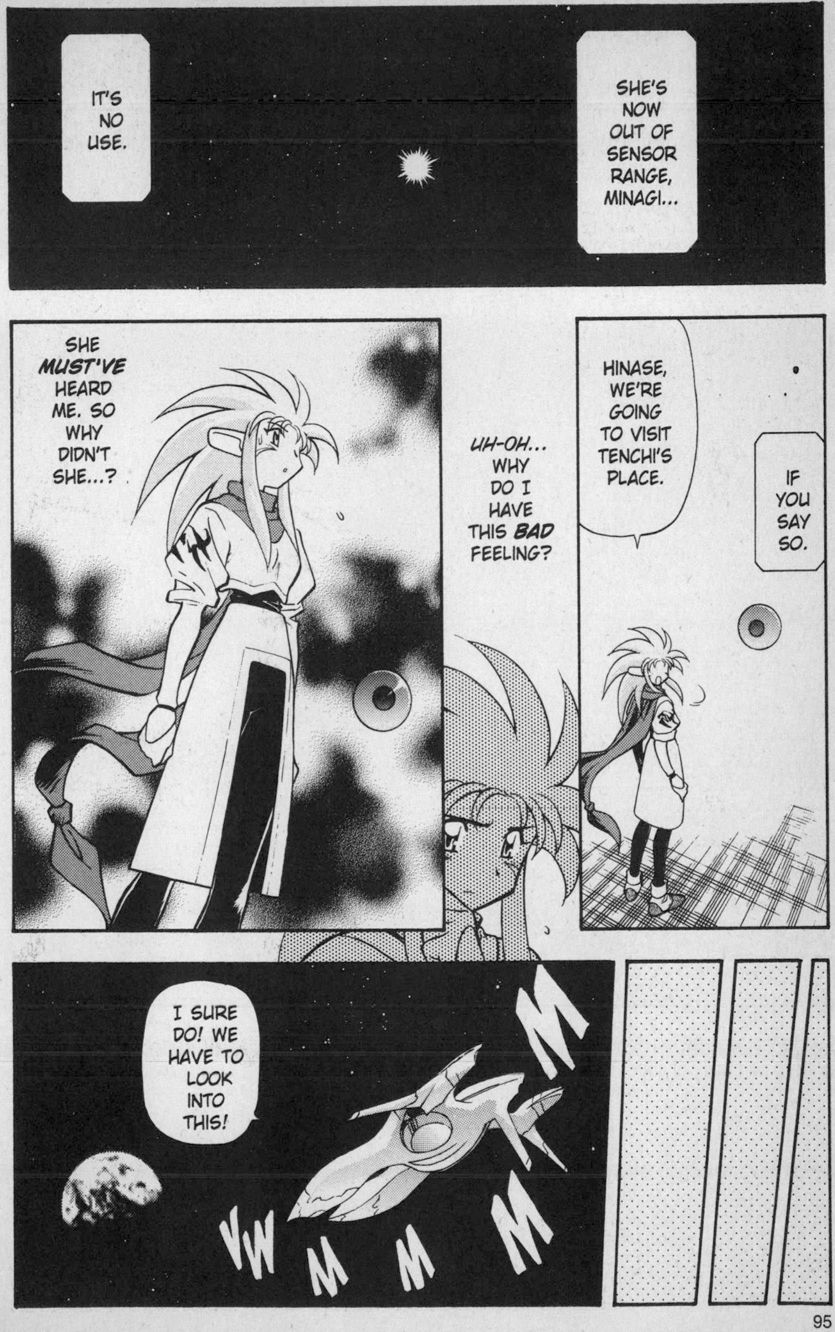
IT'S NO USE.
SHE'S NOW OUT OF SENSOR RANGE, MINAGI...
SHE *MUST'VE* HEARD ME. SO WHY DIDN'T SHE...?
UH-OH... WHY DO I HAVE THIS *BAD* FEELING?
HINASE, WE'RE GOING TO VISIT TENCHI'S PLACE.
IF YOU SAY SO.
I SURE DO! WE HAVE TO LOOK INTO THIS!
VWMMMMMM

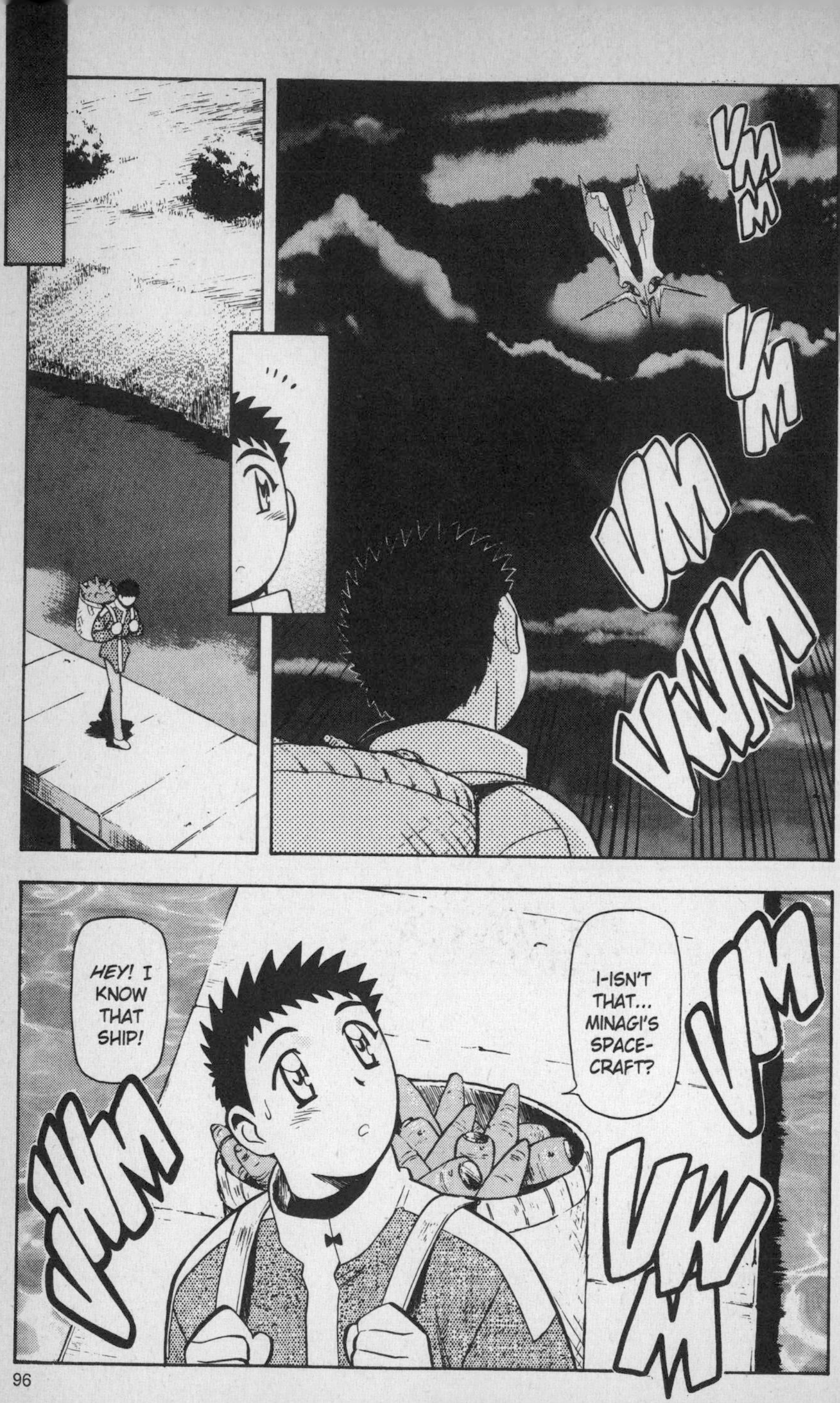
HEY! I KNOW THAT SHIP!
I-ISN'T THAT... MINAGI'S SPACE-CRAFT?

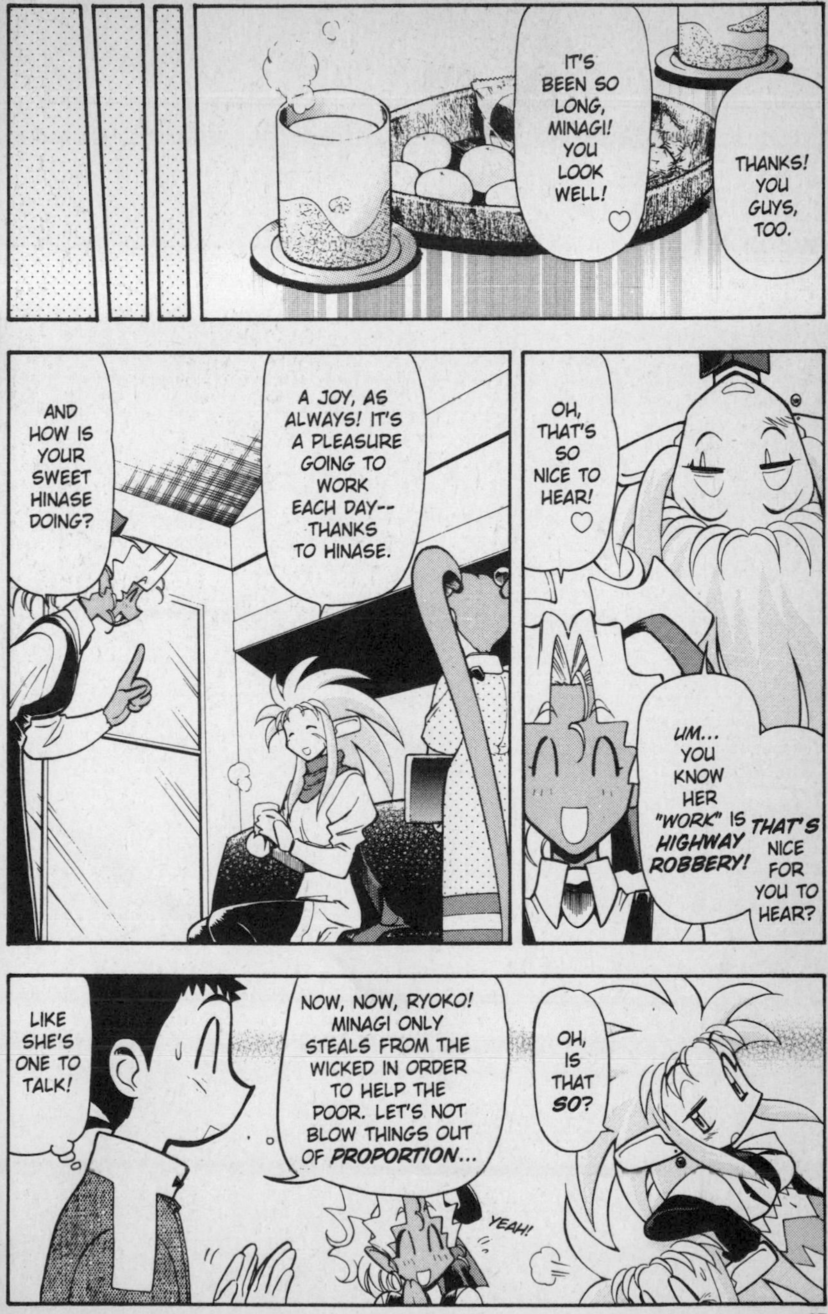
IT'S BEEN SO LONG, MINAGI! YOU LOOK WELL! ♡
THANKS! YOU GUYS, TOO.
AND HOW IS YOUR SWEET HINASE DOING?
A JOY, AS ALWAYS! IT'S A PLEASURE GOING TO WORK EACH DAY--THANKS TO HINASE.
OH, THAT'S SO NICE TO HEAR! ♡
UM... YOU KNOW HER "WORK" IS *HIGHWAY ROBBERY!* *THAT'S* NICE FOR YOU TO HEAR?
LIKE SHE'S ONE TO TALK!
NOW, NOW, RYOKO! MINAGI ONLY STEALS FROM THE WICKED IN ORDER TO HELP THE POOR. LET'S NOT BLOW THINGS OUT OF *PROPORTION*...
YEAH!
OH, IS THAT *SO*?

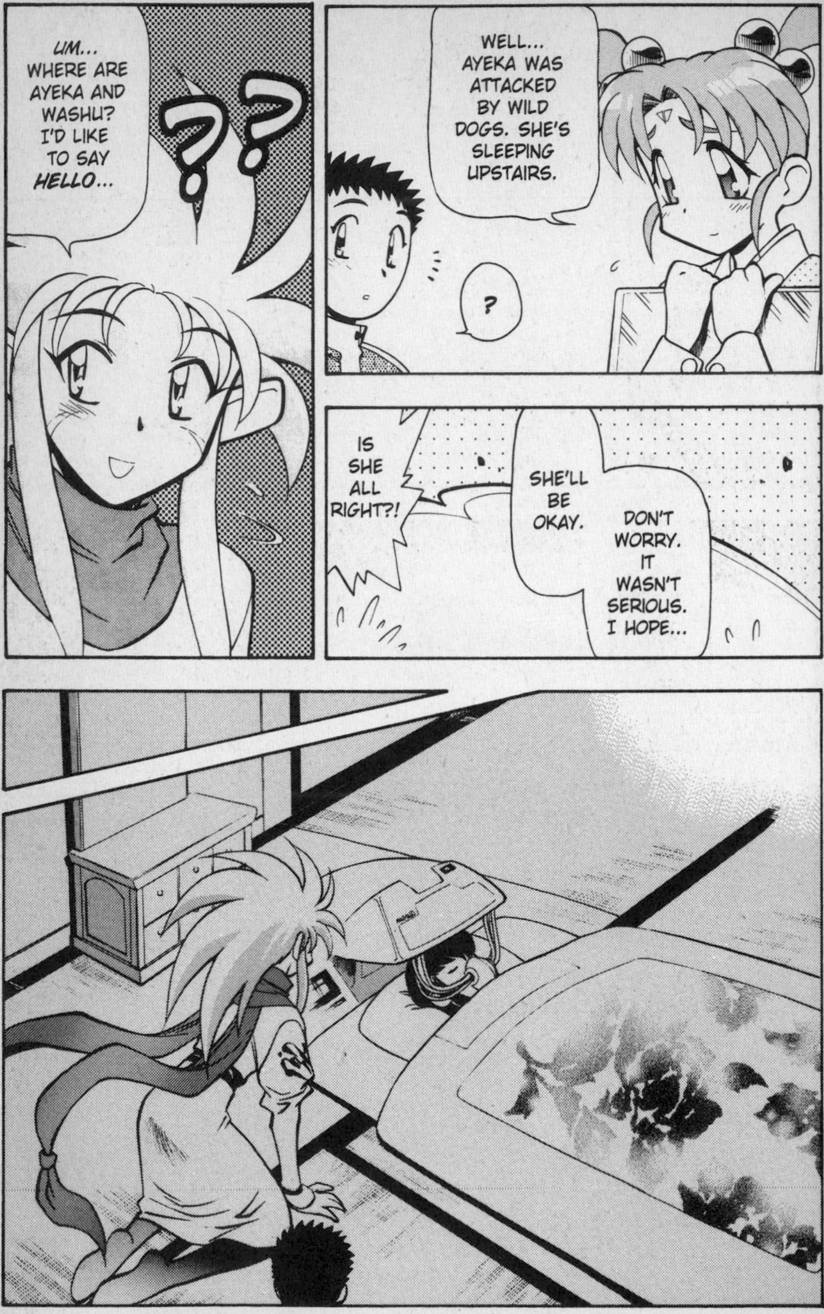
UM... WHERE ARE AYEKA AND WASHU? I'D LIKE TO SAY HELLO...
??
WELL... AYEKA WAS ATTACKED BY WILD DOGS. SHE'S SLEEPING UPSTAIRS.
?
IS SHE ALL RIGHT?!
SHE'LL BE OKAY.
DON'T WORRY. IT WASN'T SERIOUS. I HOPE...

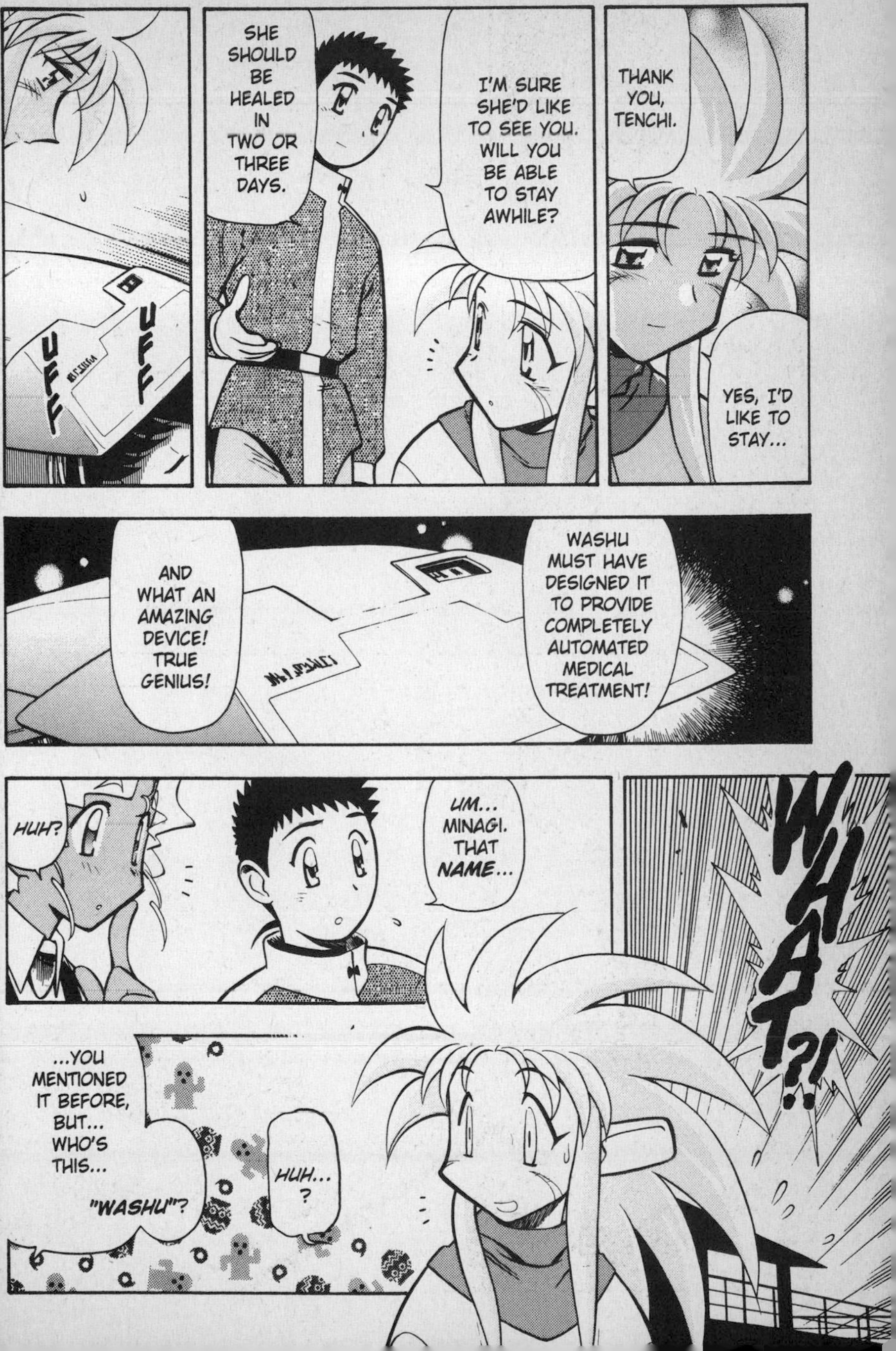
SHE SHOULD BE HEALED IN TWO OR THREE DAYS.
I'M SURE SHE'D LIKE TO SEE YOU. WILL YOU BE ABLE TO STAY AWHILE?
THANK YOU, TENCHI.
YES, I'D LIKE TO STAY...
AND WHAT AN AMAZING DEVICE! TRUE GENIUS!
WASHU MUST HAVE DESIGNED IT TO PROVIDE COMPLETELY AUTOMATED MEDICAL TREATMENT!
HUH?
UM... MINAGI. THAT *NAME*...
WHAT?!
...YOU MENTIONED IT BEFORE, BUT... WHO'S THIS... "WASHU"?
HUH...?

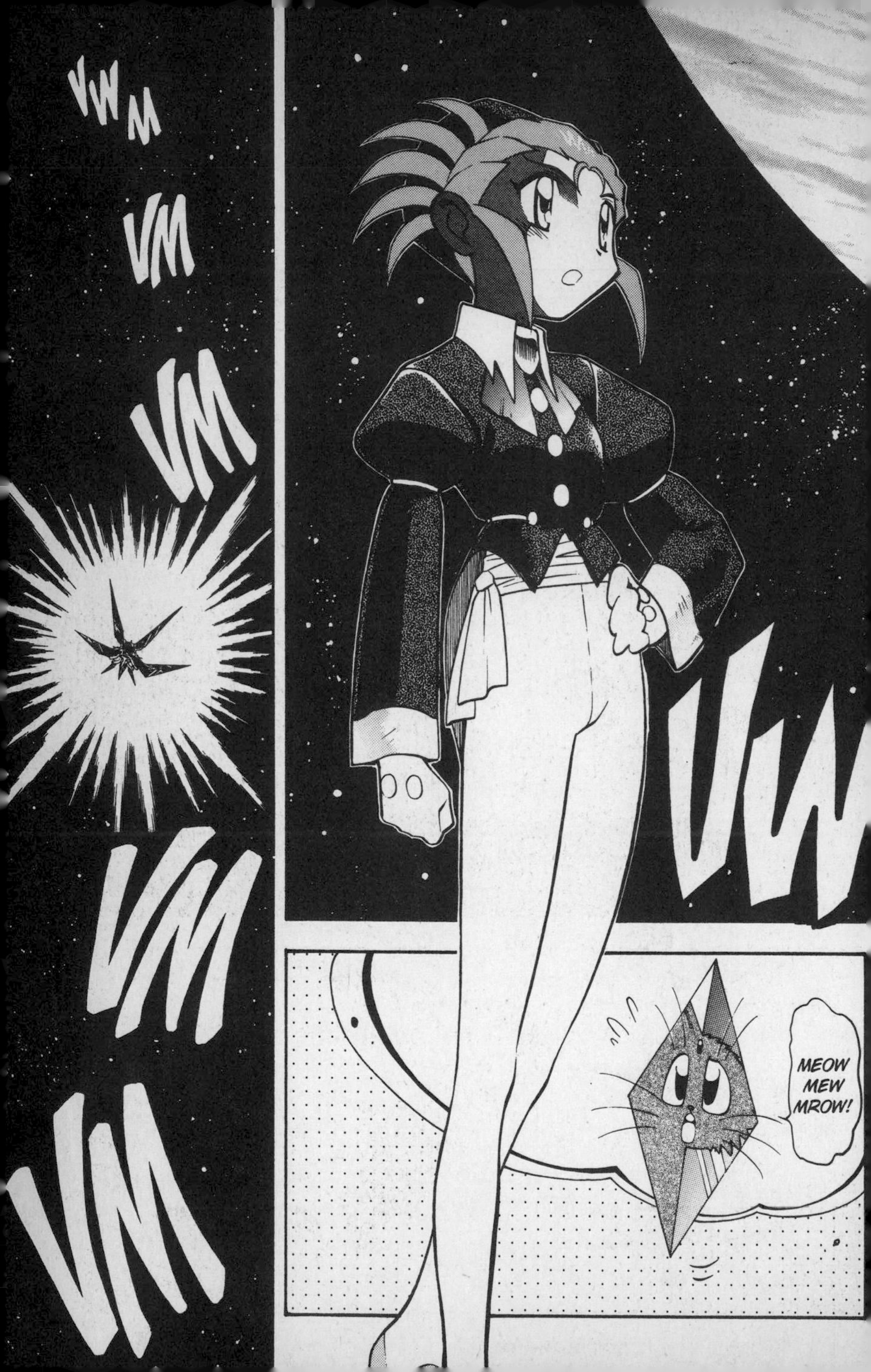
VWM
VM
VM
VM
VM
VW
MEOW MEW MROW!

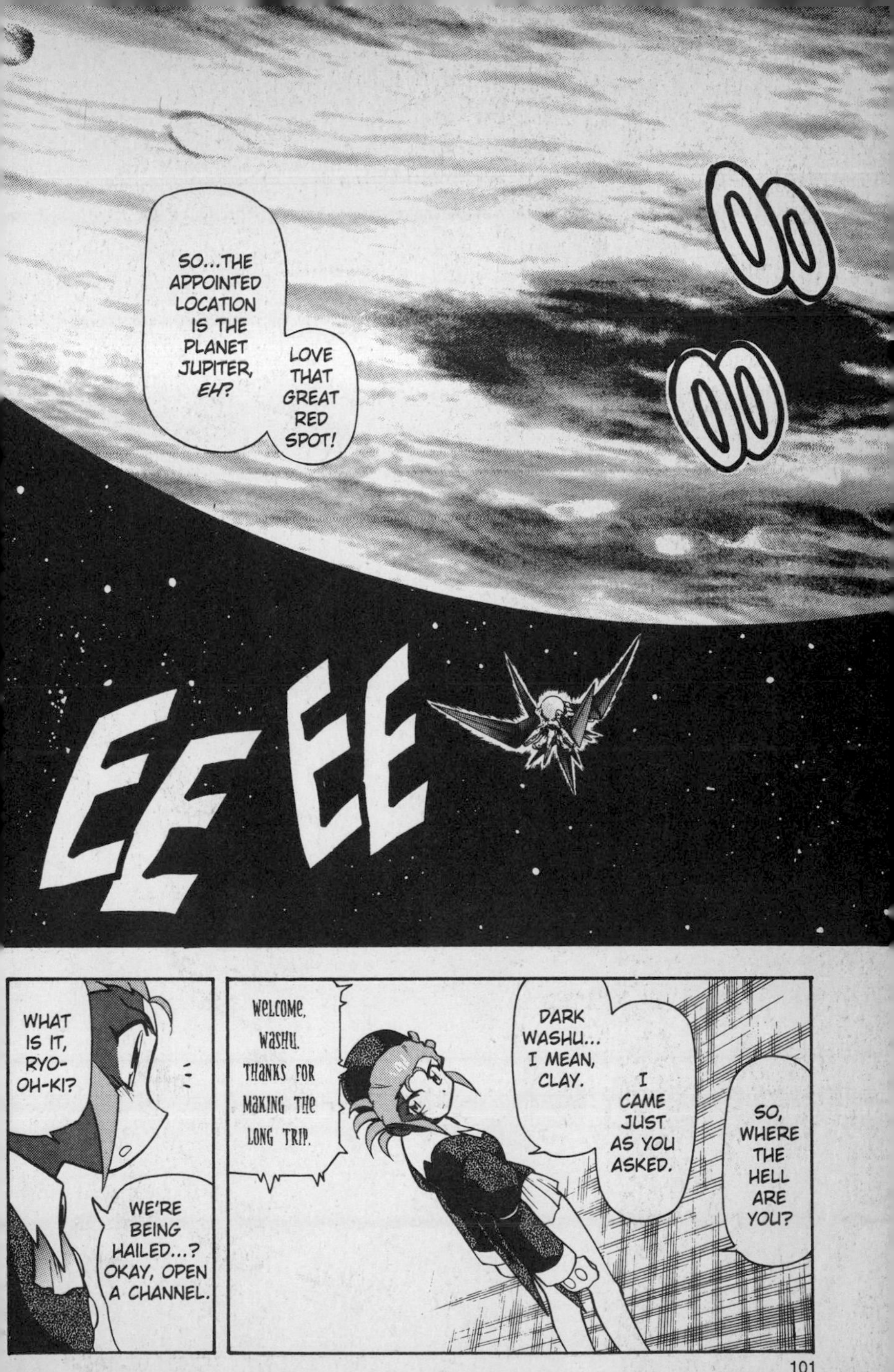
SO...THE APPOINTED LOCATION IS THE PLANET JUPITER, EH?
LOVE THAT GREAT RED SPOT!
OO
OO
EE EE
WHAT IS IT, RYO-OH-KI?
WE'RE BEING HAILED...? OKAY, OPEN A CHANNEL.
Welcome, Washu. Thanks for making the long trip.
DARK WASHU... I MEAN, CLAY.
I CAME JUST AS YOU ASKED.
SO, WHERE THE HELL ARE YOU?

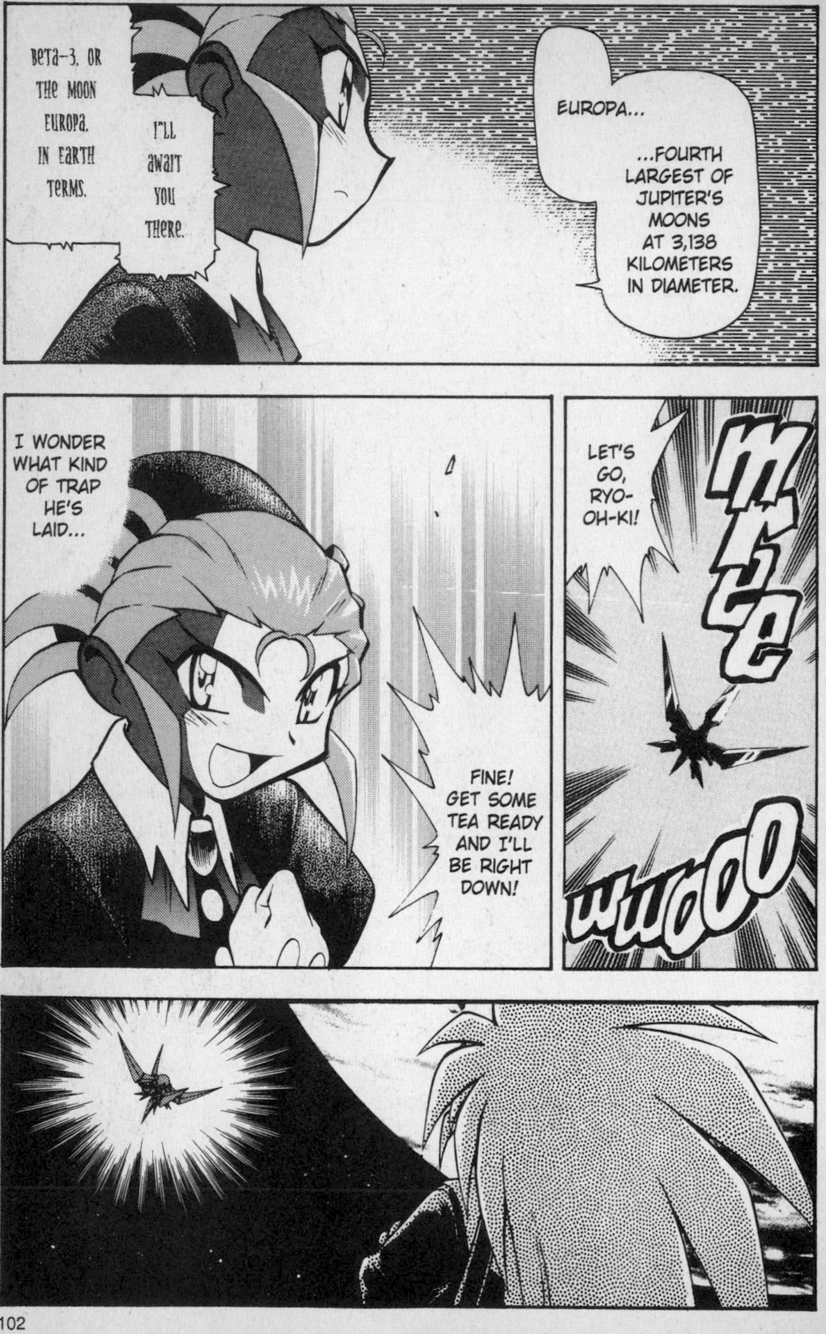
BETA-3, OR THE MOON EUROPA, IN EARTH TERMS.
I'LL AWAIT YOU THERE.
EUROPA...
...FOURTH LARGEST OF JUPITER'S MOONS AT 3,138 KILOMETERS IN DIAMETER.
I WONDER WHAT KIND OF TRAP HE'S LAID...
FINE! GET SOME TEA READY AND I'LL BE RIGHT DOWN!
LET'S GO, RYO-OH-KI!
WUOOOO

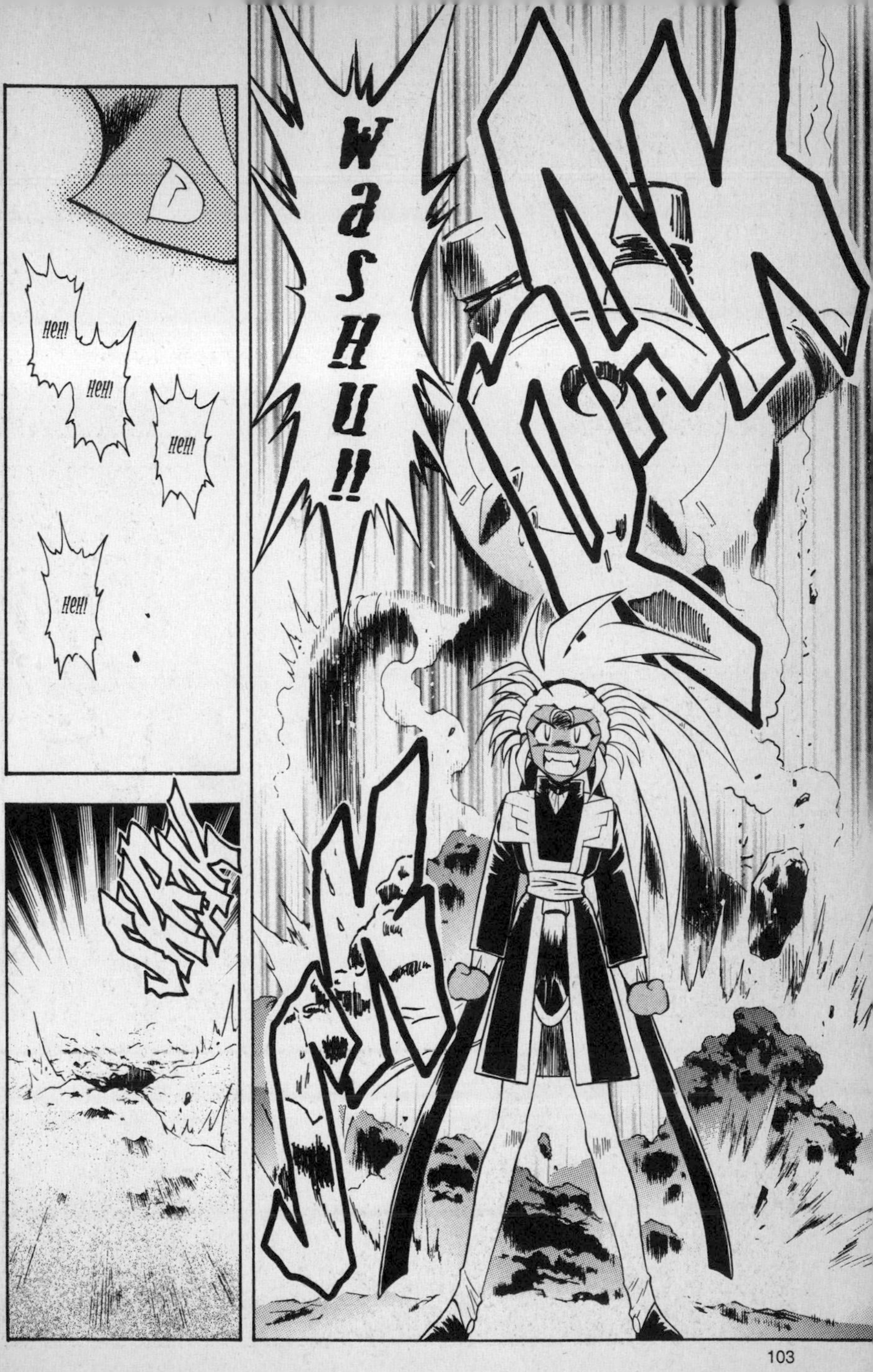
HEH!
HEH!
HEH!
HEH!
WASHUU!!

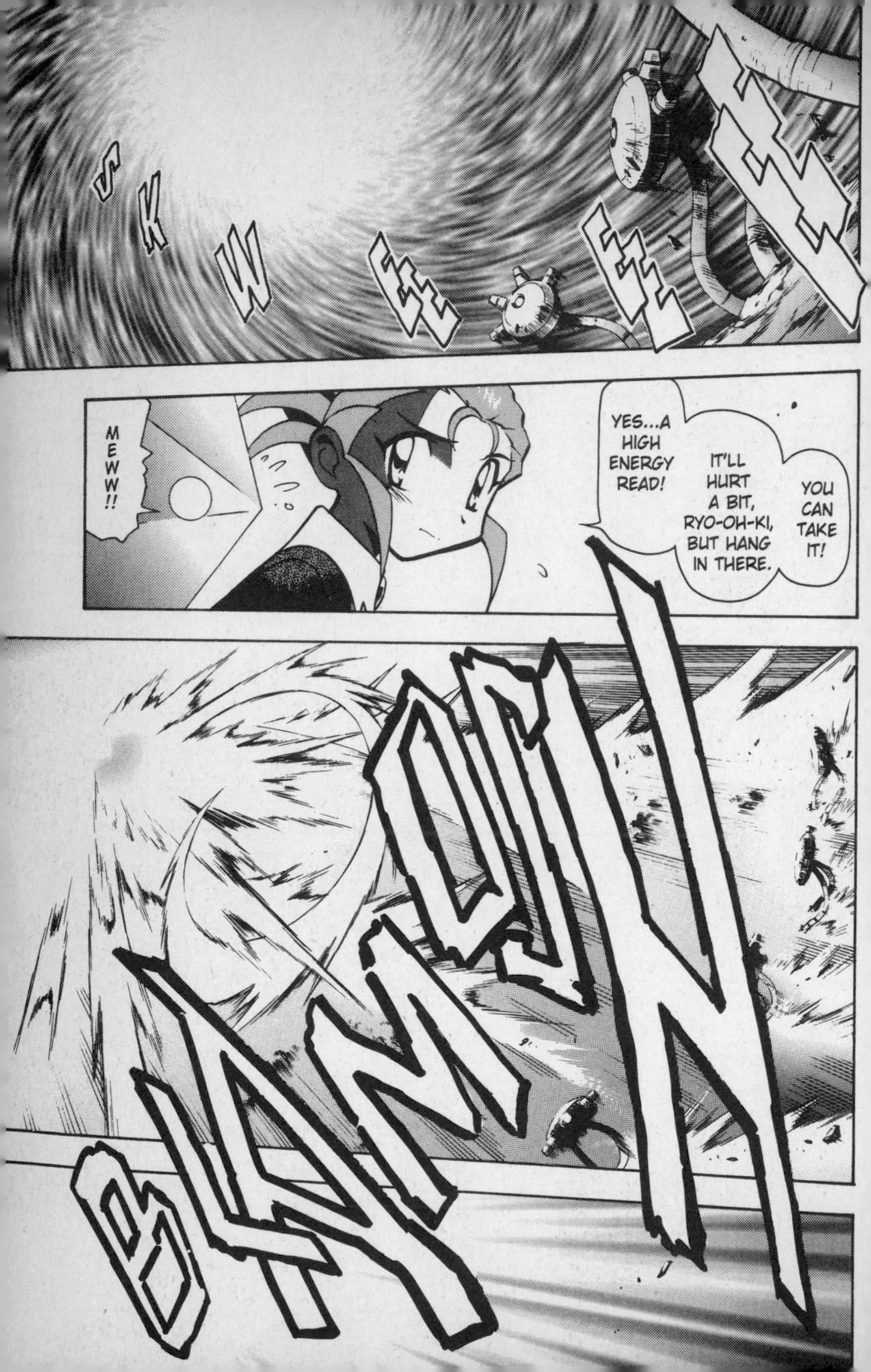
SKWEEE
MEWW!!
YES...A HIGH ENERGY READ!
IT'LL HURT A BIT, RYO-OH-KI, BUT HANG IN THERE.
YOU CAN TAKE IT!

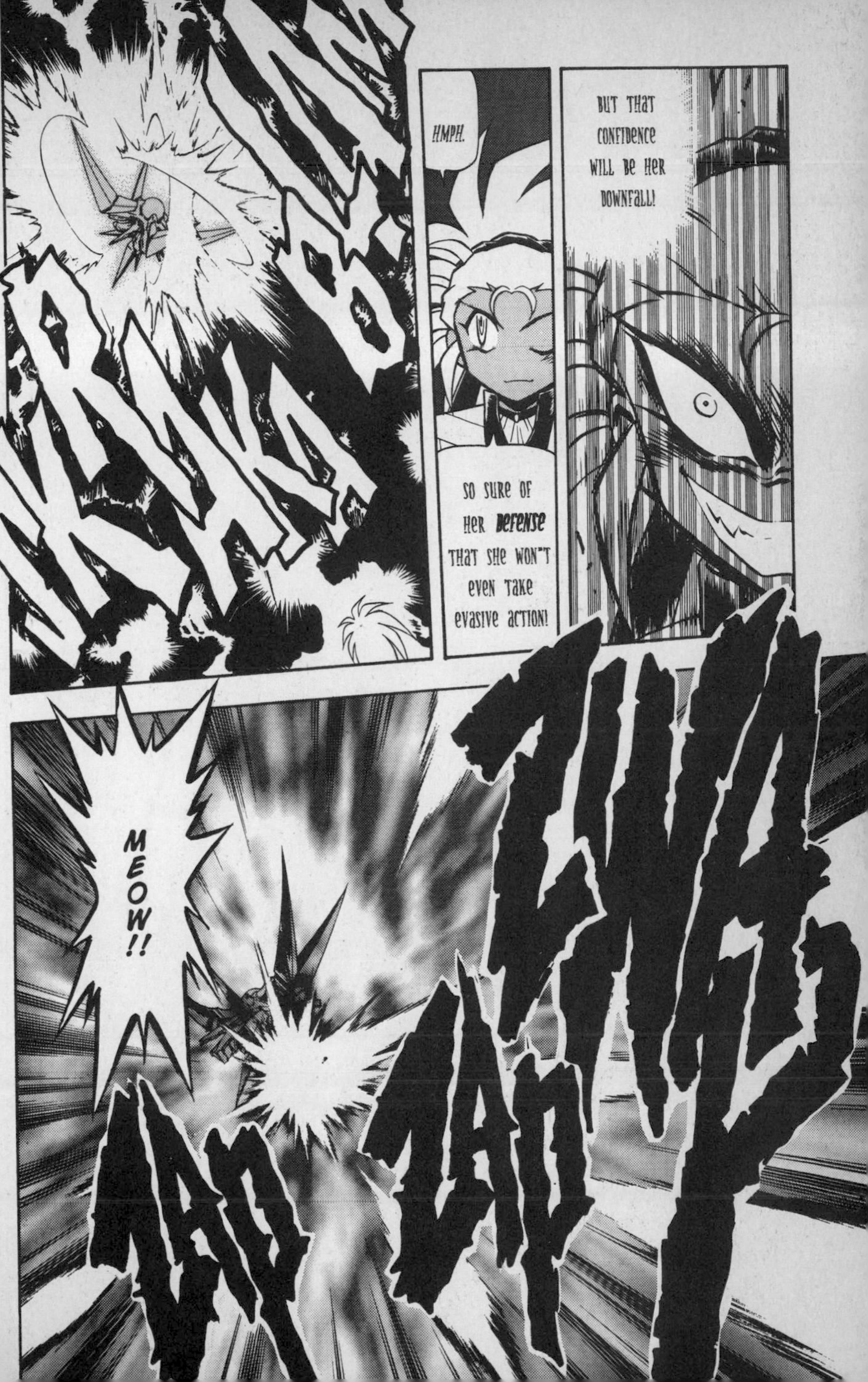
HMPH.
SO SURE OF HER **DEFENSE** THAT SHE WON'T EVEN TAKE EVASIVE ACTION!
BUT THAT CONFIDENCE WILL BE HER DOWNFALL!
MEOW!!

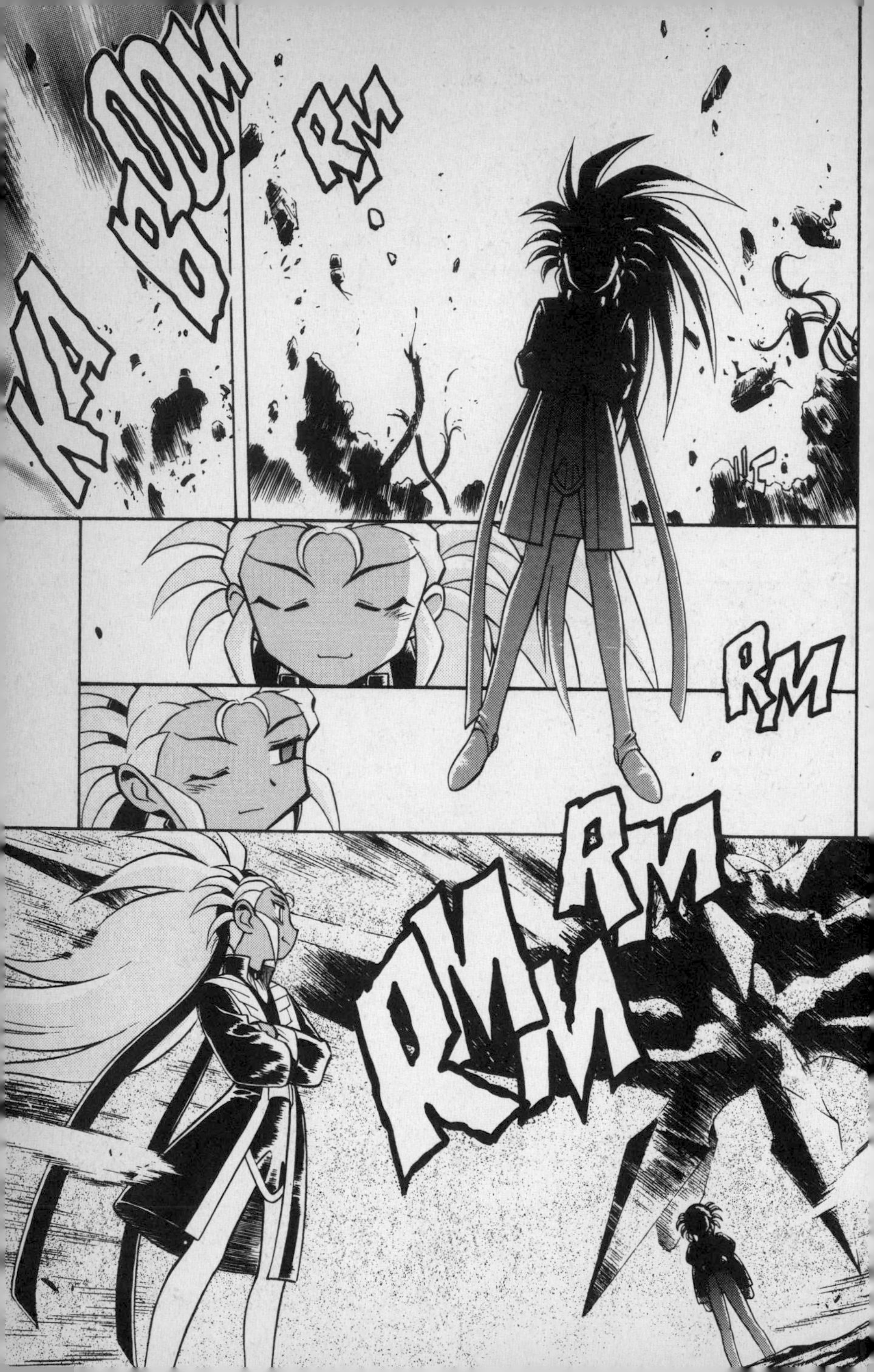
KA-BOOM
RM
RM
RM
RM

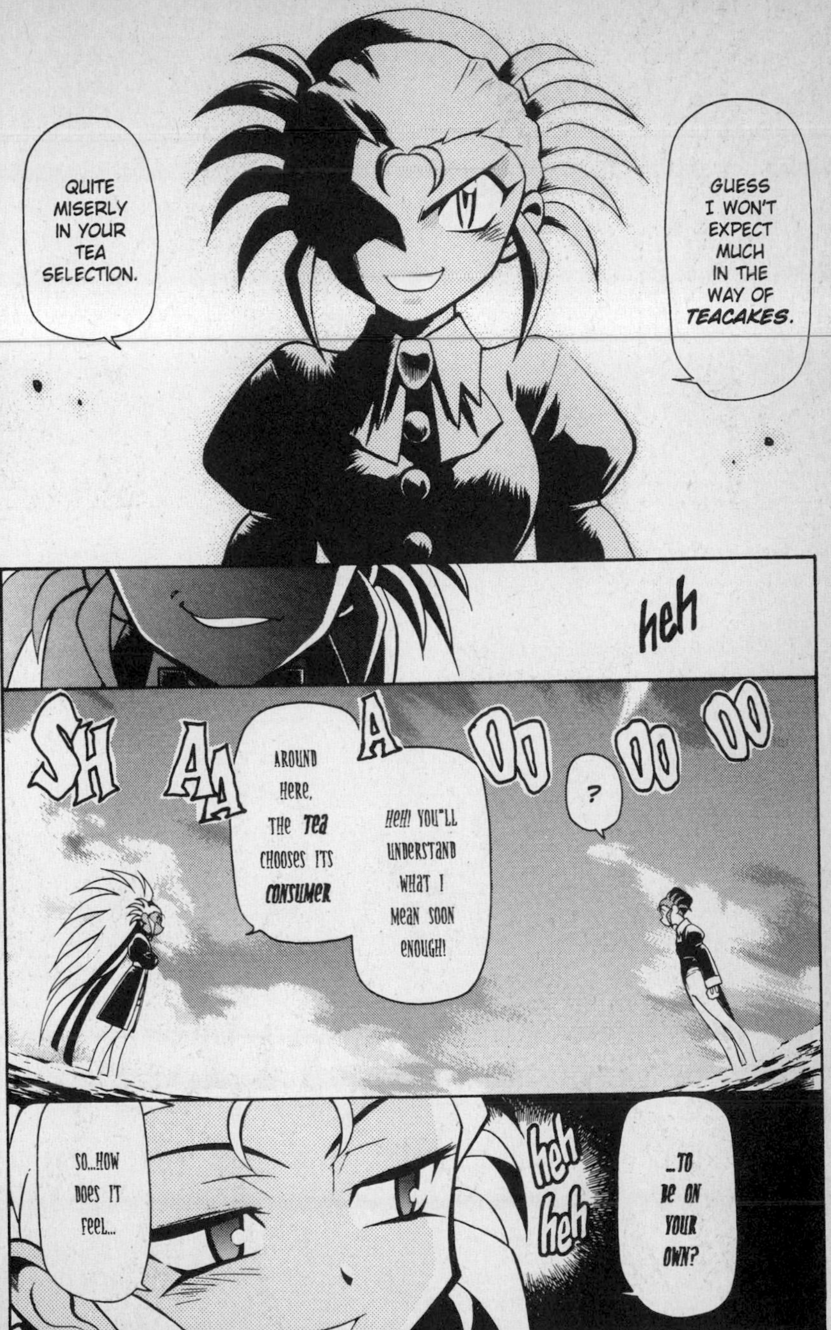
QUITE MISERLY IN YOUR TEA SELECTION.
GUESS I WON'T EXPECT MUCH IN THE WAY OF *TEACAKES*.
heh
SHAAAA
AROUND HERE, THE **TEA** CHOOSES ITS **CONSUMER**
HEH! YOU'LL UNDERSTAND WHAT I MEAN SOON ENOUGH!
OOOOOO
?
SO...HOW DOES IT FEEL...
heh heh
...TO BE ON YOUR OWN?

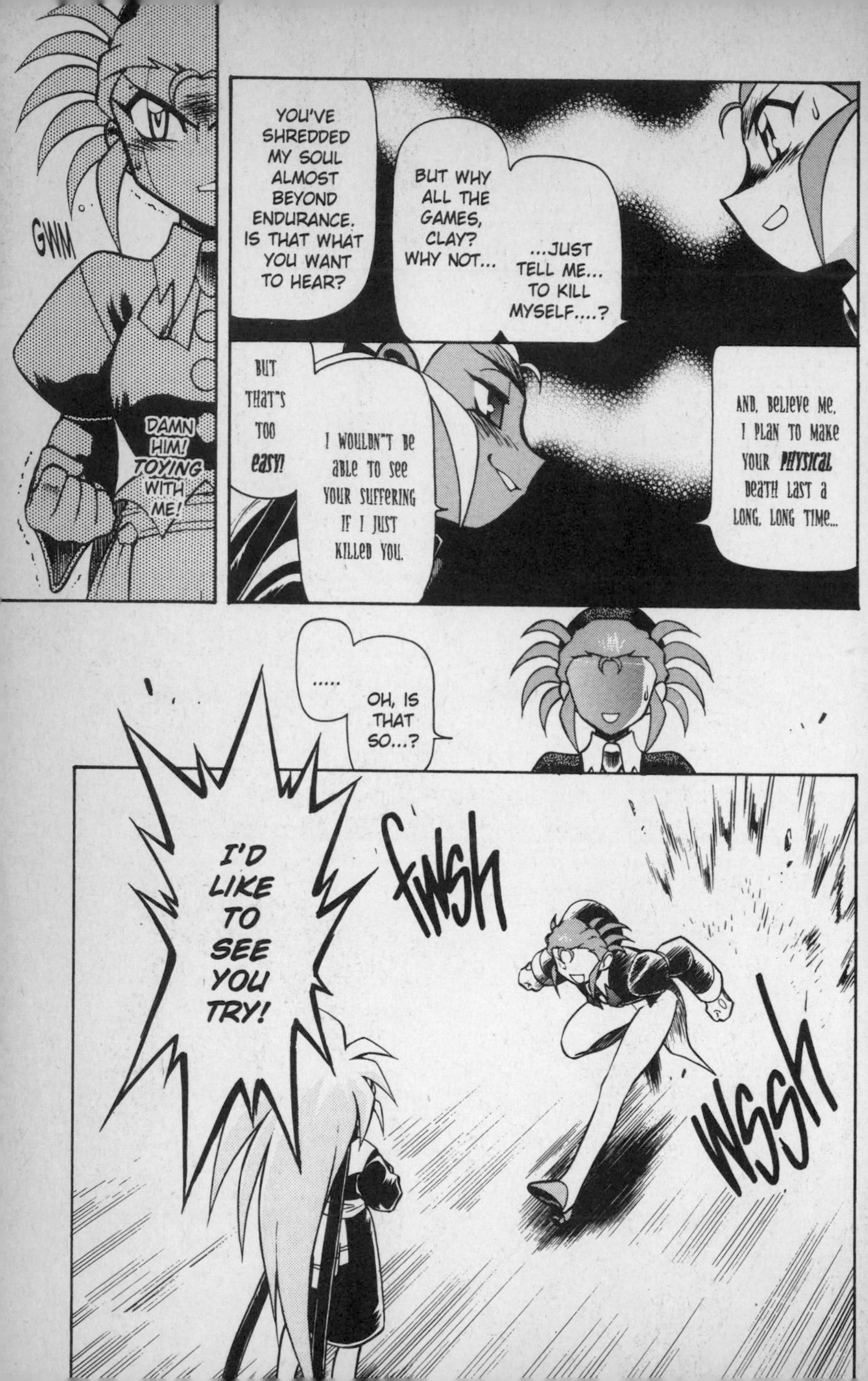
GWM
DAMN HIM! TOYING WITH ME!
YOU'VE SHREDDED MY SOUL ALMOST BEYOND ENDURANCE. IS THAT WHAT YOU WANT TO HEAR?
BUT WHY ALL THE GAMES, CLAY? WHY NOT...
...JUST TELL ME... TO KILL MYSELF....?
BUT THAT'S TOO EASY!
I WOULDN'T BE ABLE TO SEE YOUR SUFFERING IF I JUST KILLED YOU.
AND, BELIEVE ME, I PLAN TO MAKE YOUR PHYSICAL DEATH LAST A LONG, LONG TIME...
.....
OH, IS THAT SO...?
I'D LIKE TO SEE YOU TRY!
FWSH
WSSH

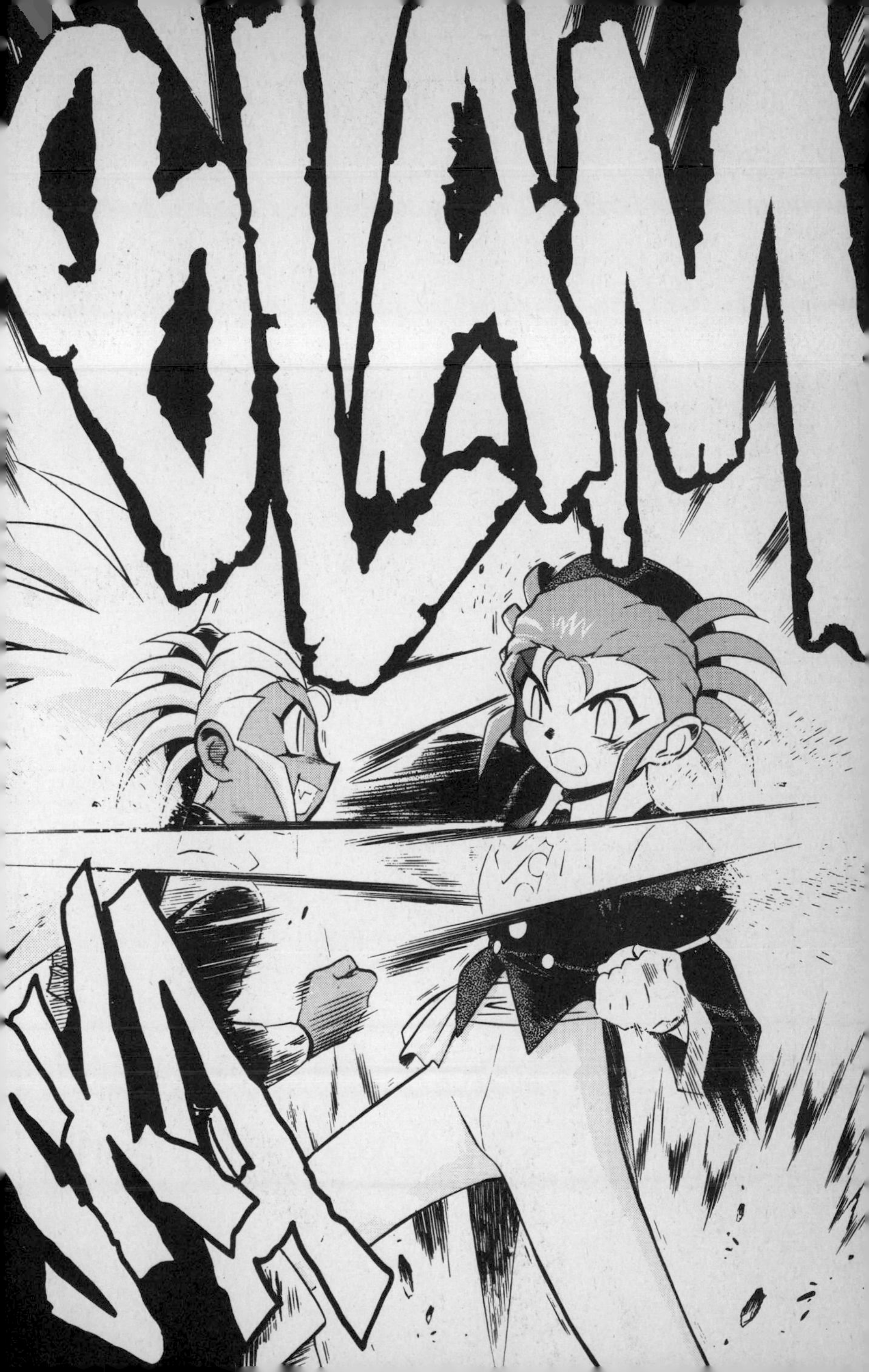
SLAM

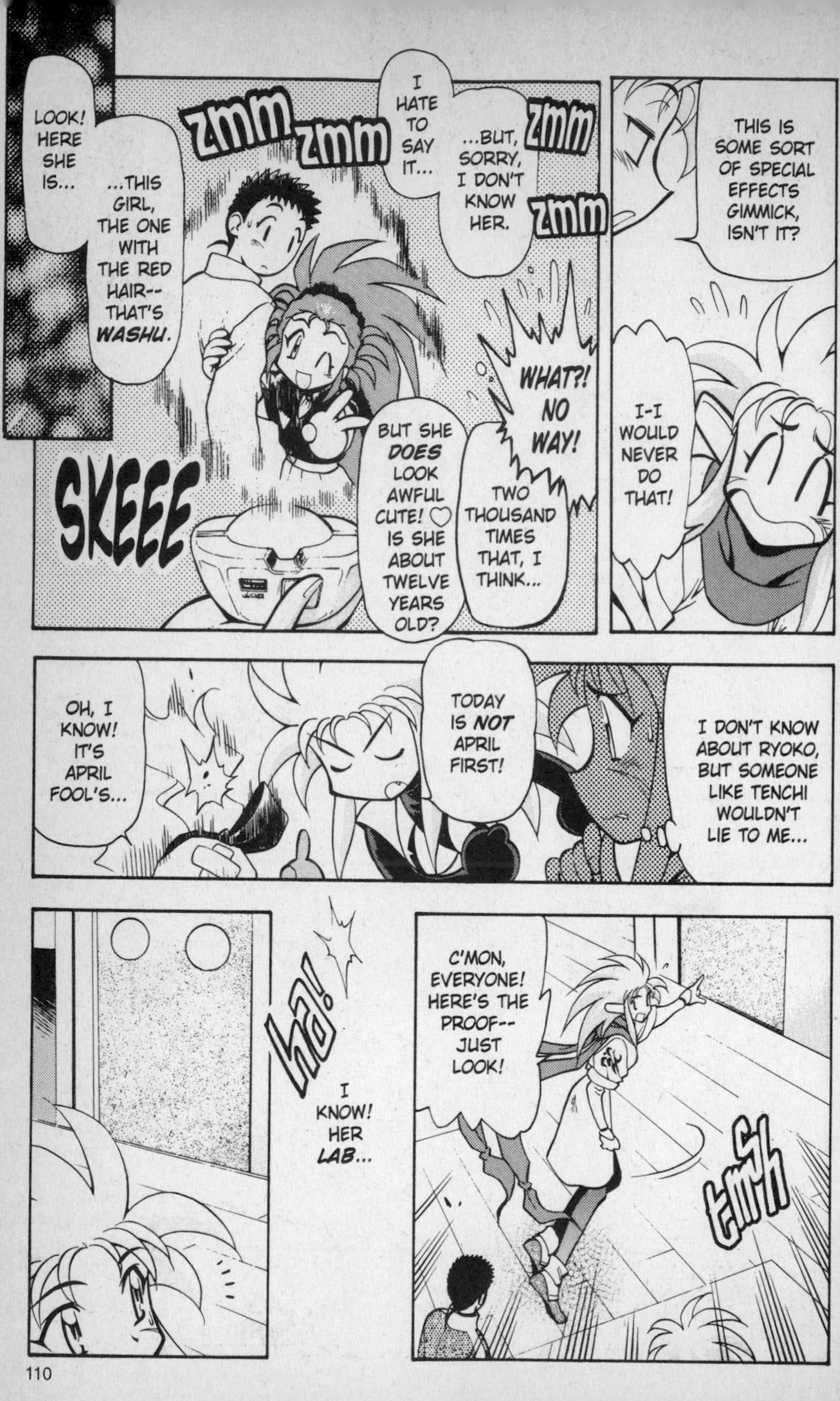

LOOK! HERE SHE IS...
...THIS GIRL, THE ONE WITH THE RED HAIR--THAT'S *WASHU*.
ZMM ZMM
I HATE TO SAY IT...
...BUT, SORRY, I DON'T KNOW HER.
ZMM
ZMM
SKEEE
BUT SHE *DOES* LOOK AWFUL CUTE! ♡ IS SHE ABOUT TWELVE YEARS OLD?
WHAT?! NO WAY!
TWO THOUSAND TIMES THAT, I THINK...
THIS IS SOME SORT OF SPECIAL EFFECTS GIMMICK, ISN'T IT?
I-I WOULD NEVER DO THAT!
OH, I KNOW! IT'S APRIL FOOL'S...
TODAY IS *NOT* APRIL FIRST!
I DON'T KNOW ABOUT RYOKO, BUT SOMEONE LIKE TENCHI WOULDN'T LIE TO ME...
HA!
I KNOW! HER *LAB*...
C'MON, EVERYONE! HERE'S THE PROOF--JUST LOOK!
TMSH

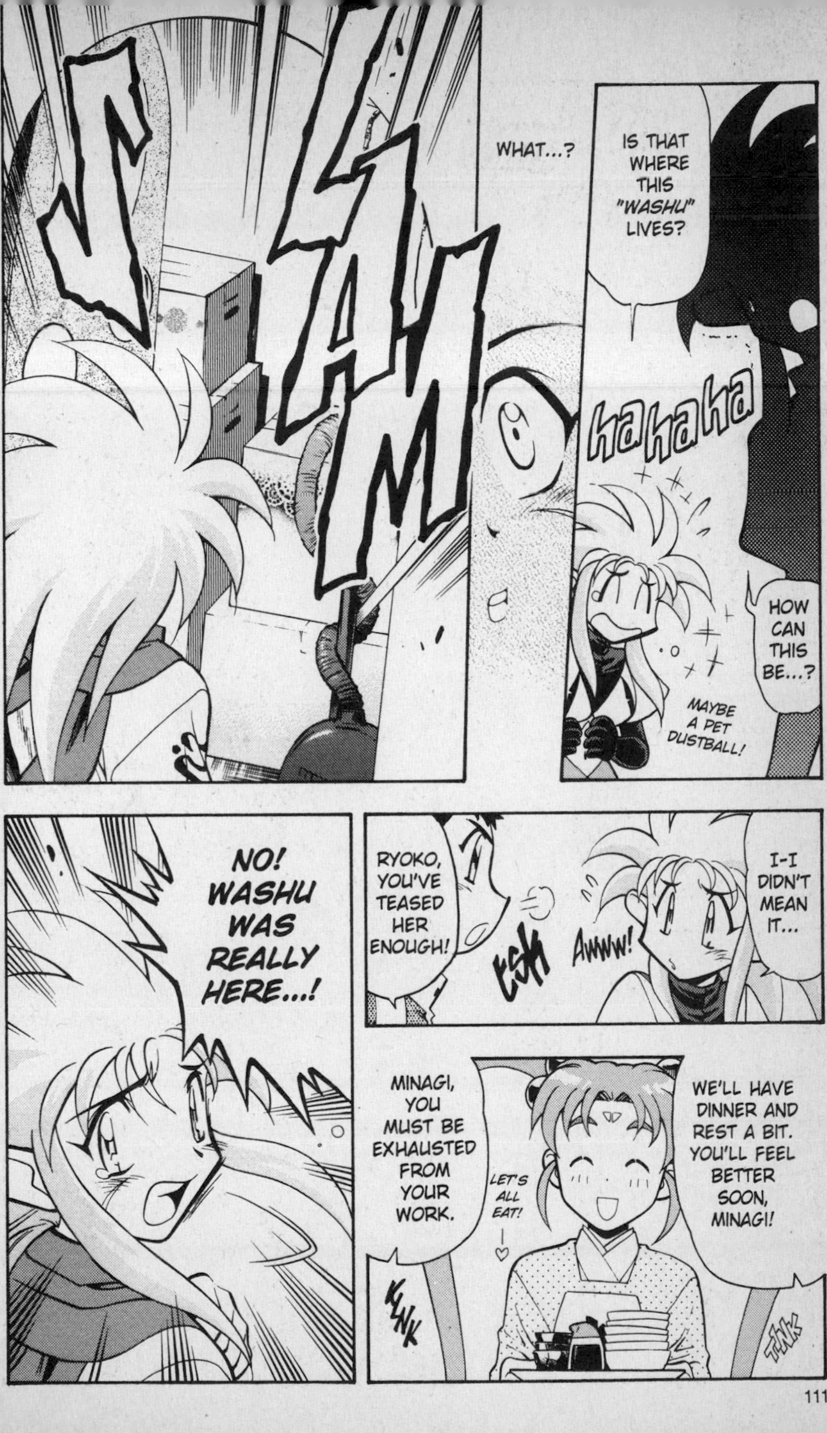
SLAM
WHAT...?
IS THAT WHERE THIS "WASHU" LIVES?
hahaha
HOW CAN THIS BE...?
MAYBE A PET DUSTBALL!
NO! WASHU WAS REALLY HERE...!
RYOKO, YOU'VE TEASED HER ENOUGH!
ESH
AWWW!
I-I DIDN'T MEAN IT...
MINAGI, YOU MUST BE EXHAUSTED FROM YOUR WORK.
LET'S ALL EAT!
WE'LL HAVE DINNER AND REST A BIT. YOU'LL FEEL BETTER SOON, MINAGI!
KLINK
TINK

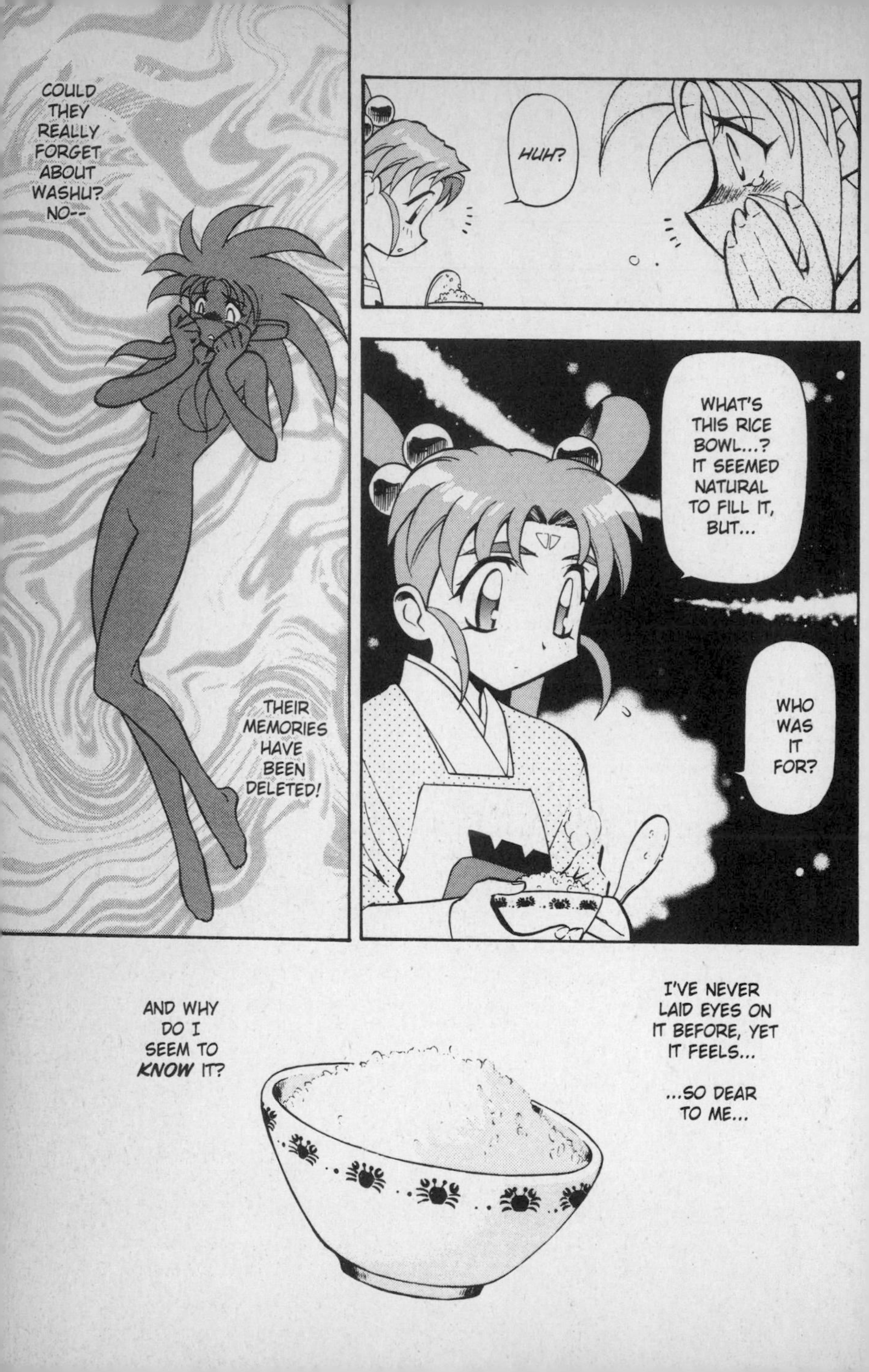
COULD THEY REALLY FORGET ABOUT WASHU? NO--
THEIR MEMORIES HAVE BEEN DELETED!
HUH?
WHAT'S THIS RICE BOWL...? IT SEEMED NATURAL TO FILL IT, BUT...
WHO WAS IT FOR?
AND WHY DO I SEEM TO *KNOW* IT?
I'VE NEVER LAID EYES ON IT BEFORE, YET IT FEELS...
...SO DEAR TO ME...

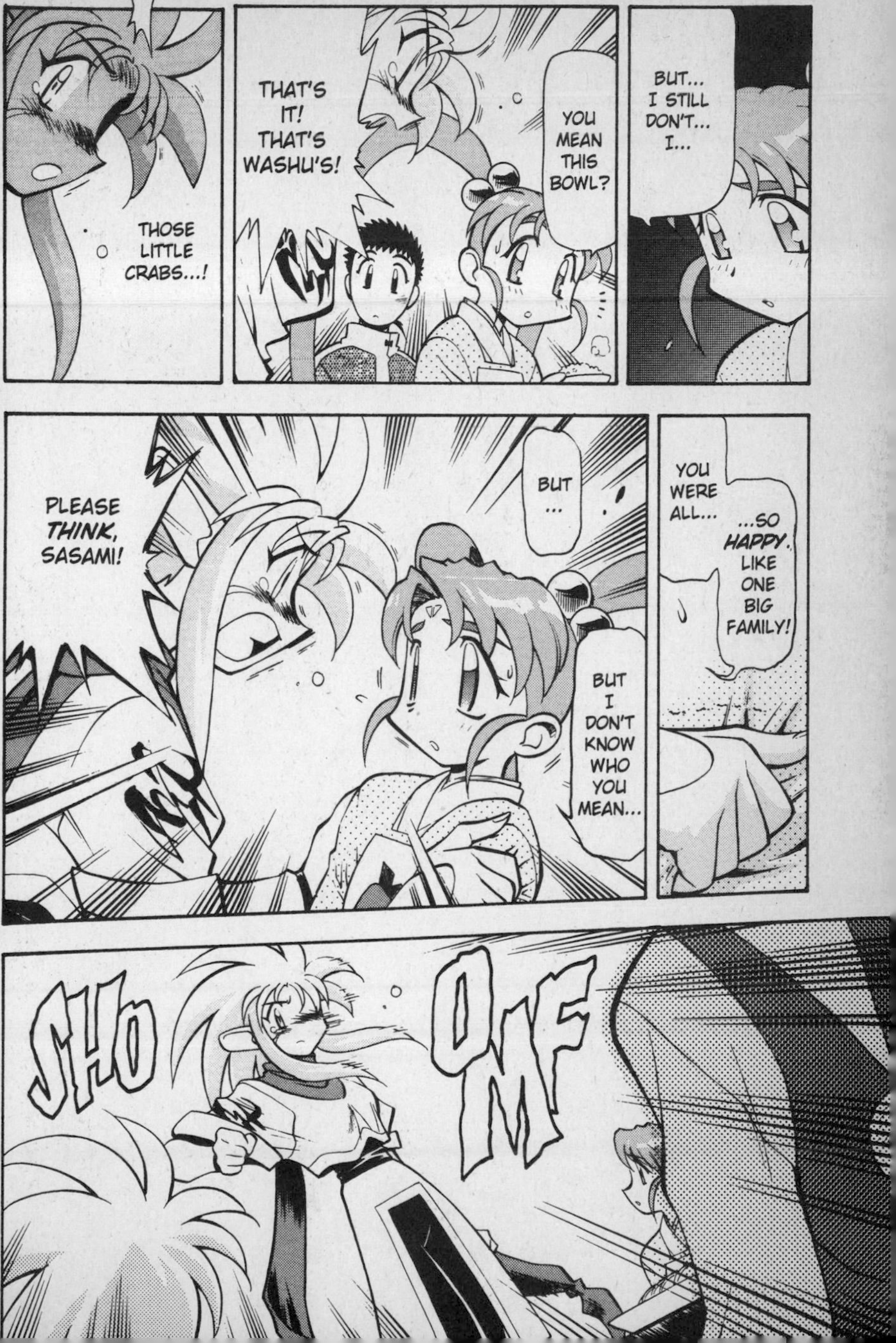
THOSE LITTLE CRABS...!
THAT'S IT! THAT'S WASHU'S!
YOU MEAN THIS BOWL?
BUT... I STILL DON'T... I...
PLEASE THINK, SASAMI!
BUT ...
BUT I DON'T KNOW WHO YOU MEAN...
YOU WERE ALL...
...SO HAPPY. LIKE ONE BIG FAMILY!
SHO
OMF
M

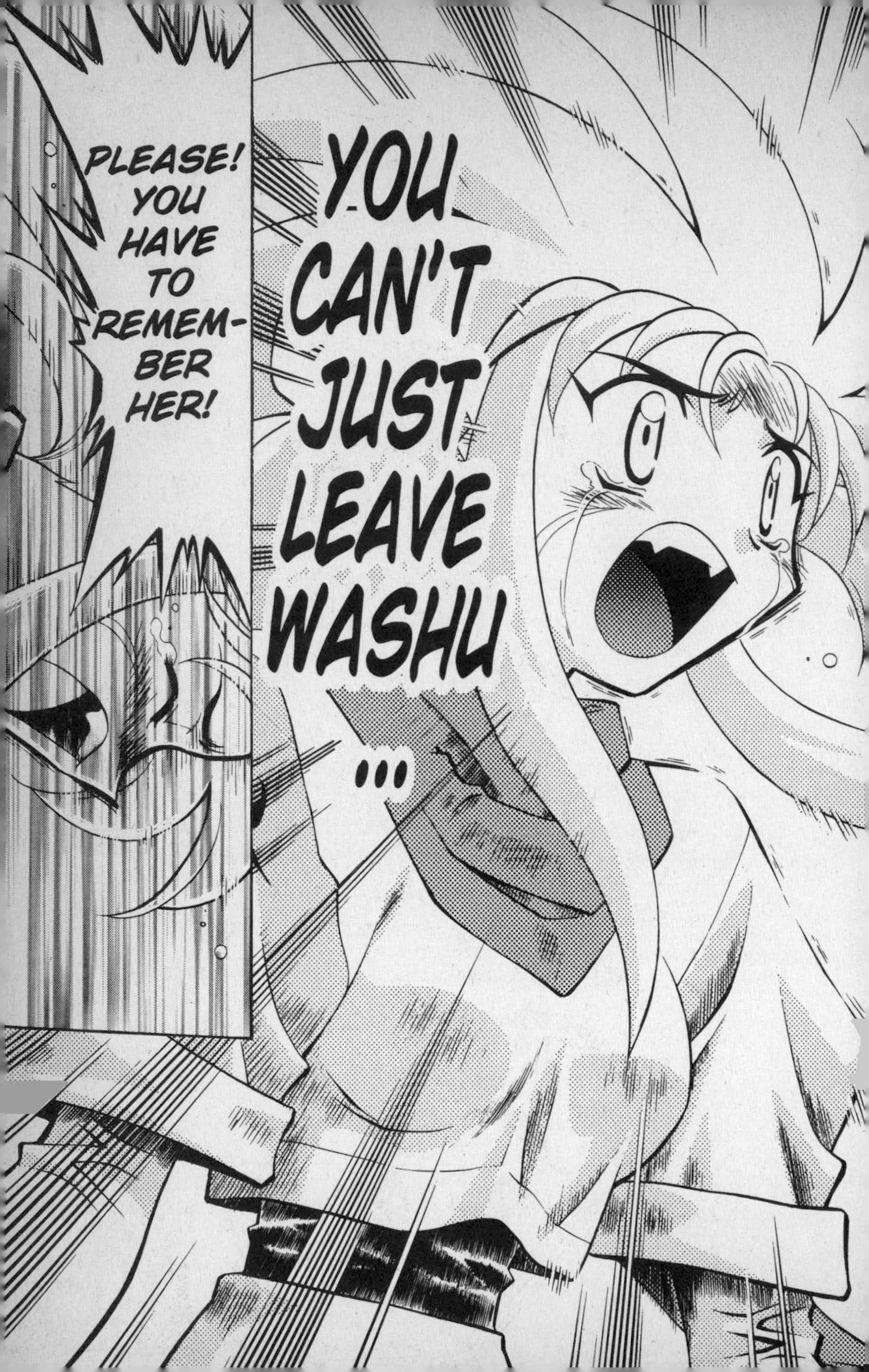
PLEASE! YOU HAVE TO REMEMBER HER!
YOU CAN'T JUST LEAVE WASHU ...

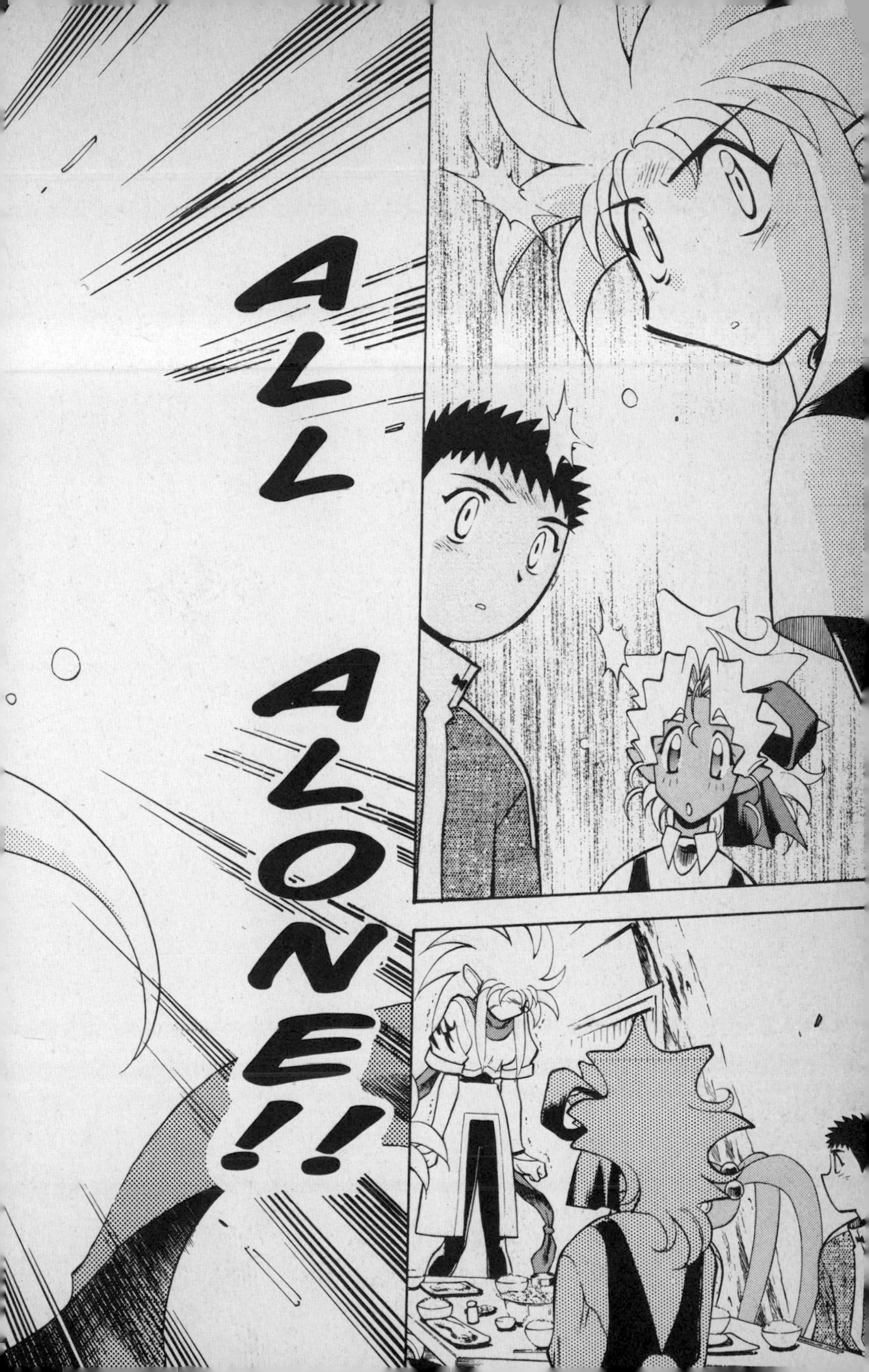
ALL ALONE!!

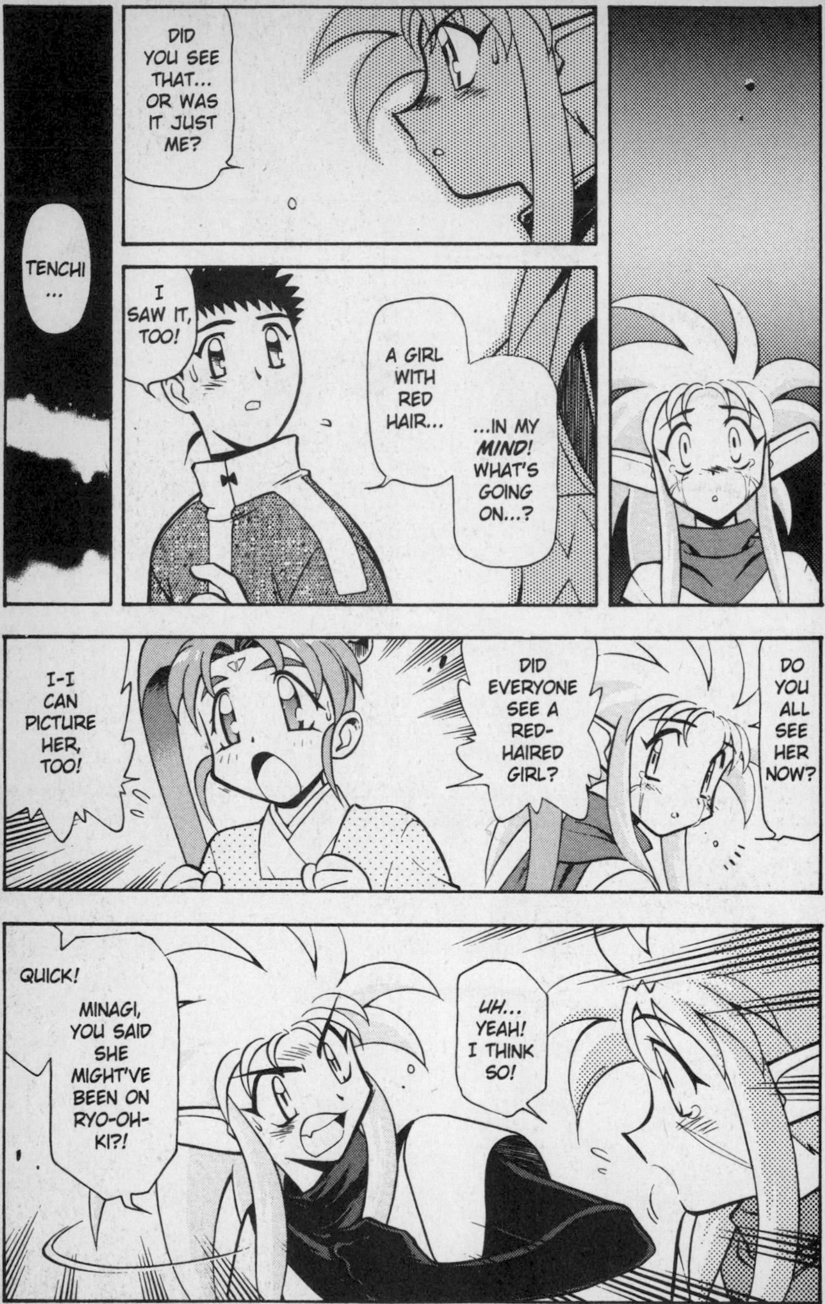
TENCHI ...
DID YOU SEE THAT... OR WAS IT JUST ME?
I SAW IT, TOO!
A GIRL WITH RED HAIR...
...IN MY *MIND!* WHAT'S GOING ON...?
I-I CAN PICTURE HER, TOO!
DID EVERYONE SEE A RED-HAIRED GIRL?
DO YOU ALL SEE HER NOW?
QUICK!
MINAGI, YOU SAID SHE MIGHT'VE BEEN ON RYO-OH-KI?!
UH... YEAH! I THINK SO!

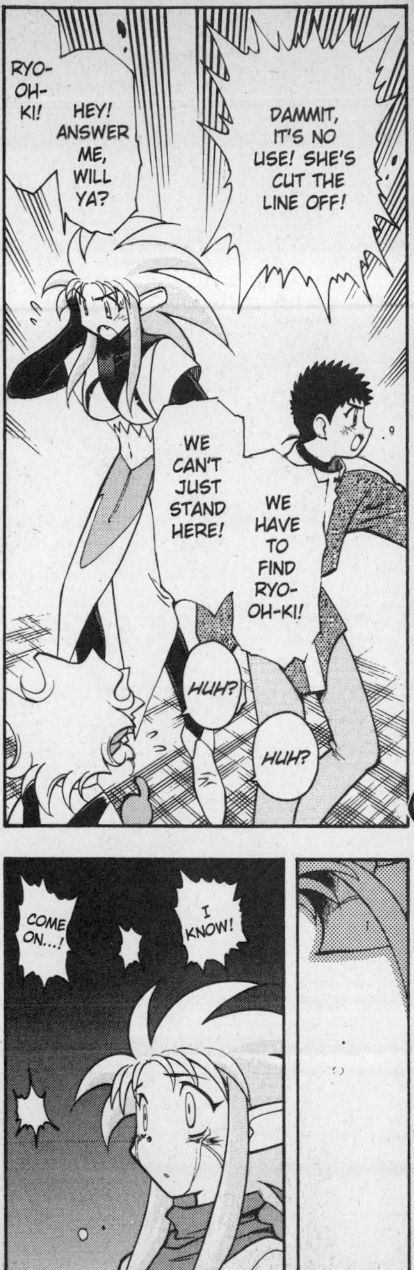
RYO-OH-KI!
HEY! ANSWER ME, WILL YA?
DAMMIT, IT'S NO USE! SHE'S CUT THE LINE OFF!
WE CAN'T JUST STAND HERE!
WE HAVE TO FIND RYO-OH-KI!
HUH?
HUH?
COME ON...!
I KNOW!
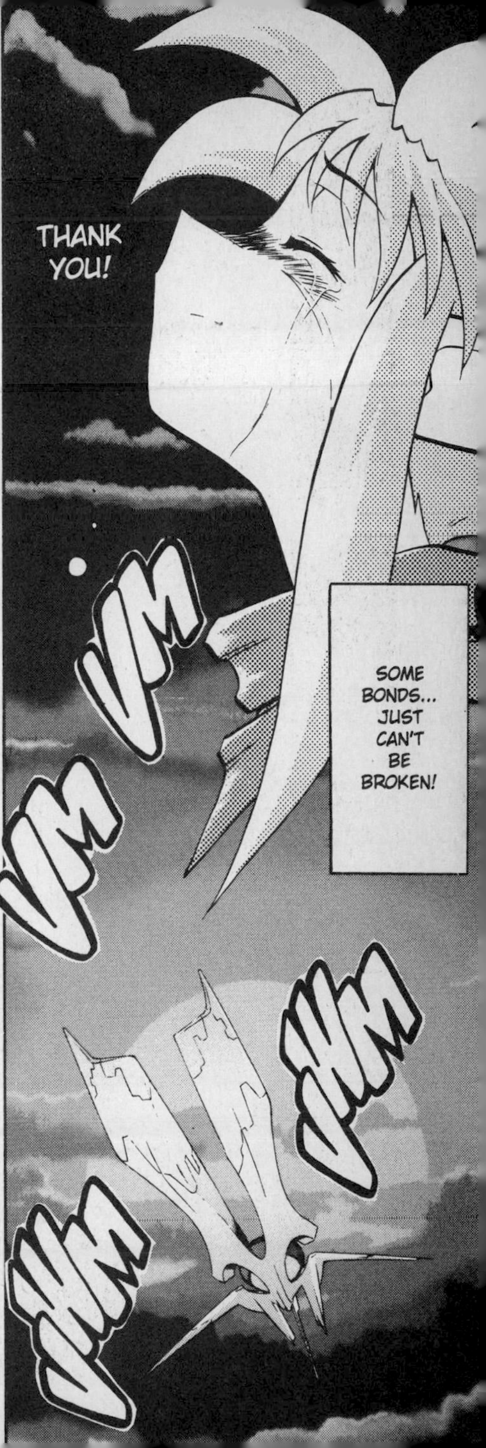
THANK YOU!
VVM VVM
SOME BONDS... JUST CAN'T BE BROKEN!
VHM VHM

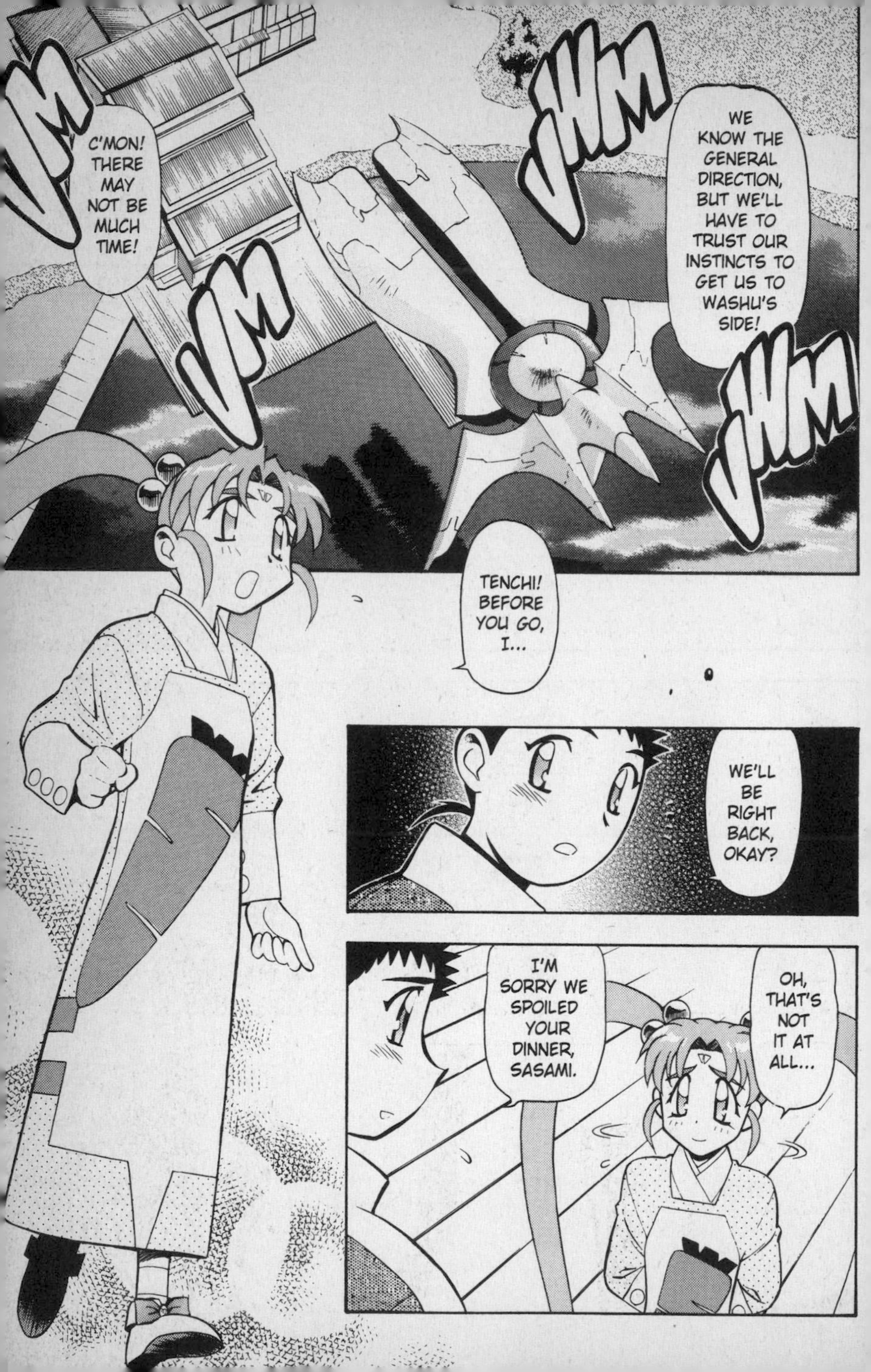
C'MON! THERE MAY NOT BE MUCH TIME!
WE KNOW THE GENERAL DIRECTION, BUT WE'LL HAVE TO TRUST OUR INSTINCTS TO GET US TO WASHU'S SIDE!
TENCHI! BEFORE YOU GO, I...
WE'LL BE RIGHT BACK, OKAY?
I'M SORRY WE SPOILED YOUR DINNER, SASAMI.
OH, THAT'S NOT IT AT ALL...

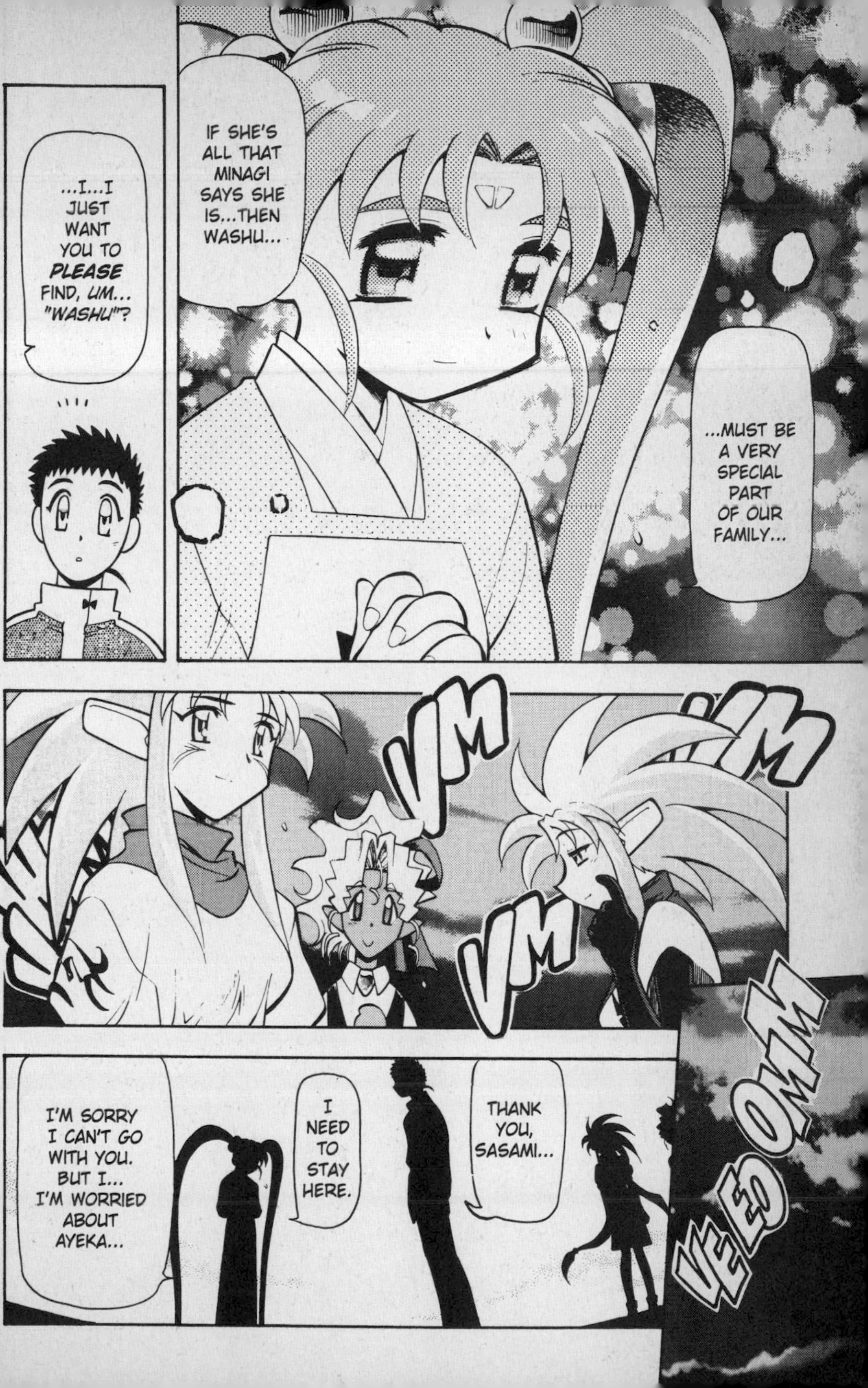
...I...I JUST WANT YOU TO *PLEASE* FIND, UM... "WASHU"?
IF SHE'S ALL THAT MINAGI SAYS SHE IS...THEN WASHU...
...MUST BE A VERY SPECIAL PART OF OUR FAMILY...
VM
VM
VM
I'M SORRY I CAN'T GO WITH YOU. BUT I... I'M WORRIED ABOUT AYEKA...
I NEED TO STAY HERE.
THANK YOU, SASAMI...
VEEOOMM

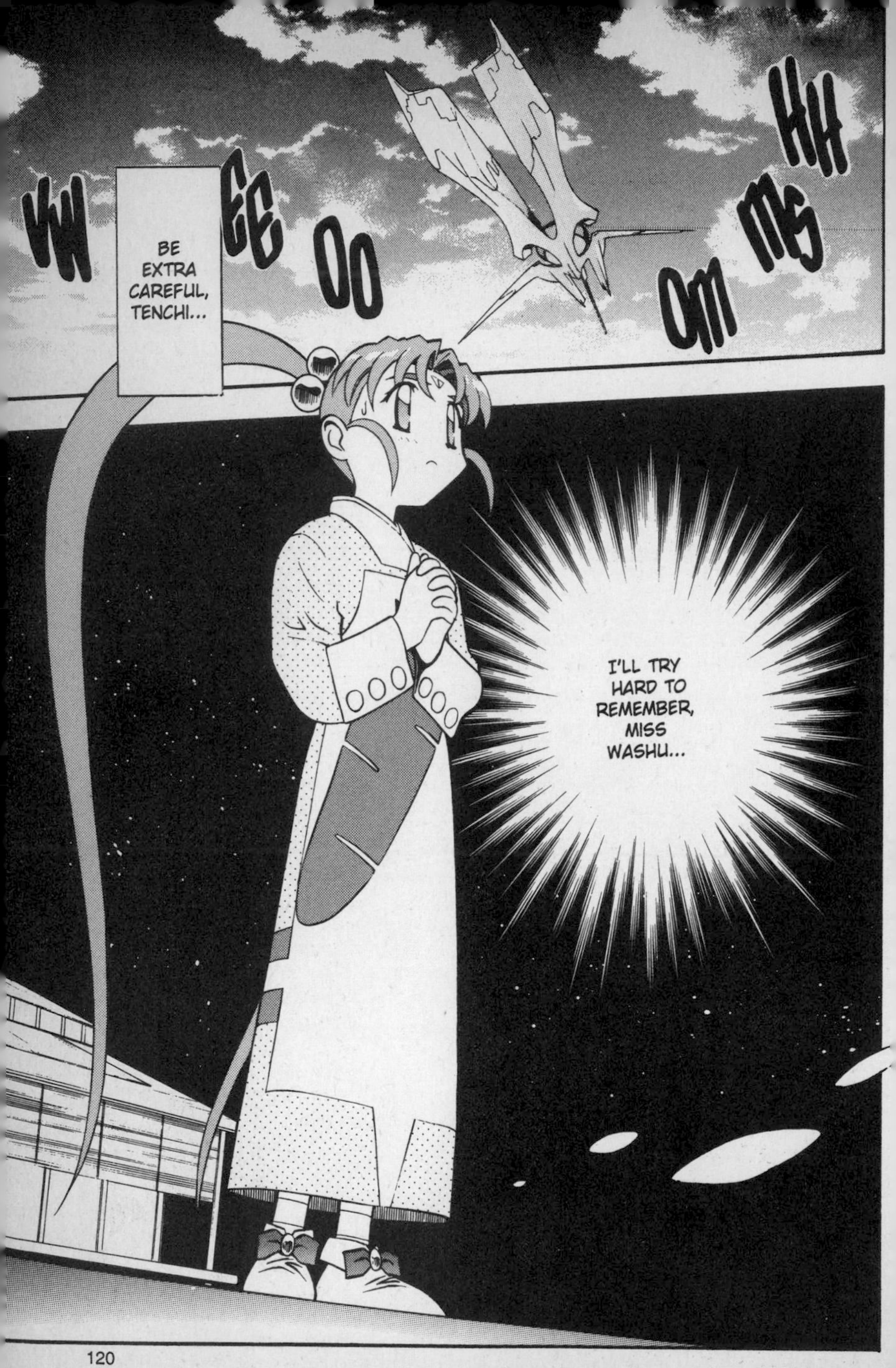
VWEEOOOMMGHH
BE EXTRA CAREFUL, TENCHI...
I'LL TRY HARD TO REMEMBER, MISS WASHU...

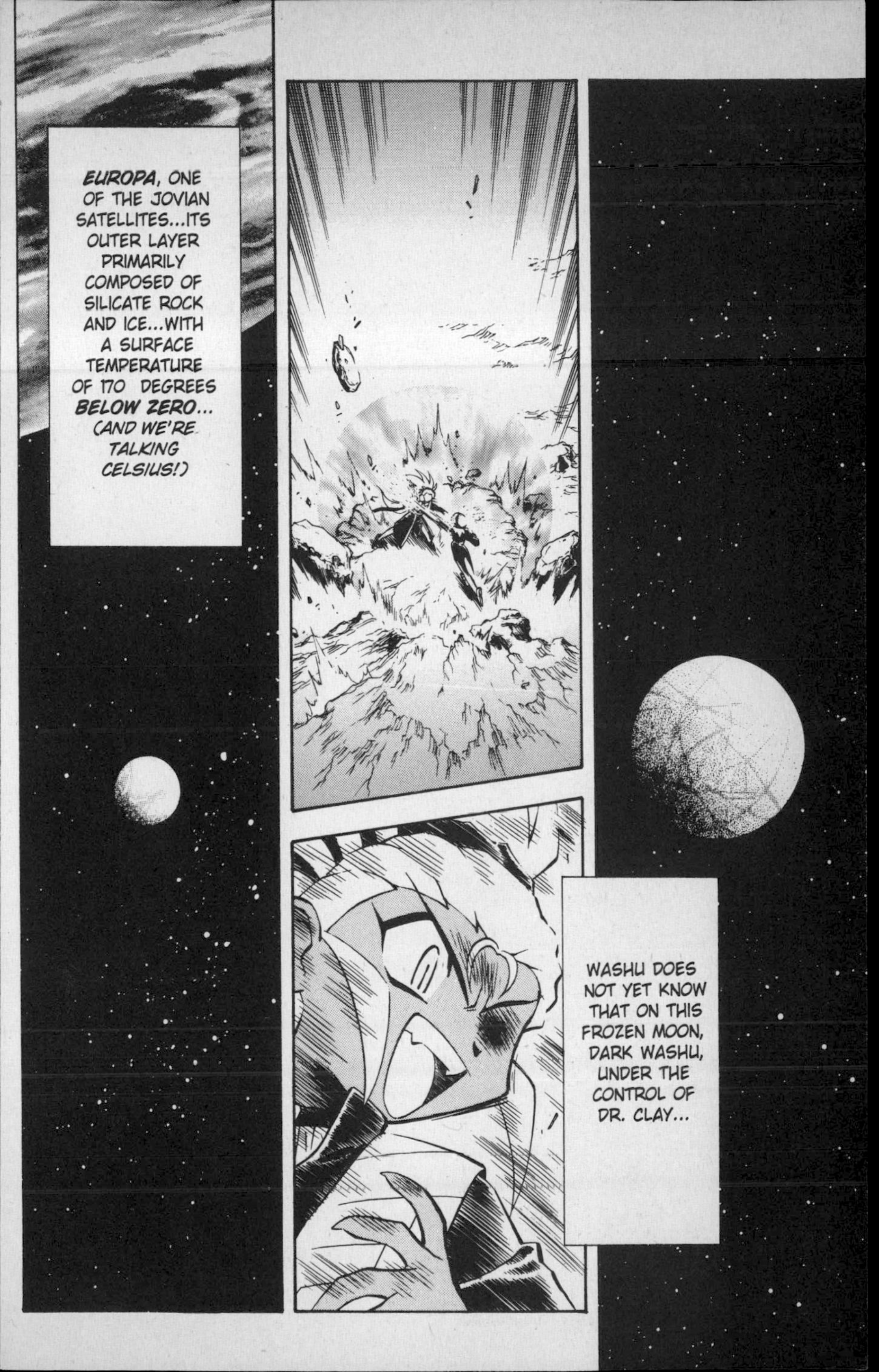
EUROPA, ONE OF THE JOVIAN SATELLITES...ITS OUTER LAYER PRIMARILY COMPOSED OF SILICATE ROCK AND ICE...WITH A SURFACE TEMPERATURE OF 170 DEGREES BELOW ZERO... (AND WE'RE TALKING CELSIUS!)
WASHU DOES NOT YET KNOW THAT ON THIS FROZEN MOON, DARK WASHU, UNDER THE CONTROL OF DR. CLAY...

Chapter 5: ASSEMBLE

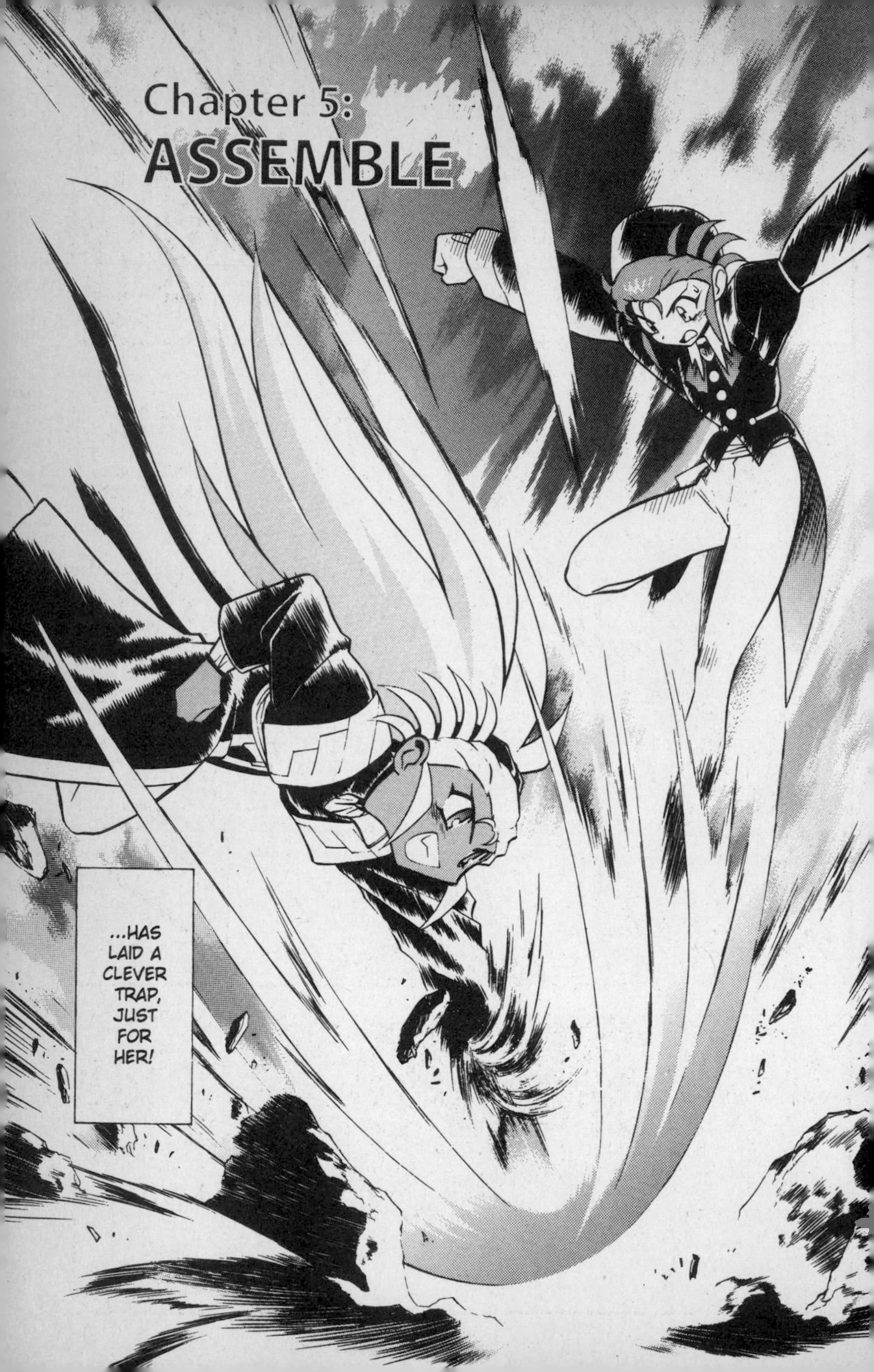
...HAS LAID A CLEVER TRAP, JUST FOR HER!

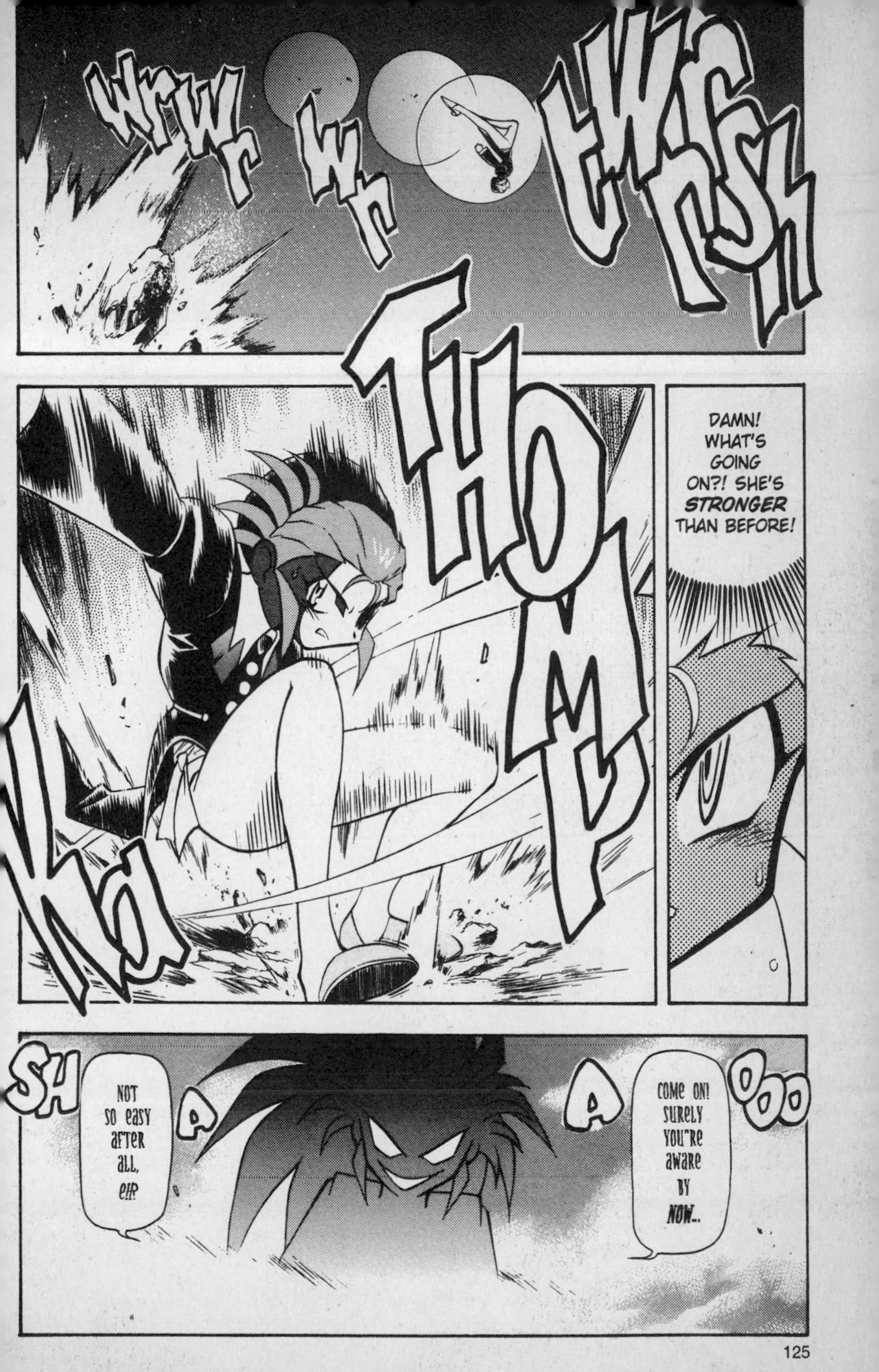
THOMP
DAMN! WHAT'S GOING ON?! SHE'S STRONGER THAN BEFORE!
NOT SO EASY AFTER ALL, EH?
COME ON! SURELY YOU"RE AWARE BY NOW..

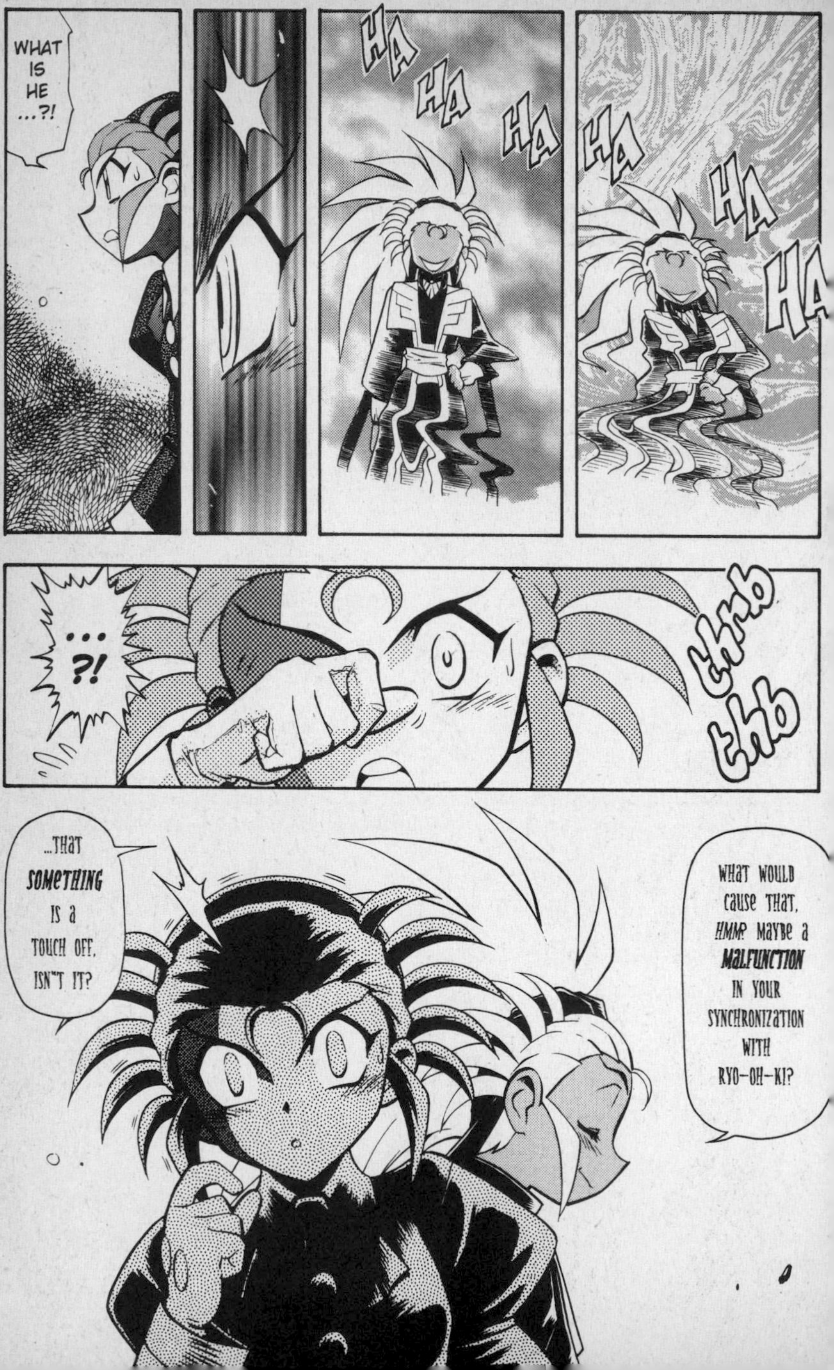
WHAT IS HE ...?!
HA HA HA
HA HA HA
...?!
thrb thb
...THAT SOMETHING IS a TOUCH OFF, ISN'T IT?
WHAT WOULD cause THAT, HMM? Maybe a MALFUNCTION IN YOUR SYNCHRONIZATION WITH RYO-OH-KI?

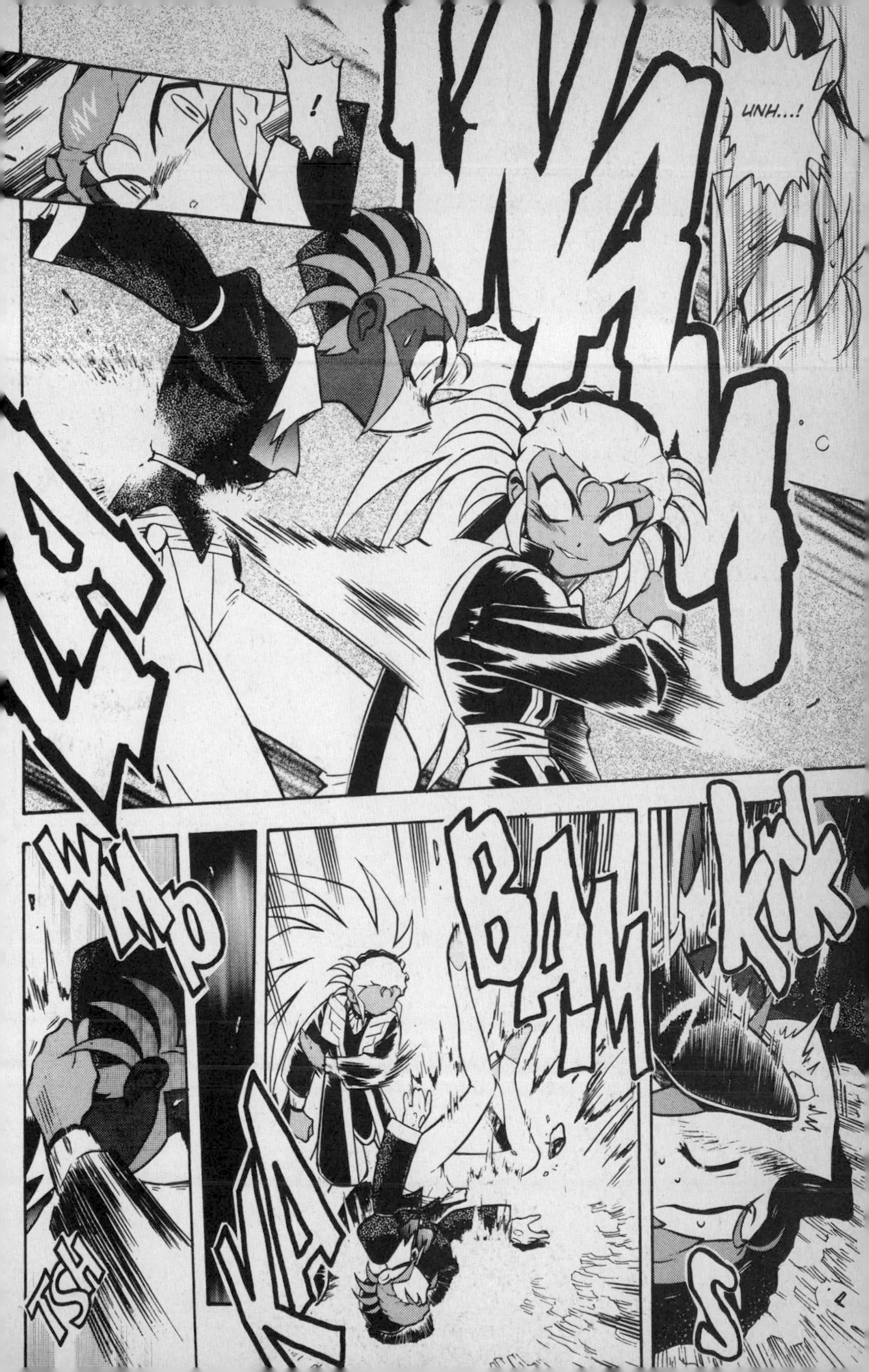
!
UNH...!
WHMP
TSH
BAM
KTK

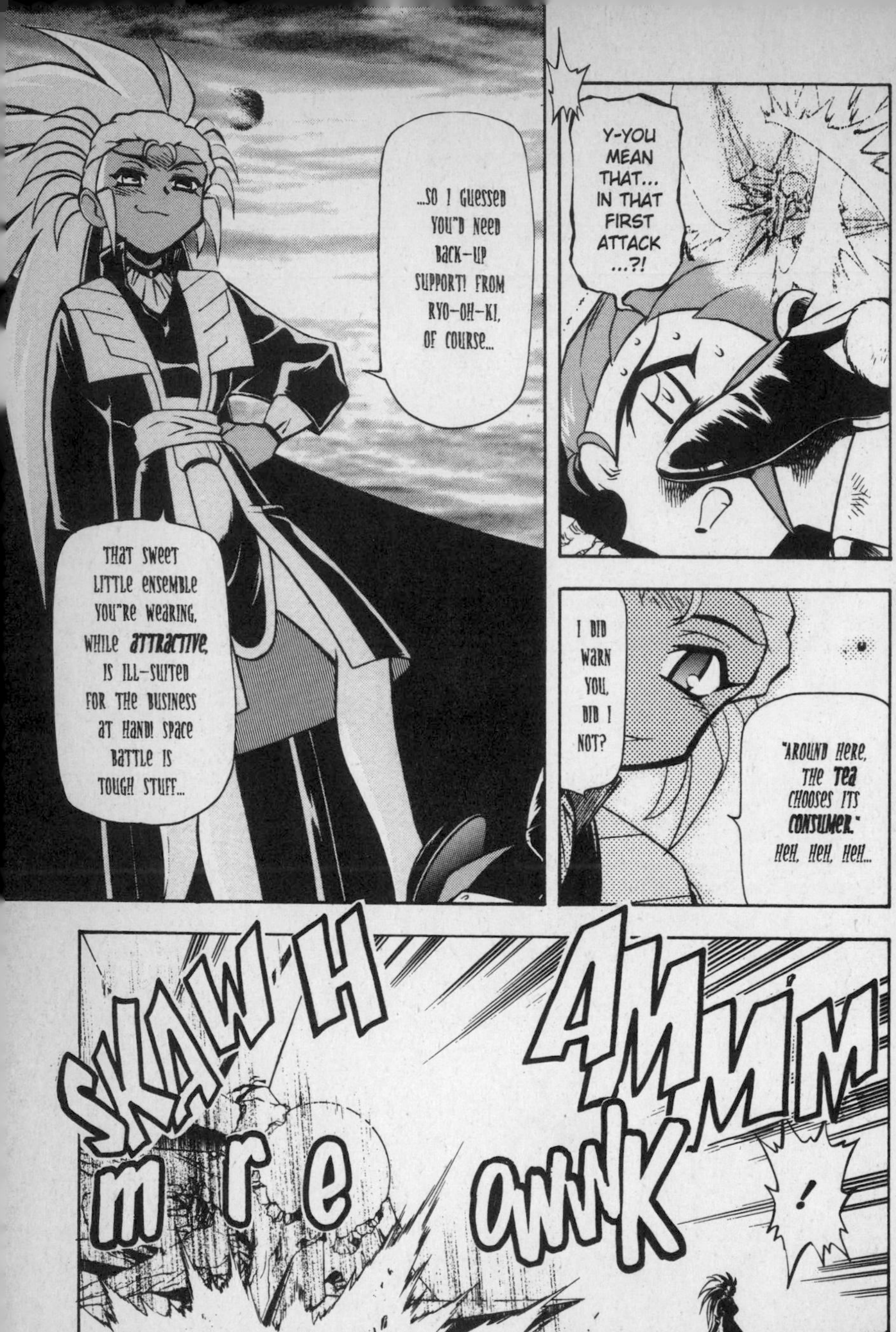
...SO I GUESSED YOU'D NEED BACK-UP SUPPORT! FROM RYO-OH-KI, OF COURSE...
THAT SWEET LITTLE ENSEMBLE YOU'RE WEARING, WHILE ATTRACTIVE, IS ILL-SUITED FOR THE BUSINESS AT HAND! SPACE BATTLE IS TOUGH STUFF...
Y-YOU MEAN THAT... IN THAT FIRST ATTACK ...?!
I DID WARN YOU, DID I NOT?
"AROUND HERE, THE TEA CHOOSES ITS CONSUMER." HEH, HEH, HEH...
SKAW-H AMMM
m r e awwK
!

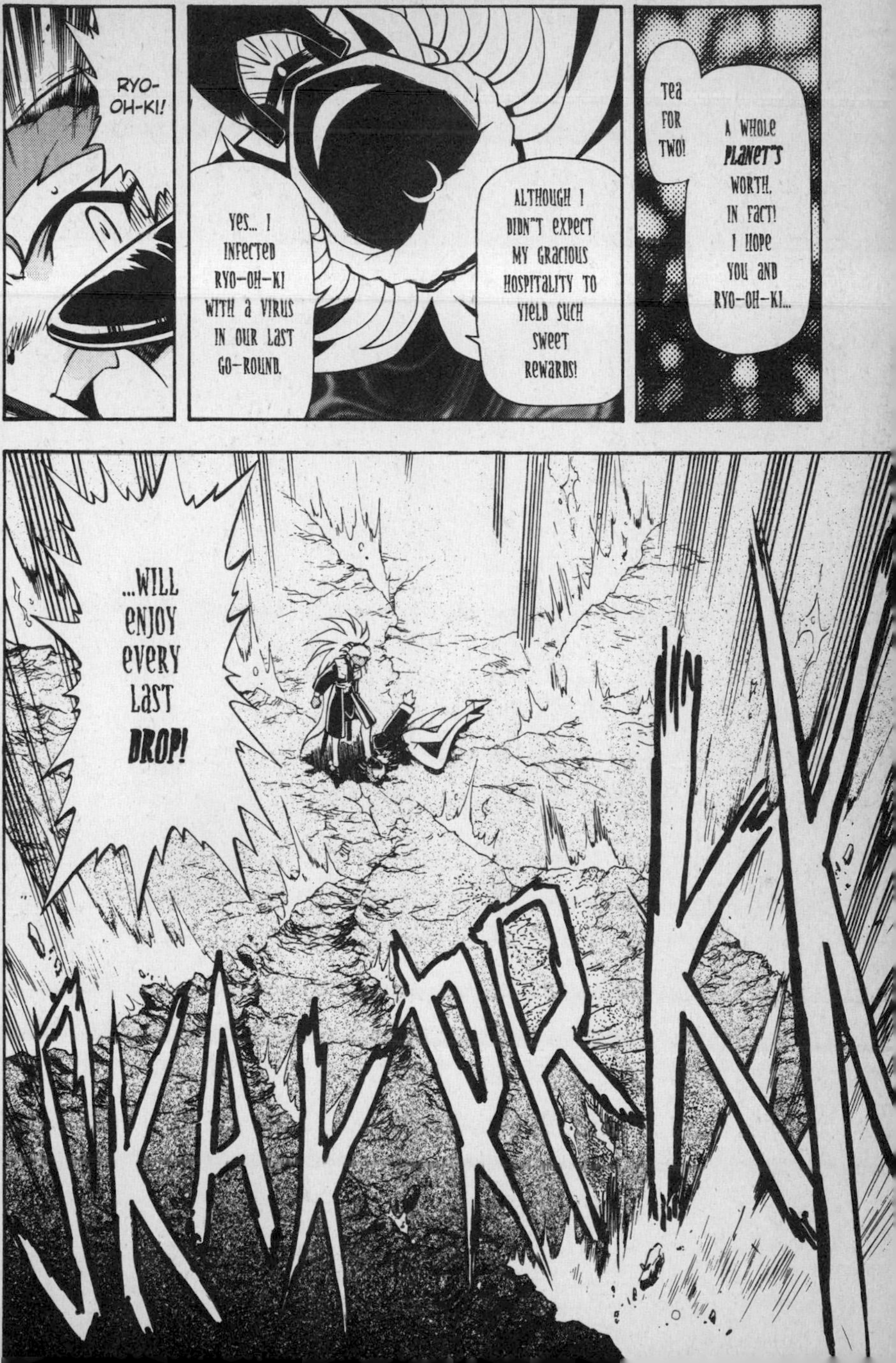
RYO-OH-KI!
YES... I INFECTED RYO-OH-KI WITH A VIRUS IN OUR LAST GO-ROUND.
ALTHOUGH I DIDN'T EXPECT MY GRACIOUS HOSPITALITY TO YIELD SUCH SWEET REWARDS!
TEA FOR TWO!
A WHOLE PLANET'S WORTH, IN FACT! I HOPE YOU AND RYO-OH-KI...
...WILL ENJOY EVERY LAST DROP!

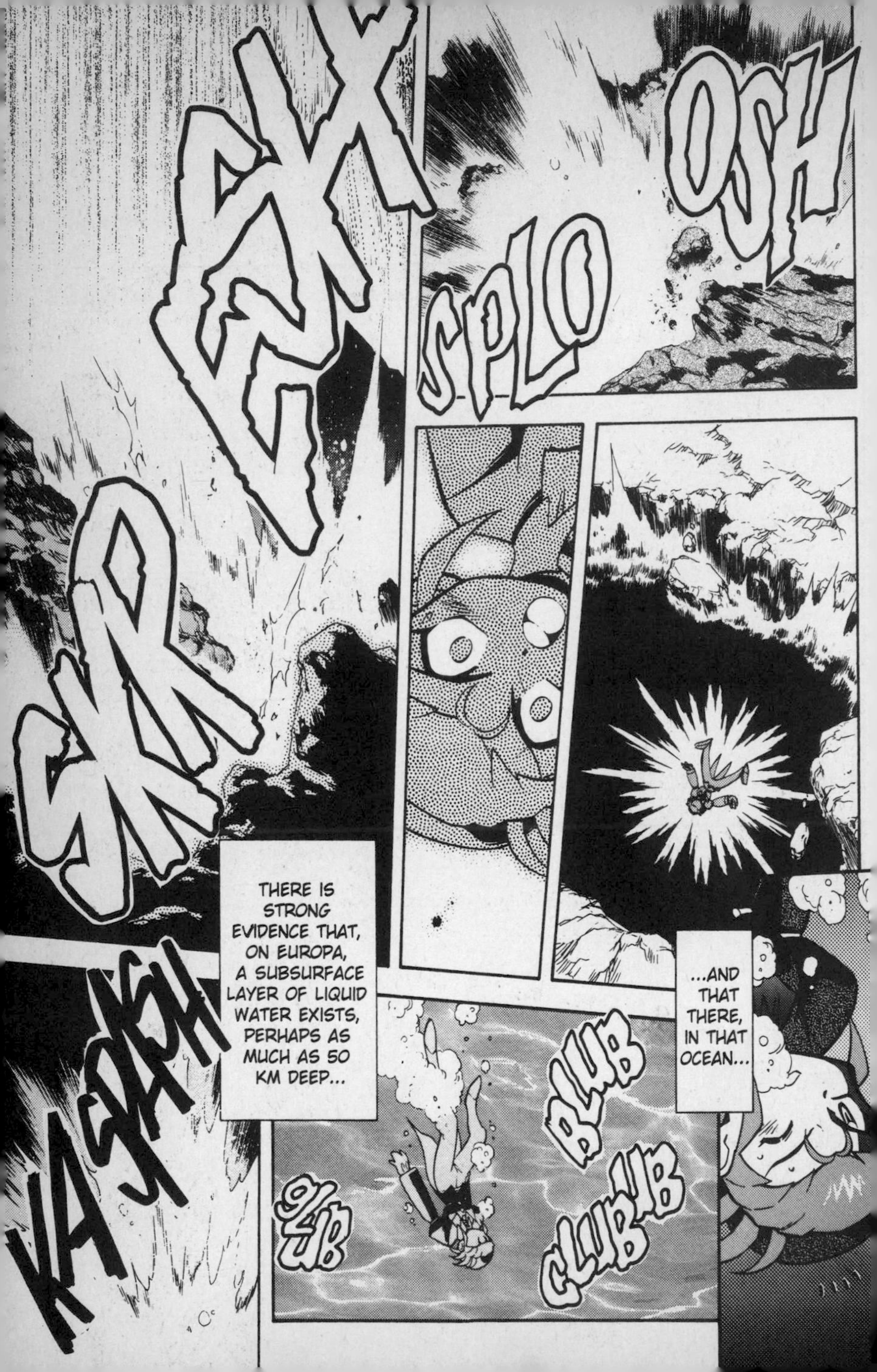
EX
SPLO
OSH
THERE IS STRONG EVIDENCE THAT, ON EUROPA, A SUBSURFACE LAYER OF LIQUID WATER EXISTS, PERHAPS AS MUCH AS 50 KM DEEP...
BLUB
...AND THAT THERE, IN THAT OCEAN...

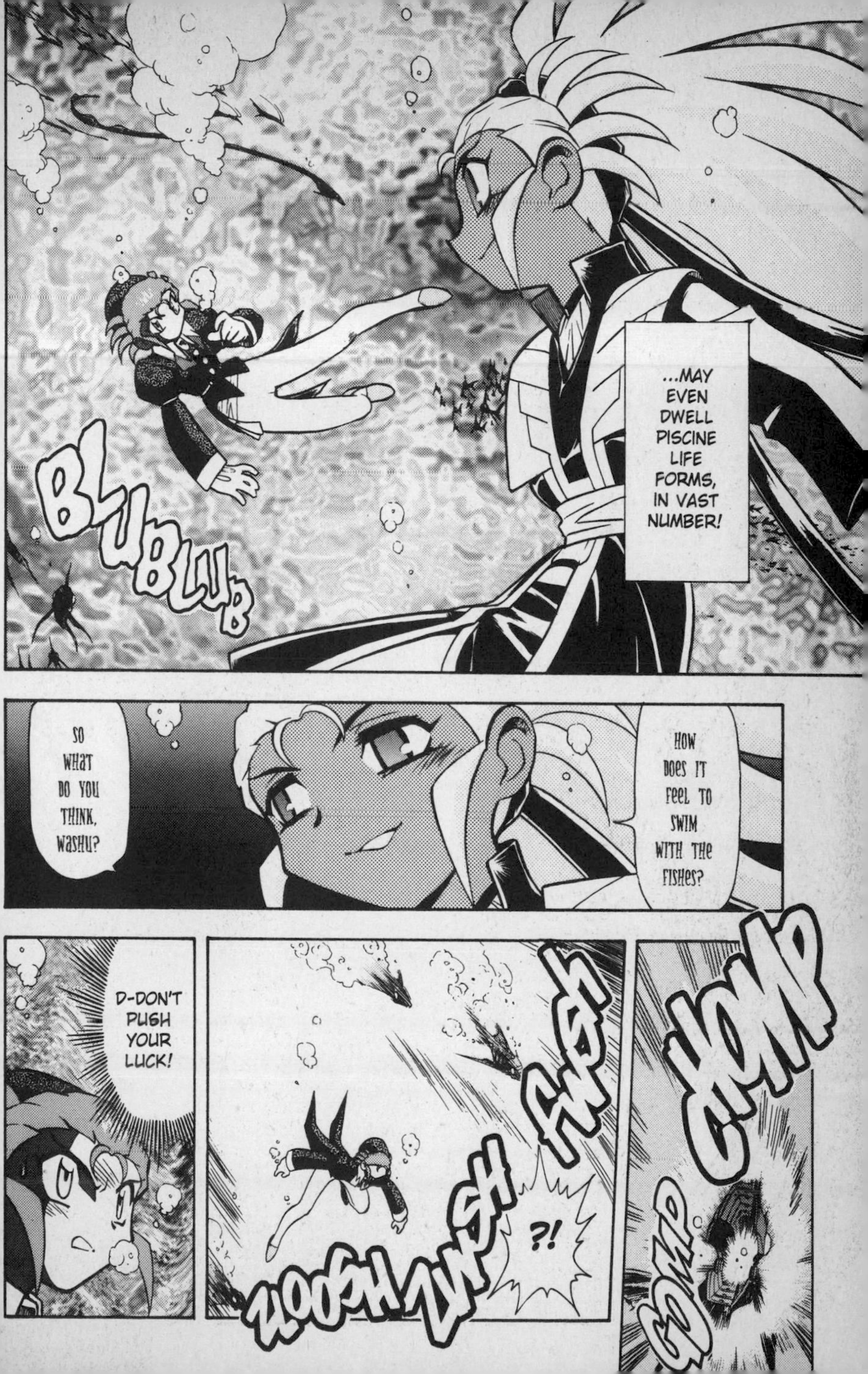
...MAY EVEN DWELL PISCINE LIFE FORMS, IN VAST NUMBER!
BLUBLUB
SO WHAT DO YOU THINK, WASHU?
HOW DOES IT FEEL TO SWIM WITH THE FISHES?
D-DON'T PUSH YOUR LUCK!
ZOOSH ZWISH FWOSH
?!
CHOMP
GOMP

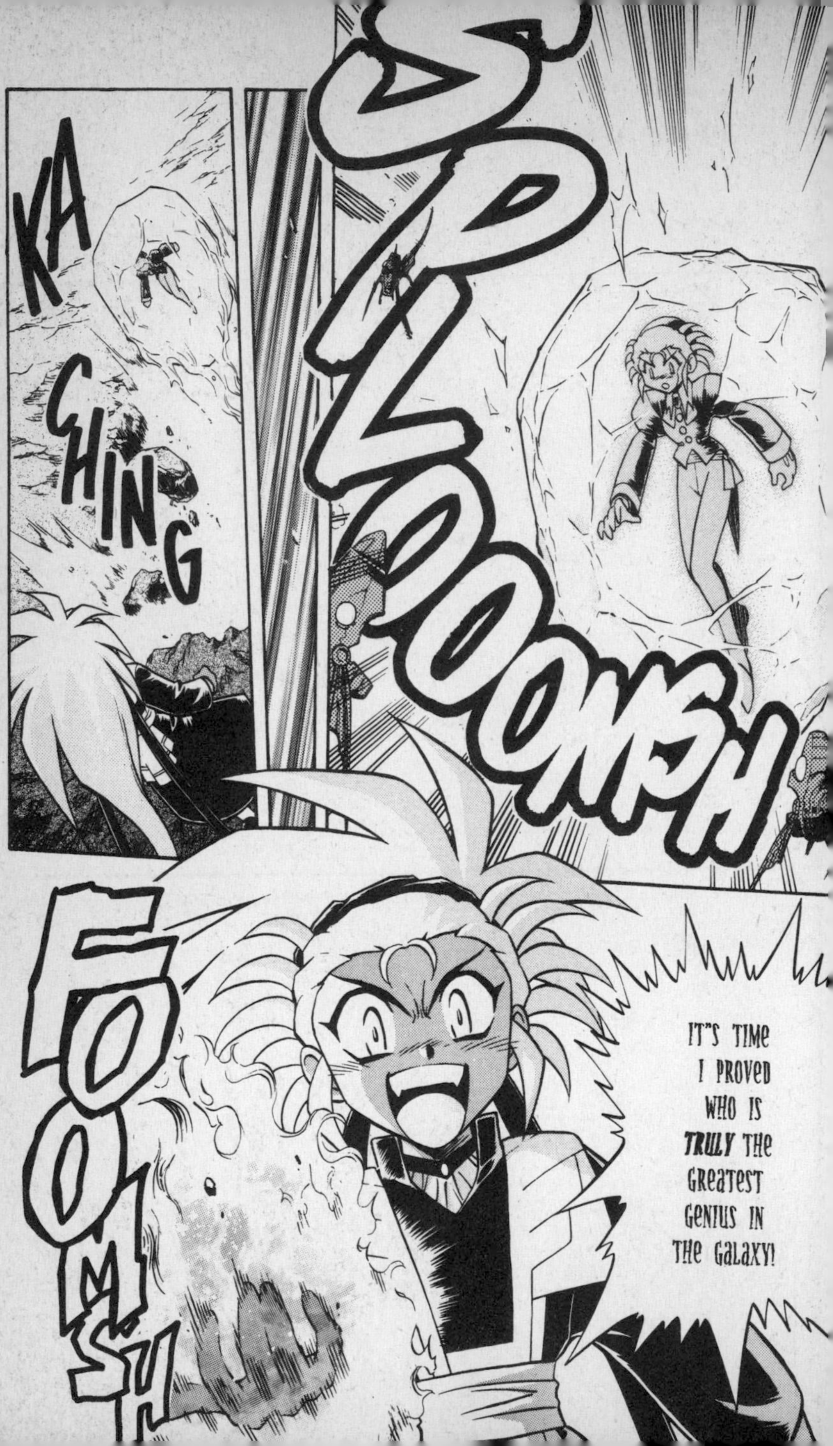
KA CHING
SPLOOOMPH
FOOMSH
IT'S TIME I PROVED WHO IS **TRULY** THE GREATEST GENIUS IN THE GALAXY!

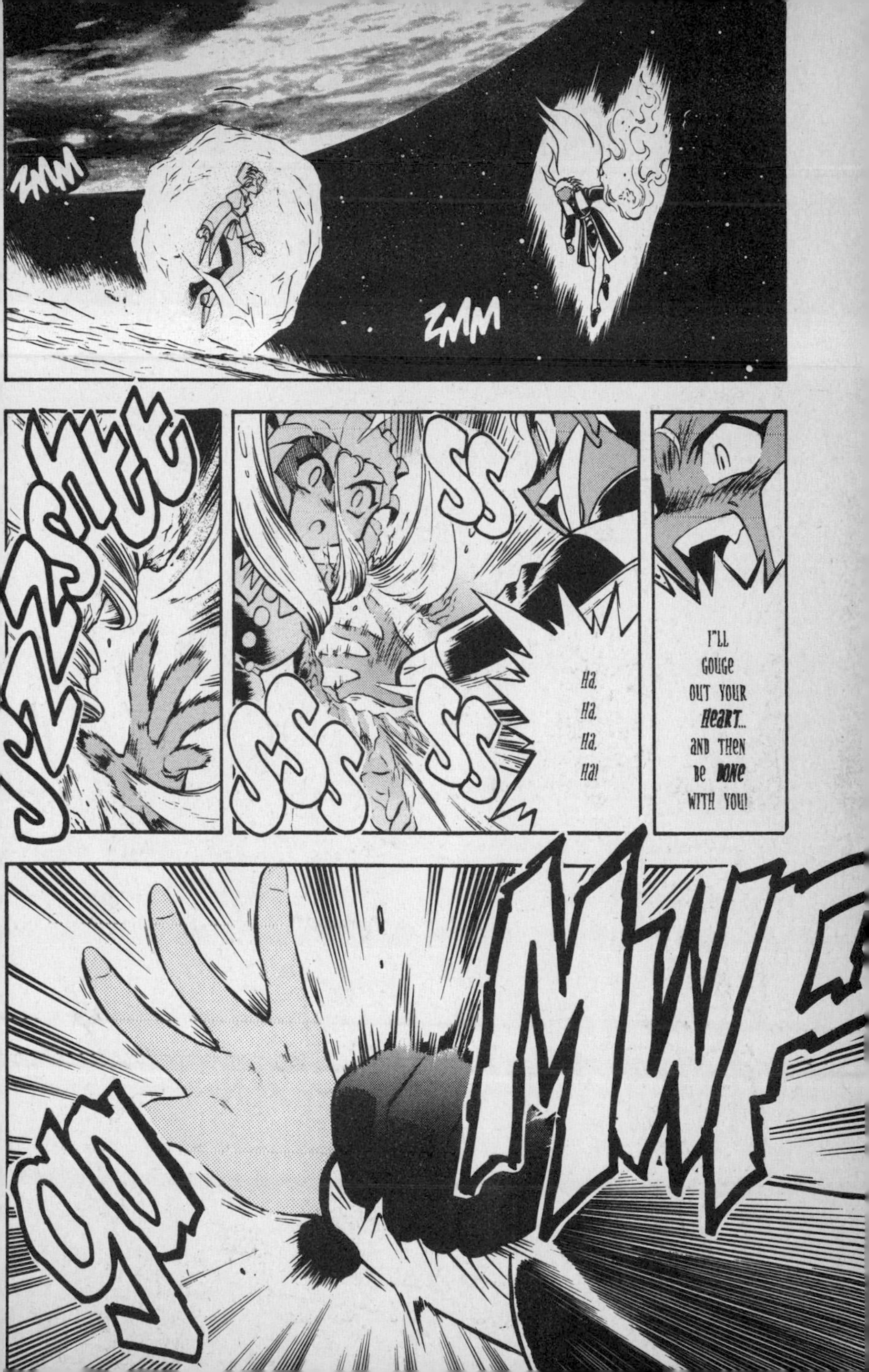
ZMM
ZMM
SS
SSS
SS
Ha, Ha, Ha, Ha!
I'LL GOUGE OUT YOUR HEART... AND THEN BE DONE WITH YOU!

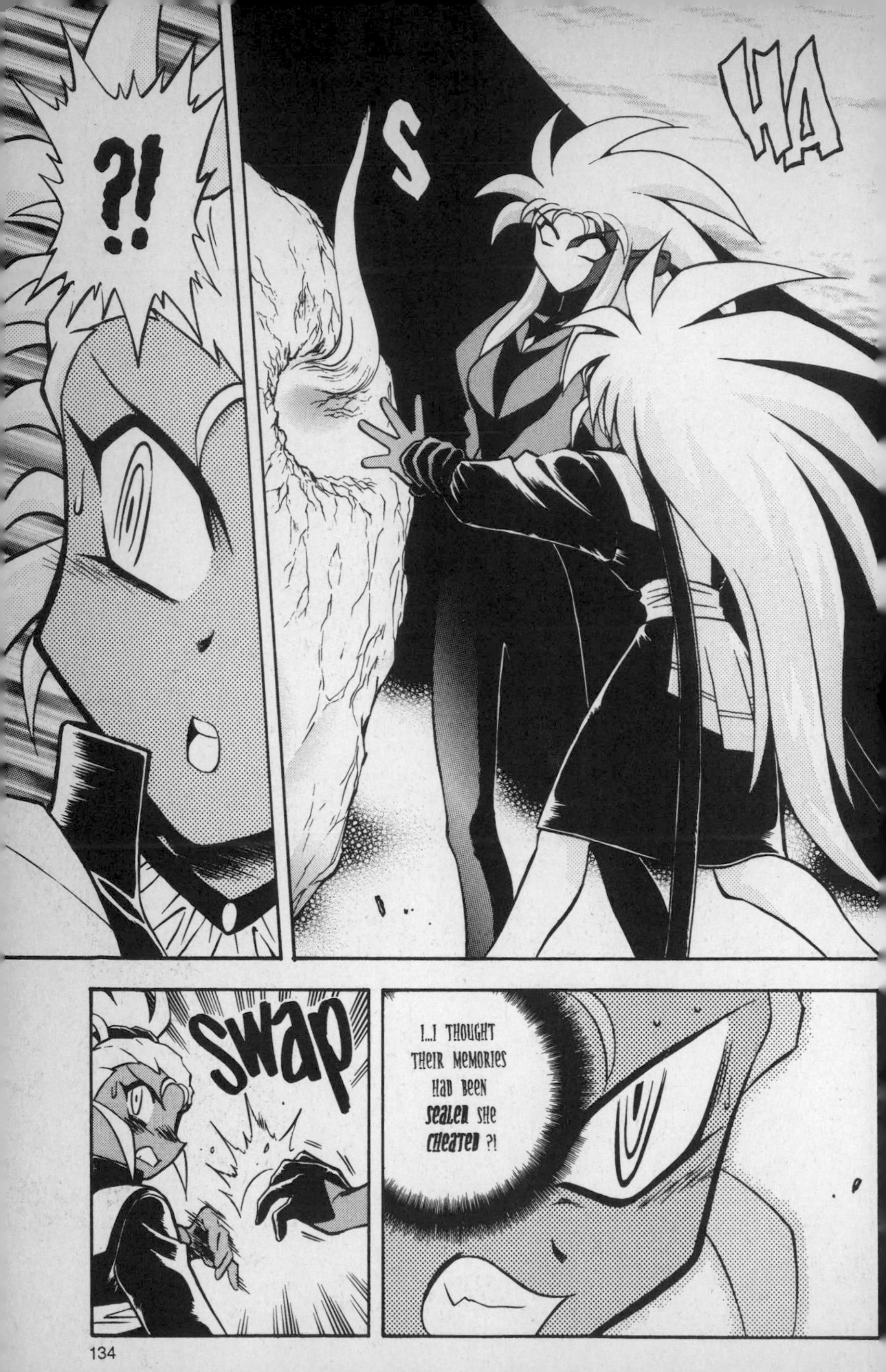
?!
S
HA
SWAP
I...I THOUGHT THEIR MEMORIES HAD BEEN SEALED SHE CHEATED ?!

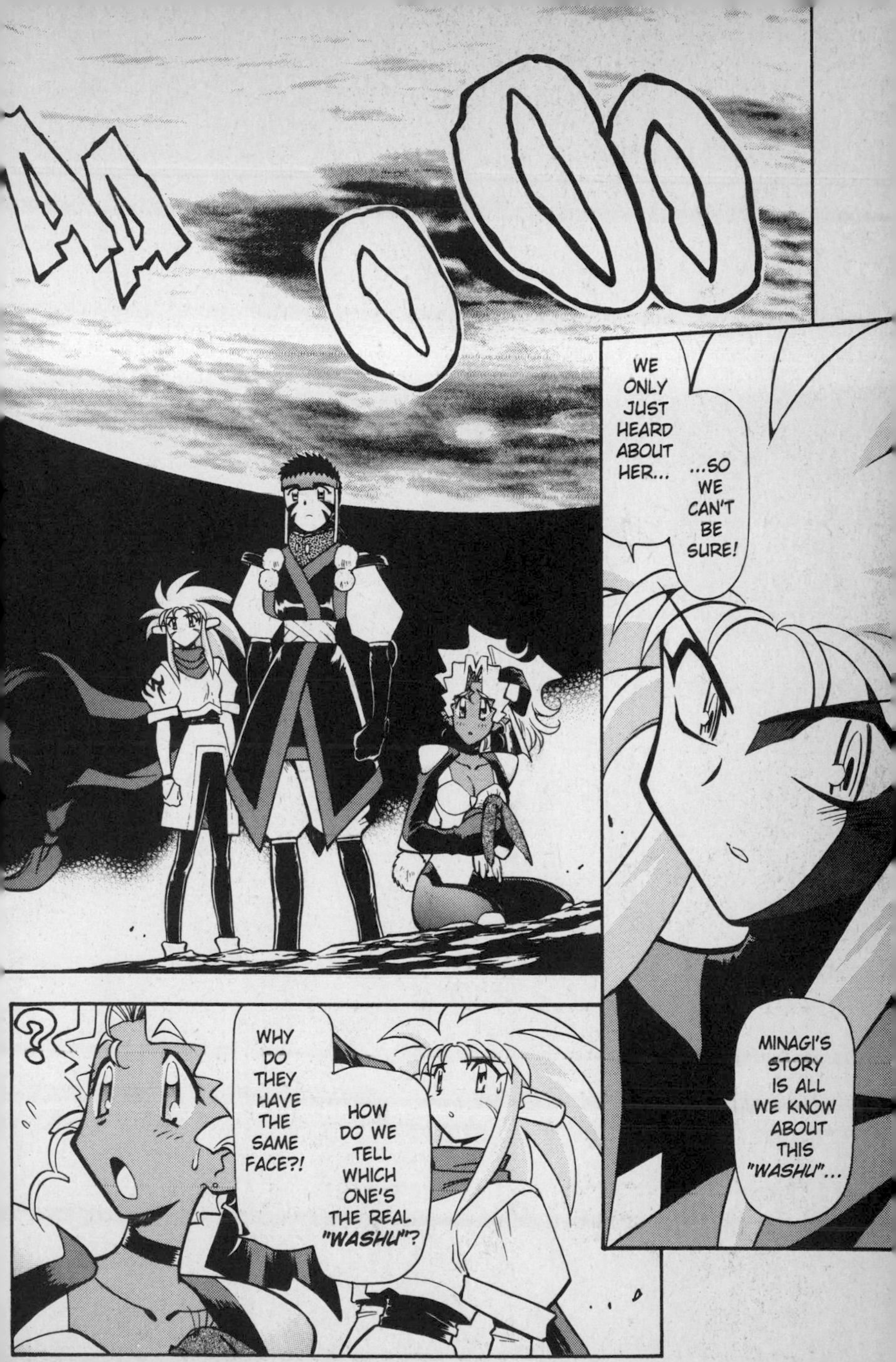

AA
OOO
?
WHY DO THEY HAVE THE SAME FACE?!
HOW DO WE TELL WHICH ONE'S THE REAL "WASHU"?
WE ONLY JUST HEARD ABOUT HER...
...SO WE CAN'T BE SURE!
MINAGI'S STORY IS ALL WE KNOW ABOUT THIS "WASHU"...

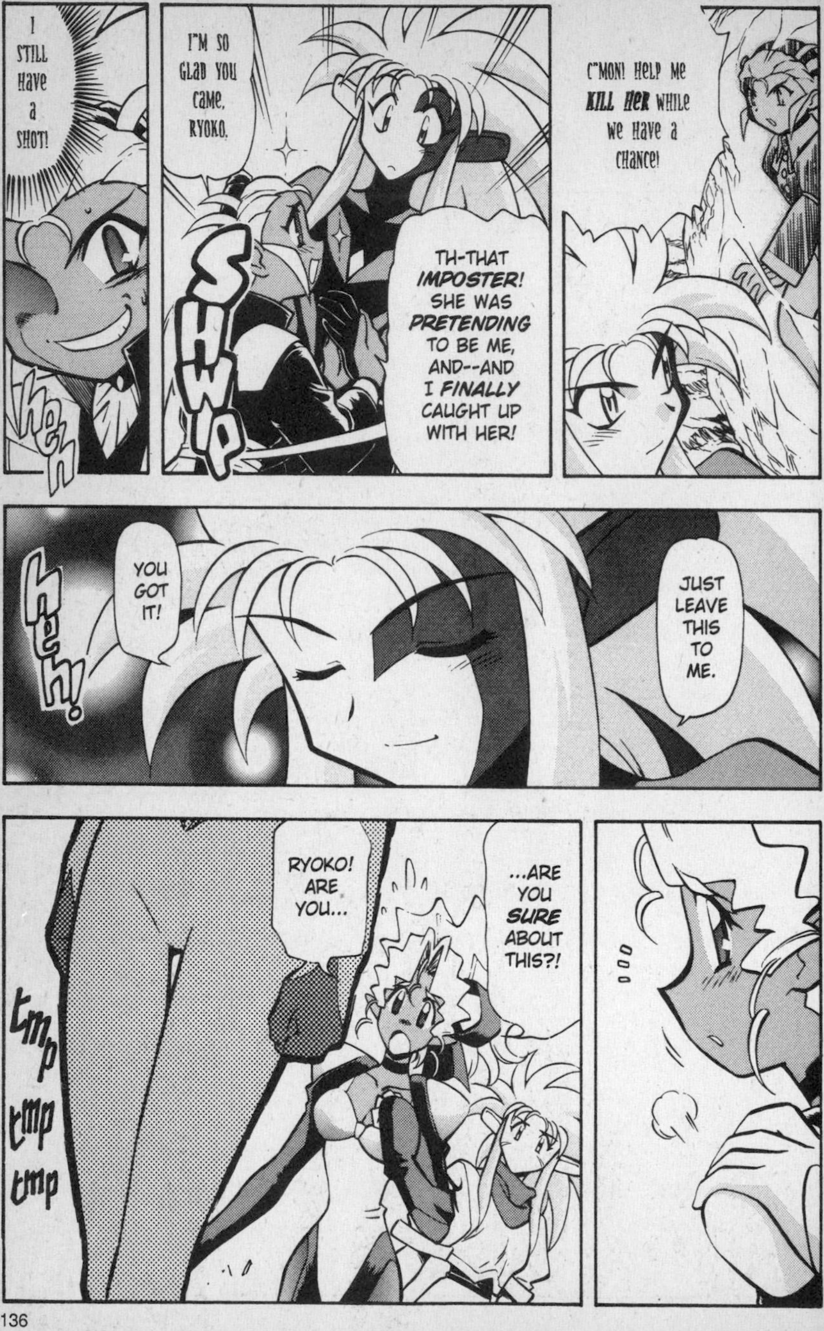
I STILL HAVE A SHOT!
HEH
I'M SO GLAD YOU CAME, RYOKO.
SHWIP
TH-THAT IMPOSTER! SHE WAS PRETENDING TO BE ME, AND--AND I FINALLY CAUGHT UP WITH HER!
C'MON! HELP ME KILL HER WHILE WE HAVE A CHANCE!
HEH!
YOU GOT IT!
JUST LEAVE THIS TO ME.
TMP TMP TMP
RYOKO! ARE YOU...
...ARE YOU SURE ABOUT THIS?!

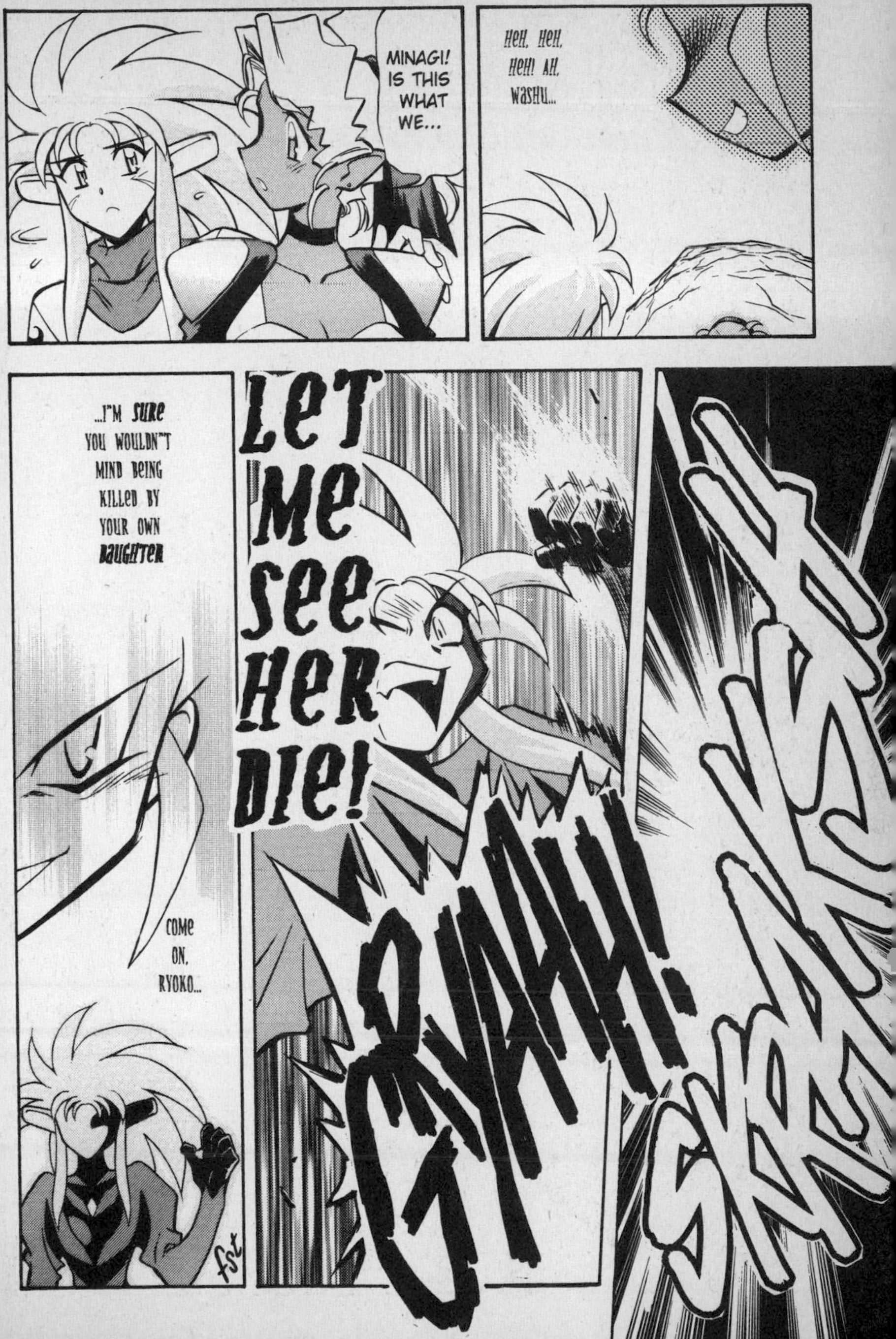
MINAGI! IS THIS WHAT WE...
HEH, HEH, HEH! AH, WASHU...
...I'M SURE YOU WOULDN'T MIND BEING KILLED BY YOUR OWN DAUGHTER
COME ON, RYOKO...
LET ME SEE HER DIE!

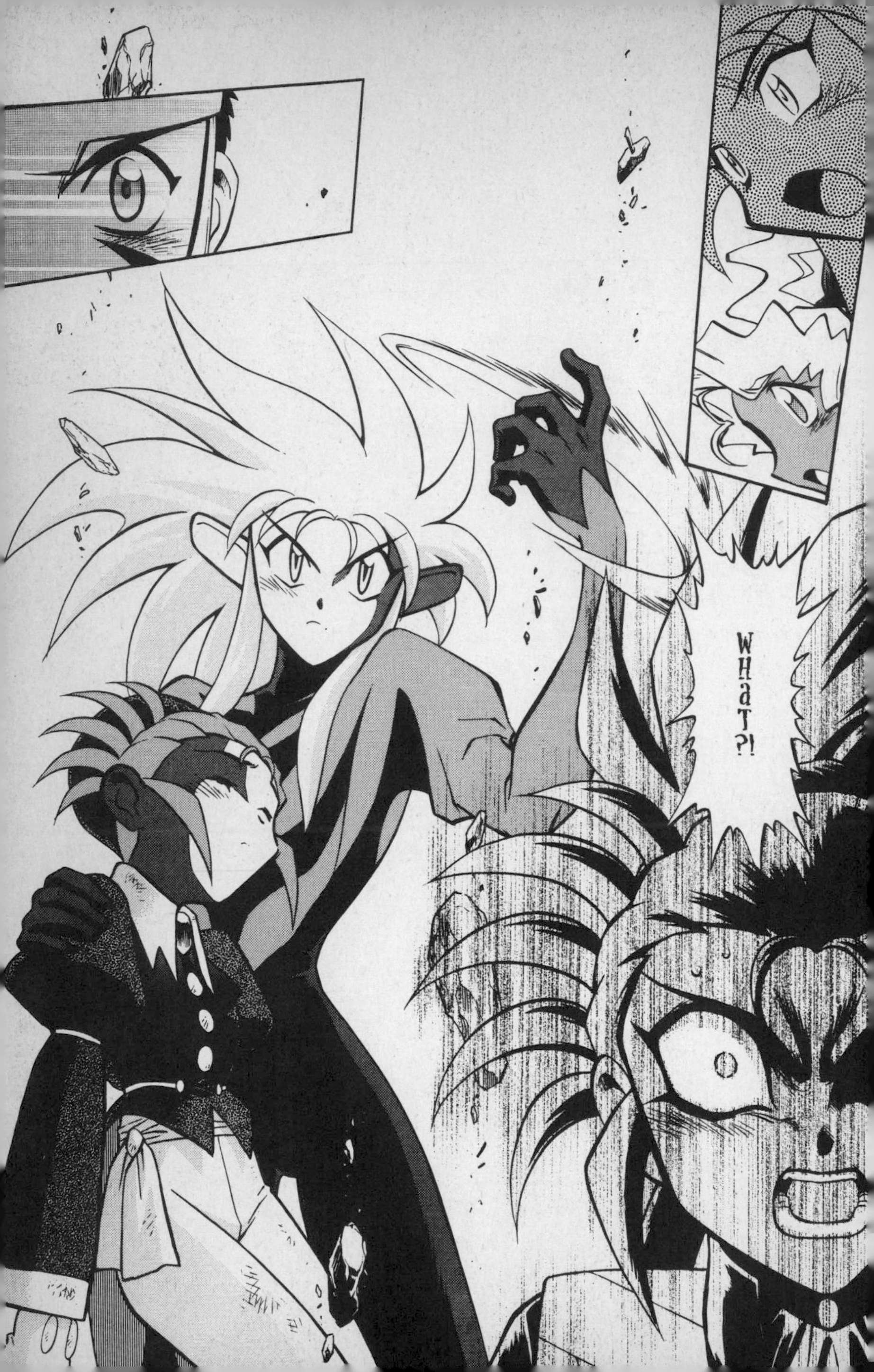
WHAT?!

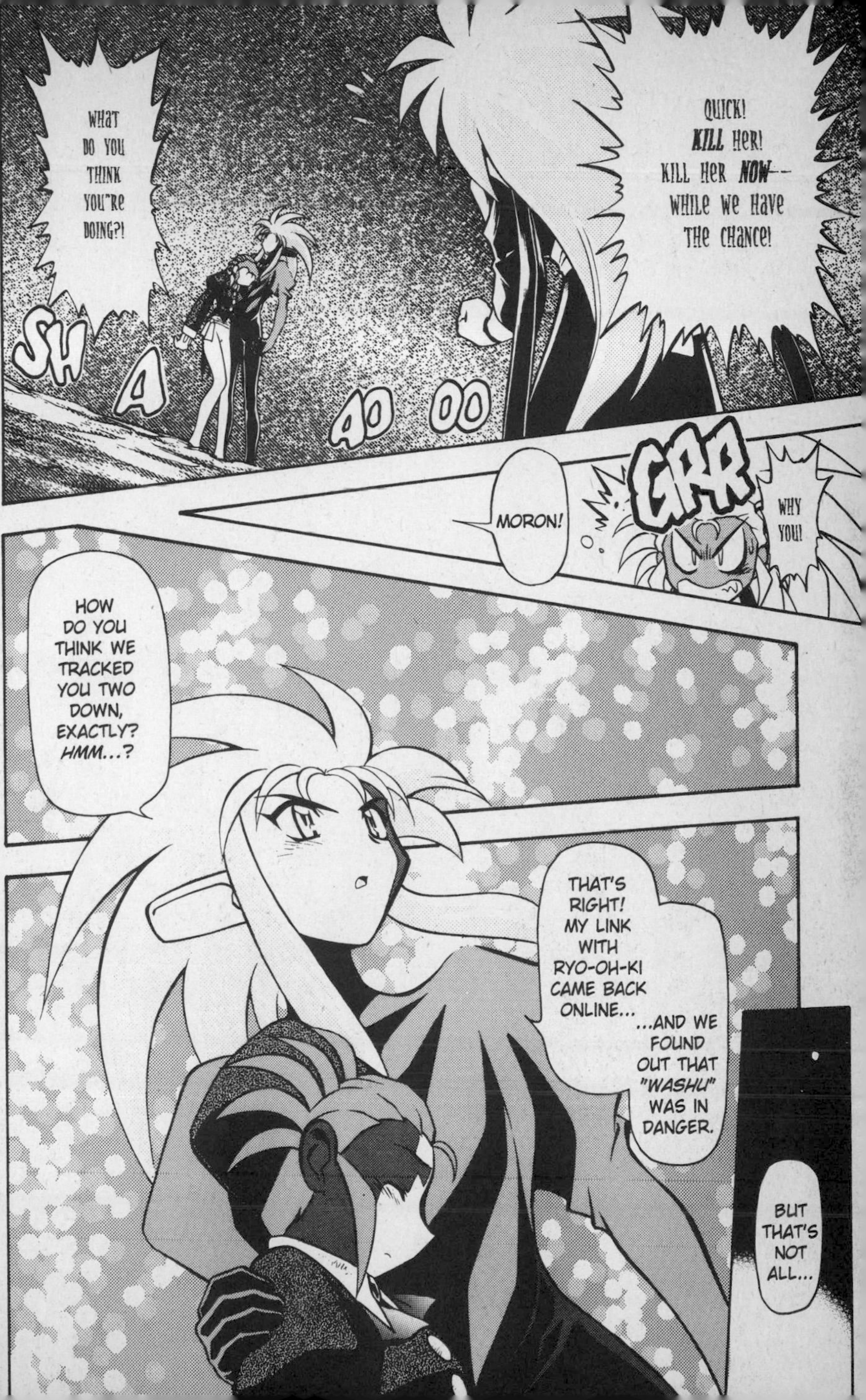
WHAT DO YOU THINK YOU'RE DOING?!
SHAAOOO
QUICK! KILL HER! KILL HER NOW-- WHILE WE HAVE THE CHANCE!
MORON!
GRR
WHY YOU!
HOW DO YOU THINK WE TRACKED YOU TWO DOWN, EXACTLY? HMM...?
THAT'S RIGHT! MY LINK WITH RYO-OH-KI CAME BACK ONLINE...
...AND WE FOUND OUT THAT "WASHU" WAS IN DANGER.
BUT THAT'S NOT ALL...

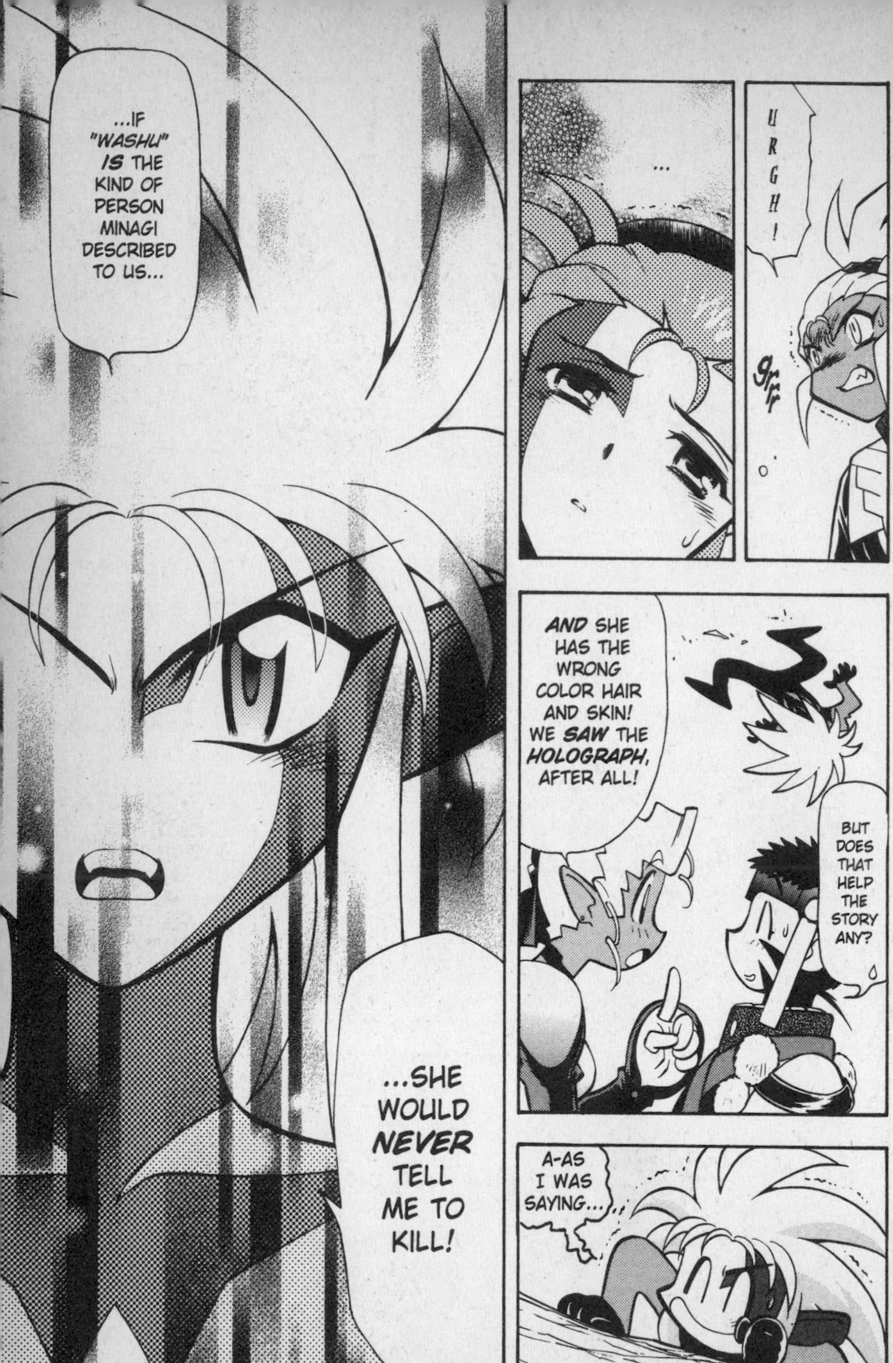
...IF "WASHU" IS THE KIND OF PERSON MINAGI DESCRIBED TO US...
...SHE WOULD NEVER TELL ME TO KILL!
...
URGH!
grrr
AND SHE HAS THE WRONG COLOR HAIR AND SKIN! WE SAW THE HOLOGRAPH, AFTER ALL!
BUT DOES THAT HELP THE STORY ANY?
A-AS I WAS SAYING...

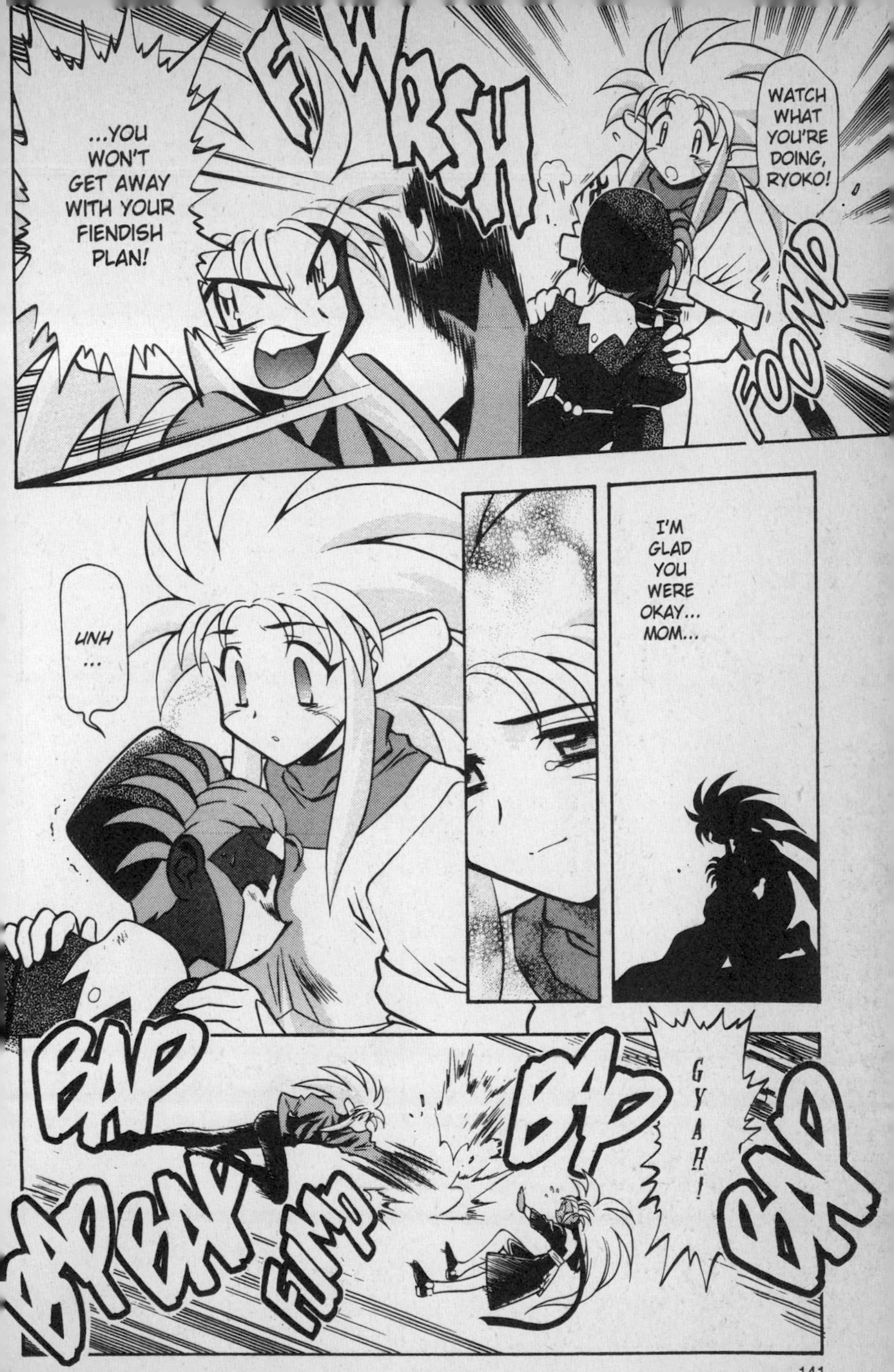
...YOU WON'T GET AWAY WITH YOUR FIENDISH PLAN!
FWRSH
WATCH WHAT YOU'RE DOING, RYOKO!
FOOMP
UNH ...
I'M GLAD YOU WERE OKAY... MOM...
BAP
FUMP
BAP
GYAH!
BAP

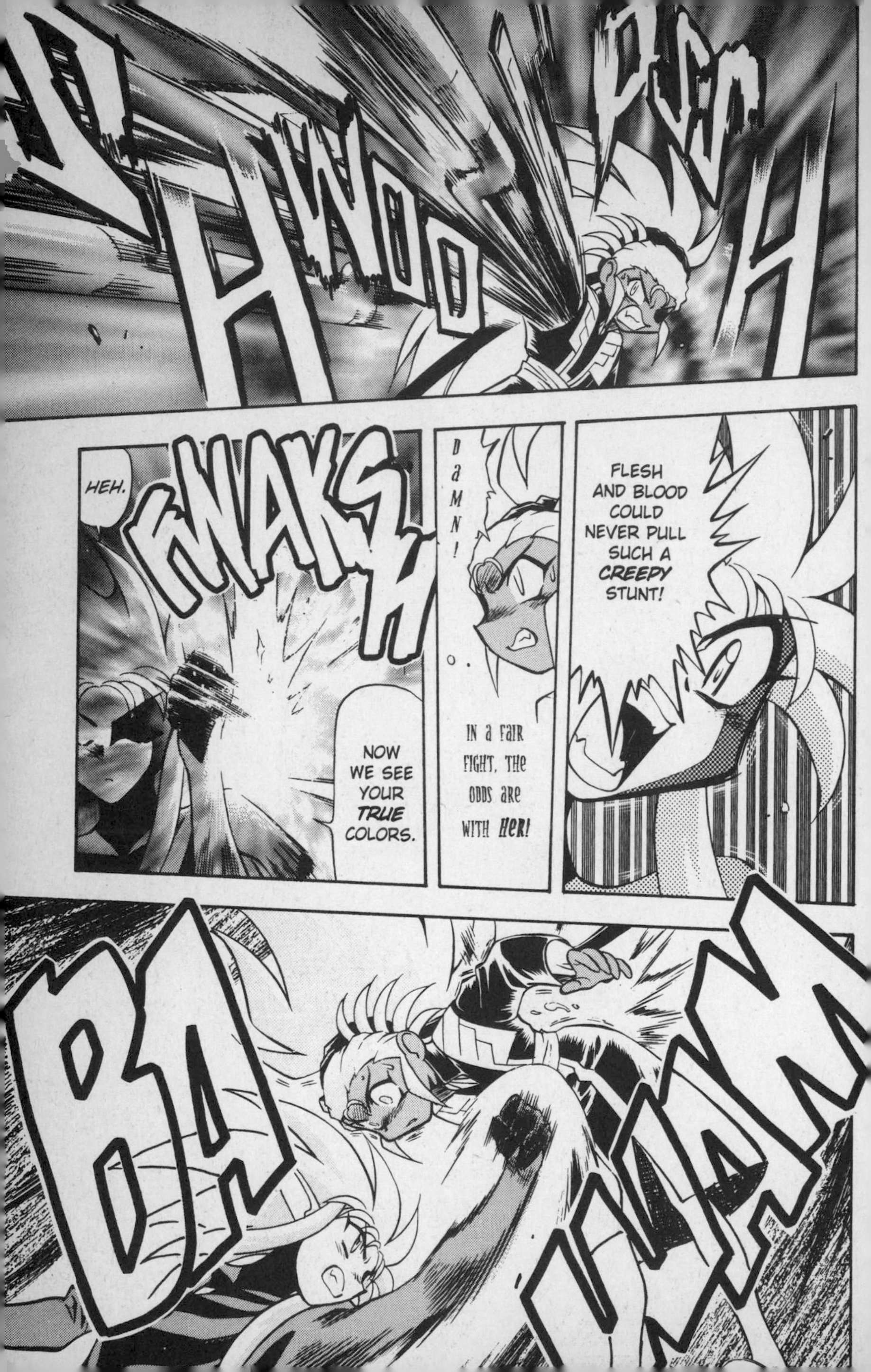
HEH.
NOW WE SEE YOUR TRUE COLORS.
DAMN!
IN A FAIR FIGHT, THE ODDS ARE WITH HER!
FLESH AND BLOOD COULD NEVER PULL SUCH A CREEPY STUNT!

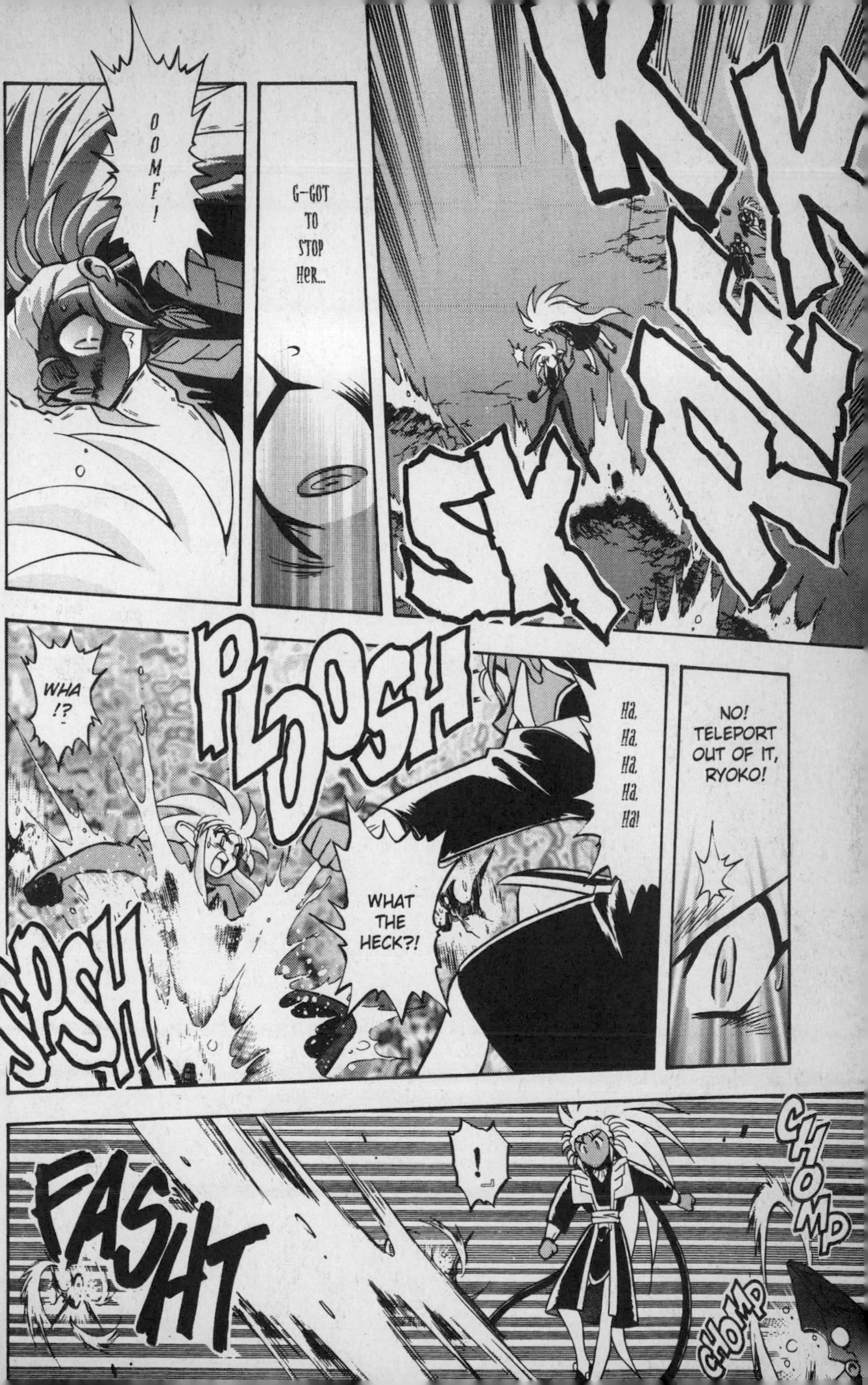
OOMF!
G-GOT TO STOP HER...
WHA!?
PLOOSH
SPSH
WHAT THE HECK?!
Ha, Ha, Ha, Ha, Ha!
NO! TELEPORT OUT OF IT, RYOKO!
FASHT
!
CHOMP
CHOMP

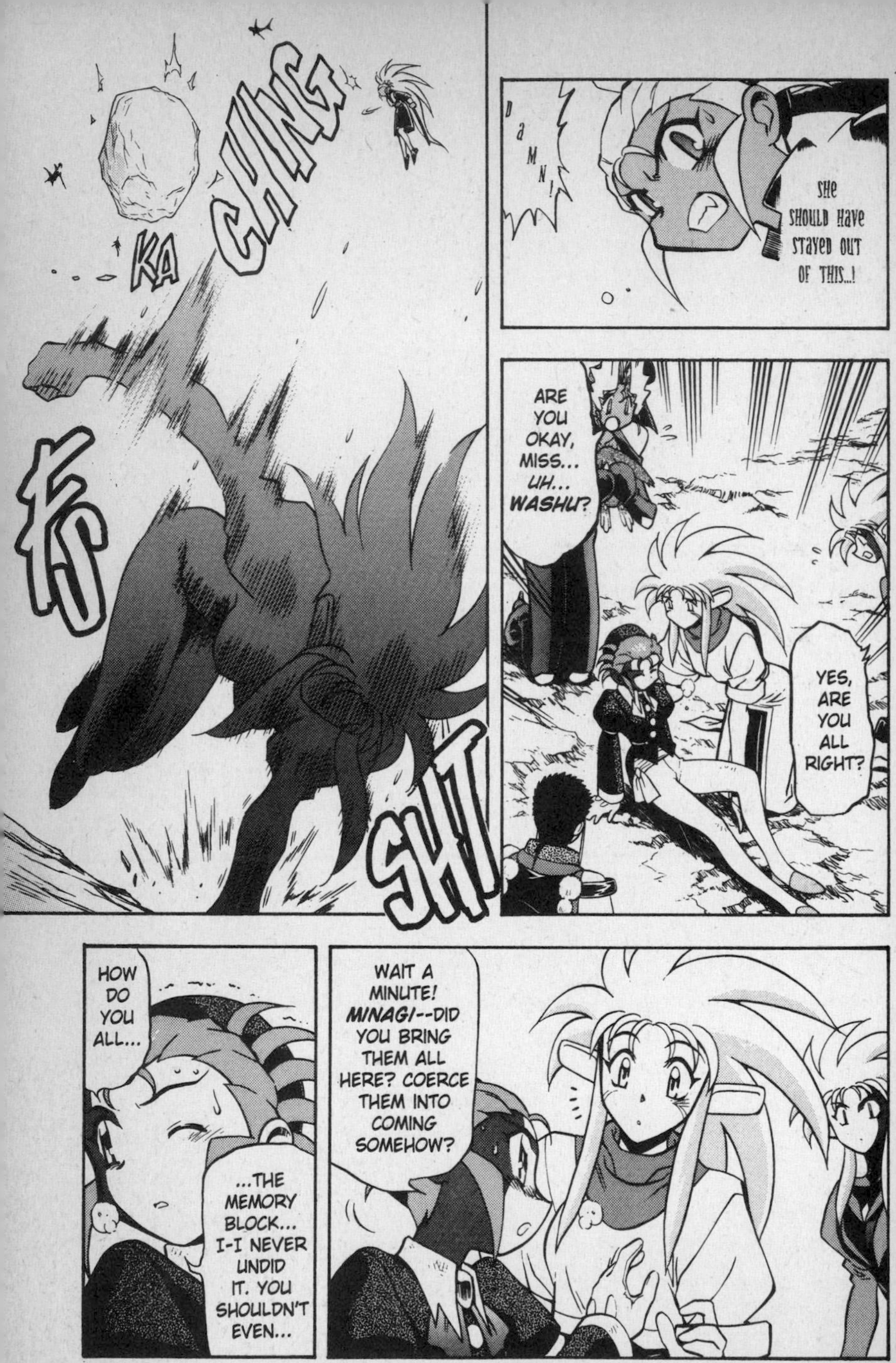
KA CHING
SHT
DAMN!
SHE SHOULD HAVE STAYED OUT OF THIS...!
ARE YOU OKAY, MISS... UH... WASHU?
YES, ARE YOU ALL RIGHT?
HOW DO YOU ALL...
...THE MEMORY BLOCK... I-I NEVER UNDID IT. YOU SHOULDN'T EVEN...
WAIT A MINUTE! MINAGI--DID YOU BRING THEM ALL HERE? COERCE THEM INTO COMING SOMEHOW?

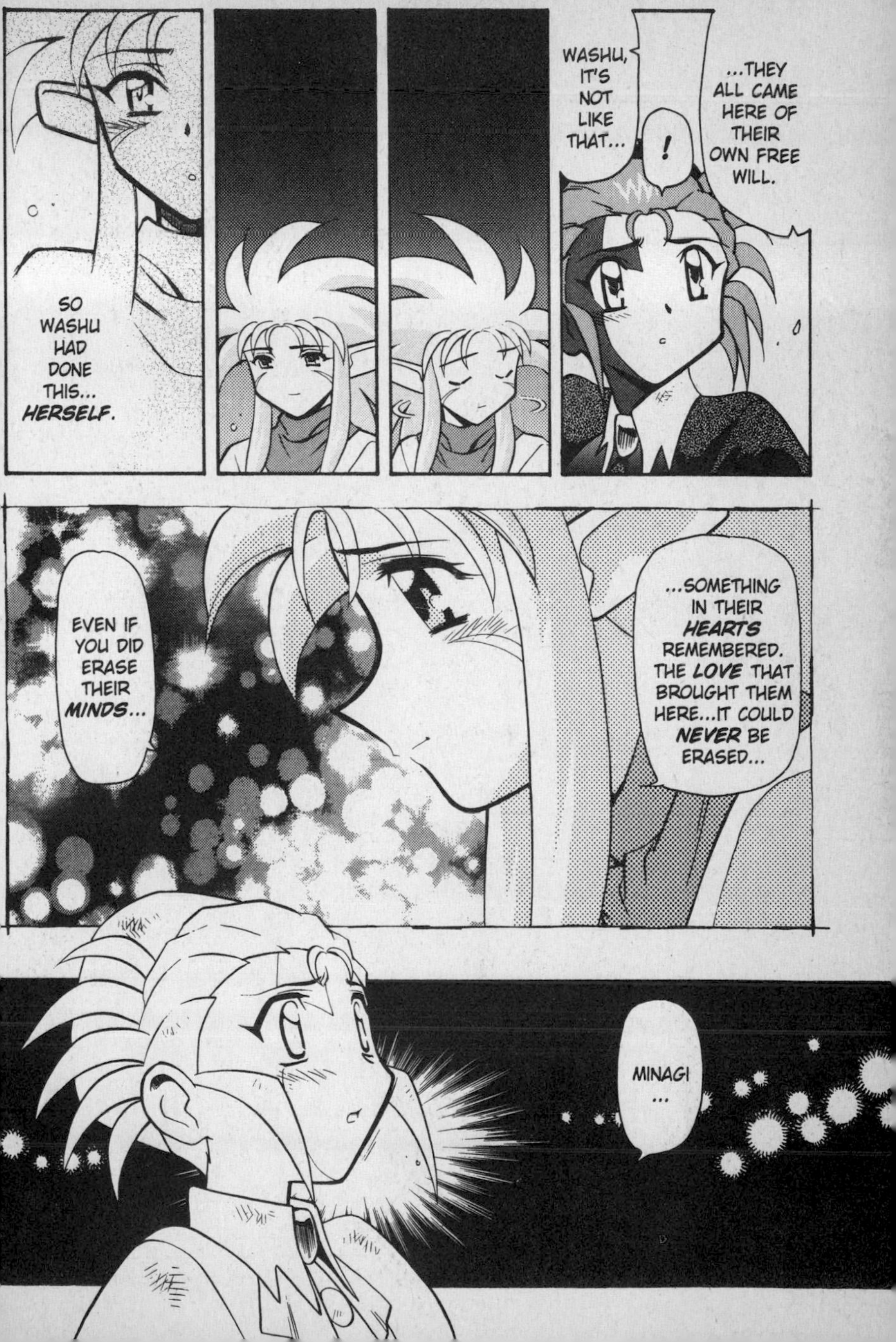
SO WASHU HAD DONE THIS... HERSELF.
WASHU, IT'S NOT LIKE THAT...
!
...THEY ALL CAME HERE OF THEIR OWN FREE WILL.
EVEN IF YOU DID ERASE THEIR MINDS...
...SOMETHING IN THEIR HEARTS REMEMBERED. THE LOVE THAT BROUGHT THEM HERE...IT COULD NEVER BE ERASED...
MINAGI ...

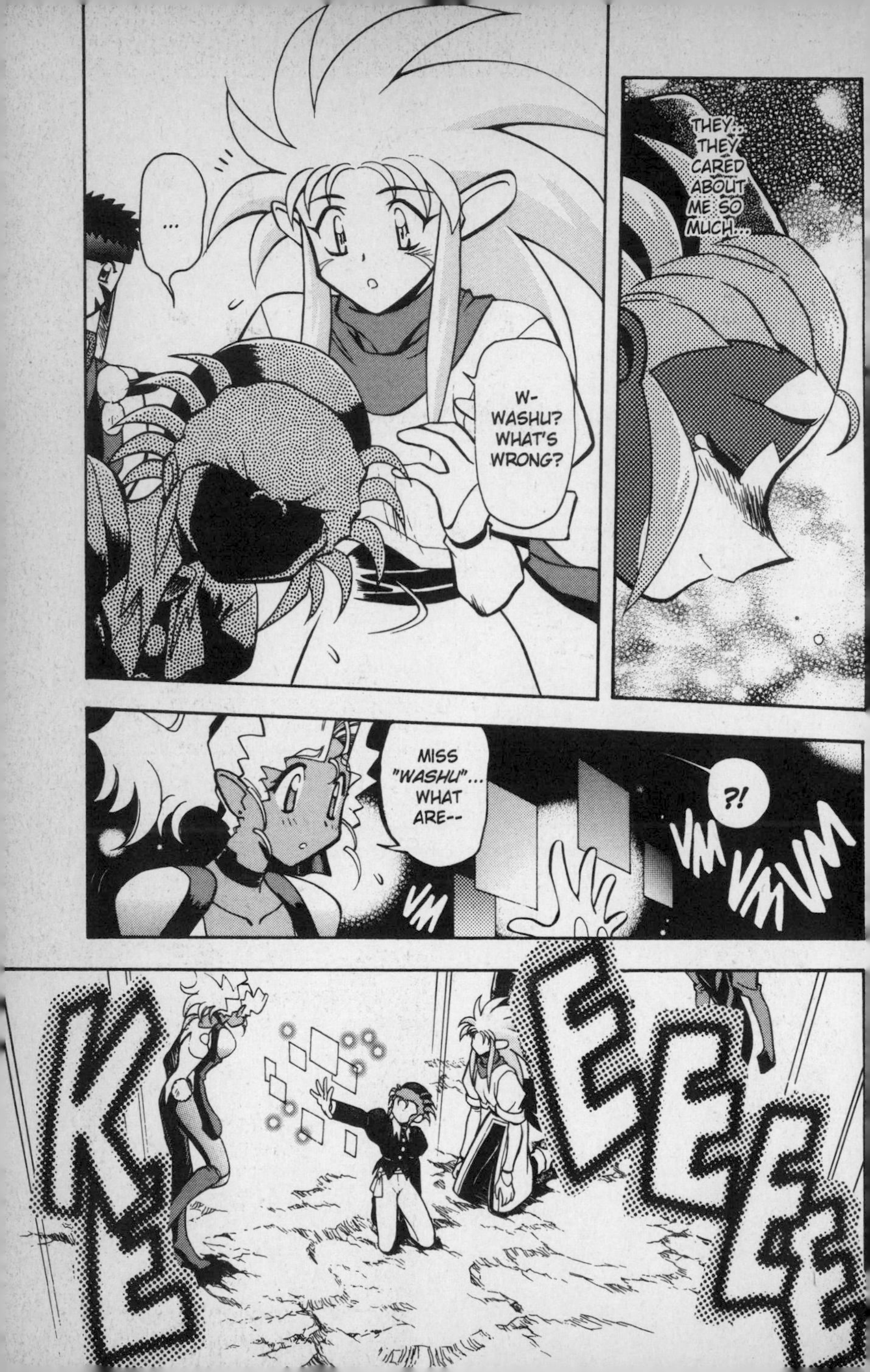
...
W-WASHU? WHAT'S WRONG?
THEY... THEY CARED ABOUT ME SO MUCH...
MISS "WASHU"... WHAT ARE--
VM
?!
VM VM VM VM

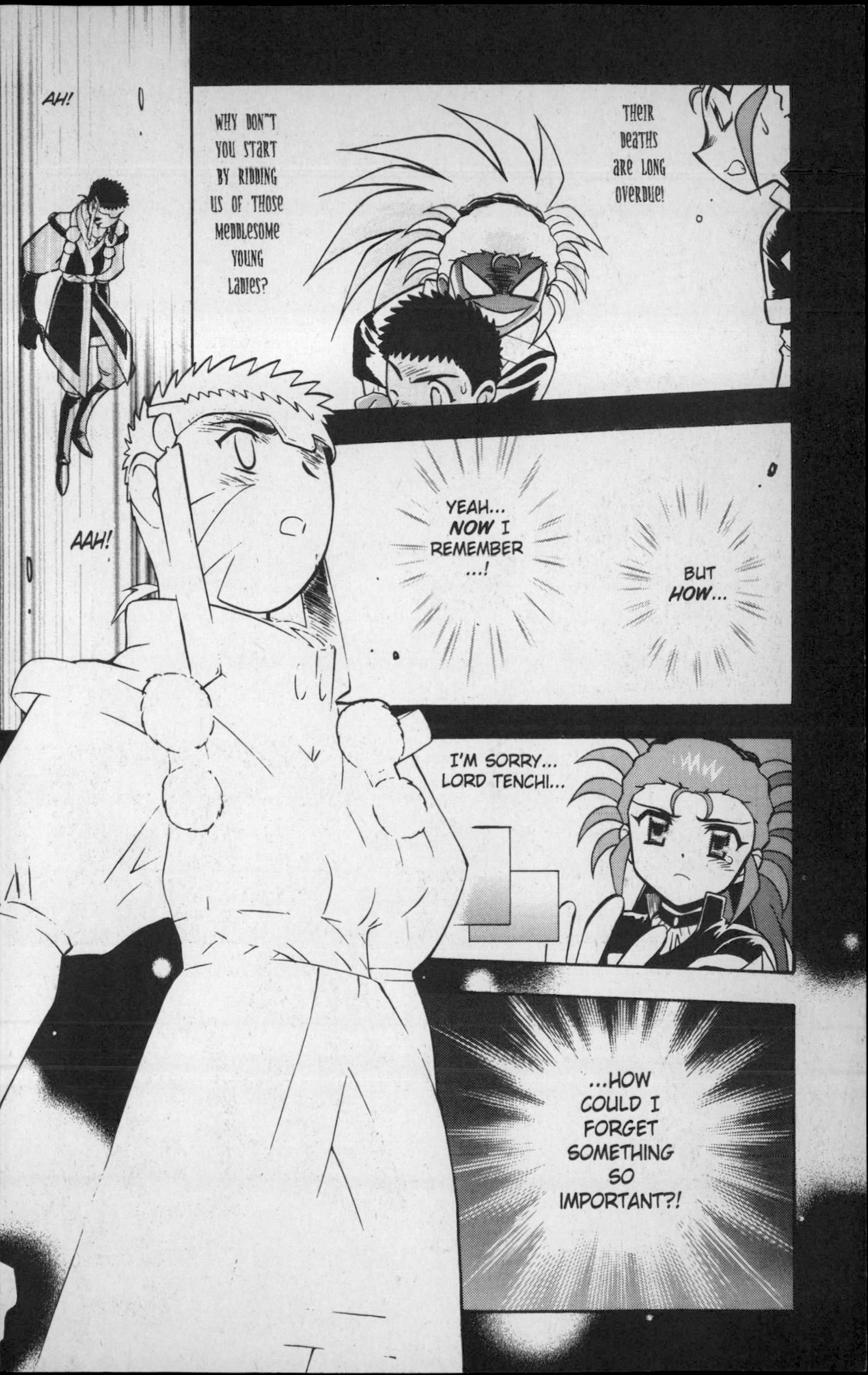
AH!
WHY DON'T YOU START BY RIDDING US OF THOSE MEDDLESOME YOUNG LADIES?
THEIR DEATHS ARE LONG OVERDUE!
AAH!
YEAH... NOW I REMEMBER ...!
BUT HOW...
I'M SORRY... LORD TENCHI...
...HOW COULD I FORGET SOMETHING SO IMPORTANT?!

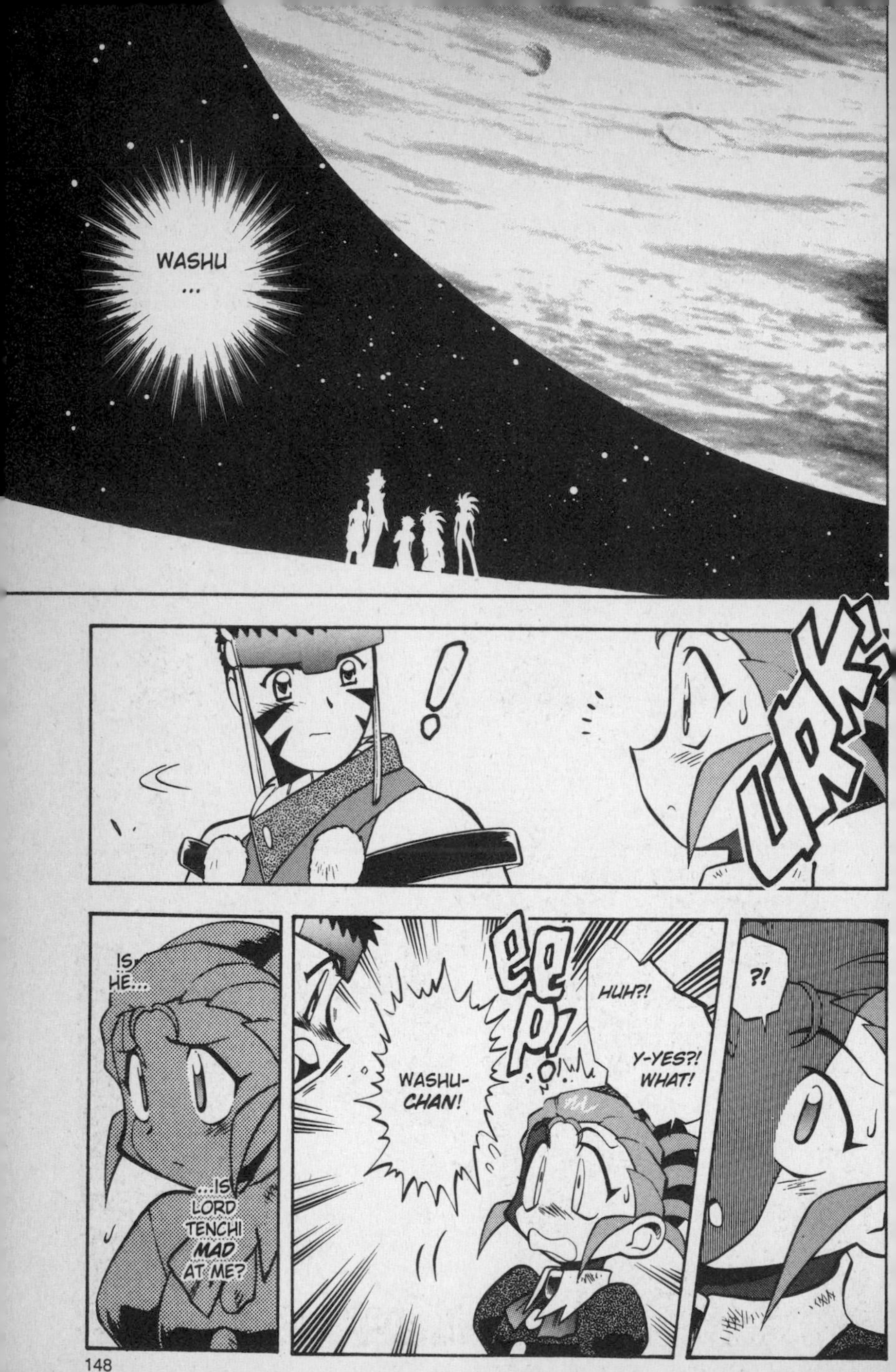
WASHU ...
!
URK!
IS... HE...
...IS LORD TENCHI MAD AT ME?
WASHU-CHAN!
EEP!
HUH?!
Y-YES?! WHAT!
?!

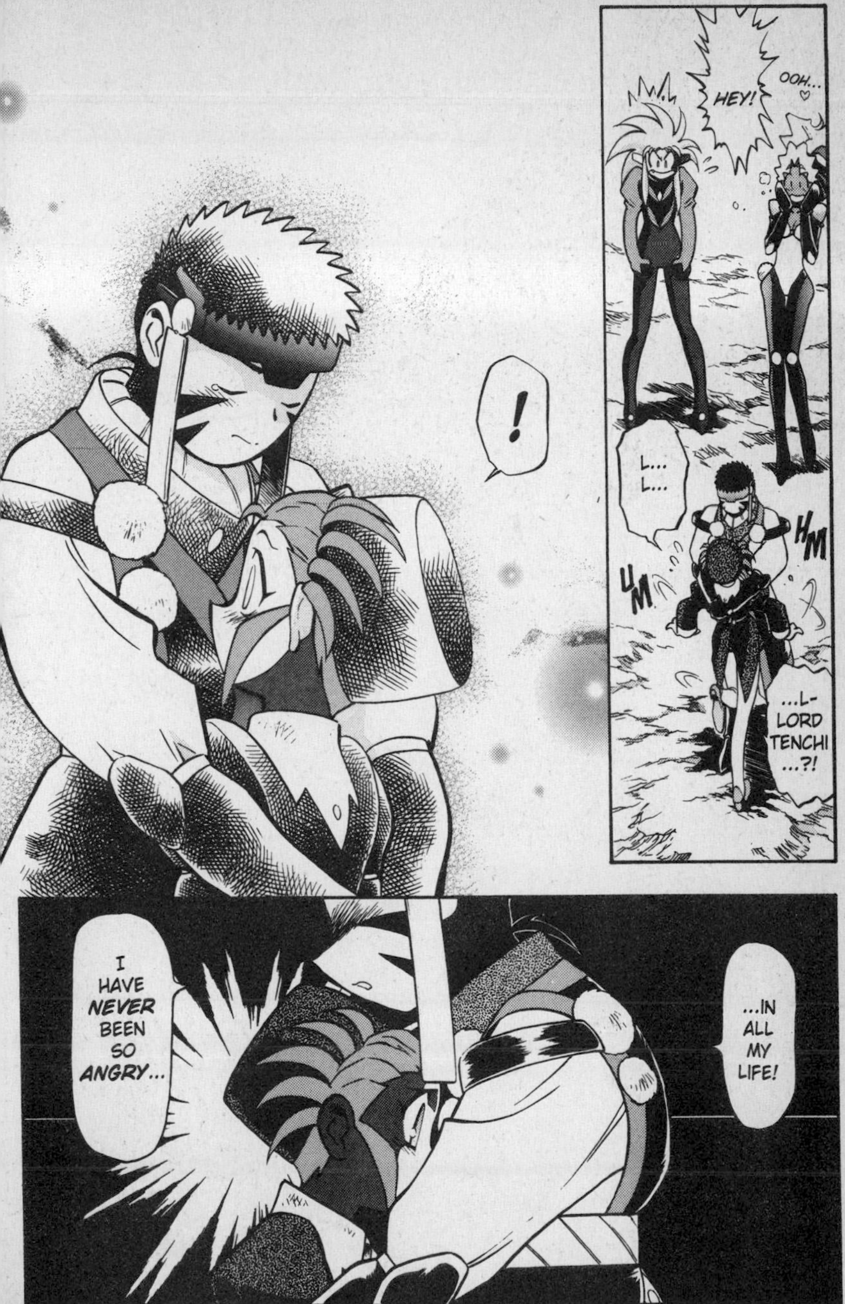
!
HEY!
OOH... ♡
L... L...
HM
UM
...L-LORD TENCHI ...?!
I HAVE NEVER BEEN SO ANGRY...
...IN ALL MY LIFE!

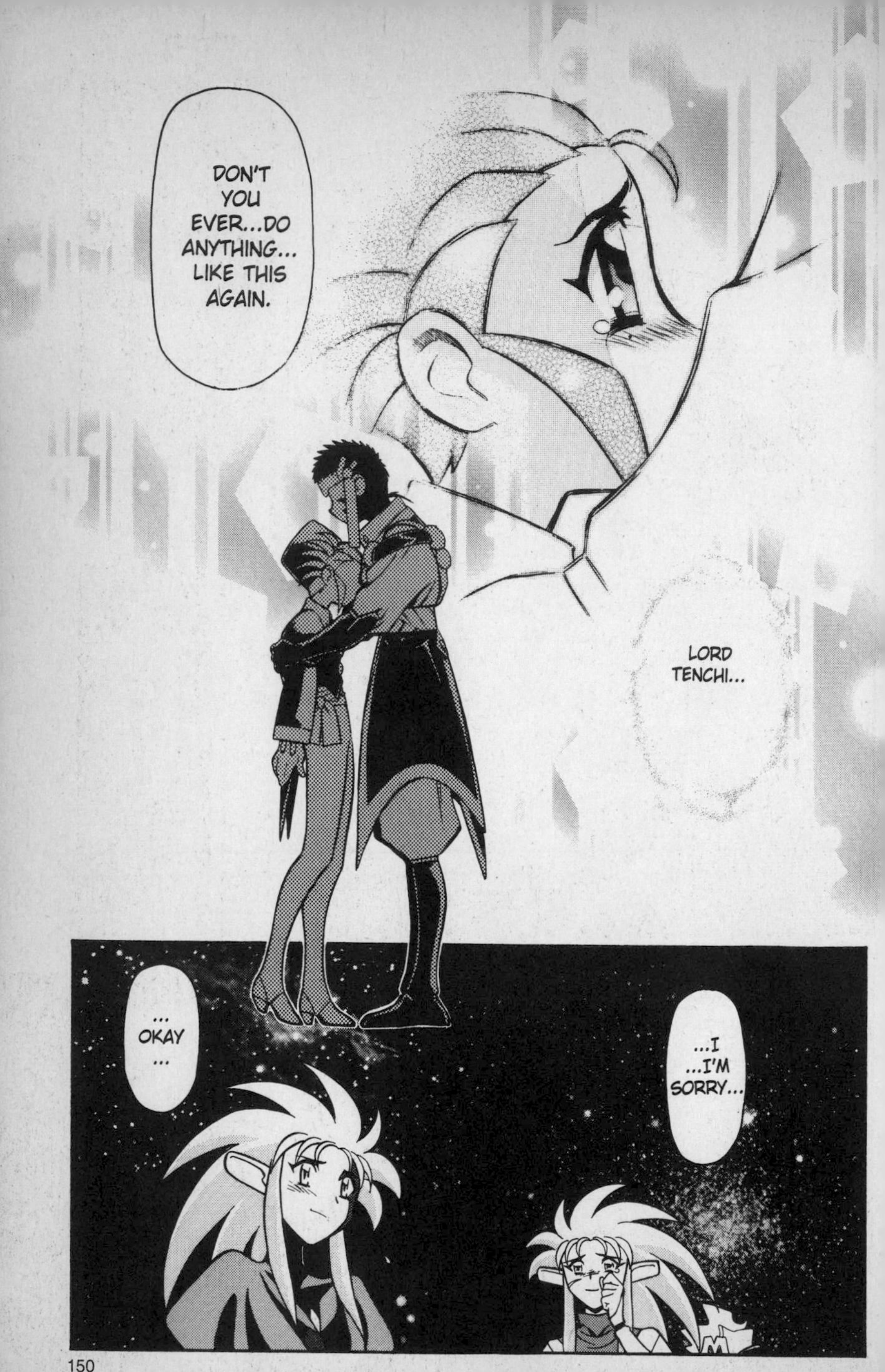
DON'T YOU EVER...DO ANYTHING... LIKE THIS AGAIN.
LORD TENCHI...
... OKAY ...
...I ...I'M SORRY...

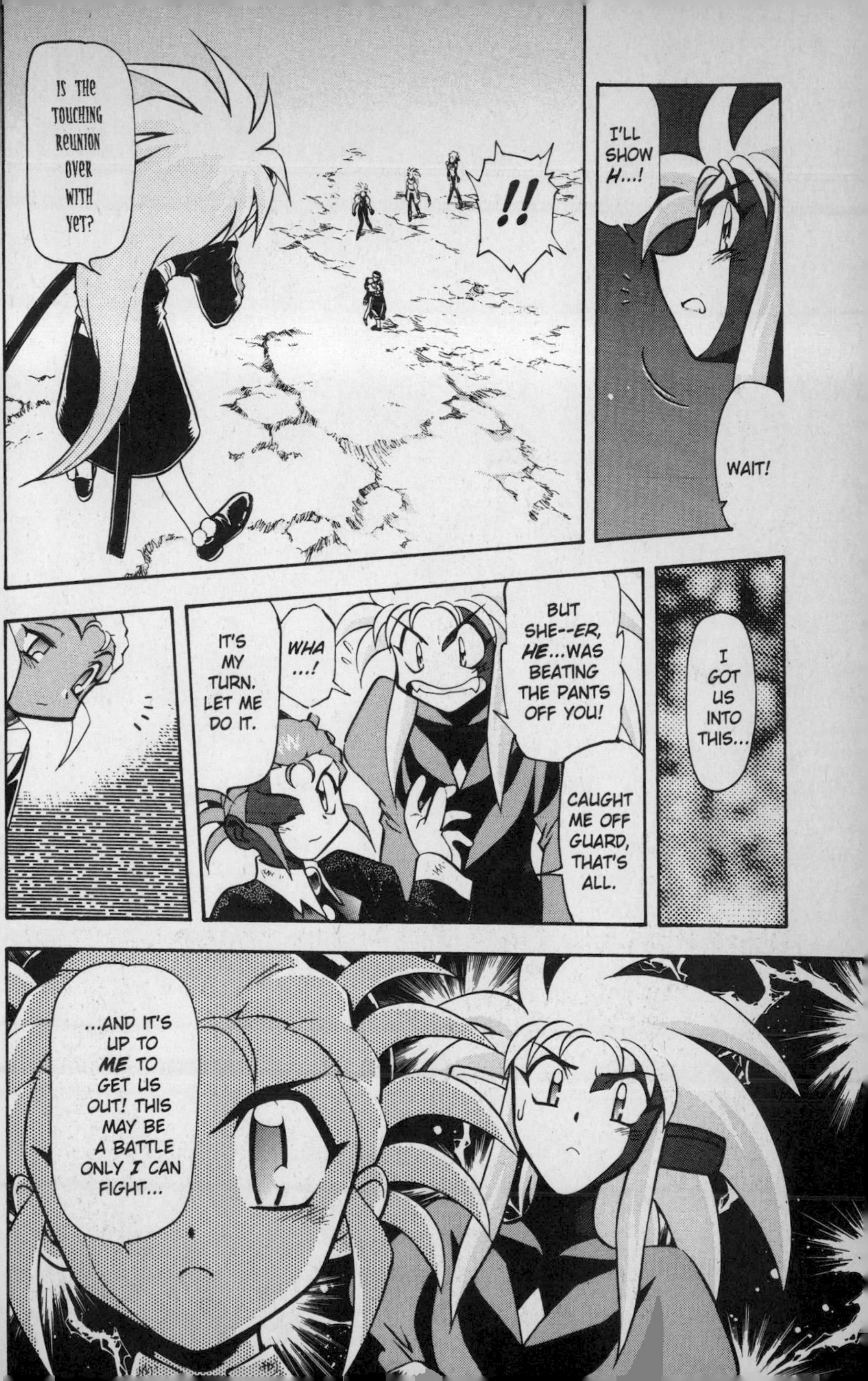
IS THE TOUCHING REUNION OVER WITH YET?
!!
I'LL SHOW *H*...!
WAIT!
IT'S MY TURN. LET ME DO IT.
WHA...!
BUT SHE--*ER*, *HE*...WAS BEATING THE PANTS OFF YOU!
CAUGHT ME OFF GUARD, THAT'S ALL.
I GOT US INTO THIS...
...AND IT'S UP TO *ME* TO GET US OUT! THIS MAY BE A BATTLE ONLY *I* CAN FIGHT...

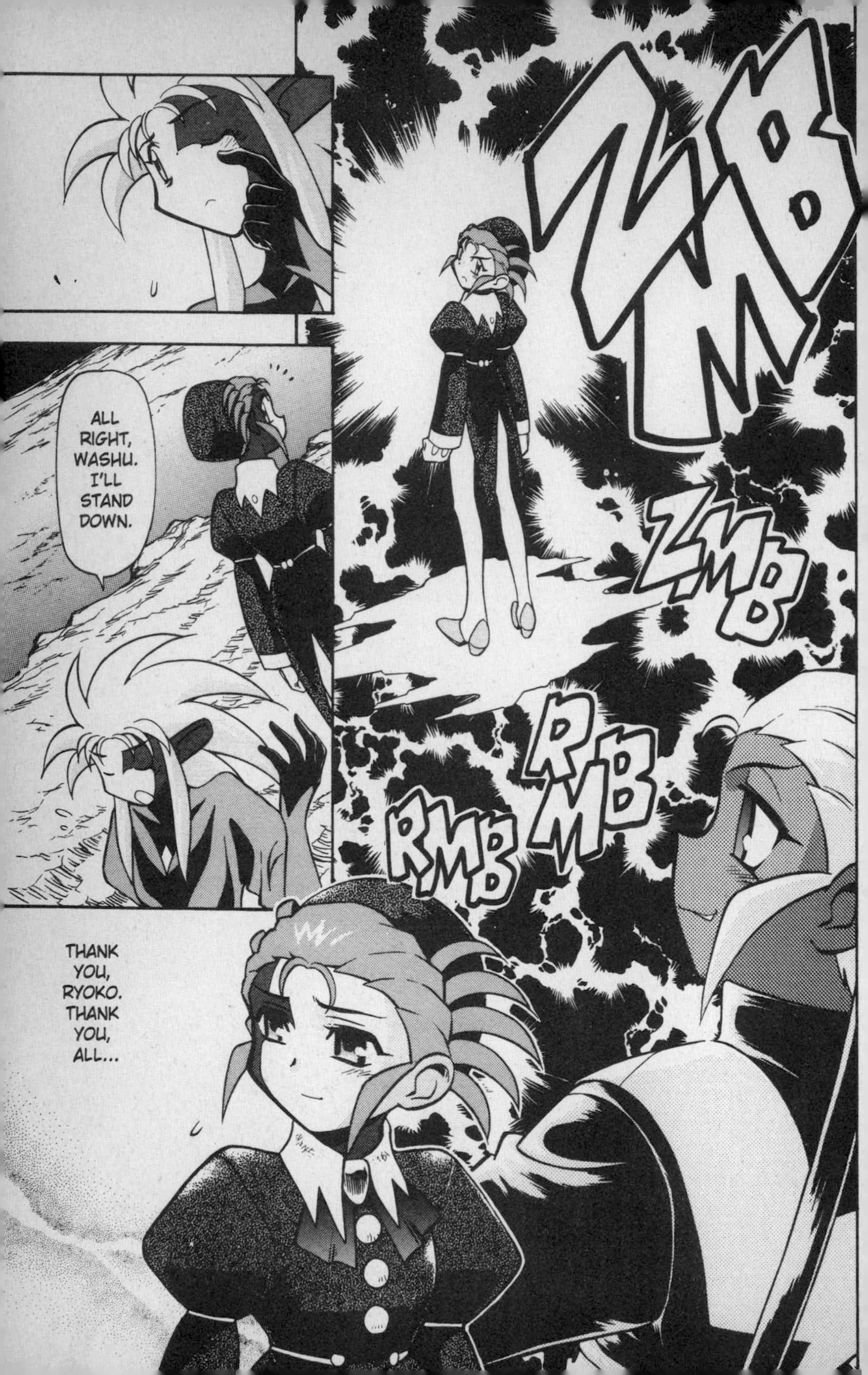
ALL RIGHT, WASHU. I'LL STAND DOWN.
ZMB
ZMB
RMB
RMB
THANK YOU, RYOKO. THANK YOU, ALL...

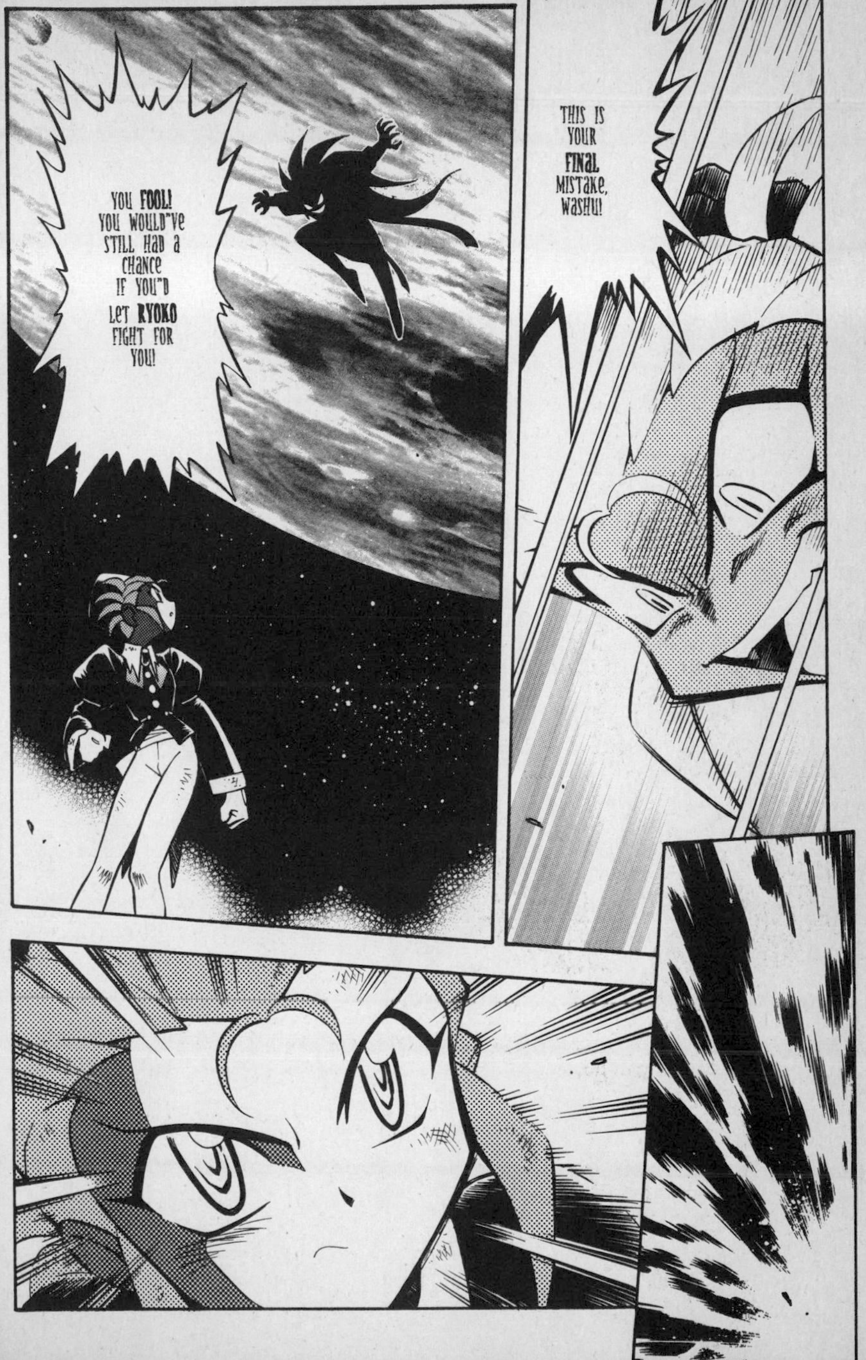
YOU FOOL! YOU WOULD'VE STILL HAD A CHANCE IF YOU'D LET RYOKO FIGHT FOR YOU!
THIS IS YOUR FINAL MISTAKE, WASHU!

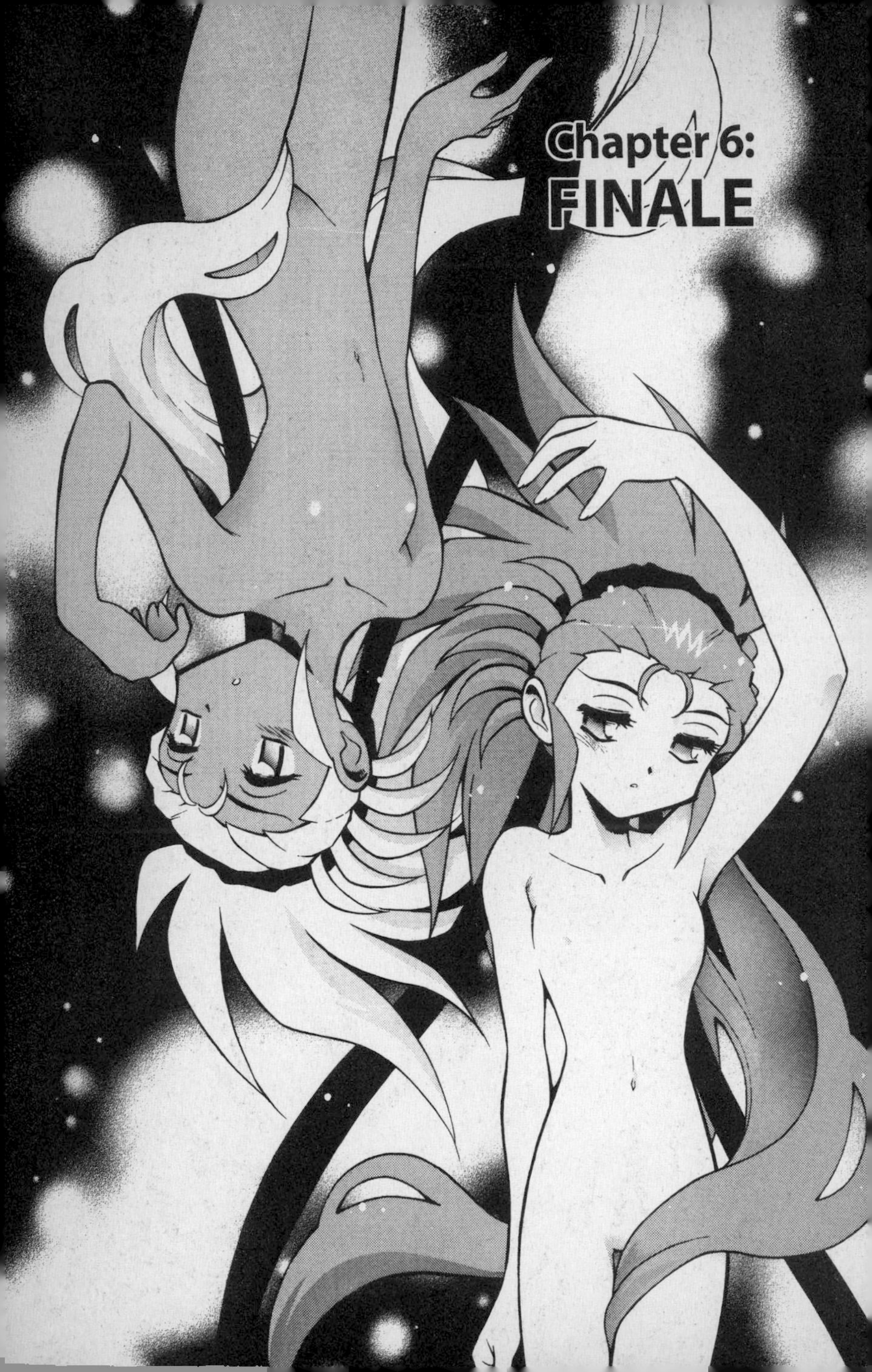
Chapter 6:
FINALE

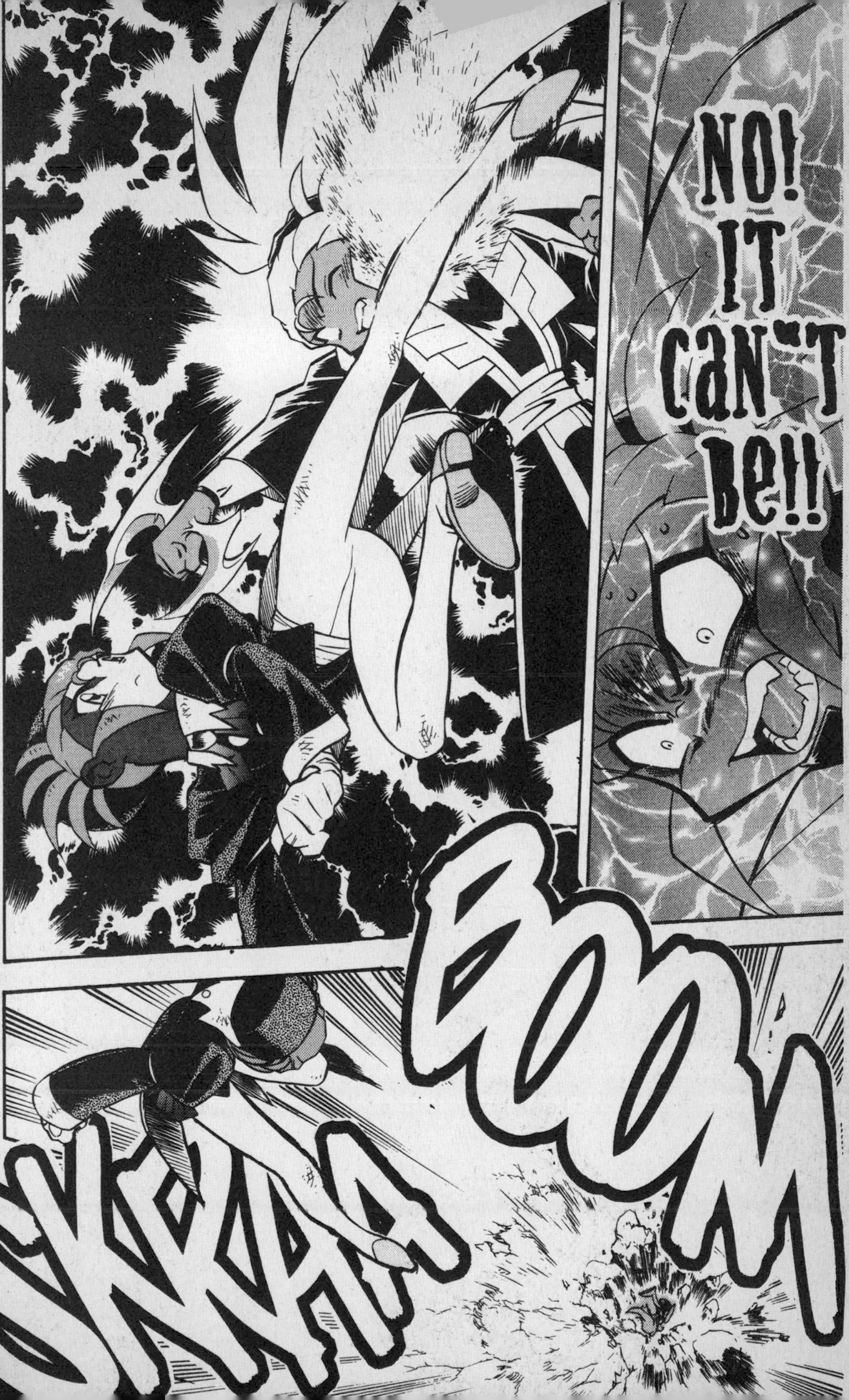
NO! IT CAN'T BE!!
SKRAA BOOM

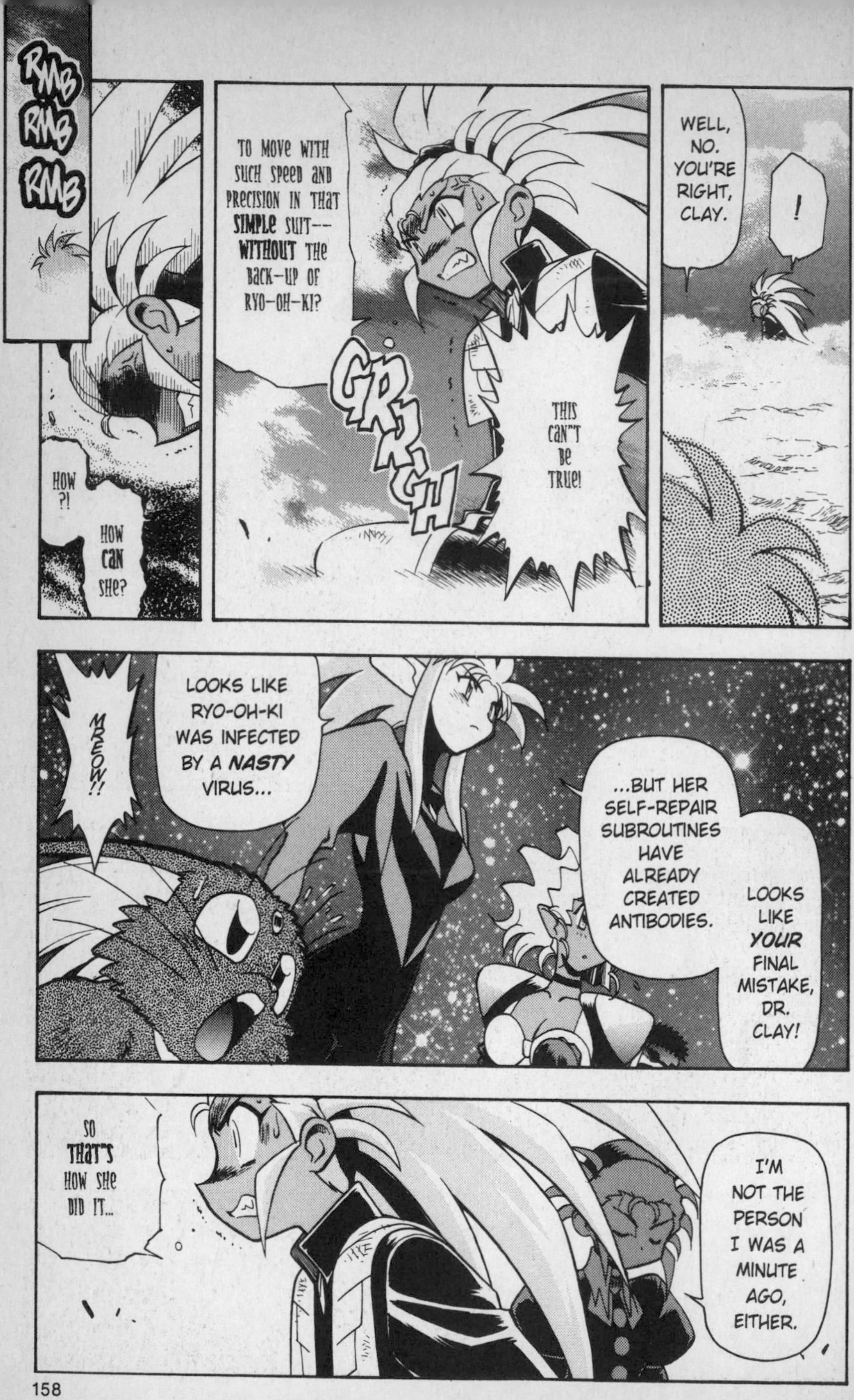
RMB RMB RMB
HOW ?!
HOW CAN SHE?
TO MOVE WITH SUCH SPEED AND PRECISION IN THAT SIMPLE SUIT-- WITHOUT THE BACK-UP OF RYO-OH-KI?
GRRRGH
THIS CAN'T BE TRUE!
WELL, NO. YOU'RE RIGHT, CLAY.
!
MREOW!!
LOOKS LIKE RYO-OH-KI WAS INFECTED BY A NASTY VIRUS...
...BUT HER SELF-REPAIR SUBROUTINES HAVE ALREADY CREATED ANTIBODIES.
LOOKS LIKE YOUR FINAL MISTAKE, DR. CLAY!
SO THAT'S HOW SHE DID IT...
I'M NOT THE PERSON I WAS A MINUTE AGO, EITHER.

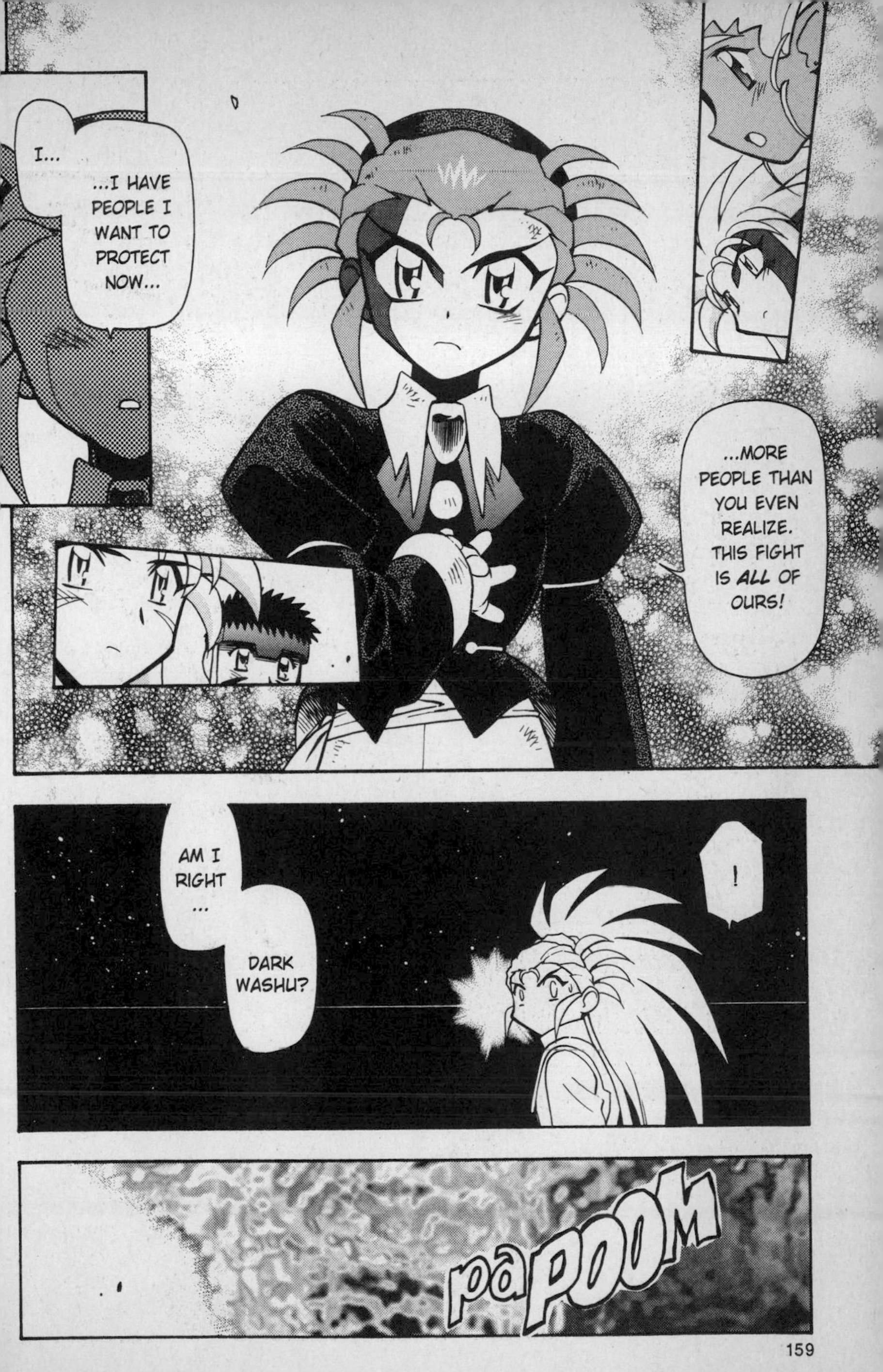
I...
...I HAVE PEOPLE I WANT TO PROTECT NOW...
...MORE PEOPLE THAN YOU EVEN REALIZE. THIS FIGHT IS ALL OF OURS!
AM I RIGHT ...
DARK WASHU?
!
paPOOM

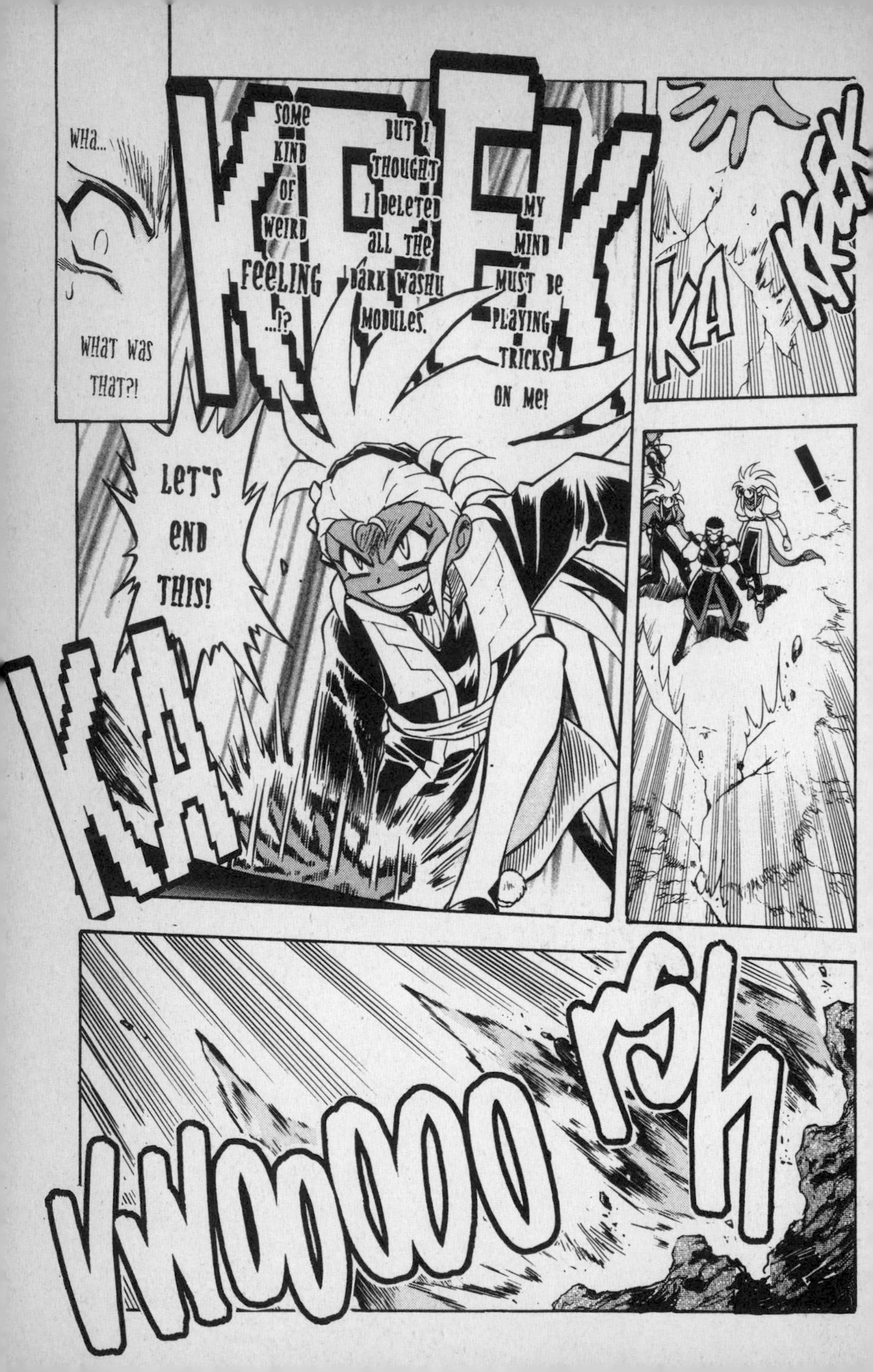
WHA...
WHAT WAS THAT?!
SOME KIND OF WEIRD FEELING ...!?
BUT I THOUGHT I DELETED ALL THE DARK WASHU MODULES.
MY MIND MUST BE PLAYING TRICKS ON ME!
LET'S END THIS!
!

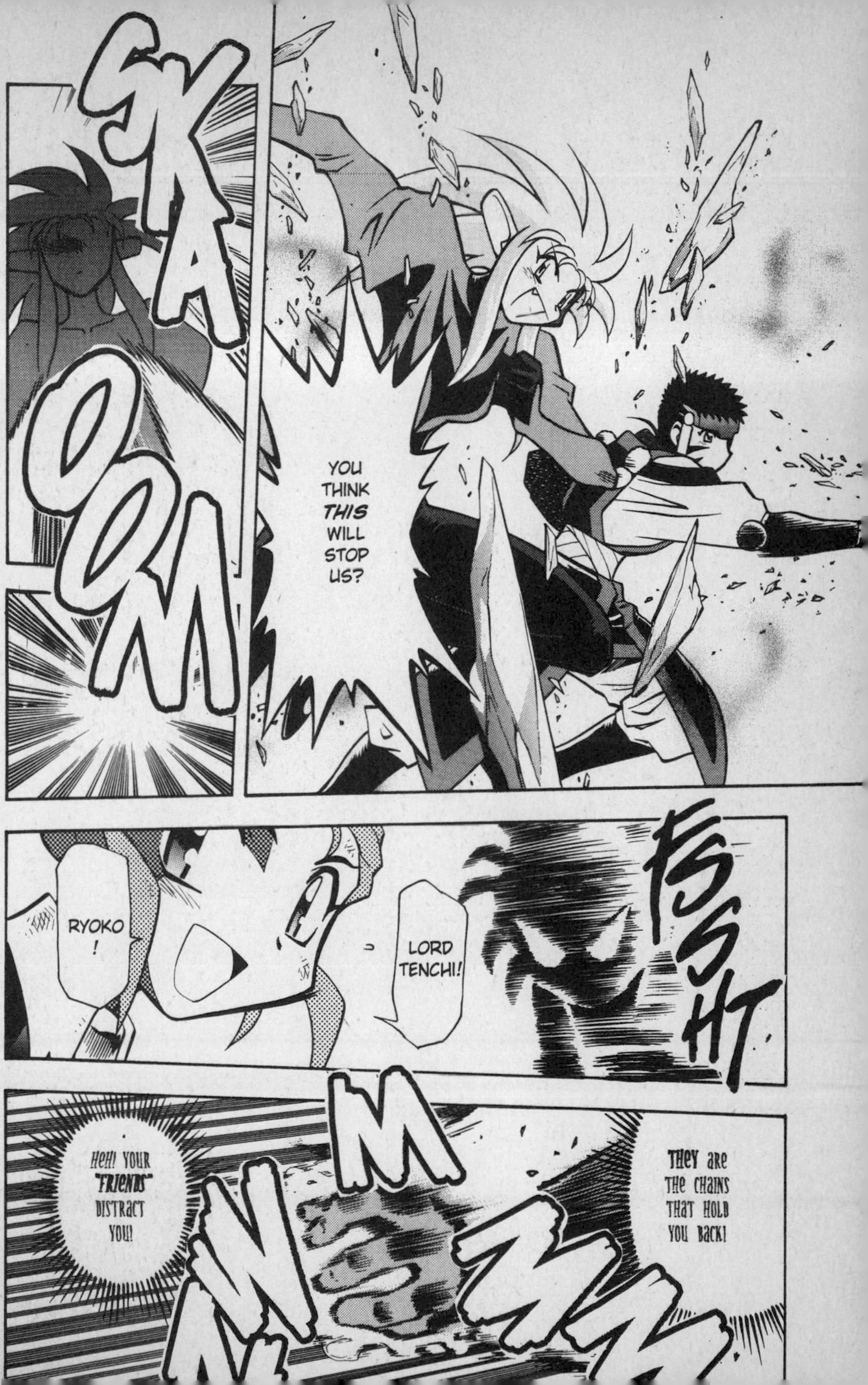
SKA
BOOM
YOU THINK THIS WILL STOP US?
RYOKO!
LORD TENCHI!
FSSHT
MMMMM
HEH! YOUR "FRIENDS" DISTRACT YOU!
THEY ARE THE CHAINS THAT HOLD YOU BACK!

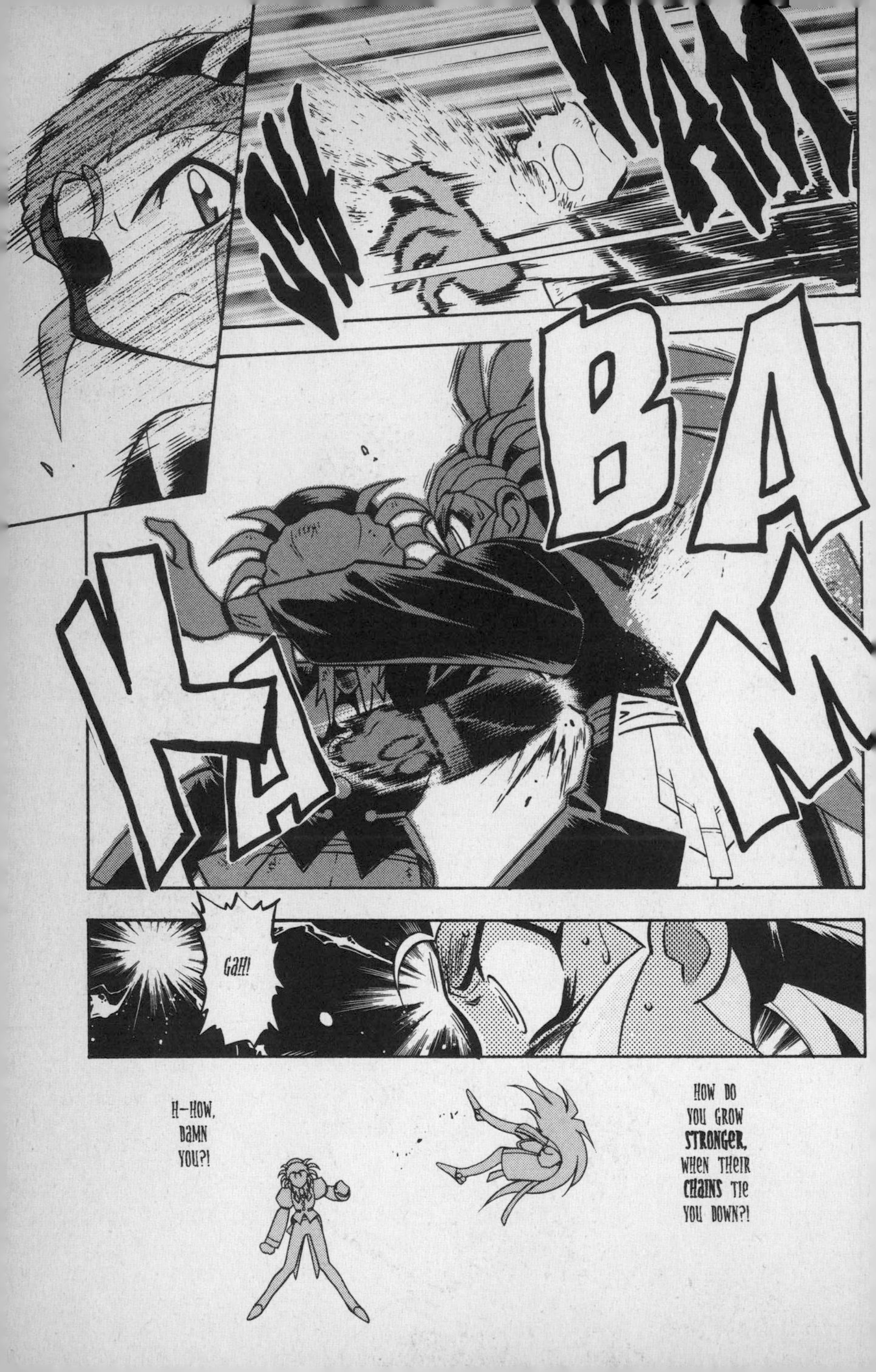
BAM
GAH!
H-HOW, DAMN YOU?!
HOW DO YOU GROW STRONGER, WHEN THEIR CHAINS TIE YOU DOWN?!

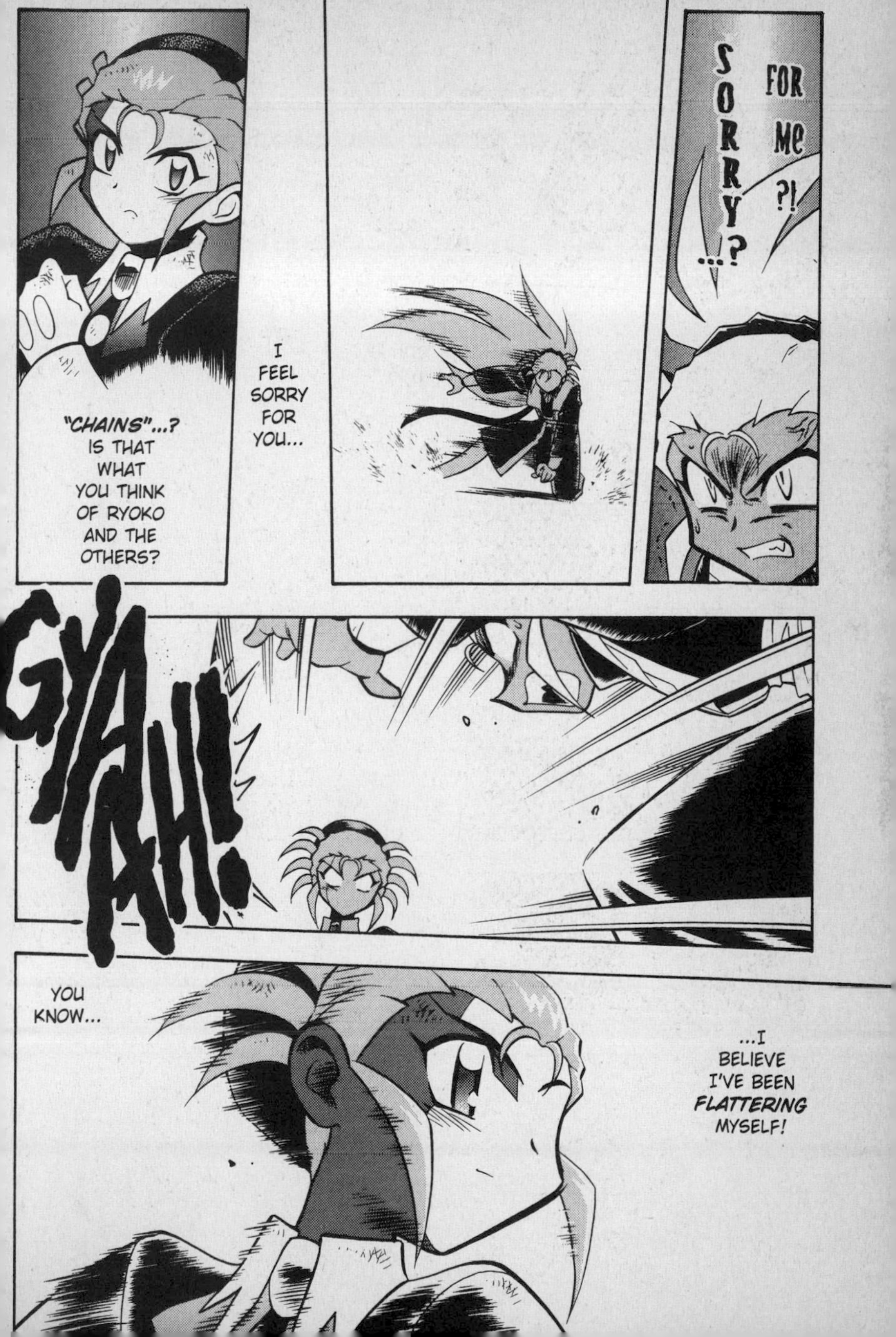
"CHAINS"...? IS THAT WHAT YOU THINK OF RYOKO AND THE OTHERS?
I FEEL SORRY FOR YOU...
SORRY...?
FOR ME?!
GYAAH!!
YOU KNOW...
...I BELIEVE I'VE BEEN FLATTERING MYSELF!

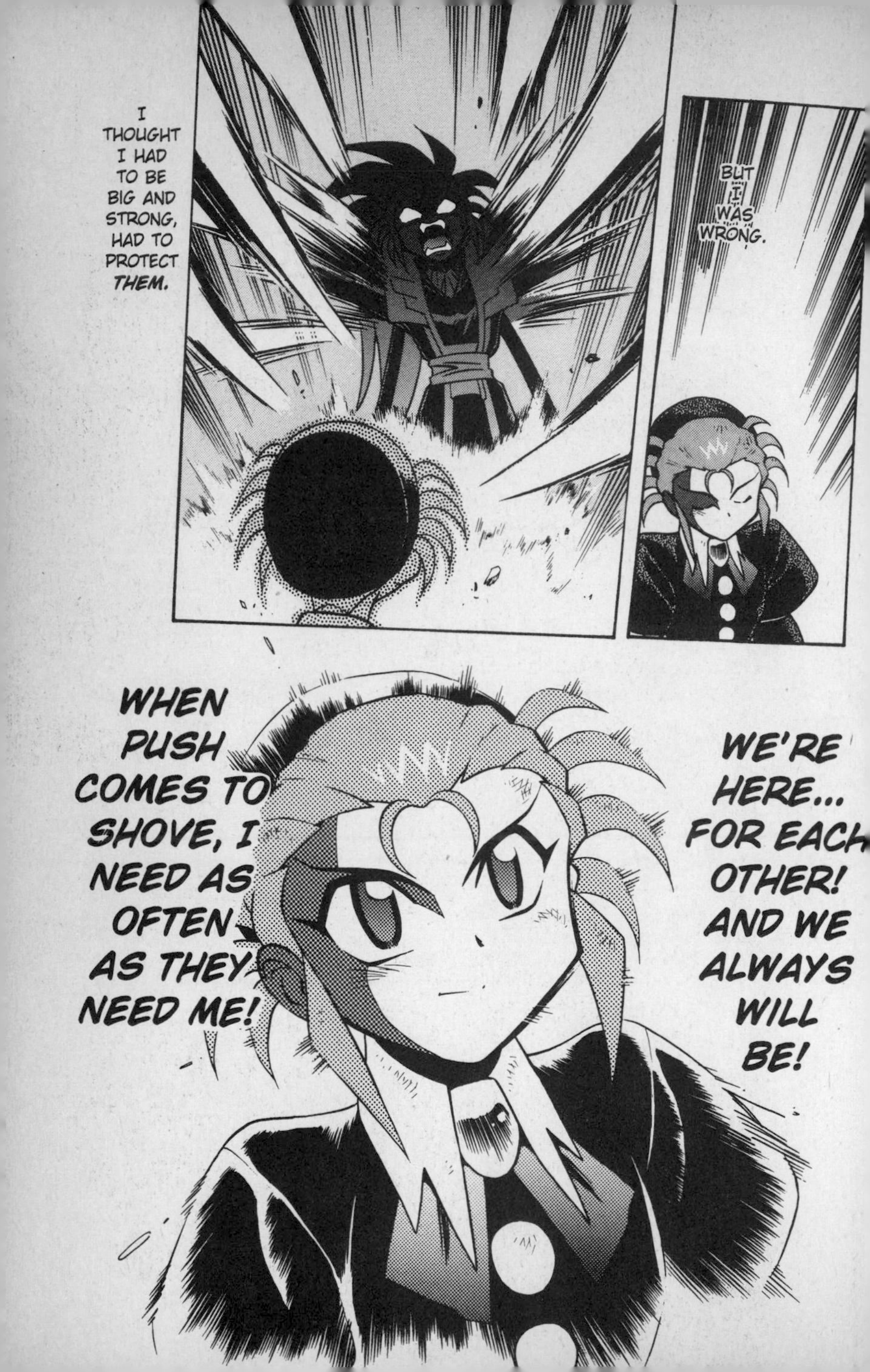
I THOUGHT I HAD TO BE BIG AND STRONG, HAD TO PROTECT THEM.
BUT I WAS WRONG.
WHEN PUSH COMES TO SHOVE, I NEED AS OFTEN AS THEY NEED ME!
WE'RE HERE... FOR EACH OTHER! AND WE ALWAYS WILL BE!

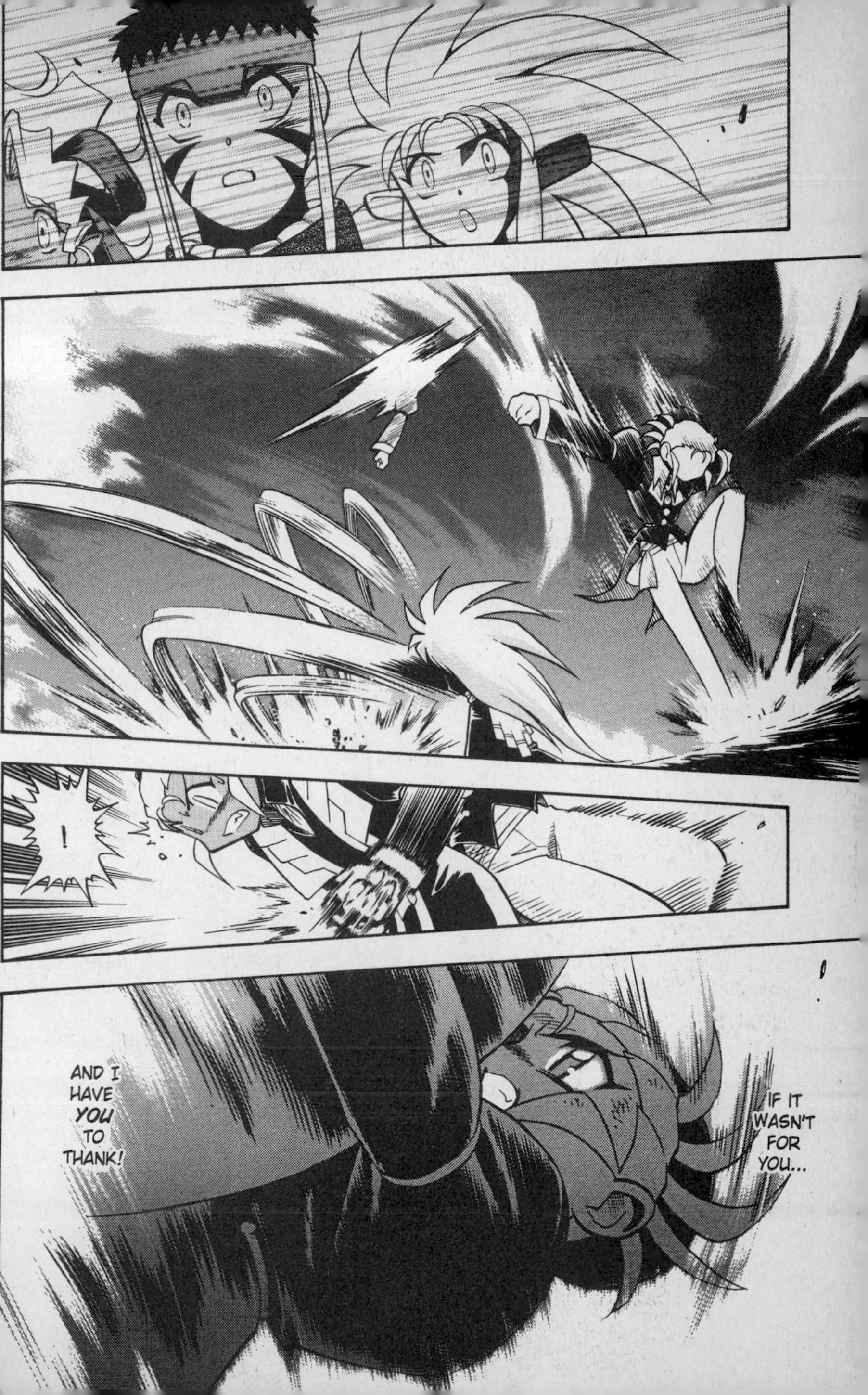
!
AND I HAVE YOU TO THANK!
IF IT WASN'T FOR YOU...

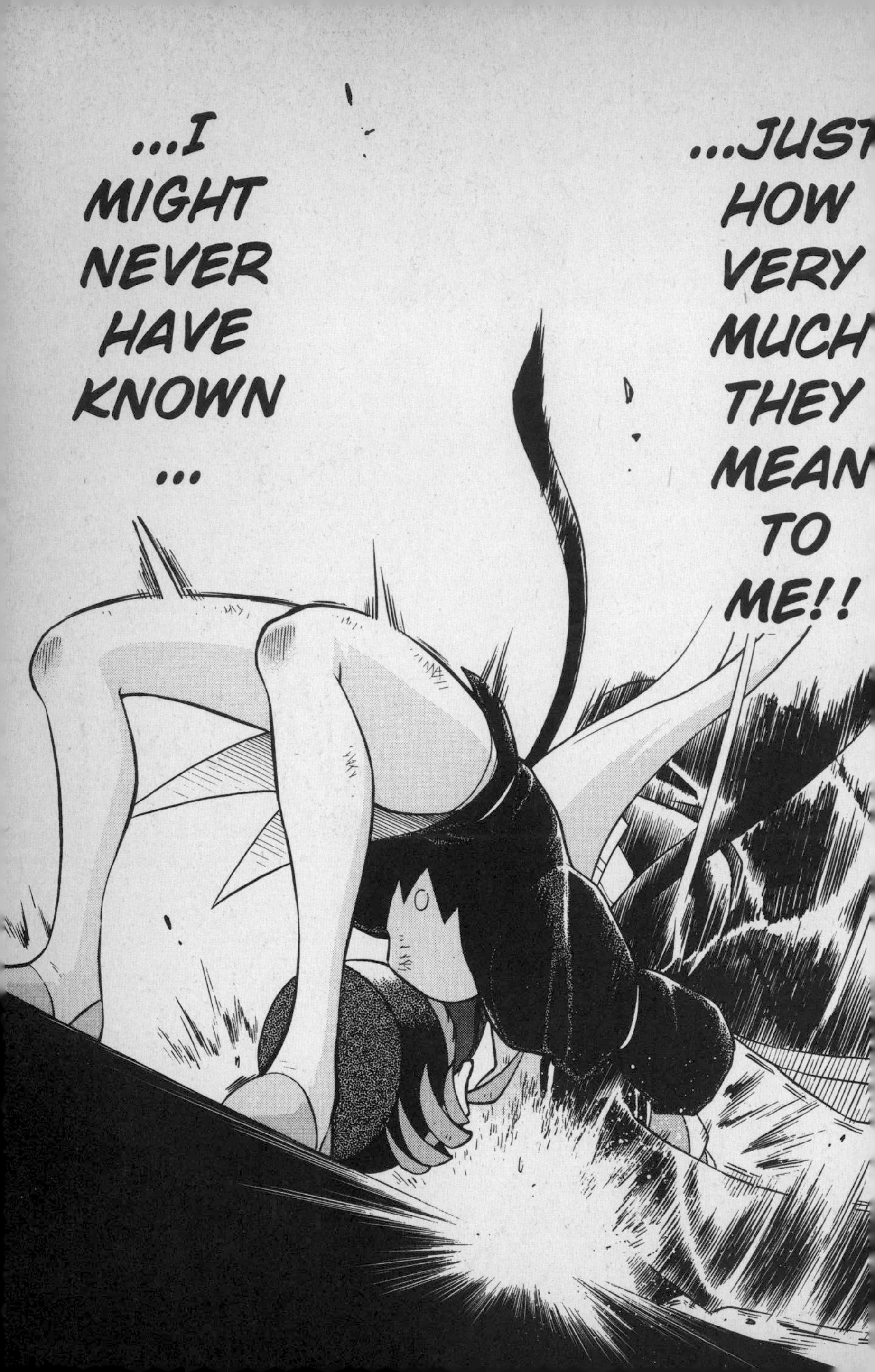
...I MIGHT NEVER HAVE KNOWN ...
...JUST HOW VERY MUCH THEY MEAN TO ME!!

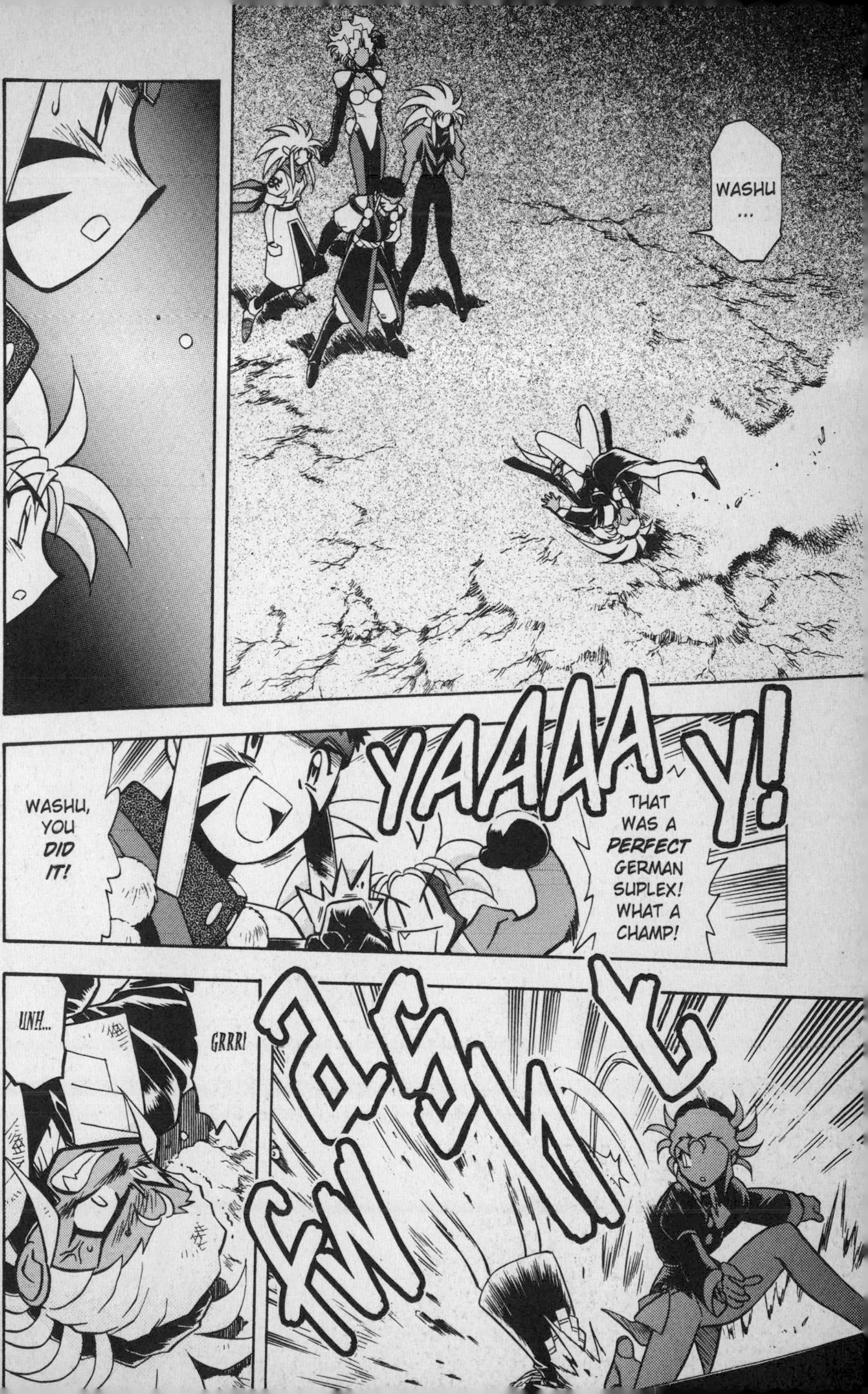
WASHU ...
WASHU, YOU *DID IT!*
YAAAAY!
THAT WAS A *PERFECT* GERMAN SUPLEX! WHAT A CHAMP!
UNH...
GRRR!

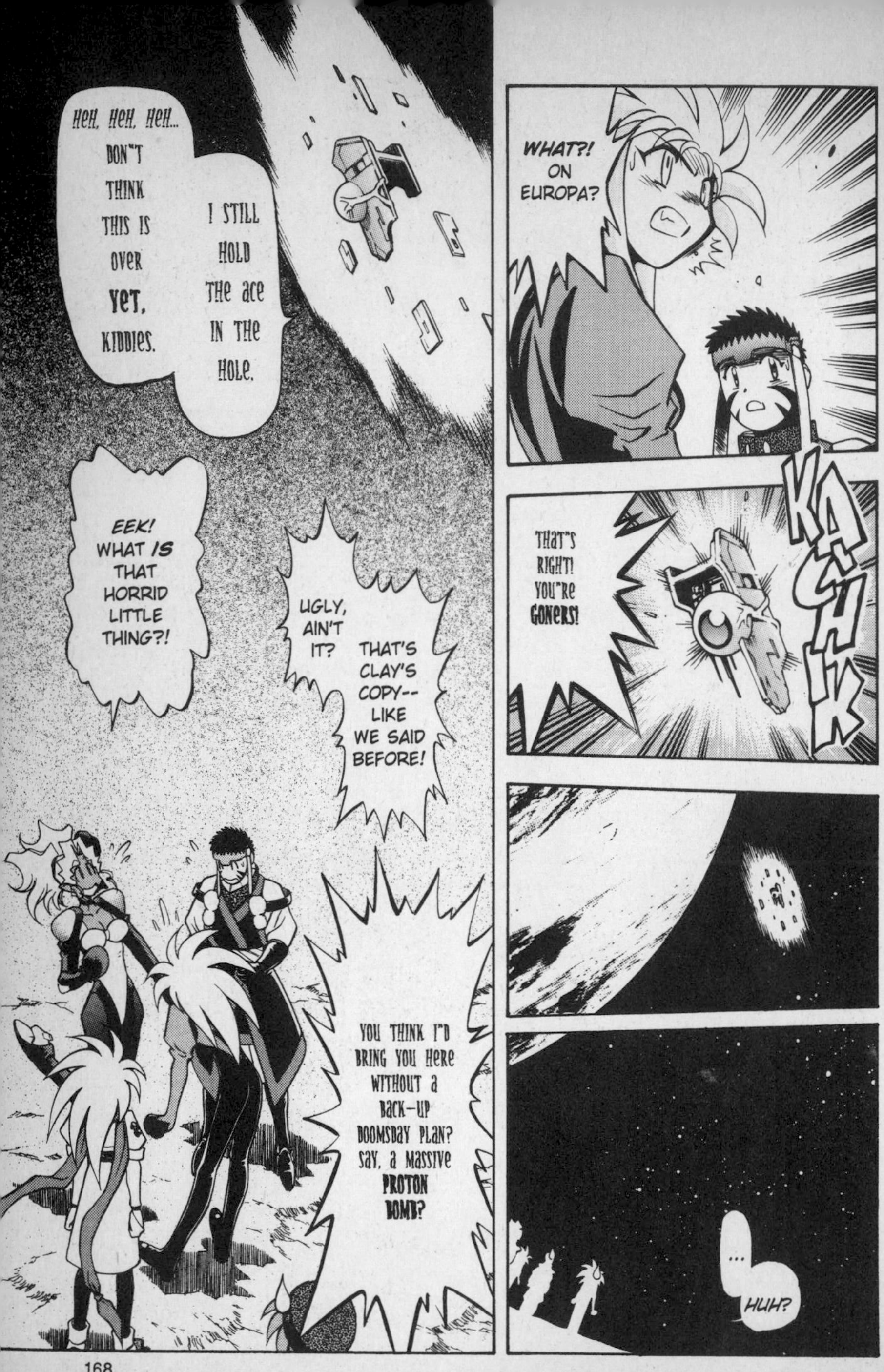
HEH, HEH, HEH... DON'T THINK THIS IS OVER YET, KIDDIES.
I STILL HOLD THE ACE IN THE HOLE.
EEK! WHAT IS THAT HORRID LITTLE THING?!
UGLY, AIN'T IT?
THAT'S CLAY'S COPY-- LIKE WE SAID BEFORE!
YOU THINK I'D BRING YOU HERE WITHOUT A BACK-UP DOOMSDAY PLAN? SAY, A MASSIVE PROTON BOMB?
WHAT?! ON EUROPA?
THAT'S RIGHT! YOU'RE GONERS!
KACHINK
...
HUH?

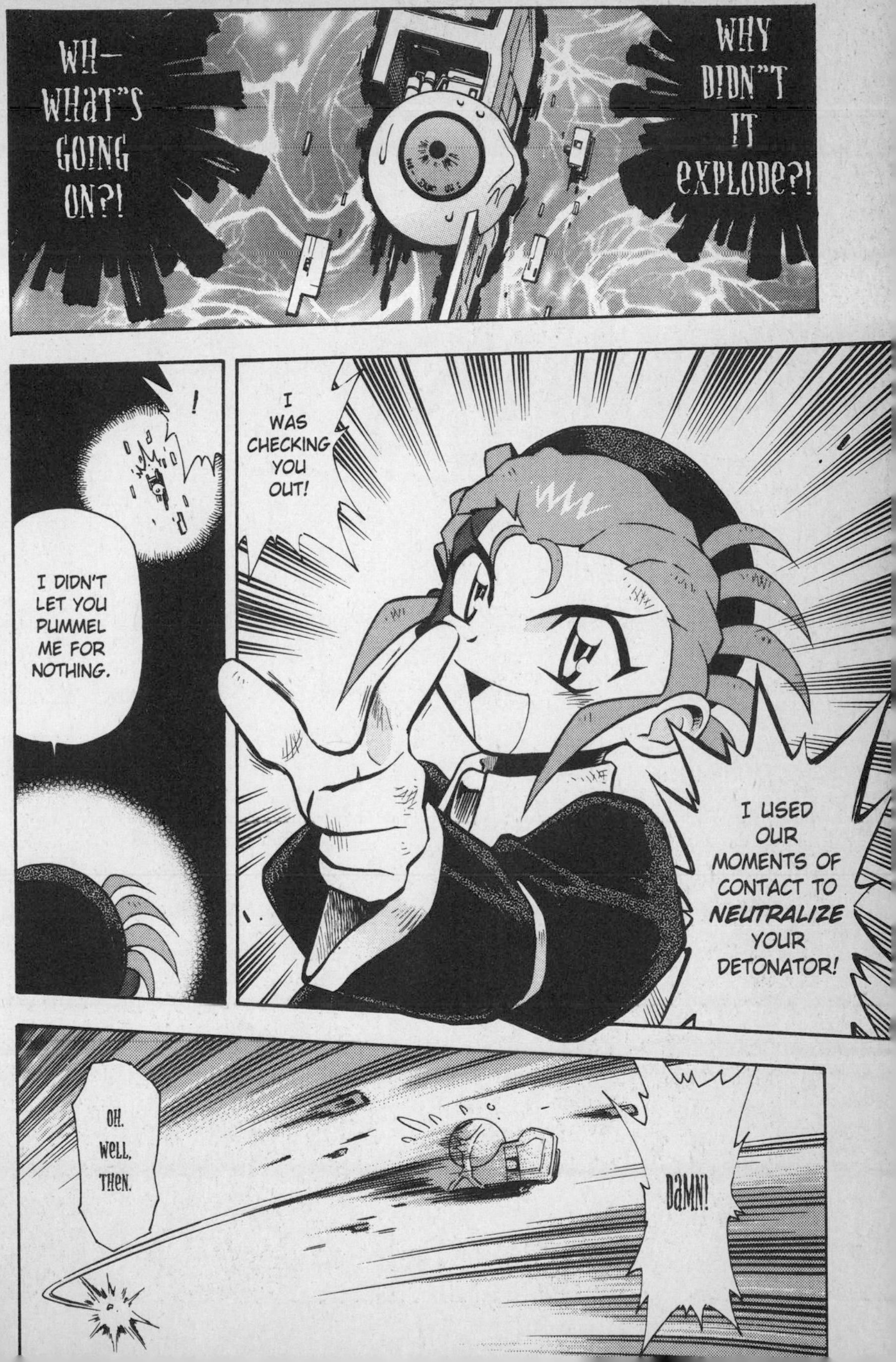
WH-WHAT'S GOING ON?!
WHY DIDN'T IT EXPLODE?!
!
I DIDN'T LET YOU PUMMEL ME FOR NOTHING.
I WAS CHECKING YOU OUT!
I USED OUR MOMENTS OF CONTACT TO **NEUTRALIZE** YOUR DETONATOR!
OH. WELL, THEN.
DAMN!

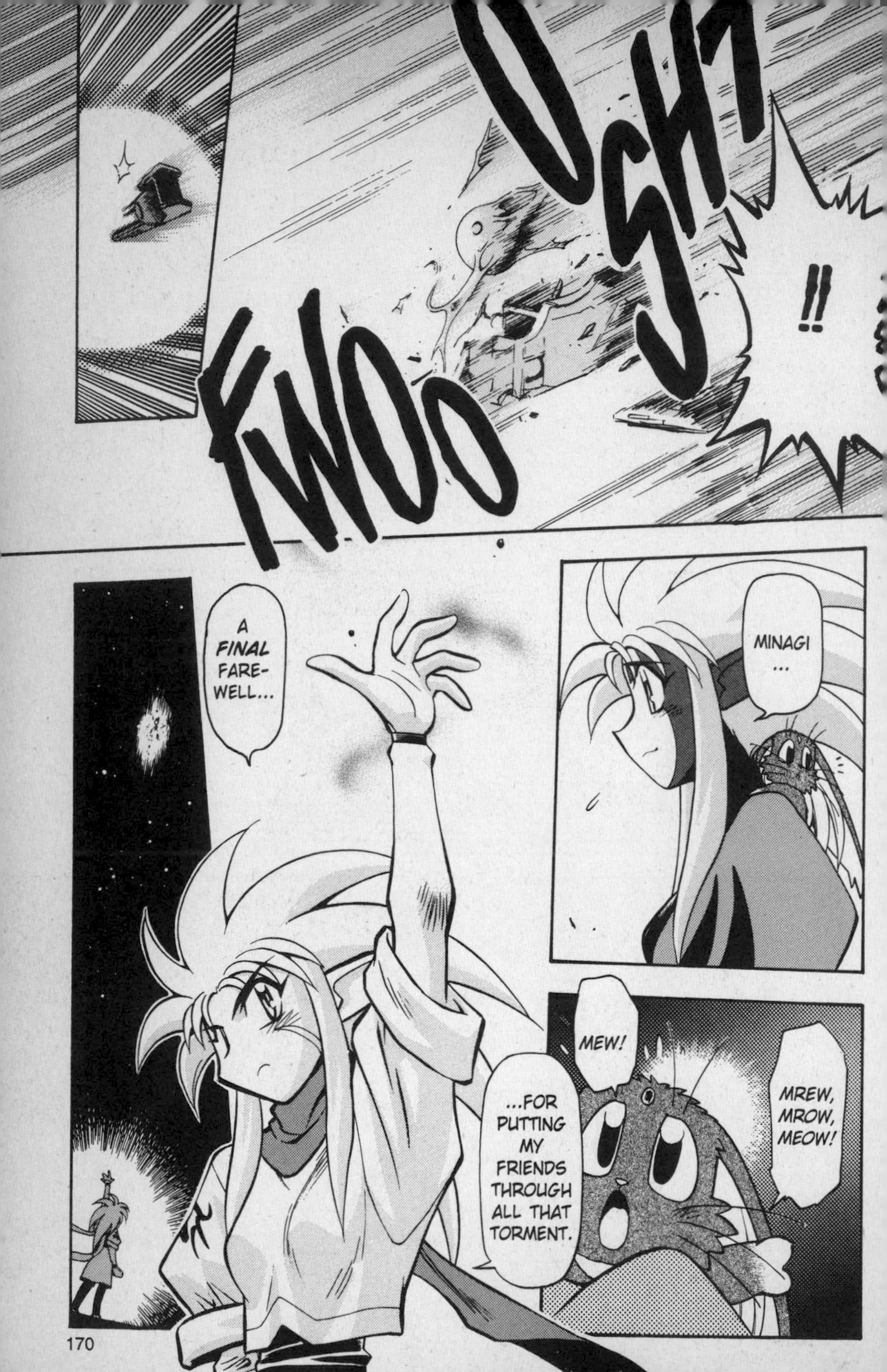
FWOOSH!!
A FINAL FAREWELL...
...FOR PUTTING MY FRIENDS THROUGH ALL THAT TORMENT.
MINAGI...
MEW!
MREW, MROW, MEOW!

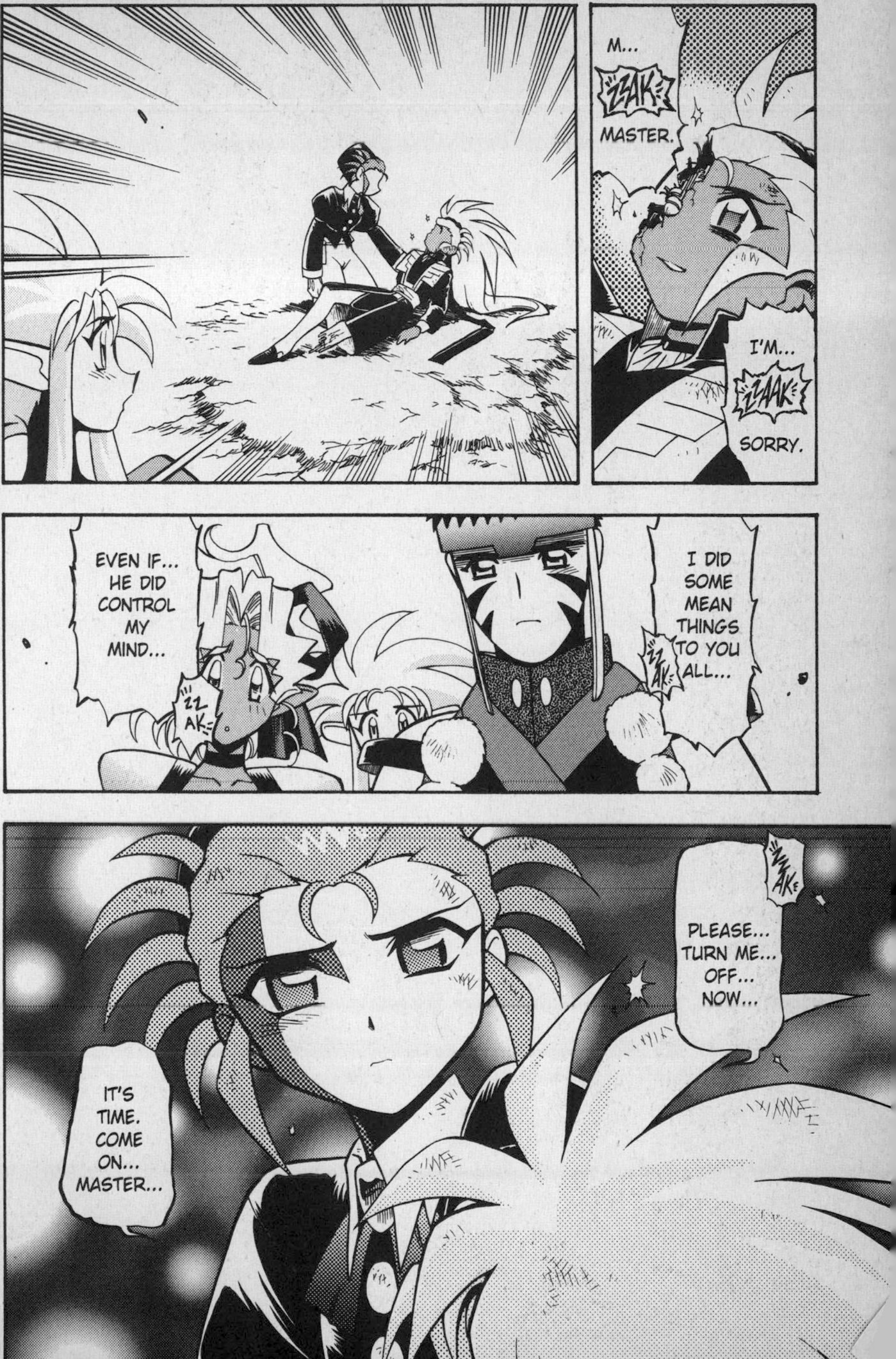
M...
ZZAK
MASTER.
I'M...
ZZAAK
SORRY.
EVEN IF... HE DID CONTROL MY MIND...
ZZ AK
I DID SOME MEAN THINGS TO YOU ALL...
ZZ AK
ZZAK
PLEASE... TURN ME... OFF... NOW...
IT'S TIME. COME ON... MASTER...

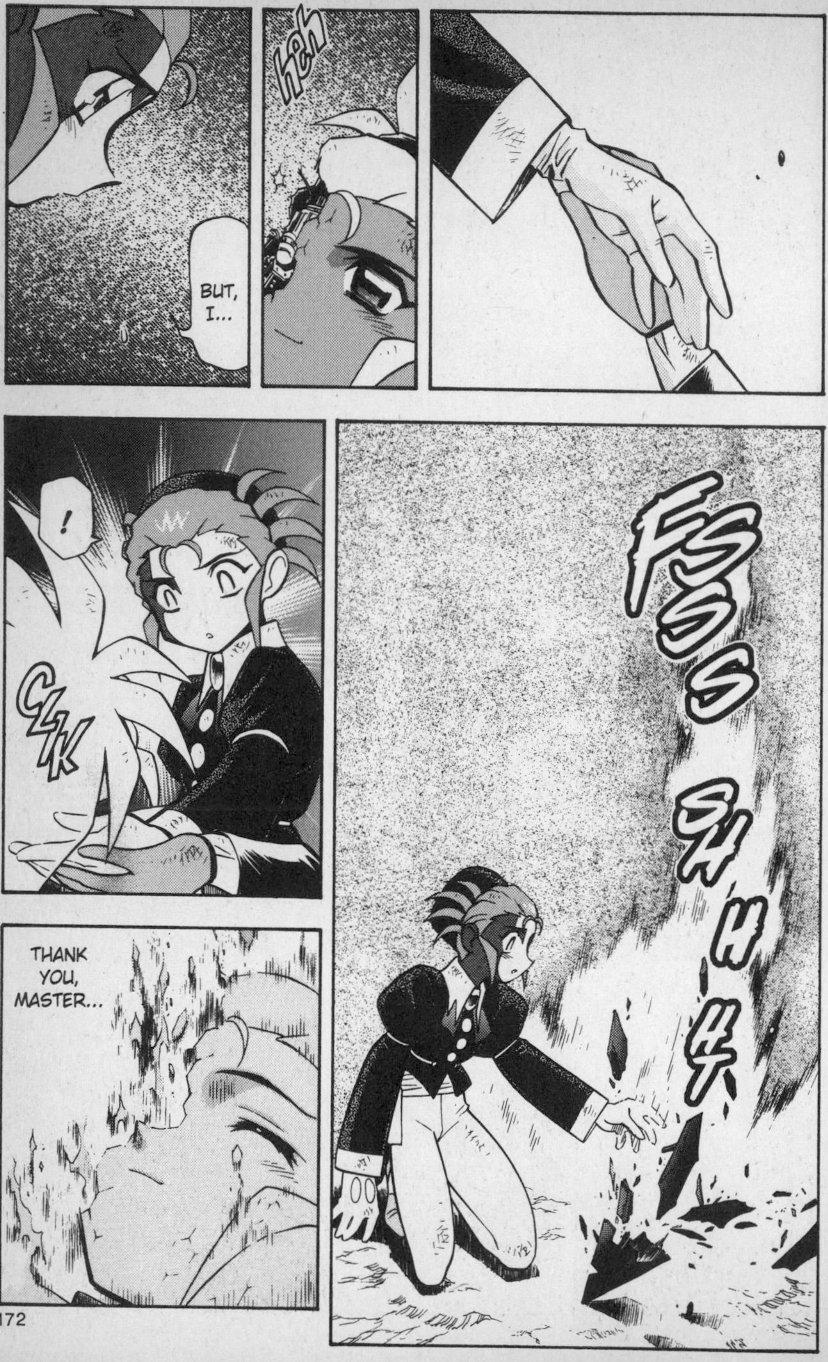
BUT, I...
HEH
!
CLIK
THANK YOU, MASTER...
FSSSHHK

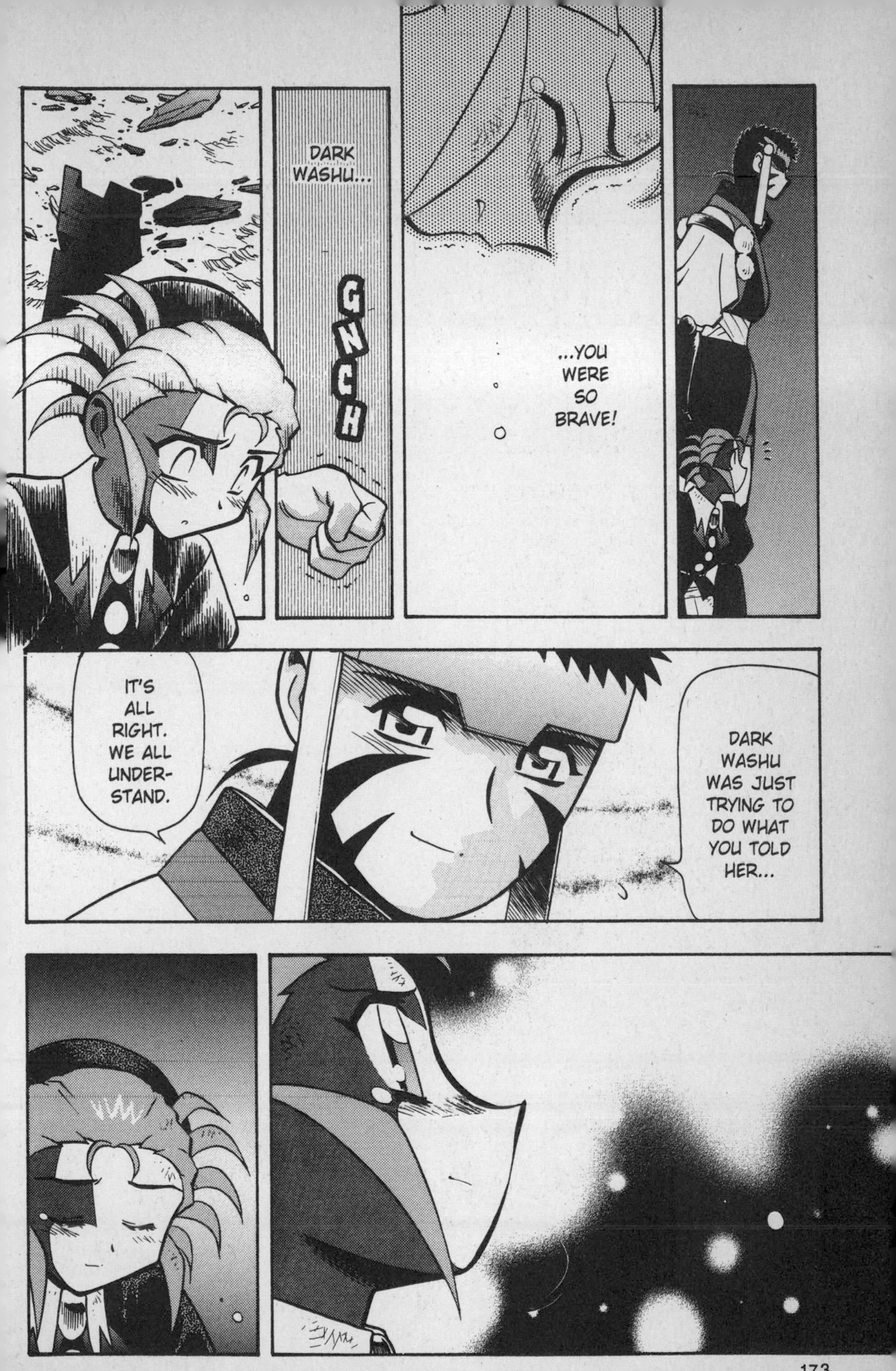
DARK WASHU...
GNCH
...YOU WERE SO BRAVE!
IT'S ALL RIGHT. WE ALL UNDER-STAND.
DARK WASHU WAS JUST TRYING TO DO WHAT YOU TOLD HER...

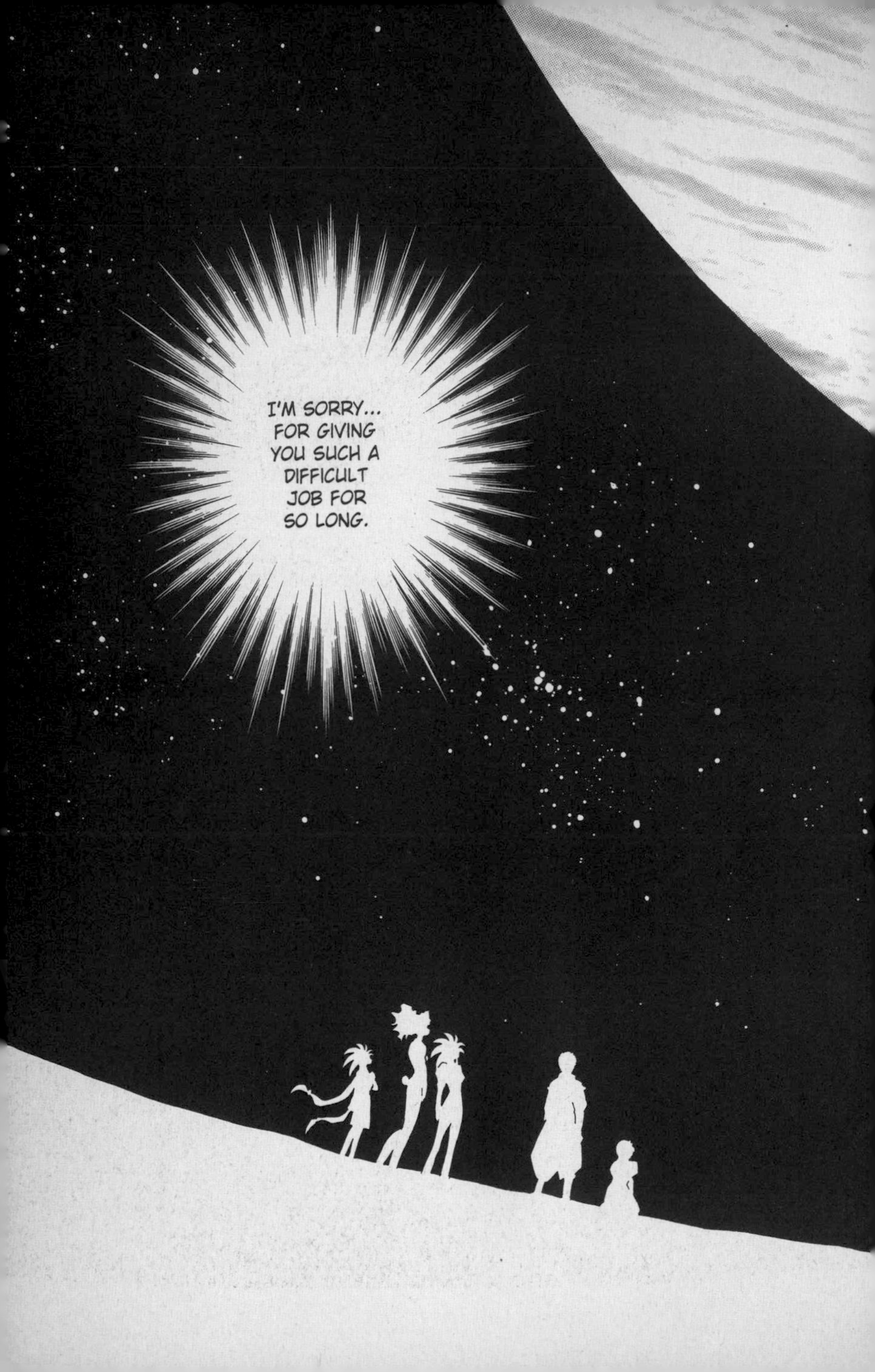
I'M SORRY... FOR GIVING YOU SUCH A DIFFICULT JOB FOR SO LONG.

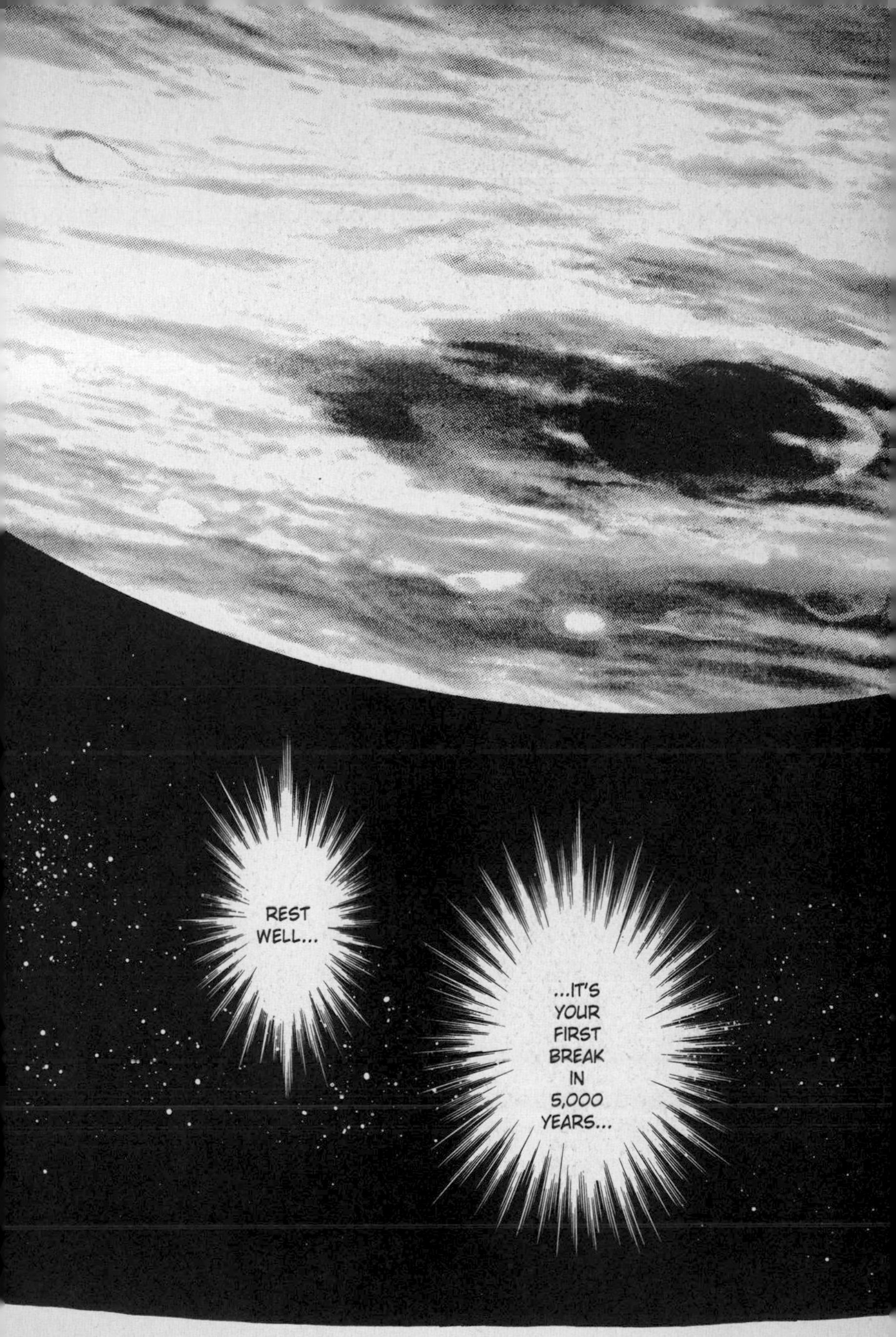
REST WELL...
...IT'S YOUR FIRST BREAK IN 5,000 YEARS...

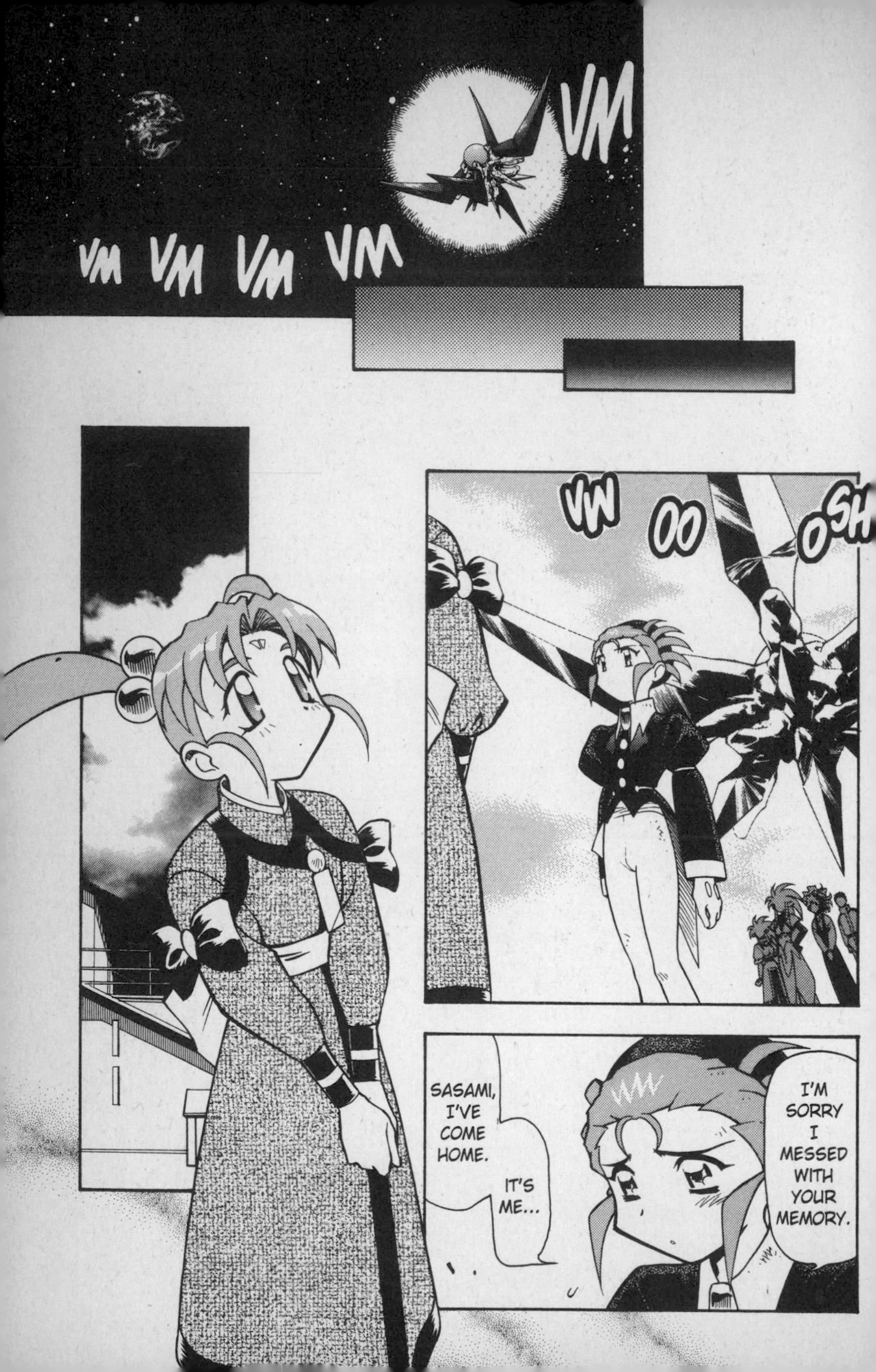
VM
VM VM VM VM
VW OO OSH
SASAMI, I'VE COME HOME.
IT'S ME...
I'M SORRY I MESSED WITH YOUR MEMORY.

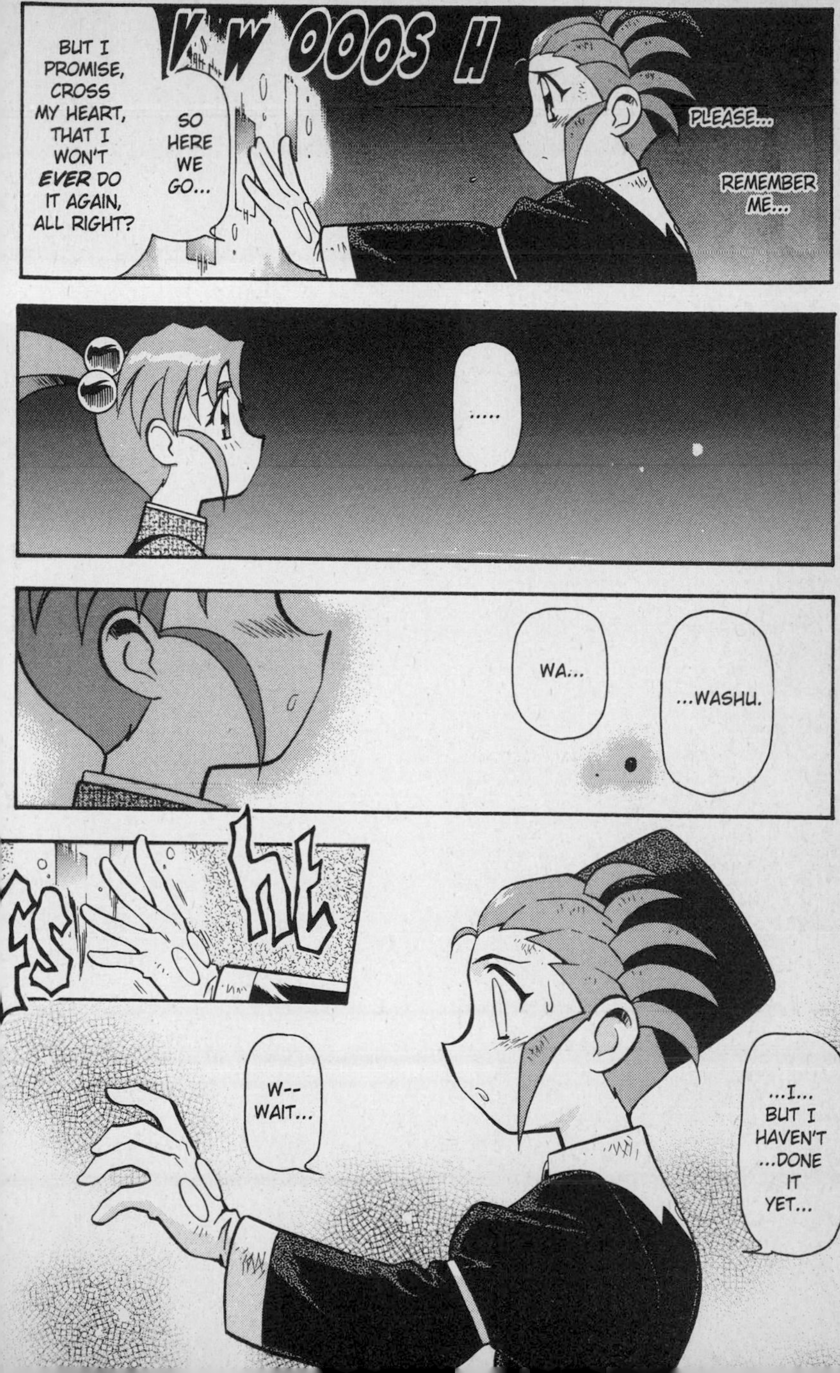
BUT I PROMISE, CROSS MY HEART, THAT I WON'T *EVER* DO IT AGAIN, ALL RIGHT?
VWOOOSH
SO HERE WE GO...
PLEASE...
REMEMBER ME...
.....
WA...
...WASHU.
FSHT
W-- WAIT...
...I... BUT I HAVEN'T ...DONE IT YET...

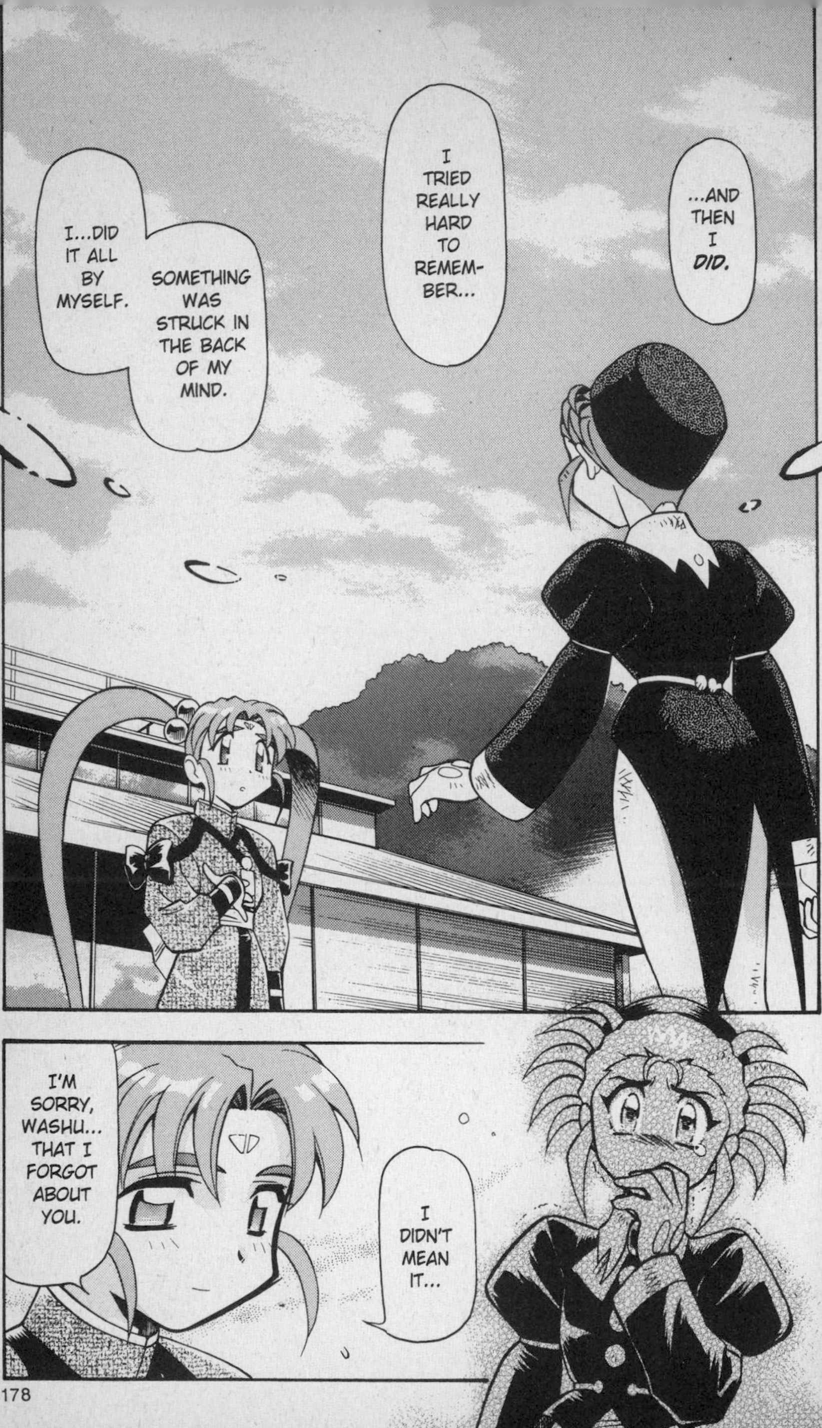
I...DID IT ALL BY MYSELF.
SOMETHING WAS STRUCK IN THE BACK OF MY MIND.
I TRIED REALLY HARD TO REMEMBER...
...AND THEN I *DID.*
I'M SORRY, WASHU... THAT I FORGOT ABOUT YOU.
I DIDN'T MEAN IT...

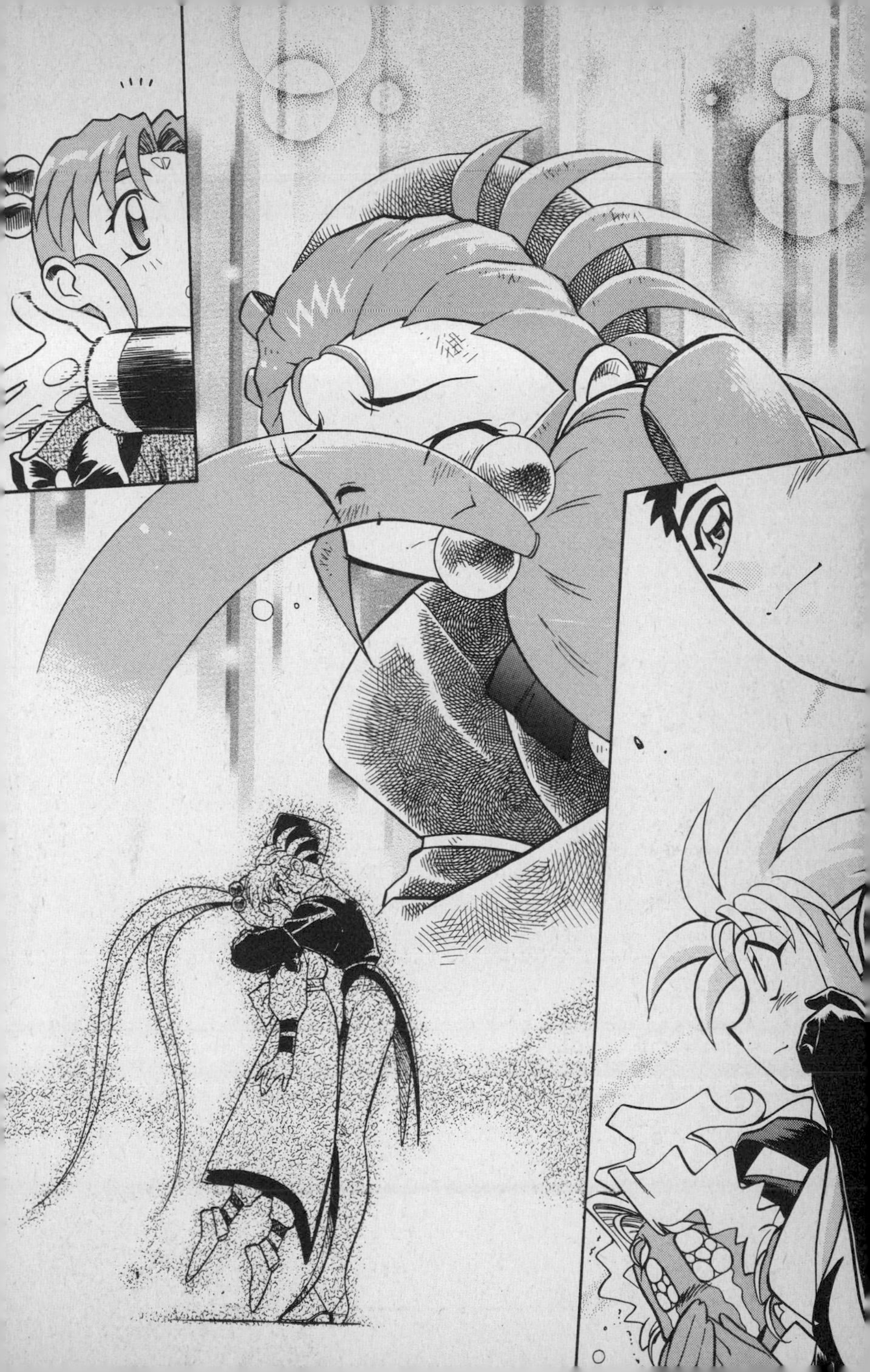

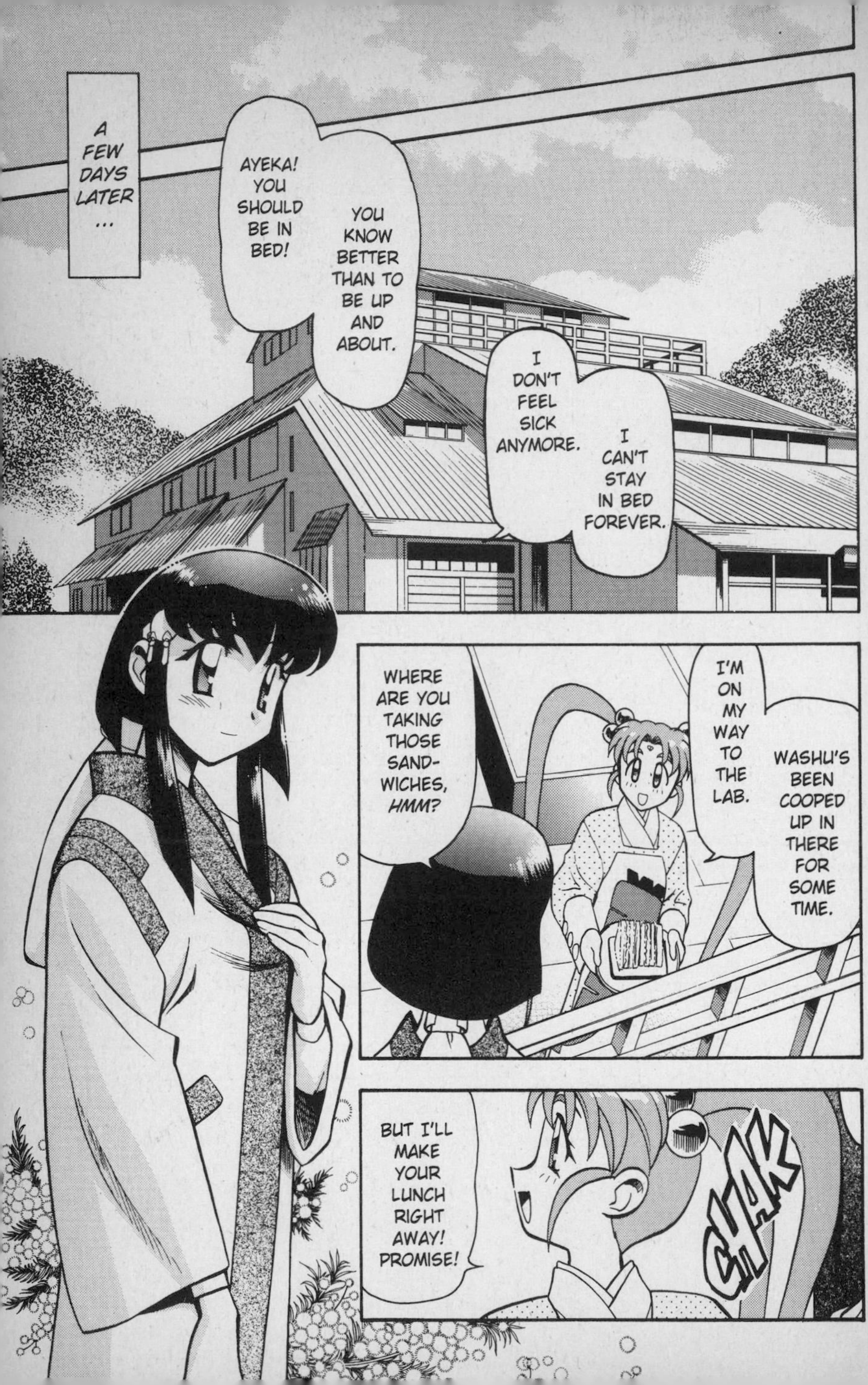
A FEW DAYS LATER...
AYEKA! YOU SHOULD BE IN BED!
YOU KNOW BETTER THAN TO BE UP AND ABOUT.
I DON'T FEEL SICK ANYMORE.
I CAN'T STAY IN BED FOREVER.
WHERE ARE YOU TAKING THOSE SAND-WICHES, *HMM?*
I'M ON MY WAY TO THE LAB.
WASHU'S BEEN COOPED UP IN THERE FOR SOME TIME.
BUT I'LL MAKE YOUR LUNCH RIGHT AWAY! PROMISE!
CHAK

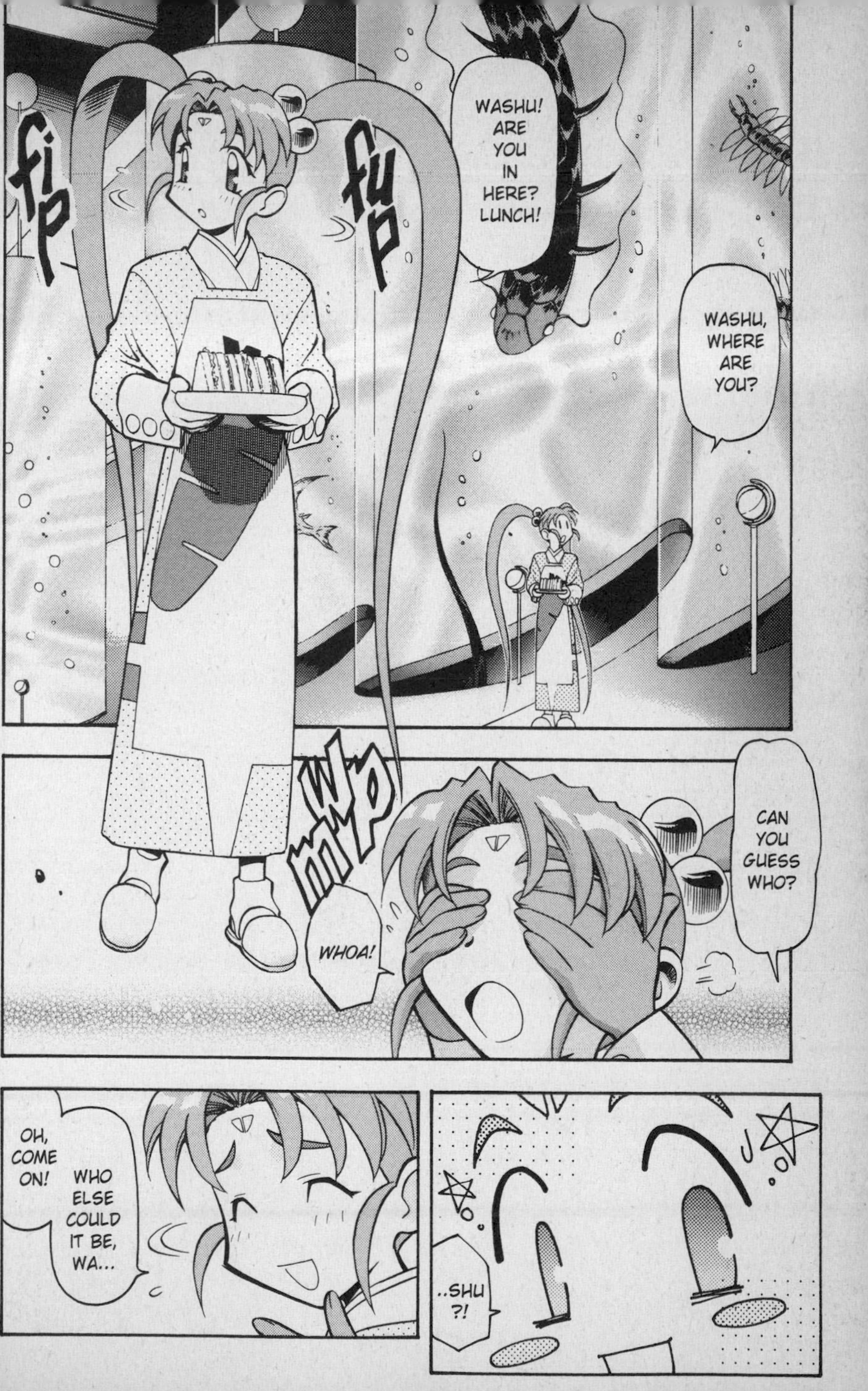
fip
fup
WASHU! ARE YOU IN HERE? LUNCH!
WASHU, WHERE ARE YOU?
wmp
WHOA!
CAN YOU GUESS WHO?
OH, COME ON!
WHO ELSE COULD IT BE, WA...
..SHU ?!

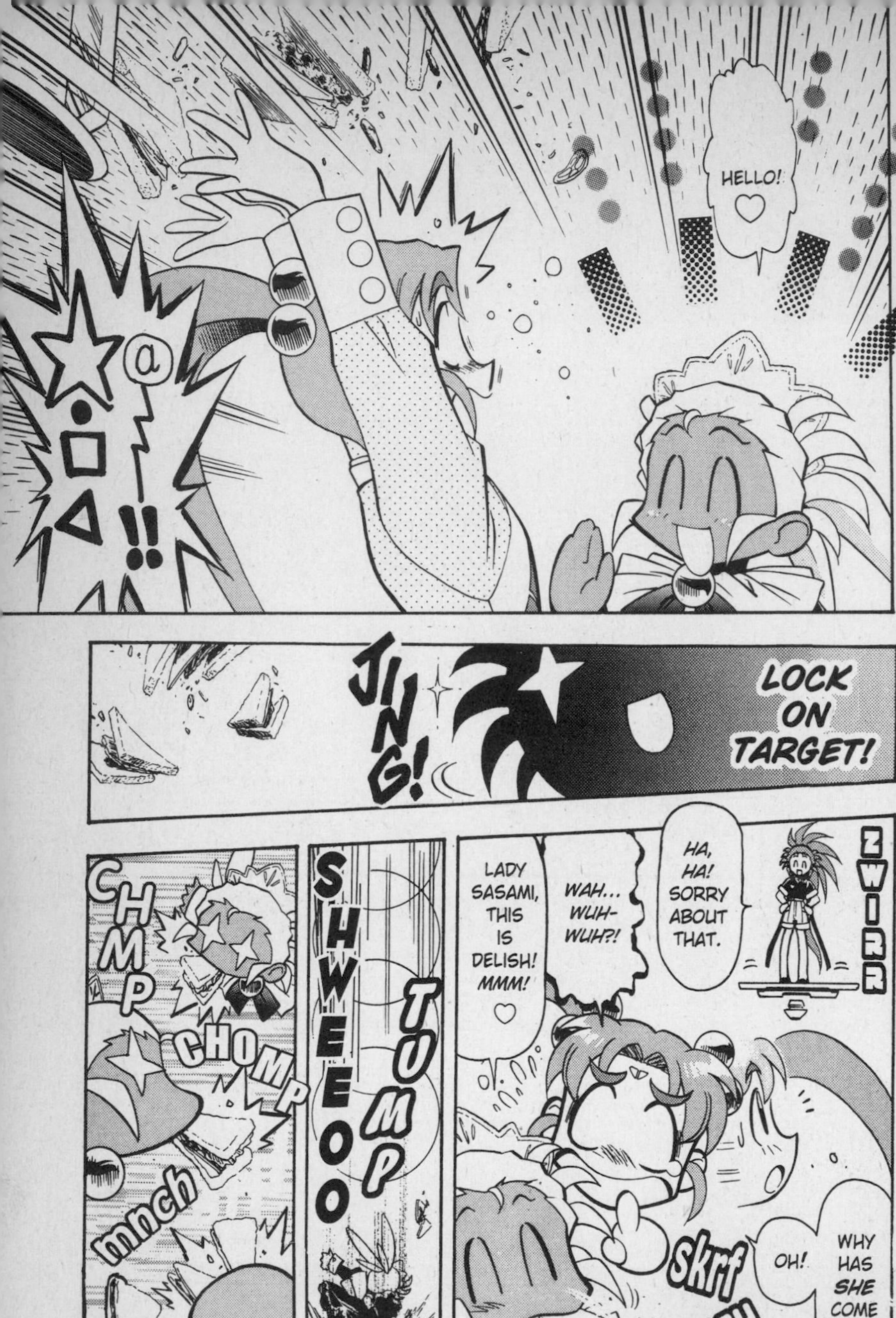
@ ● □ △ !!
HELLO! ♡
JING!
LOCK ON TARGET!
CHMP
CHOMP
mnch
SHWEEOO
TUMP
LADY SASAMI, THIS IS DELISH! MMM! ♡
WAH... WUH-WUH?!
HA, HA! SORRY ABOUT THAT.
ZWIRR
skrf
MNCH
OH!
WHY HAS SHE COME BACK?!

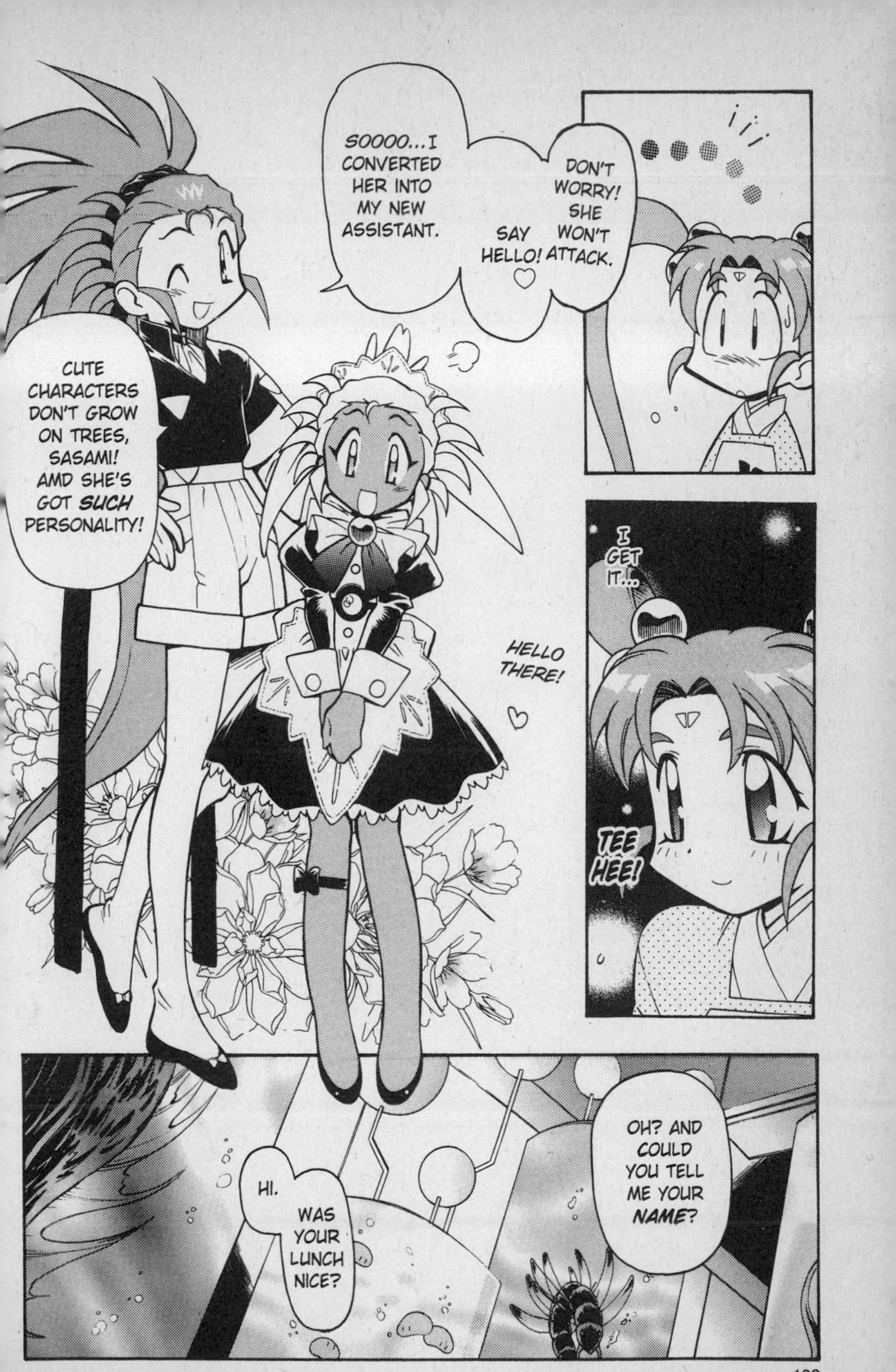
SOOOO...I CONVERTED HER INTO MY NEW ASSISTANT.
DON'T WORRY! SHE WON'T ATTACK.
SAY HELLO! ♡
CUTE CHARACTERS DON'T GROW ON TREES, SASAMI! AMD SHE'S GOT SUCH PERSONALITY!
HELLO THERE! ♡
I GET IT...
TEE HEE!
HI.
WAS YOUR LUNCH NICE?
OH? AND COULD YOU TELL ME YOUR NAME?

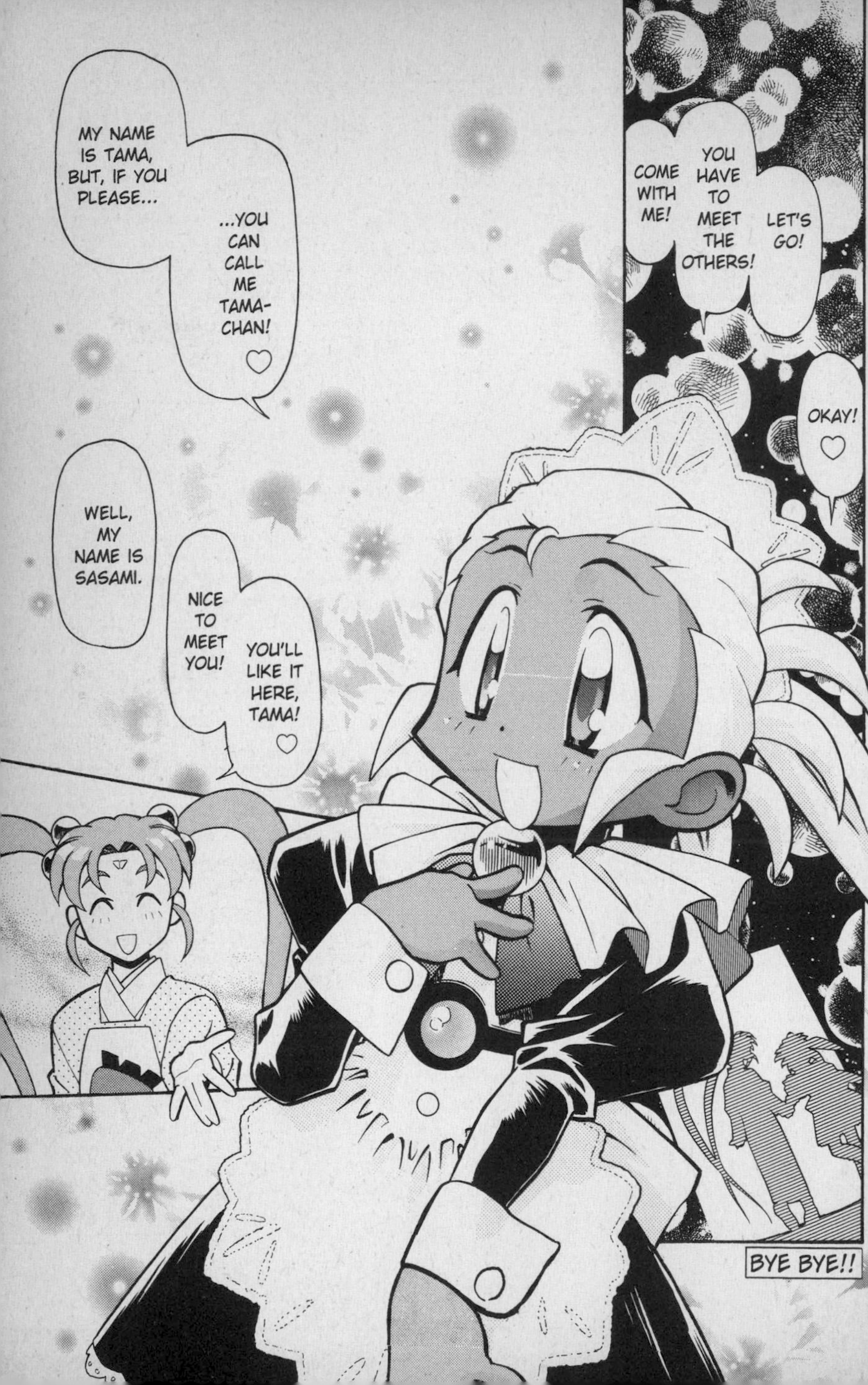
MY NAME IS TAMA, BUT, IF YOU PLEASE...
...YOU CAN CALL ME TAMA-CHAN! ♡
WELL, MY NAME IS SASAMI.
NICE TO MEET YOU!
YOU'LL LIKE IT HERE, TAMA! ♡
COME WITH ME!
YOU HAVE TO MEET THE OTHERS!
LET'S GO!
OKAY! ♡
BYE BYE!!

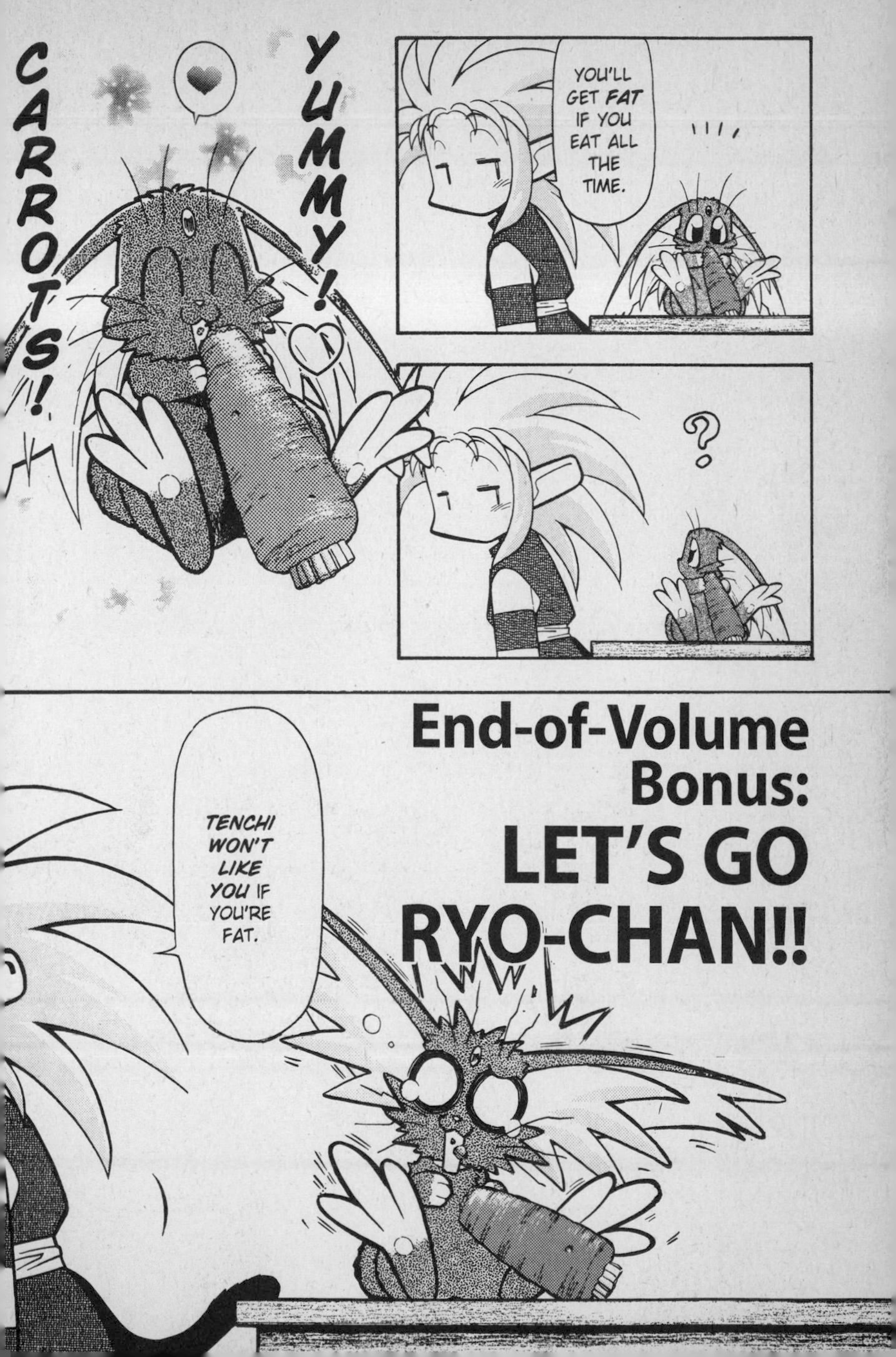
CARROTS!
YUMMY!
YOU'LL GET FAT IF YOU EAT ALL THE TIME.
End-of-Volume Bonus: LET'S GO RYO-CHAN!!
TENCHI WON'T LIKE YOU IF YOU'RE FAT.

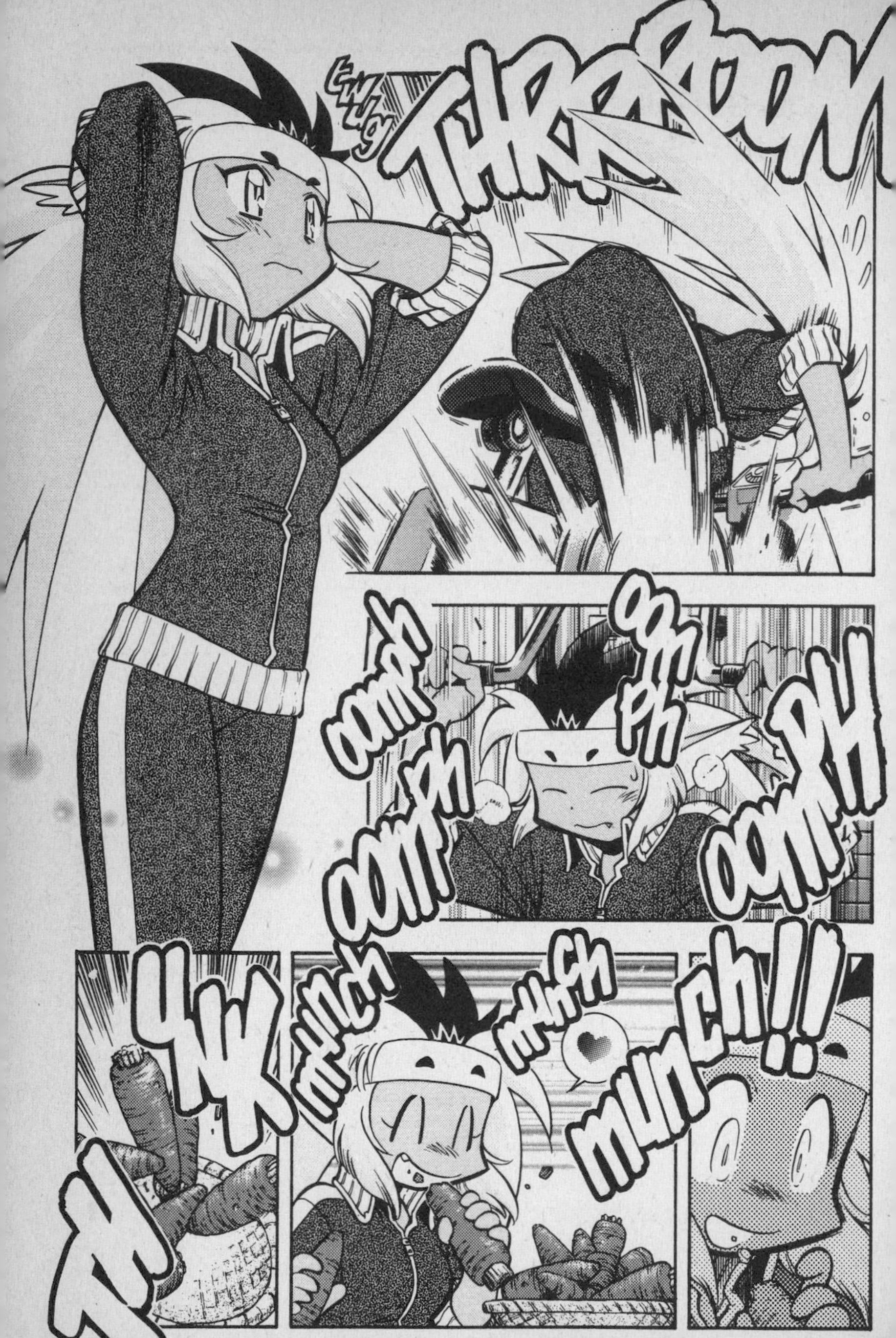
twug
THRRROOM
oomph
oomph
oomph
OOMPH!!
THUNK
munch
munch
munch!!

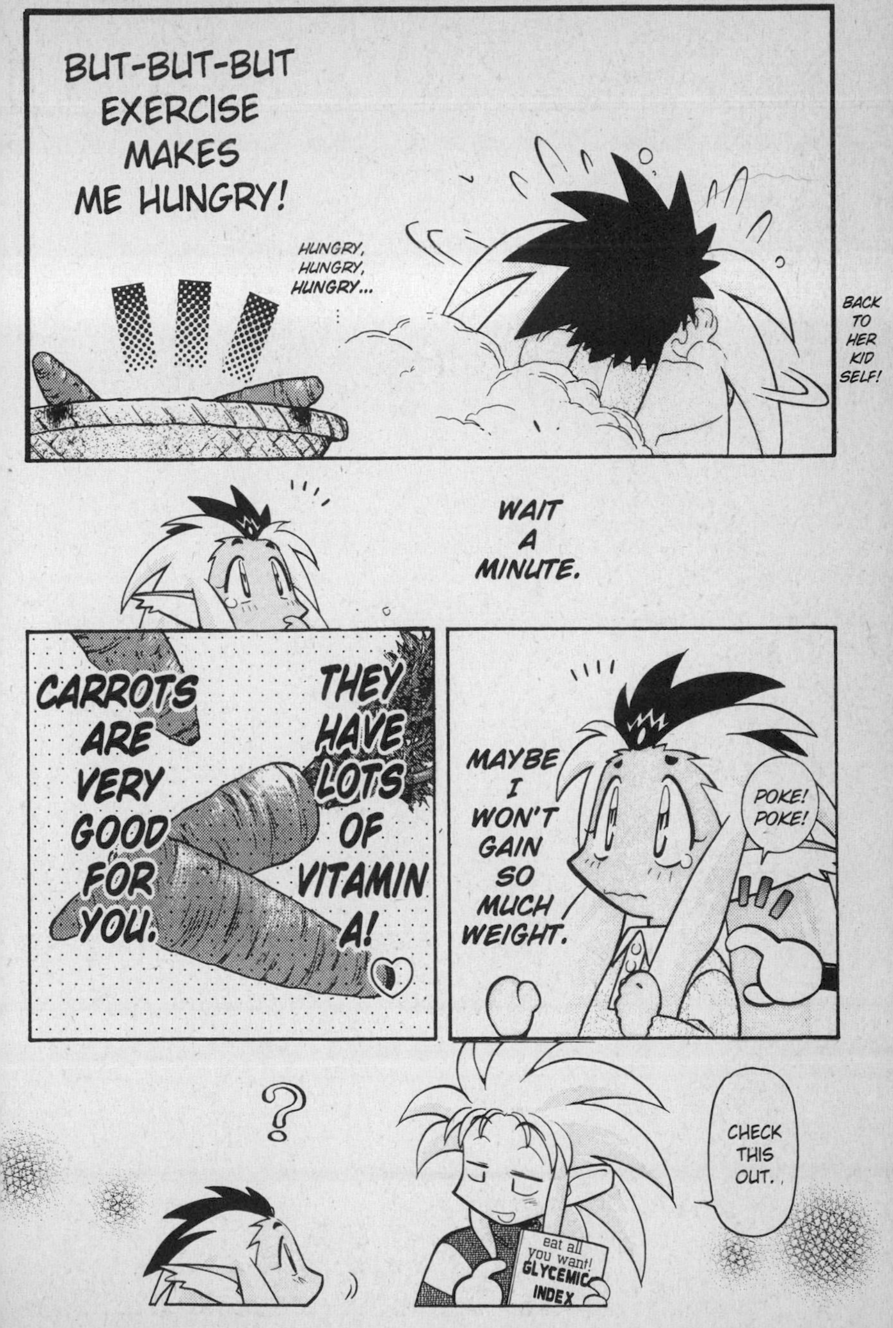
BUT-BUT-BUT EXERCISE MAKES ME HUNGRY!
HUNGRY, HUNGRY, HUNGRY...
BACK TO HER KID SELF!
WAIT A MINUTE.
CARROTS ARE VERY GOOD FOR YOU.
THEY HAVE LOTS OF VITAMIN A!
MAYBE I WON'T GAIN SO MUCH WEIGHT.
POKE! POKE!
?
CHECK THIS OUT.
eat all you want! GLYCEMIC INDEX

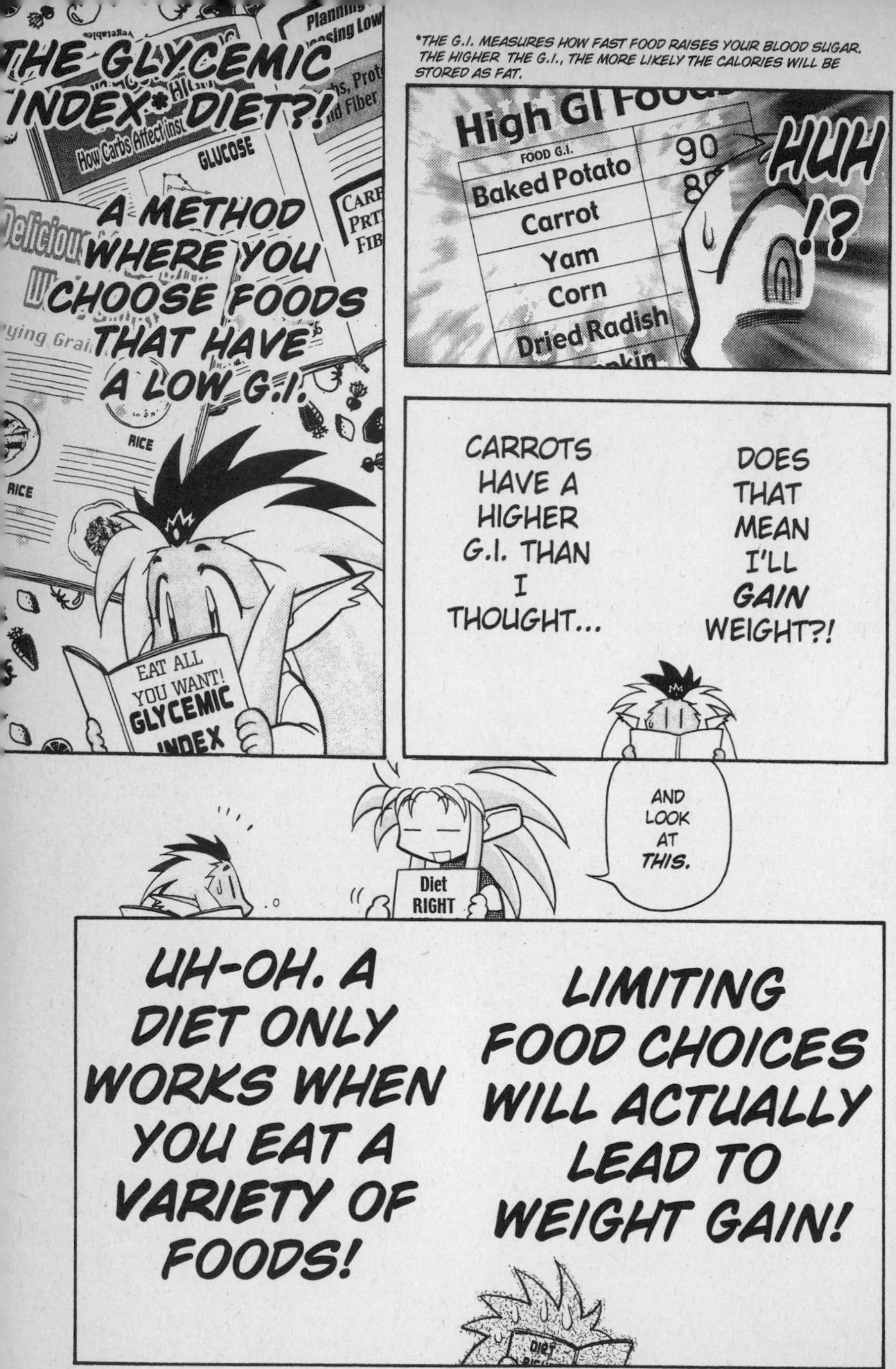
THE GLYCEMIC INDEX* DIET?!
A METHOD WHERE YOU CHOOSE FOODS THAT HAVE A LOW G.I.
GLUCOSE
RICE
RICE
EAT ALL YOU WANT! GLYCEMIC INDEX
*THE G.I. MEASURES HOW FAST FOOD RAISES YOUR BLOOD SUGAR. THE HIGHER THE G.I., THE MORE LIKELY THE CALORIES WILL BE STORED AS FAT.
FOOD G.I.
Baked Potato
90
Carrot
Yam
Corn
Dried Radish
HUH!?
CARROTS HAVE A HIGHER G.I. THAN I THOUGHT...
DOES THAT MEAN I'LL GAIN WEIGHT?!
AND LOOK AT THIS.
Diet RIGHT
UH-OH. A DIET ONLY WORKS WHEN YOU EAT A VARIETY OF FOODS!
LIMITING FOOD CHOICES WILL ACTUALLY LEAD TO WEIGHT GAIN!

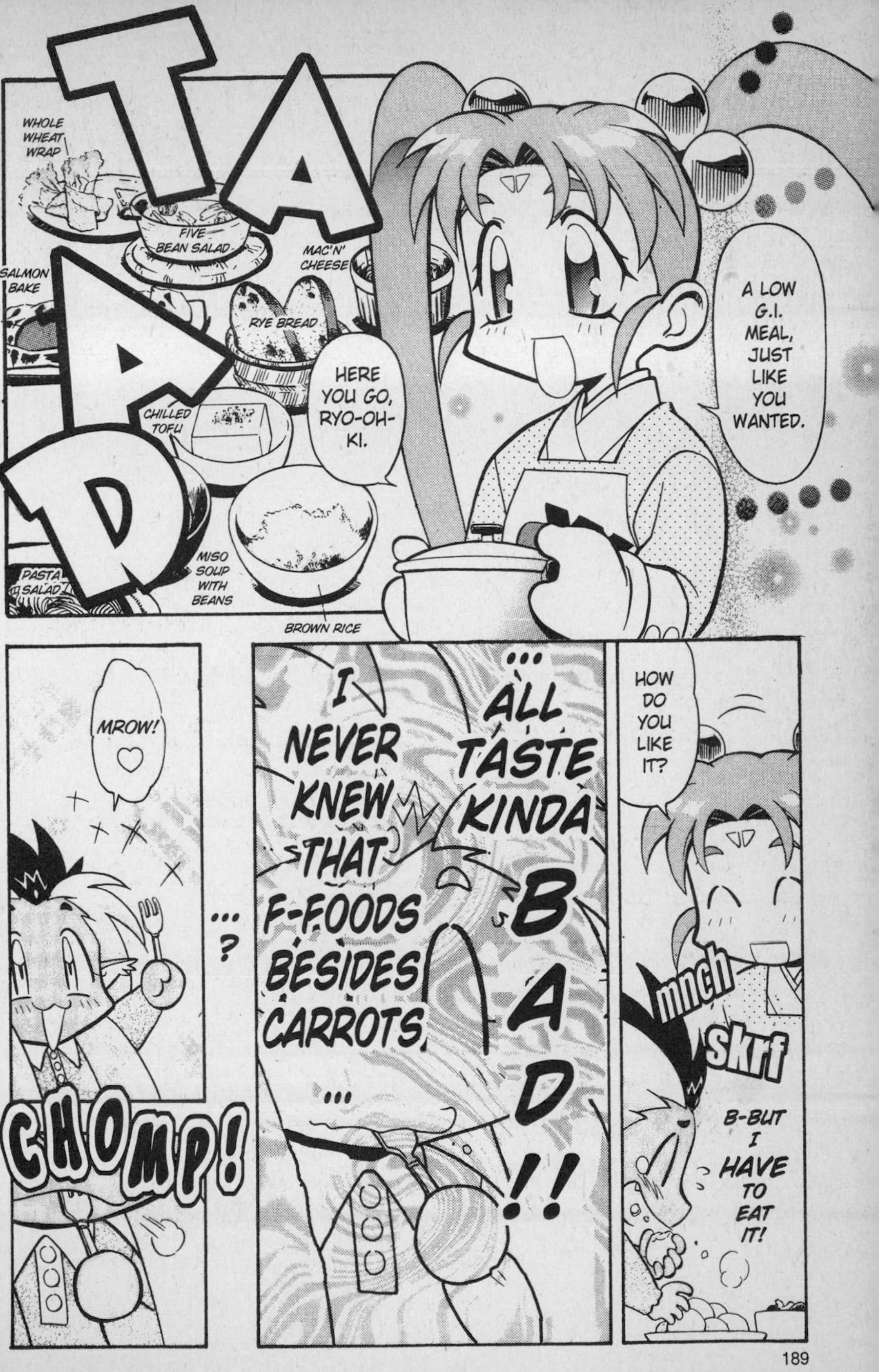

TA-DA
WHOLE WHEAT WRAP
FIVE BEAN SALAD
MAC'N' CHEESE
SALMON BAKE
RYE BREAD
CHILLED TOFU
PASTA SALAD
MISO SOUP WITH BEANS
BROWN RICE
HERE YOU GO, RYO-OH-KI.
A LOW G.I. MEAL, JUST LIKE YOU WANTED.
MROW! ♡
CHOMP!
...?
I NEVER KNEW THAT F-FOODS BESIDES CARROTS...
...ALL TASTE KINDA BAD!!
HOW DO YOU LIKE IT?
mnch
skrf
B-BUT I HAVE TO EAT IT!

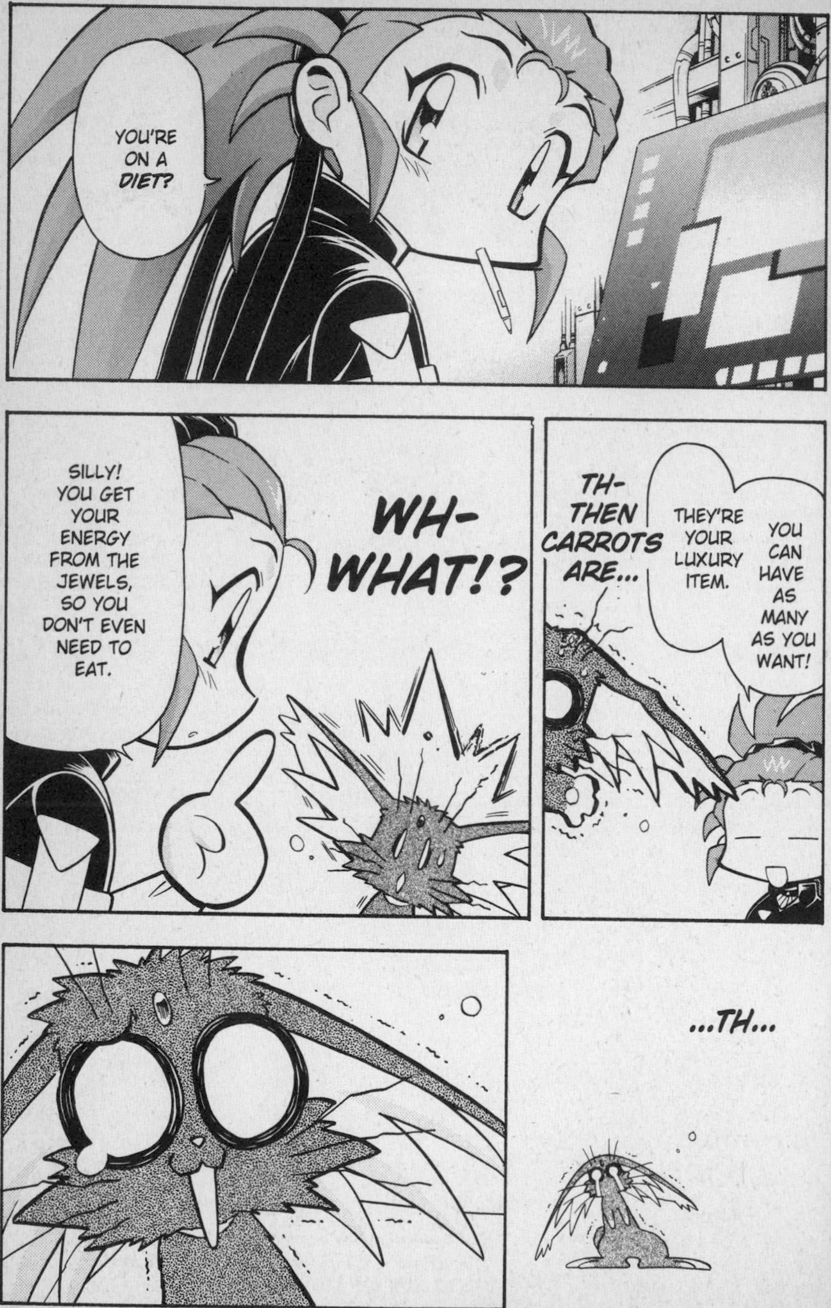
YOU'RE ON A DIET?
SILLY! YOU GET YOUR ENERGY FROM THE JEWELS, SO YOU DON'T EVEN NEED TO EAT.
WH-WHAT!?
TH-THEN CARROTS ARE...
THEY'RE YOUR LUXURY ITEM.
YOU CAN HAVE AS MANY AS YOU WANT!
...TH...

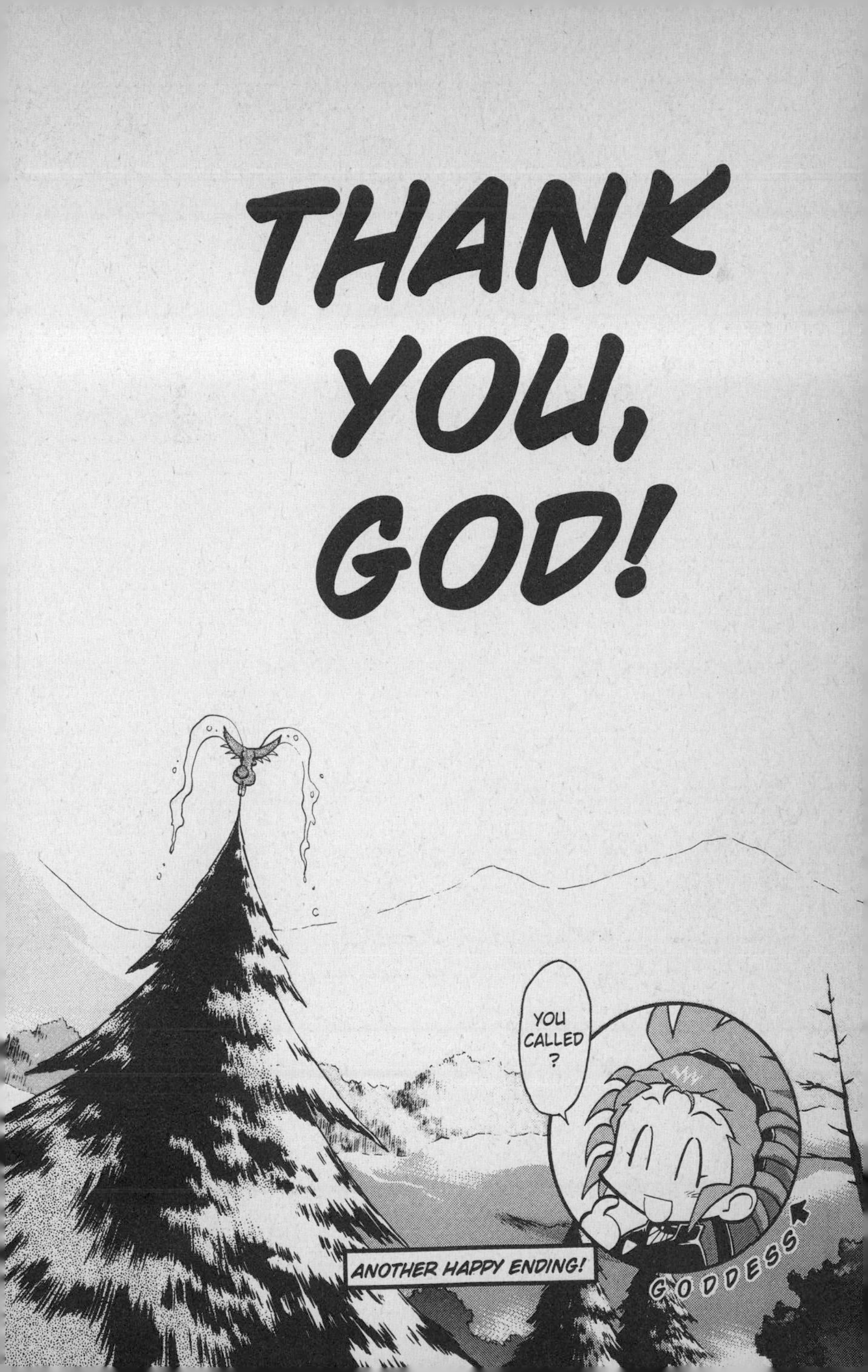
THANK YOU, GOD!
YOU CALLED ?
GODDESS
ANOTHER HAPPY ENDING!

Under the Big Tent

As editor of **The All-New Tenchi Muyô!** I get a lot of mail plopped on my desk every week. Much of it is fan mail with capital letters, multiple exclamation marks and a cherry on top. In other words, these letters are from readers who truly love **Tenchi** comics.

To you fans I say: THANK YOU! And I don't mind using the caps-lock key on my keyboard to express how much I dig your enthusiasm.

There's something about Tenchi and his pals that people really respond to… especially young readers. There are **Tenchi** fans of all ages, of course, but the bulk of letters I receive come from pre-teens.

And think about this: most of these **Tenchi** fans are girls. Why is that?

After all, this is the mother of all harem comics. **Love Hina**, **Oh My Goddess!** and **El-Hazard** are just a few of the titles that represent this popular genre. The set-up is simple: an amiable (and somewhat clueless) young man finds himself surrounded by a gaggle of girls. Some of them are ditzy; some of them are motherly; and, let's be honest, some of them are knock-out sexy.

Doesn't that sound like a male fantasy to you? You'd think guys would be hanging posters of curvy Mihoshi on their dorm room walls. And how about tomboy Ryoko? She's available for a little wrestling and romancing. She's every boy's dream date.

But despite all this, **Tenchi Muyô!** is predominately read by young girls. And judging by all the letters I've read, the reason is obvious. Inside every young girl there's a Ryoko waiting to get out. There's also a little bit of Mihoshi, Ayeka, Sasami and Washu, too.

Watch out guys. The next generation of **Tenchi Muyô!** fans are growing up fast. Will you be ready for them?

Eric Searleman

Editor of **The All-New Tenchi Muyô!**

Are you a *big* Tenchi fan?

If so, here are three other books the editor thinks you'll enjoy:

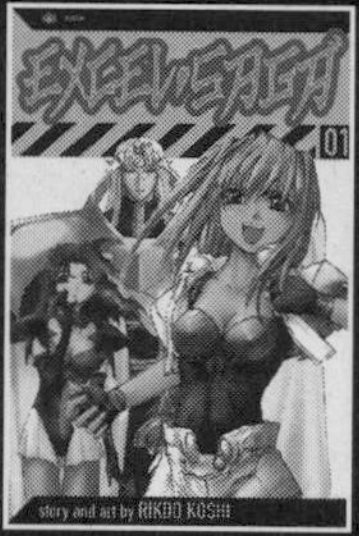
EXCEL SAGA
01
story and art by RIKDO KOSHI

- **Excel Saga**: The fun begins when dreamy dictator IL Palazzo recruits a couple of teenage girls into his secret organization. Together, the threesome begin making plans to take over a city in Japan. XS bubbles with a satirical edge sure to amuse all rebels and revolutionaries.

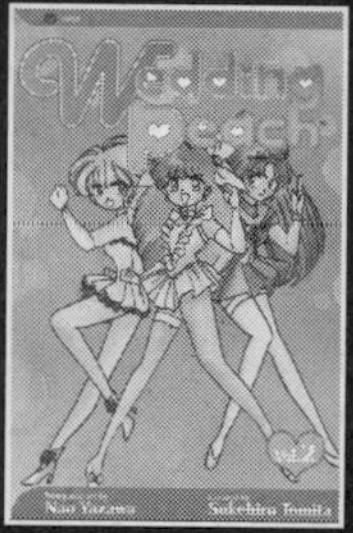
Wedding Peach
vol.2
Nao Yazawa
Sukehiro Tomita

- **Wedding Peach**: In a world where the wedding chapel has become a war zone between good and evil, three young girls transform into the mighty morphin' warriors of love.

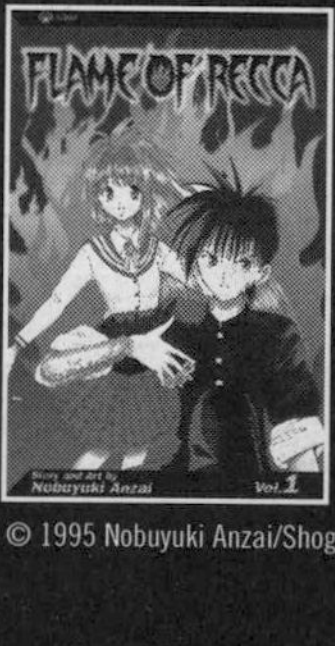
FLAME OF RECCA
Story and Art by Nobuyuki Anzai
Vol.1

- **Flame of Recca**: Fireworks explode (literally) when classmates Recca Hanabishi and Yanagi Sakoshita meet for the first time. As their love grows, the flame of Recca grows hotter and hotter. Explosive!

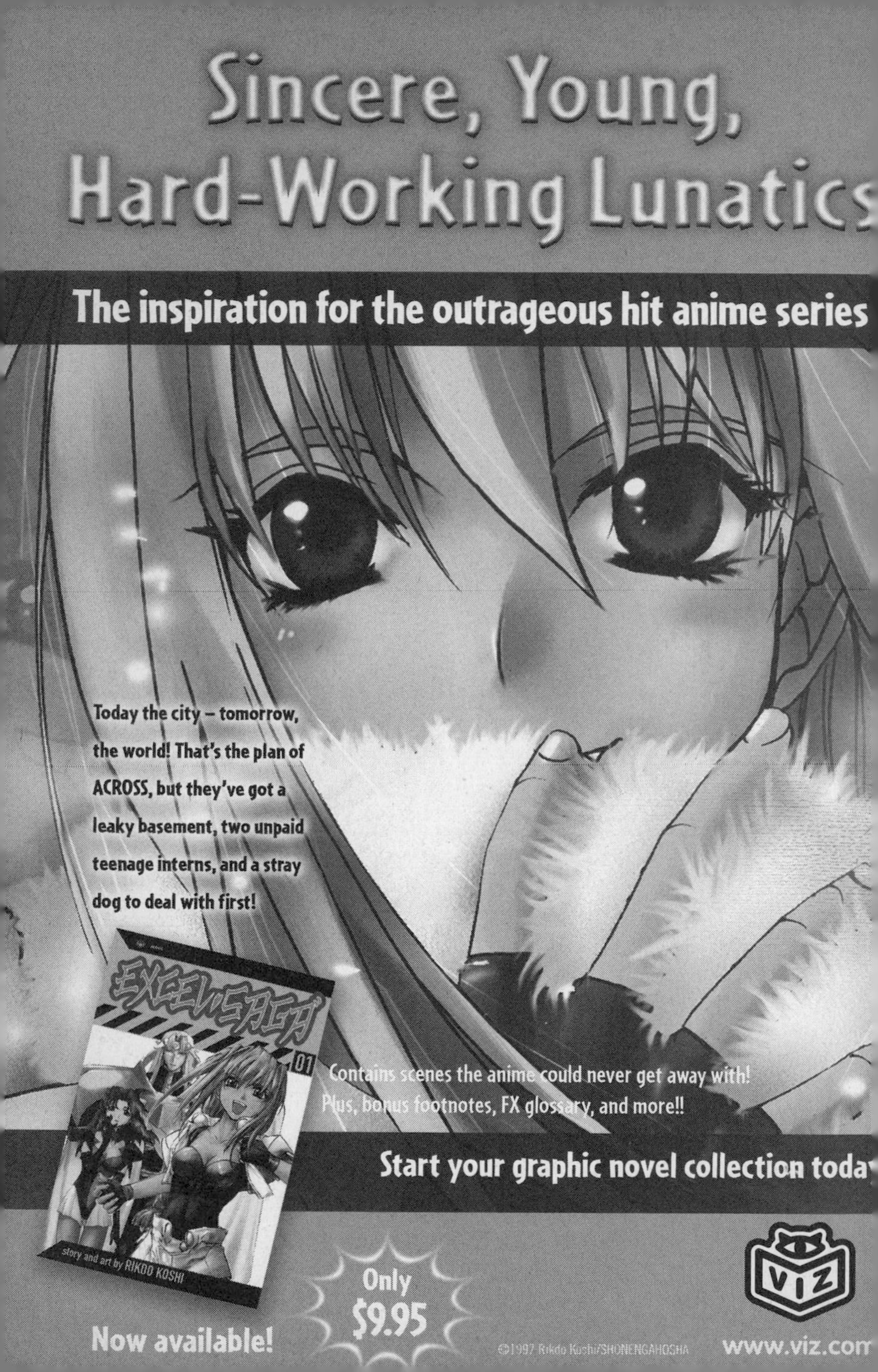
Sincere, Young, Hard-Working Lunatics
The inspiration for the outrageous hit anime series
Today the city – tomorrow, the world! That's the plan of ACROSS, but they've got a leaky basement, two unpaid teenage interns, and a stray dog to deal with first!
EXCEL SAGA
01
story and art by RIKDO KOSHI
Contains scenes the anime could never get away with! Plus, bonus footnotes, FX glossary, and more!!
Start your graphic novel collection today
Only $9.95
Now available!
VIZ
©1997 Rikdo Koshi/SHONENGAHOSHA
www.viz.com